GROUP THERAPY IN BRITAIN

Open University Press
Psychotheraphy in Britain series
Series Editor: Windy Dryden

GROUP THERAPY IN BRITAIN

Edited by
Mark Aveline and Windy Dryden

Open University Press
Milton Keynes · Philadelphia

Open University Press
Celtic Court
22 Ballmoor
Buckingham
MK18 1XW

and
1900 Frost Road, Suite 101
Bristol, PA 19007, USA

First published 1988
Reprinted 1993

British Library Cataloguing in Publication Data

Group therapy in Britain.
    1. Medicine. Group therapy.
    I. Aveline, Mark.   II. Dryden, Windy
    III. Series
    616.89' 152

    ISBN 0–335–09839–8
    ISBN 0–335–09829–0 Pbk

Library of Congress Cataloging-in-Publication Data

Group therapy in Britain/edited by Mark Aveline and Windy Dryden.
        p.   cm. – (Psychotherapy in Britain)
    Includes indexes.
    1. Group psychotherapy.   2. Group psychotherapy – Great Britain.
    I. Aveline, Mark.   II. Dryden, Windy.
    III. Series: Psychotherapy in Britain series.
    RC488.G73   1987
    616.89'152 – dc19   88–12452 CIP

    ISBN 0–335–09839–8
    ISBN 0–335–09829–0 (pbk.)

Typeset by Scarborough Typesetting Services
Printed in Great Britain by Redwood Books, Trowbridge, Wiltshire

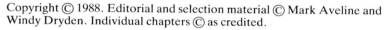

To Anna and Louise

CONTENTS

THE EDITORS

MARK AVELINE

Mark Aveline F.R.C. Psych. is Consultant Psychotherapist to the Nottingham Health Authority, and Clinical Teacher in the Medical School. His research and clinical publications are on teaching dynamic psychotherapy, reforming the membership examination of the Royal College of Psychiatrists, group therapy, action techniques, psychodrama, diabetes and the use of questionnaires in assessment for psychotherapy.

WINDY DRYDEN

Windy Dryden is Professor of Counselling at Goldsmiths' College, University of London. He has edited or written over fifty books; and he is the editor of six series of books, of which two *Psychotherapy Handbooks* and *Therapeutically Speaking* are published by Open University Press.

THE CONTRIBUTORS

Waseem Alladin M.Phil., Dip. Psych. Senior Clinical Psychologist with the Clwyd Health Authority and Lecturer in the Department of Psychology, University College of North Wales, Bangor. Also editor of *Counselling Psychology Quarterly: An International Journal of Theory, Research and Practice.*

Sidney Bloch Ph.D., F.R.C. Psych. Trained at the University of Melbourne, the Maudsley Hospital and Stanford University. Is Consultant Psychotherapist, Warneford Hospital and Clinical Lecturer in Psychiatry, University of Oxford. Author of many papers on psychotherapy and psychiatric ethics. Books include *What is Psychotherapy?* (Oxford University Press, 1982), *Introduction to the Psychotherapies* (ed.) (Oxford University Press, 2nd edition, 1986) and *Therapeutic Factors in Group Psychotherapy* (with Eric Crouch; Oxford University Press, 1985).

Martin H. Davies F.R.C. Psych. Was educated at Cambridge University and St. Mary's Hospital Medical School. After National Service as a Medical Officer, he specialized in psychiatry at the Birmingham Teaching Hospital where he has since been a Senior Lecturer and Consultant. He learned psychodrama in Dean Elefhery's first British training group and has since practised, demonstrated and written articles on the method.

Nona W. Ephraim Currently a Development Worker with Lambeth MIND. Having followed a career in nursing, she completed a Social Science degree at the Polytechnic of Central London. Subsequently, she worked for Grouplinks, which is a MIND project that supports self-help groups.

Barrie Hinksman B.D., A.K.C. Educated at Westminster School and Kings College, London. He practises psychotherapy in Warwickshire, and teaches psychotherapy for the Gestalt Training Service and the English Gestalt Institute.

Keith Hyde M.B., B.S., M.R.C. Psych. Member of the Institute of Group Analysis, London. Consultant Psychotherapist at Hope Hospital, Salford, and the Red House Psychotherapy Day Unit. Co-ordinator of the Manchester Course in Group Psychotherapy.

David Kennard Regional Tutor for the Trent Regional Training Scheme in Clinical Psychology and Principal Clinical Psychologist at Rampton Hospital. He is a member of the Institute of Group Analysis and Honorary Lecturer in the Department of Psychology, Leicester University.

Eric J. Miller M.A., Ph.D. 1947–52: Social anthropological fieldwork in India and Thailand. 1953–58: Internal Consultant in textile industry, USA and India. 1958 to date: Staff member, Tavistock Institute of Human Relations, engaged in a wide range of research and consultancy, and from 1969, Joint Director of Group Relations Training Programme. Visiting Professor of Organizational Behaviour, Manchester Business School, 1971–3; board member of A. K. Rice Institute, Washington D.C., since 1970; policy adviser and founder member of OPUS, 1975 to date.

Jane Price Trained at Barts, qualifying in 1974. After house jobs and junior psychiatric training in Southampton, she moved to Nottingham as a Senior Registrar in Psychotherapy. Alongside of the growing commitment to psychotherapy in the NHS, she was also exposed to the London Women's Therapy Centre and went on to found and co-direct the Nottingham Women's Therapy Service and to co-found CATS (Counselling and Therapy Service for Women in Southampton) between 1981–5. Since June 1985, she has been Consultant Psychotherapist to the West Berkshire Health Authority.

Bernard Ratigan Ph.D. Head of the Student Counselling Service at Loughborough University of Technology, visiting supervisor and group therapist at the Nottingham Psychotherapy Unit and supervisor at the Leicester Counselling Centre.

Brian Thorne Has been Director of Student Counselling at the University of East Anglia and a co-Director of the Facilitator Development Institute (Britain) since 1974. In 1980, he co-founded the Norwich Centre for Personal and Professional Development which remains the primary agency in Britain committed to the person-centred approach. He is co-author of *Student Counselling in Practice* and author of *Intimacy* and *The Quality of Tenderness*.

CHAPTER 1

GROUP THERAPY IN BRITAIN: AN INTRODUCTION

Mark Aveline and Windy Dryden

The three sections of this chapter provide an overview of the subject, detail the structure of the book, and describe the fundamentals of forming a group.

OVERVIEW

The first recorded use of group therapy was by Joseph Pratt in 1905. His 'classes' brought together patients with tuberculosis who took it in turns to present themselves to their fellow members and tell how they had successfully struggled with their illness. Participation in the group mobilized group support, aroused hope and corrected misinformation; the experience was valued by the members (Hadden, 1955). This positive beginning, only 12 years after Freud's seminal publication in psychoanalysis (Breuer and Freud, 1893), led to many developments in theory, practice and application on both sides of the Atlantic. Yet despite its particular advantages as a therapeutic modality (see below), group therapy has never equalled the attention given by psychotherapists to individual therapy and, indeed, has been overtaken by work with *natural groups*, namely married couples in the 1950s and 1960s and the larger constellation of the family in the 1970s and 1980s. We hope that *Group Therapy in Britain* will make a contribution to redressing the balance.

Human beings are born in groups, live in groups and die in groups. Without the support and co-operation of others, individual efforts count for little or are unsustainable. Attitudes and social behaviour are learnt from interaction and are expressed in interaction. It is in interaction that many of the sources of personal emotional satisfaction and growth are to be found. Each person is influenced by group pressures and, in turn, through their personal contribution, has an impact on the behaviour of others which, then, modifies what was first done. Interpersonal and intrapersonal learning are inextricably linked. Adult personality is born out of inherited potentials which are facilitated or inhibited by childhood learning and social culture, and then, fortunately for the psychotherapy enterprise, is subject to useful though minor modification by new learning later in life. One planned situation for helpful learning is the *stranger group* whose many forms are documented in this book.

The informed reader who has scanned the contents page will be quick to discern two problems with the title of the book – the singular form of the term therapy and the word itself. Just as in individual therapy, it is no longer appropriate to speak of a single therapy and do justice to the breadth of the field. In groups, therefore, one should speak of the group therapies (this point is elaborated by Sidney Bloch in Chapter 13). The *group therapies* described in this book differ markedly in their size, membership and purpose. Their practitioners draw on analytic, interpersonal, systems, humanistic and learning theories, among others, in conceptualizing what happens and should happen in their approach; each of these gives a distinct cast to their work. While little or no evaluative research has been carried out on their relative merits, clinical experience suggests that people and problems vary in their responsiveness to different approaches – we contend that the same is likely to be true of therapists. Hence, one purpose of this book is to acquaint inexperienced and more experienced therapists with the range of group therapies being practised in Britain in a format that will allow ready comparison between the approaches.

The word *therapy* suggests that what is involved is treatment of patients by health-care professionals. Such a formulation would be an anathema to many working in self-help groups, where the source of help is located in the person of the sufferer and a peer-group of fellow-sufferers, or to members of a women's group committed to the view that the position of women has been adversely affected by a narrow, male perspective imposed by that sex's dominance of medicine and other culturally formative occupations. Some approaches such as gestalt, psychodrama and the person-centred model have developed outside the purview of the Health Services and tend to see their members as clients or, simply, as people. Leaders of cognitive-behavioural groups may see themselves primarily as educators providing skills to customers. Yet others offer experiences which are not intended to be *therapy* but which may often be *therapeutic* – examples are the Leicester Conference where the metaphor is of education and the large person-centred group where it is encounter. What they have in common is *the context of a group and the hope of the members that they will derive some special benefit from their membership for problems that have been framed, by and large, in interpersonal terms.*

Even the term *group* presents some difficulties in definition. Technically a group is formed when two or more people come together. Group therapy occurs when those people interact and influence each other to a therapeutic end (Shaw, 1976). In the analytic group therapies, which rely heavily on identifying and working with group processes and to a lesser extent in the interpersonal approach, a minimum number of about five is necessary for these processes to occur and an optimal number is eight. Other approaches make far less use of inter-member interaction and group-as-a-whole phenomena but, on a practical basis, tend to have between 7 and 14 members. The large groups of therapeutic communities, the Leicester Conference and person-centred events, have at least 15 members and may have as many as 70 or more.

How group leaders conceptualize the therapeutic locus of their role has considerable significance for their practice. Glassman and Wright (1983) discerned a continuum of leadership goals for the group with clusters around three points: therapy *in* the group, *with* the group and *of* the group.

The first is what Parloff (1967) terms the classicist approach, the early dominant mode in the USA. The leader, prototypically a psychoanalyst (Slavson, 1959), works with one member at a time, elucidating their past and present conflicts and making intrapersonal interpretations. The leader's role is central; members are passive learners, observers or surrogate therapists. Gestalt group therapy, transactional analysis, psychodrama and be-haviourally orientated groups often follow this pattern.

Therapy *with* the group makes use of some of the special properties of groups. The focus is on the interpersonal relationships, issues and conflicts that evolve out of the group process. Analytic group therapies, as developed in Britain by Foulkes, fall in this category with the conductor having an expert role in clarifying unconscious group and individual processes, the latter often with an historical perspective. The leader attends to the social matrix formed in the group. The interpersonal group as typified in the work of Yalom (1985), though classified by Glassman and Wright in the *with* category, also belongs in the *of* grouping and, hence, is properly termed by Parloff as an integrationist approach. The task of the leader is to mobilize the ability of members to help themselves and each other; the focus is principally on the 'here and now' experience of interactions within the group.

British workers have also made major contributions to the development of therapy *of* the group. The treatment efforts of the leader are directed towards the group as a whole and only minimally to individual members – the aim is the development of a healthy group which will of itself be the vehicle for therapeutic change. In small groups, Bion (1961), first at

Northfield and later at the Tavistock Clinic, made pioneering observations about the way in which groups, collectively, may avoid working; his technique of group interpretation was further refined by Ezriel. Similar group interpretations were developed by Whitaker and Lieberman (1964). The larger living and learning group of the therapeutic community owes much to the innovations made by Maxwell Jones at Belmont Hospital (later renamed the Henderson Hospital) and, subsequently, at Dingleton, Tom Main at the Cassel and David Clark at Fulbourn.

All too often group therapy is seen as second-best therapy, i.e. an economical way of spreading therapist time between many or, less flatteringly, as a way of avoiding contact with people who might be too draining or too hopeless for individual work. Consequently, the highly skilled role of leader may be given as a chore to well-intentioned but usually ill-informed staff members whose input confirms the negative stereotype and, thereby, both therapist and members miss the opportunity of experiencing the therapeutic power of a mature, working group.

In contrast to individual therapy, groups offer a rich opportunity for interaction with several others, each of whose experience of life and style of coping is different. Where one may be weak, another will be strong. Where one may be beginning, another may be some way down a similar path of personal difficulty and can offer guidance and assistance with the unfamiliar terrain. These roles are not fixed but may alternate within sessions and over time. Groups provide the chance to be altruistic and discover that one can be of assistance to others with all that that implies for improving an inner sense of worthlessness. Being a member of a cohesive, purposeful group may be a uniquely encouraging experience in a person's life. No other treatment setting allows such opportunities for interpersonal learning through testing out how one is seen, how one's inner self may be received and what effects negative acts have, and for recognizing and undoing defensive strategies. The reactions of fellow members have great force, because they are seen as coming from unbiased peers and not from therapists who are compelled, professionally and financially, to be supportive. In the stranger group, risks in the form of new interaction may be undertaken which might be too disruptive in the natural group of the family and the marriage or which might be opposed by a dynamic wish in others to maintain the status quo. Careful consideration by the leader of the purpose of the group will lead to the construction of a group whose form and membership – whether it be small group or therapeutic community, single-sex, special problem or mixed – will provide a varied, relevant, new forum for personal learning.

The power of the group should not be taken lightly. Poorly constructed and poorly led groups, where a discouraging or even destructive culture has developed, can exert a strong negative influence which is hard for the individual to resist. These and other issues which are important in group leadership are repeatedly considered in this book.

THE STRUCTURE OF THE BOOK

Comprehensive coverage and comparable format were our twin objectives in structuring the book. We intend that the reader be given sufficient practical detail of each approach in order to have a clear view of what is involved, how experienced leaders conceptualize their role and the role of members, and how problems may be grappled with and overcome. Our focus is on the contemporary practice of group therapy in its principal forms in Britain.* Of necessity, the focus has had to be wider in the chapters on research and training. While in each chapter European and North American innovations in the development of the history and underlying assumptions of the approach have been documented, each contributor was specifically asked to bring out the contribution of British workers.

The book is in three parts. In Part 1, various forms of small-group therapy, from the analytic through the interpersonal to the cognitive-behavioural, are considered. Part 1 ends with a comparative review. In Part 2, the therapeutic value of other group approaches is addressed, namely three forms of large-group and two special applications. In Part 3, the issues of research and training are taken up.

Contributors to Part 1 were asked to follow the same chapter structure; other contributors were made aware of the schema and were encouraged to make use of this as and when it met their purpose. The chapter structure is as follows:

Historical context and development in Britain
Underlying assumptions
● Theoretical underpinnings citing research evidence if available
● Key concepts with definitions
Practice
● The goals of the group – includes special inclusion and exclusion factors
● The role of the leader (and co-leader) – includes what the leader(s) does and why (style, technique, nature and form of interpretations/interventions)
● The role of group members
● Group development over time – includes the natural history of this kind of group

---

* An account of encounter groups may be found in *Innovative Therapy in Britain* (1988), edited by Rowan and Dryden. Open University Press.

- Mechanisms of change – linking back to 'goals of the group' and 'role of the leader', includes mechanisms that are both assumed and those that have been demonstrated to occur
- Typical problems and their resolution – includes what problems typically occur in this kind of group as the result of group and individual process and how they may be resolved
- Limitations of the approach
- Typical qualities of effective leaders

Contributors were asked to illustrate points with examples from group practice, to emphasize the distinctive features of the described approach or application, and to elucidate the role of the leader.

In the interests of editorial consistency, it was suggested that the male pronoun be used. No implication of leadership exclusivity is implied by this convention. Some contributors of necessity or by choice have used the female form.

FUNDAMENTALS OF FORMING A GROUP

To avoid duplicating information in later sections of the book, an account is now given of the fundamental principles in forming a group. The following account refers particularly to small groups which formally make use of group interaction to facilitate change in personal functioning. However, all groups need careful planning and stage-setting by the leader, especially in the early phase, if they are to reach their optimal level. In this section, we are indebted to the clear accounts set out by Yalom (1985) and Whitaker (1985).

Undertaking group therapy is a serious commitment for leader and members alike. While it is beyond the power of the leader to ensure that the experience will be helpful, much can be done to create favourable conditions. In nearly all forms of group therapy, the leader has the role, firstly, of creating and maintaining the group and, secondly, of making a fundamental contribution to building the culture of that group.

Creating and maintaining the group

(a) *Context, need* and *ability* are the determining parameters in the all important planning stage weeks or months before the first meeting of the group. The leader(s) needs to ask himself the question: in the setting(s) available to me, what is the need of the patient or client group, and have I the necessary time, skills and ability to meet that need? If the skills and ability are insufficient, how may a sufficiency be acquired?

(b) The leader creates the formal structure of the group by deciding its form, size, duration and membership. In a *closed* group, members contract to stay together for the entire life of the group; this form provides an intense, shared, complete experience of beginning, working together and ending. Despite this contract, in the real world of group therapy there is likely to be a modest change in membership, but, even so, a closed group is less subject to the disruptions of members joining and leaving and, thus, can develop high levels of familiarity and trust within the group – essential elements in interpersonal change. In an *open* group, length of membership is, primarily, determined by need. New members join when there is a vacancy and leave when their difficulties are resolved or their situation alters, as when an in-patient departs from the ward-group on discharge. This form allows members to work at their own pace – some in an analytic or interpersonal group joining for months and others for years – and takes account of the differing severity of problems among members. An open group provides a temporal sense of achievement. Newcomers can see where the more experienced have got to and help the latter recognize their progress. Once issues of sibling rivalry have been dealt with, the experienced can speed the newcomers' learning of how to make the best use of their time in the group. In a *slow open* group, there is a gradual change of membership.

(c) The leader will decide the *size* of the group (commonly 7–10 in a small group), the *duration* (usually 1½ hours), the *frequency* (typically weekly), and the *time* of meeting (the fixed time conveys a message of reliable constancy). The *overall duration* of the group will depend on the nature of the objectives embedded in the theory of change in the particular approach or may be determined by an external factor of, for example, a planned cycle of group experiences in a day-centre.

(d) Careful attention needs to be given to securing an appropriate room for the group. The room must be big enough to easily accommodate the members with comfortable, informal, identical seating that can be arranged in a circle. It should be quiet and private, free from interruptions and available without question for each group meeting.

(e) The leader may choose to work alone or with one or more co-leaders. Especially for the less experienced leader, co-leadership is desirable, because it helps alleviate leader anxiety, provides alternative perceptions of what is going on and fosters a reflective attitude. Co-leadership is like marriage; leaders need to ensure as far as possible that they can have a respectful, trusting and stimulating professional relationship. Potential difficulties in the working relationship, such as disparity in experience or style, should be anticipated in prior discussion, perhaps with the aid of the supervisor. Role differences, if one leader is to have junior status or to be an observer, should be clarified. Though it may seem to be stating the obvious, it is vitally important that the same leaders or principal leader conduct the group; a group is not a parcel that can be handed on without damaging the contents.

(f) Having established a secure foundation for the group, the members may now be selected. Three aspects are important: *suitability, composition* and *informed agreement*. In general, suitability is a function of the potential member's readiness to learn from the approach and the judgement of the leader and others that the learning may be fruitful. Specific inclusion and exclusion factors are addressed in the following chapters and the comparative review (Chapter 7). A well-balanced group has the best chance of being productive, and two criteria may be within the leader's control. Firstly, while some groups will intentionally be made up of members with a common problem or demographic characteristic, in all groups it is wise to compose a membership that is *homogeneous for severity of problem and heterogeneous for coping style*. This has the consequence that no one member will be held back in their progress by more fearful others and that the latter will not be terrified by levels of disclosure and intimacy that are achieved too rapidly for them. The variety in coping style enriches the matrix for learning in the group and undermines the tendency for similar individuals to collude with each other in promoting the same self-handicapping solution. Secondly, *avoid isolates*. These are members in a minority of one who, through some difference in race, physique or problem, are at risk of having their isolation further accentuated in the group and may then leave prematurely.

Informed agreement is an essential ingredient in the collaborative psychotherapy enterprise. The decision to offer a place in a group and to accept is an active one for both leader and member. Both must feel that they can work together productively. This demands accurate information about what will be asked of members in the group. Some leaders supplement their verbal description with a written statement of expectations and ground-rules. New members need to be *prepared* for group life through, perhaps, several pre-group individual sessions with the leader. In these sessions, conflicts which may be activated at an early stage in the group have their drop-out effect reduced by anticipation and partial working through.

(g) Once the group has begun, the leader has ultimate responsibility for its maintenance, though the maturation of the group will be marked by its increasing participation in this task. The leader will ensure that the room is ready and the chairs set out; he will gather and relay messages from absentees, initiate and close the meeting, and encourage the group to consider the issues stirred by changes in membership. In short, the leader *holds the boundaries* of the group.

Building the culture of the group

(a) While the group has an inherent potential to be a powerful instrument for improving interpersonal relationships, this good result is not achieved by chance; chaos and demoralization are possible alternatives. Particularly in the early stages of the group, the leader is active in building through personal example and style of intervention a *facilitative culture* or set of *norms* in the group.

(b) The techniques deployed and the structure of the group varies between approaches. However, most leaders will wish to encourage the special opportunities for learning that the group presents, namely (i) interaction with different people with different experience and different styles of coping, (ii) disclosure and feedback, (iii) the development of trust through sharing and being close, (iv) being accepted and supported by peers, and (v) taking the risk of being different.

(c) *Spontaneity* and *authenticity* are the hallmarks of a mature working group. The leader can set the tone by:

   (i) encouraging members to address each other directly, in the first person, by speaking of their own experience and not attributing experience to others;
  (ii) being respectful and even-handed in his interaction with members;
 (iii) making space for the silent member;
  (iv) addressing important disregarded issues;
   (v) adjusting the pace of the group so that the risk of harm is minimized;
  (vi) fostering the potential of the group to take responsibility for its actions and direction;
 (vii) actively seeking to release the therapeutic force in members and the group;
(viii) cultivating in the group a reflective, analytic attitude to its processes; and
  (ix) modelling openness and tolerance of faults by being open, spontaneous and honest, i.e. being responsive and responsible.

(d) Finally, the thoughtful leader will take steps to reflect on the work. Weekly supervision is the ideal back-up for group leadership. But, at the very least, a written record of the events of each meeting should be kept and reviewed before the next meeting. Co-leaders will need a few minutes together before the session to get up to date with any developments and a longer time afterwards to discuss and try to understand what has and has not occurred.

Having set the scene, different approaches to small group therapy are now described in Part 1.

REFERENCES

Bion, W. R. (1961). *Experiences in Groups*. London, Tavistock.

Breuer, J. and Freud, S. (1893). On the physical mechanism of hysterical phenomena: a preliminary communication. *Standard Edition*, Vol.2. London, Hogarth Press.

Glassman, S. M. and Wright, T. L. (1983). In, with, and of the group. A perspective on group psychotherapy. *Small Group Behavior* **14**: 96–106.

Hadden, S. B. (1955). Historic background of group psychotherapy. *International Journal of Group Psychotherapy* **5**: 162–8.

Parloff, M. B. (1967). Advances in analytic group therapy. *In* J. Marmor (ed.), *Frontiers of Psychoanalysis*. New York, Basic Books.

Shaw, M. (1976). *Group Dynamics: the Psychology of Small Group Behavior*. New York, McGraw-Hill.

Slavson, S. R. (1959). *Analytic Group Therapy with Children, Adolescents and Adults*. New York, Columbia University Press.

Whitaker, D. S. (1985). *Using Groups to Help People*. International Library of Group Psychotherapy. London, Routledge and Kegan Paul.

Whitaker, D. S. and Lieberman, M. A. (1964). *Psychotherapy Through the Group Process*. London, Tavistock.

Yalom, I. D. (1985). *The Theory and Practice of Group Psychotherapy*, 3rd edition. New York, Basic Books.

PART 1

SMALL GROUP THERAPIES

CHAPTER 2

ANALYTIC GROUP PSYCHOTHERAPIES

Keith Hyde

INTRODUCTION

This chapter examines four theoretical approaches to analytical group therapy – that of Bion, the Tavistock approach, Group Analysis, and the Group Focal Conflict Model. In the first section the author describes the historical development of these ideas, emphasizing contributions he considers of prime importance, outlining the development and practice of analytic group therapy in Britain, and comparing it with analytic group therapy in North America.

The second section enlarges on the key concepts in these theories, emphasizing some differences between them. The section on practice describes the group analytic approach of the author which integrates aspects of the Group Focal Conflict Model. Group Analysis is now the most influential approach to analytic group therapy in Britain.

HISTORICAL CONTEXT AND DEVELOPMENT IN BRITAIN

During the 1920s and 1930s there was a shift from the study of the individual to the study of interpersonal relationships and their influence on the development of personality; and the traditional psychoanalytic view of the mind developing through the influence of primitive instincts was reviewed. Freud himself integrated a number of sociological concepts, discussing the role of groups in society in *Group Psychology and Analysis of the Ego*, published in 1921. During the 1920s Trigant Burrow, an American psychoanalyst, described how individuals behaved in the group as they thought others expected them to behave: maintaining these *social images* impedes spontaneous interaction and leads to isolation (Durkin, 1974).

In the 1930s there was a spread of new concepts to Britain and North America as people left Germany and Austria. Melanie Klein settled in London and played a central role in the development of object relations theory which influenced Bion and his colleagues, and the later development of the Tavistock approach of Ezriel and Sutherland. It was through the delineation of projection and projective identification by Klein that Bion was able to develop his theories of group process.

Foulkes, the father of group analysis, came to England in 1933, having studied medicine and neurology, and having practised as a psychoanalyst in Frankfurt. Foulkes, like Fritz Perls, worked under the neurologist Kurt Goldstein who considered that individual neurones always functioned as part of a communicating network. Goldstein adapted the *gestalt psychology* of Koffka and Kohler, and considered the neurone as a *nodal point* in the *network* of cells forming the brain. Foulkes described the individual as a nodal point within the network of relationships in the group. Gestalt psychology provided the theoretical concepts to understand the relationship of the individual to the group: the group always functioned as a whole, and parts could only be understood when their relationship to the whole was considered. The *figure* was part of the *ground*, and what was happening in the group was viewed in the context of the whole group.

In Frankfurt Foulkes was acquainted with a group of sociologists who attempted to integrate Marxist and Psychoanalytic theory. In reviewing the work of Norbert Elias, Foulkes (1938) commented that psychoanalysis should consider the whole network of relationships in which the individual was involved, there being no clear difference between the inside and outside, individual and environment.

Kurt Lewin had moved from Germany to America, and was the originator of 'T' groups. He developed *Field Theory*, which offered a way to conceptualize the forces in the group. In the *force field* of the group there were both *restraining forces*, which pushed the individual away from the *goal* (the preferred state), and *driving forces*, which propelled the individual towards the goal. If these forces were equal there was no movement towards or away from the goal. It was easier to weaken the restraining force so that movement towards the goal occurred than to increase the driving force. Lewin considered a group had unique and particular qualities which were different from those of the individuals who made up the group. The group influenced the individual, and the individual influenced the group, together forming a gestalt or whole.

Developments during the Second World War

The Second World War created the impetus in Britain for these new concepts to be integrated into psychiatry. Bion and Rickman from the Tavistock Clinic played a major part in developing a group approach to selecting army officers. Following their success they were posted to the Northfield Military Neurosis Centre in 1942. The first Northfield Experiment, as it is now known, only lasted a few weeks but demonstrated Bion's approach to groups.

First Northfield experiment
Bion was placed in charge of the military training and rehabilitation wing, with the task of preparing for war up to 200 men who were suffering from neurotic disorders. He considered that the role of the leader in a group was to make the members aware of what they were doing; it was not to be helpful through providing solutions. He considered there was a direct relationship between the organization of a group and the interactions of the members of that group. A 'leaderless' ward system was established where treatment of the individual patient and his neurotic difficulties became a problem for the whole ward group. Bion based his approach on a number of principles (Trist, 1985):

(i)   the wing was to study its internal tensions in a real life situation which went on 24 hours a day;
(ii) a problem could only be tackled when the majority of the group understood its nature, and considered it worth studying;
(iii) the solution for any problem was only accepted after careful scrutiny by the group; and
(iv) the aim was to let the patients learn a way of coping and adapting to intra-group tensions.

Initially the patients met in small groups, Bion did not take control, and the ward became more disorganized. When patients started complaining about the chaos and squalor of their ward, large group meetings took place. The patients began to realize that if they wanted an organized ward, a reasonable environment in which to live, then they had to resolve their interpersonal difficulties, and take responsibility for their situation. Bion's approach confronted those soldiers who expressed their resentment of military organization by being disorganized, and was very successful in rehabilitating them. The 'authorities' could not accept an approach which challenged their view of what should happen in the army and Bion and Rickman were transferred.

Second Northfield experiment
Foulkes was posted to Northfield in 1943, joining among others Bridger, Main and Bierer. The changes which occurred in the hospital were as dramatic and effective as in the first experiment, but occurred more slowly, and did not

directly challenge the established order. Main coined the term 'therapeutic community' (Main, 1946) to describe the approach that developed. Foulkes viewed the wards, different groups, staff and individual patients at Northfield as 'an interrelated group with a common aim'. His interventions were to 'intensify and promote the hospital activities *in toto*' (Foulkes, 1948, p. 113).

Development of analytic group therapy

Following the war the staff at Northfield dispersed. Bion, Sutherland (Sutherland, 1985) and Bridger went to the Tavistock Clinic, where they were joined by Ezriel. Foulkes became a consultant at the Maudsley Hospital. At the Cassel Hospital, Main developed a more analytically orientated therapeutic community than Maxwell Jones (see Chapter 8). Bierer established the Marlborough Day Hospital.

Group analysis
In this approach, developed by Foulkes, not only the transference to the therapist, but also transference relationships with other group members, and extratransference relationships are important in therapy. Transference means the experience in the present of feelings, attitudes and fantasies displaced from important early relationships. Man is a social creature, and neurotic symptoms are an expression of difficulties in personal relation-ships. The individual is treated within the context of the group, and it is in the matrix of the group as it slowly develops that the individual matures and individuates.

In 1952, as the network of people interested in developing these ideas increased, the Group Analytic Society was formed, and the journal *Group Analysis* became a forum for a network of people communicating and developing ideas, as occurs in the free-floating discussion in a group. More formal training developed with the formation of the Institute of Group Analysis (see Chapter 14).

Group analysis is practised in a variety of settings, and its influence has spread beyond psychotherapy into education, management, therapeutic communities, literature and family therapy. In large groups the emphasis is on socio-cultural learning, and group analysts continue to work with and develop concepts from large groups (de Mare, 1975).

Group focal conflict model
The group focal conflict model defines how the group resolves issues that arise, how the group culture develops, and when an intervention may be necessary if the group is to develop a therapeutic culture. It is compatible

with group analysis (Whitaker, 1985a), and provides a way of understanding the group process and the relation of the individual to the group. As will be seen, there are a number of similarities between the tripartite interpretation of the Tavistock model and the formulation of the group focal conflict.

The approach was developed in Chicago by Whitaker, Lieberman and Whitman (Whitaker and Lieberman, 1964), who had researched hypotheses developed from Bion and Lewin. The theory developed from the nuclear conflict model of French who worked with them. Whitaker is now resident in Britain.

Bion

Bion made a unique contribution to the study of group dynamics in his recognition of the recurrent emotional states that arose in groups, in his strict orientation to the group as a whole, and in his view of the individual and society.

He was very influential in the development of the Tavistock Clinic after the war, and in the establishment of its psychoanalytic orientation, but only led a few therapeutic groups, stopping in the early 1950s; even so, his approach remains highly influential. His papers on groups, mainly published in *Human Relations*, the house journal of the Tavistock Clinic, were collected together in *Experiences in Groups* (Bion, 1961).

Bion made many original contributions to psychoanalytic theory, and his ideas on thinking, projective identification and containment have been creatively integrated into group analysis (James, 1984).

Tavistock Clinic and Tavistock model of group therapy

The Tavistock Clinic responded to the establishment of the NHS by developing a form of psychoanalytic treatment which could be made available to a much larger population. Ezriel and Sutherland applied the principles of individual therapy to the group setting – the primary focus was on the group as a whole, as in all the British approaches to analytic group therapy. The Tavistock model offers a specific tripartite way of interpreting the transference in the group and emphasizes that this is the key therapeutic factor. Unlike group analysis it does not emphasize the value of other group-specific factors.

Other staff of the Tavistock Clinic emphasized different aspects of this approach; for instance, Schindler (1966) described group transferences which resulted in the analyst being viewed as father, and the group itself being viewed as mother.

The Tavistock Clinic has a major role in training professionals of all disciplines in psychoanalytical psychotherapy and its application; its approach to groups has influenced people in medicine, education, business management, criminology and anywhere that group processes and dynamics are studied.

Analytic group therapy in America contrasted with the British approach

The Tavistock model is psychoanalysis of the group, whereas group analysis is psychoanalysis of the group by the group. In America, Wolf and Schwartz (1962) consider the focus should be on the individual. Conflicts are manifested in the transference, and therapy is essentially individual psychoanalysis in the group. The format of the group increases the opportunities for transference to develop, thus creating more material for individual analytic work.

Others in America consider the group as a whole, emphasizing the therapeutic potential of the group. There are similarities with the group analytic approach, but the concept of the social nature of the personality is not fully accepted, and factors unique to each person are considered of crucial importance in development, and thus in therapy (Kauff, 1979; Glatzer *et al.*, 1983).

The comparability of the British analytic group therapies

Though the four models considered have in common the fundamental tenets of psychoanalysis, maintaining the importance of the historical development of the individual, and understanding present relationships to a greater or lesser extent as transference relationships, they are not directly comparable. Bion studied group processes; the Tavistock model applies concepts from individual therapy to groups, whereas Foulkes and group analysis developed a theory of group therapy, and demonstrated its application in practice. The focal conflict model applies specifically to groups, but of itself is not a model of group therapy, though Whitaker (1985b) has integrated it with other concepts to provide a theoretical and practical approach to group therapy.

UNDERLYING ASSUMPTIONS

The theoretical underpinnings and key concepts of the four major schools will be considered in turn.

Theoretical underpinnings – group analysis

The rationale behind this approach is that man is a social animal, born and brought up in a social situation through and within which personality develops.

Psychological disturbance commonly originates in relationships, and the destructive aspects of this disturbance results in withdrawal from the social situation, from its support and from the potential to develop and flourish within it.

Faced with a number of strangers in a situation where the task does not appear clearly defined, most people behave and respond to others in a typical way that reduces their anxiety. This behaviour is based on assumptions about themselves and others which those individuals consider to be unassailably true. These recurrent patterns of behaviour become manifest in the *here-and-now* of the group – the nature of the relationships which moulded and shaped the personality in the past being now expressed in a modified form.

The more *heterogeneous* the membership of the group, the more it is representative of the society from which its members come. The members have in common the mature, healthy aspects of themselves which can interact with others to produce creative relationships; but opposing such interactions are the members' difficulties which lead them to be self-centred, and which result in them acting in a manner that is destructive of social relationships and of open communication. The group supports the healthy functioning which leads to increasing maturity, while the responses of the individual which block the development of relationships become unaccept-able to the group. This produces a force in the group which pushes the members towards maturation, towards co-operating with others and away from an isolated, egocentric, neurotic position.

The aim in the group is that members should talk freely, without censoring what they say or think, so that a *free-floating discussion* becomes estab-lished. Foulkes (1975, p. 95) wrote of '*free group association*' as equivalent in the group to free association in individual therapy. It differs in that what arises in each member's mind is in response to what previously has been said or has occurred in the group, a form of *resonance*. Each member responds personally to the group content, as it raises specific issues in that member's mind.

Group analytic therapy attends to the patient's current life situation more directly than individual analytic therapy, emphasizes the *here-and-now*, and reveals less of the patient's past developmental experiences. This focus on the here and now does not imply that group analysis is a superficial approach as compared with psychoanalysis, because *communication* is viewed as occurring simultaneously at a number of levels. Foulkes (1964) described four levels:

(i) The level of current reality;
(ii) The transference level;
(iii) The level of part-object relations;

(iv) The level of the collective unconscious, of transpersonal processes that bind mankind together.

The following example may clarify how the same words are understood as a communication at a number of different levels.

> Clive talks on, listening neither to himself or others. Jane suddenly opens her eyes, sits up in her chair from her slouched position, and yells at Clive to 'shut up'. She then tells him all he does is turn up and remain silent, or pour out his worries listening to nobody. Jane is reacting to Clive's behaviour, the level of current reality, but her aggressiveness is inappropriate. She is responding to Clive as if he is her selfish brother, which is the transference level. Jane understands Clive because she, likewise, tends to be at the centre of the group or effectively absent; he represents a needy part of her which she disowns by projecting into him, the level of the part object relationship.

In preferring the term *conductor* to therapist or leader group analysts are describing the way they support the maturation of the group. The conductor acts as a model facilitating the group process while maintaining a psychoanalytic attitude of being non-directive, and available as a transference figure who is non-judgemental and accepting of the group members. The initial attempts of the group to establish a dependent relationship with the conductor will be accepted, to increase the security of the group; but as the group matures, authority both for the group and treatment of its members is given back to the group.

Key concepts – group analysis

The individual is a *nodal point* within a *network* of communication (see p. 14). Symptoms are an expression of a disturbance in that person's networks: in their family, work or social networks. This disturbance, this block to communication, is then recreated in the group.

Through a neurotic symptom the individual achieves both some expression of a conflict in a symbolic but unintelligible form, and some recompense for it being kept unconscious. The symptom is a *communication*, but is unintelligible to others, and is a block to open communication with them. As the group works towards an ever more articulate form of communication, focusing not only on what is said, but how and why, *translation* of the manifest communication occurs, and its latent meaning is understood. The underlying conflict becomes expressed in articulate language. Foulkes described the conductor striving 'to broaden and deepen' the group members' range of expression, this process having 'much in common with making the unconscious conscious' (Foulkes, 1964, p. 112).

The significance of any communication can only be understood fully if seen within the web of communication and relationships in the group, the *matrix* inside which all processes take place. This is the shared ground of the group which ultimately gives meaning to the events and communications that occur. It is through this fundamental concept of the matrix that the group analyst, focusing on the total interaction of the group, understands how the contributions of each individual effects the other group members, and the group as a whole.

The conductor actively supports the *integration of the group*, the significant involvement of the members with each other, despite upsets and difficulties in their relationships. Analysis and interpretation may threaten this involvement, and there should be a balance between the integrative and analytic forces in the group. Interpretations from other group members are often less disturbing than those from the conductor, as they side-step the issues of authority that need to be resolved with the conductor.

Discovering one is not alone with incongruous, absurd or obscene thoughts and impulses, but is accepted – with the reciprocal requirement that one accepts others and their struggles – draws the group member out of an isolated position, and consequently *socialization* occurs.

Transference is when feelings, attitudes and fantasies are experienced in the present, but are a displacement from an important early relationship. In the group, transference occurs to the group members as well as to the conductor. Any member who attempts to gain relief and satisfaction from their transferential fantasies solely from the conductor will be frustrated, because the conductor's time and interest has to be shared. The group may absorb some of the transference feelings towards the conductor, and support the member who is struggling to understand these feelings, taking over some of the roles of the therapist in individual therapy. The transference phenomemon of individual therapy is diluted in the group, and worked through in the interactions between the group members.

Mirror, chain and condenser phenomena describe specific patterns of communication which occur in groups. It is easier to see in others what one cannot recognize in oneself – *the mirror phenomenon*. Having confronted the other person, and understood their behaviour, the member may begin to recognize the trait in him/herself, and understand this sensitivity to it in the other (see example of Jane and Clive, p. 20).

When the group pools its associations – *the chain phenomenon* – particularly to symbolic material such as dreams, there is a loosening up of group resistances and a sudden discharge of deep unconscious material – *the condenser phenomenon*. These phenomena resulted in one group suddenly being aware of the rivalry which had been avoided by the group treating one member as special, while the others suppressed their desires to have a special relationship with the conductor. In very condensed form, the sequence was:

Three dreams are told one after the other. The group moved from a feeling of innocent happiness and freedom, to thoughts of self-denial in the interest of others, a suggestion that the group was asexual, and finally to members becoming aware of their sexual desires and rivalry.

Theoretical underpinnings – group focal conflict model

Though the focal conflict perspective and group analysis developed independently, and utilize different terms, the approaches have many similarities. One difference is that the focal conflict model emphasizes the shared emotions of the group, whereas group analysis stresses the transference relationships which emerge between group members.

Group members are invited to discuss their concerns, whatever is important to them. Open discussion develops, and there is a *flow of associations* from the different members. Each member only responds to part of what has previously been said, and participates verbally or silently, by being attentive or inattentive, sprawled out, restless or tense. As the conductor listens to these interactions, in time a theme emerges. The *group theme* has some relevance to all the members of the group, each member responding individually to the theme, as it arouses thoughts and feelings specific to that individual's past and present experience.

Key concepts – group focal conflict model

The theme arouses feelings in the group, which slowly become clear. A fear, the *reactive motive*, is in conflict with a wish, the *disturbing motive*. This is the *focal conflict*, and the group searches for a solution (Whitaker and Lieberman, 1964). Solutions are of two types: *restrictive solutions* which reduce anxiety and guilt, and satisfy the demands of the reactive motive, and *enabling solutions* which increase anxiety by responding to the disturbing motive (wish), but open up the theme to full discussion. The *group culture* is established by the successive solutions to the focal conflicts which become group history. Whether these solutions are enabling or restrictive will fundamentally shape the therapeutic potential of the group. The conductor assists the group in developing enabling solutions, by helping the group to cope with anxiety and guilt through focusing interpretations on the reactive motive (fear).

Group solutions are sometimes quite complex, because they need the support of all the group's members. In the following example the enabling solution allows the group to explore feelings about parents and the conductor.

Figure. 2.1 Group focal conflict.

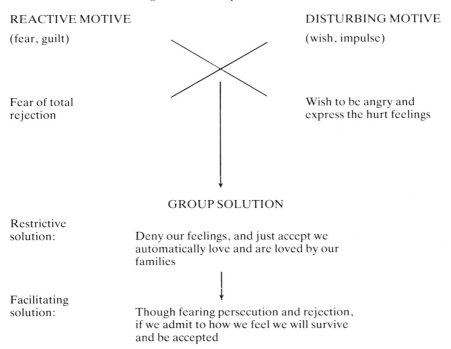

REACTIVE MOTIVE   DISTURBING MOTIVE

(fear, guilt)   (wish, impulse)

Fear of total   Wish to be angry and
rejection   express the hurt feelings

GROUP SOLUTION

Restrictive
solution: Deny our feelings, and just accept we
                             automatically love and are loved by our
                             families

Facilitating
solution: Though fearing persecution and rejection,
                             if we admit to how we feel we will survive
                             and be accepted

In the first group meeting following a break Brian describes how close he feels to his family – they just accept each other as they are. Peter disagrees with his attitude, stating he despises his family, but fears being rejected by his fiancée's family. Maurice is shocked, stating one should never criticize one's parents; Peter is told how good his parents are, and is pushed to withdraw his statement. Others insist 'we love our families and are loved by them', and when Peter refuses to change his view the other members become desperate, Maurice pleading 'you can't turn against your own family'. The group members wish to express their feelings of discontentment, hurt and anger with their families, but fear being rejected (see Fig. 2.1). The group has similar feelings about the conductor following him failing them by going away on leave. Peter refuses to accept this restrictive solution – 'of course we love and are loved by our families' – and the group searches for other solutions, finally focussing on David who is wearing a pink triangular badge: 'so you've come out.' David is unable to tell his parents he is homosexual, fearing he will be thrown out of home. The group is told the pink badge is a symbol originally used in Nazi concentration camps, and now this symbol of persecution is worn with pride. This enabling solution symbolically expresses the fear of annihilation, the resentment and wish to turn against the family, and the proof that one can survive persecution and rejection.

French (1952) developed the *nuclear conflict model* to explain how recurrent patterns of behaviour are established. In early life, the individual

Figure. 2.2 Nuclear conflict model – applied to Peter.

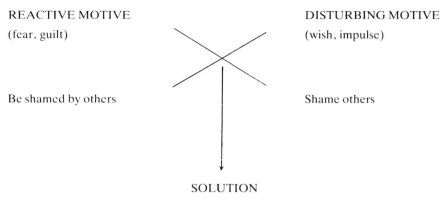

REACTIVE MOTIVE   DISTURBING MOTIVE

(fear, guilt)   (wish, impulse)

Be shamed by others   Shame others

SOLUTION

Be isolated, self-sufficient, and different
from the family

is faced with situations where behaving as one wishes will have some disastrous consequence, and complex restrictive patterns of thought and behaviour are developed to resolve such dilemmas. In later life, feelings are aroused which resonate with the nuclear conflict, and commonly the same solution, no matter how restrictive or inappropriate to the present situation, is instigated (see Fig. 2.2).

Theoretical underpinnings – the Tavistock model

Ezriel (1952, 1973) and his colleagues applied the principles of psychoanalysis to the group situation. Interpretations of the transference relationship established by the group as a whole to the therapist, are given initially to the group and then to each individual. The therapist does not pay attention to the transference relationships between group members, as in group analysis. The key factor that produces change is the interpretation of the transference as it is expressed in the here and now of the group situation. All material, including gestures and movements, as well as dreams and lies, is treated as transference material. Transference is present from the moment the patient meets the analyst.

The tension on meeting new people stems from an individual's fear of the other person because of the fantasies projected onto them. Members attempt to reduce this tension by imposing their own patterns of relationships on the group. The unconscious group tension that arises when several people meet together results in the members selecting, supporting, distorting, and pushing others into and being pushed into alien roles.

Key concepts – the Tavistock model

The therapist works to understand why this *common group tension*, or group theme, is presenting itself now, clarifying the three kinds of object relations which each individual is attempting to establish. Each individual expresses in the common group tension the *required relationship* which the patient is trying to establish with the therapist, the *avoided relationship* which is the relationship the patient would dearly love to have with the therapist (at an unconscious, fantasized level), and the *calamity* which is the disastrous consequence that would ensue if the avoided relationship was consciously expressed.

The therapist will first make a group interpretation, then show the relevance of this to the individual members, pointing out how each is behaving now in the group, and how this is a repetition of responses stemming from early life experiences. First the defence against the anxiety (the required relationship) is interpreted, then the anxiety (the calamity), and later the unconscious impulse (the avoided relationship). A correct group interpretation results in a feeling of warmth, and a moving sense of closeness in the group.

There are a number of similarities between this model and the focal conflict model, but applying this approach to the example given previously (see p. 23) creates a slightly different emphasis. By stating that he despises his parents, Peter arouses considerable anxiety which is associated with the avoided relationship; this prompts the group to insist that members of families love and accept each other (the required relationship), and do not criticize their parents. Peter also expresses the calamity by describing the fear that his future in-laws may reject him.

These statements about parents and in-laws are understood and interpreted as transference communications about the therapist. The therapist would first describe the group's insistence that they accept and love him (the required relationship), and are loved by him they fearing being rejected (the calamity) should they express their feelings about the despicable therapist who goes away and leaves them.

This approach provides a clear, precise way of interpreting group phenomena; interpretations in individual therapy are often formulated in these terms. The group focal conflict model provides a similar structure, but in considering the nature of the group solution, the therapist considers the effect of an intervention on the further development of the group, and may actively support group integrative solutions which lead to increasing maturity of the group. The Tavistock approach maintains a classical analytic position in which the role of the therapist is to provide understanding, not to accept responsibility for helping the patient or group, nor to provide support, give direction to the group, nor to make rules.

The therapist is distant from the emotional turmoil of the group and its members, and is not considered part of the group, influencing and being influenced by the group.

The transference to the therapist is always interpreted, in contrast to group analysis, where initially it is accepted and used to support the development of the individual and the group. This therapist-centred approach encourages regression, and there is no attempt to work with the healthy, social, group-supportive aspects of the individual as in group analysis. What the members say is treated as free associations, and interpretations are often made about deep, sexual material.

The benefits of group therapy compared with individual therapy are not clear in the Tavistock model. Though it accepts the social nature of man, it does not demonstrate how this is used for the further development of the individual. It is likely that patients who are mature enough to analyse themselves will gain considerably from this approach, but many patients report a lack of warmth, support or care. A follow-up study of the Tavistock Clinic (Malan *et al.*, 1976) pointed to the need for careful selection and preparation for this approach.

Theoretical underpinnings – Bion

Bion produced a general theory of small group processes which is used in study and training groups, and which has influenced research (Stock and Thelen, 1966). Though the approach is not directly applied in clinical work, at times the theoretical ideas are valuable in understanding small therapeutic groups.

The sole task of the analyst is to interpret the group phenomena, not offer help or guidance. The group learns as the analyst points out what it is doing. The analyst models not a way of behaving but a way of looking at behaviour and thinking about it. Interpretations are often made on the basis of the feelings and impulses the analyst feels as the object of projections from the group. They are not directed at individuals, as this supports the basic assumption mode established by the group.

A group carrying out its allotted, consciously decided-upon task is a *working group*. Often, however, if one observes the *work group*, it acts instead 'as if' its aim is to obtain support, or avoid the task, or find strength from a new leader who will supply what the group wants. Opposed to the conscious *work group* are three unconscious *basic assumption states* of dependency, fight – flight and pairing. The individual contains certain innate patterns which become apparent in the unorganized group. These patterns or basic assumptions bond the group members together, creating a sense of security and unity, and the group then runs on the basis of fantasies, the individual losing the ability to resolve issues rationally from personal experience of reality.

Key concepts – Bion

In the *work group*, organization and structure results from the co-operation of the members, but the basic assumption group is not organized, and Bion used the term '*valency*' to describe the way individuals are compelled to behave according to the prevalent basic assumption.

Individual contributions to the group become part of the collective *group mentality* if they are supported by the comments of others. The group mentality, because of its defensive origins, is opposed to the aims of the individual members of the group. The *group culture* relates to the atmosphere in the group, and the way members relate to each other.

In the *dependent group*, the group behaves as if someone will magically satisfy the group's needs and longings. Initially the group expects both knowledge and solutions from the analyst, but when these are not forthcoming there is often initial denial, and then the analyst is attacked and the group searches for an alternative leader.

In the *fight – flight group*, the accepted leader is one who creates opportunities for the group to avoid work activity, possibly by leading the group in criticizing administrators, politicians, society or some force outside the group. The group is united against external threats and to protect itself from in-fighting.

In the *pairing group*, two members are involved in a discussion and the remaining group members listen attentively, giving no indication of wishing to discuss their own problems. In the pairing basic assumption, there is a shared unconscious fantasy that the pair will create a person or idea which will save the group, but for this basic assumption to continue it is important the saviour remains unborn.

These group phenomena are observable in a group conducted by a detached, imperturbable therapist, and are a function of that style. Basic assumption states occur when there is an avoidance of meaningful personal contact and the group functions at a primitive level of communication with a loss of individual distinctiveness. This is intentional in some group situations, and is a response to difficulties and resistance in therapeutic group situations (Brown, 1985). While it is important that regression occurs in group therapy, the individual must be in touch with reality and be able to reflect on the experience.

In this approach, the individual's need for security is emphasized in the basic assumption, but there is no recognition of the individual's need for growth. In contrast, group analysis allows the individual and group to discover their interrelatedness, encourages spontaneous interaction and communication at many levels, and discourages the development of the basic assumption states.

PRACTICE

The author's approach to group analytic therapy, integrating concepts from the focal conflict model, is described in this section. The group has seven to nine members who have not had any previous relationships with each other, but who will come to know each other intimately. They meet with the conductor for 1½ hours, once or twice weekly for 18 months to 4 years, face to face in a circle, at the centre of which there is often a low table which acts as a focus for the group, and at times as a transitional object. The group may be *closed*, having fixed membership, and probably a pre-determined termination date; more commonly, it is a *slow open* group, continuing for many years, and having a stable membership for long periods.

The goals of the group

The goal of the group is the freeing of the individual from intrapsychic conflicts, and difficulties in interpersonal relationships; so that the individual may be more aware of thoughts and feelings, may learn from experience, and establish appropriate networks of relationships in which the full potential of the individual may be realized. The group provides a protected arena in which personal exploration can occur, i.e. where there is a relaxation in the functioning of the individual's super-ego, and where the group may play with ideas, metaphors and symbols.

Inclusion and exclusion criteria
Group members must establish a working alliance with the conductor and the group. Their difficulties should be understandable in psychological terms, and they should be motivated to gain insight and change. They need to become caught up in the emotional turmoil and the transference which develops in the group, and yet be able to observe and reflect on their behaviour. They must be able to cope with feelings that are aroused without responding to them impulsively, and between sessions must continue to function in their normal life. It is important to remember that the individual is selected for a particular group, so anyone may be acceptable in certain groups.

Psychotic, paranoid and severely depressed patients, and anti-social individuals, are often not suitable for group analytic therapy. Socially isolated individuals, who do not have a supporting network outside the group to sustain them, do not do well in group analysis. Those caught up in an acute crisis, such as a bereavement, are often looking for support to enable them to continue functioning, and are not able to question their defences, though this may not apply once the acute crisis is over. The group may provide structure for disorganized people, but this is not the purpose of the analytic group.

Group balance

The group should have a wide mix of people (*a heterogeneous group*), who have different problems, but also different ways of coping, expressing feelings, and patterns of defence. It is useful if they have a similar tolerance to anxiety. In a balanced group, each member gains from the strengths of the others. In the slow open group, there is the opportunity to introduce someone who will balance the group.

One or two people whose fundamental defence is by splitting (borderline personality organization) may be included in a group of people with neurotic difficulties whose primary defence is repression. These members are aware of their primitive feelings and arouse similar primitive feelings in the more rigid neurotic patients, while reciprocally gaining from that rigidity.

It is preferable that there is, for example, more than one homosexual, one person with physical disabilities, or one adolescent in the group, because isolates are always at risk of being scapegoated or isolated.

Patients with addictions or sexual perversions may do better in an *homogeneous group*, where members all have the same presenting problem. Their need for dependence or attachment may be too great for the heterogeneous group to satisfy, and still function analytically. In an homogeneous group members are confronted by others with similar needs, and have to find some way of providing mutual support. (see also 'Limitations of the approach': pp. 39–40).

The role of the leader (conductor)

The conductor is part of the group and is permeated by the group process, but has particular functions and is of particular significance. S/he will be very active in his/her own mind, but will intervene as little as possible, staying in the background. The conductor is not the leader, but the servant and guide of the group; though this does not diminish the authority and responsibility of the role. The group will be dependent on the conductor who will be taken as a model and used as a transference figure. Initially, the conductor accepts this role but does not wish to be too central, and so works towards the group taking responsibility for itself. A major distinction between group analysis and the approach of Bion and Ezriel, is that the former model accepts this dependence but works towards the group becoming independent, whereas the latter approach interprets this dependence.

The conductor's tasks can be divided into two – dynamic administration and therapeutic activity.

Dynamic administration

This is the therapeutic work of the conductor creating and maintaining the structure and boundaries of the group, which are challenged both from within and without the group.

(a) The setting. The group is part of a larger organization or society on which it is dependent. It disturbs the dynamics of the organization and the group conductor must negotiate with colleagues so that they recognize and accept the importance of its meeting at a regular time, in an appropriate room, with no disturbances. In creating and guarding the physical boundaries of the group, the conductor is establishing the psychological boundary of the group.

(b) Preparation for the group. Prior to someone joining, it is important to explore their ideas and fantasies about being in a group: what will happen to them, how they will gain what they want, and how people will respond to them. Unless the patient is encouraged to raise questions, concerns and doubts about group therapy, and understands the appropriateness of the approach, the necessary commitment cannot be made. The group needs to be a priority in the patient's life. Practical issues should also be discussed: the time of meetings, length, place, fees, number of members in the group, and any specific features.

(c) Group boundaries. The group starts punctually, absence should be notified in advance, and group members should arrange their holidays around the group. Drugs should normally be avoided and not be prescribed by the group conductor, and other displacement activities, such as smoking and eating, should be discouraged. In an out-patient setting it is preferable that members only meet during the group sessions. Meetings that occur outside the group should always be discussed in the group.

These are not rules, but boundaries necessary for the therapeutic functioning of the group, and the conductor focuses on these issues as they arise, particularly in the first few sessions of the group, so that members may understand their relevance.

The group needs plenty of notice (a minimum of 2 weeks) of a new member joining them, and it is better if the issue is discussed 4–8 weeks in advance, so that the conductor can assess how the group will respond. If the group is uncohesive, it may disintegrate on the arrival of the new member, whereas if it is cohesive, but threatened by the new family member, the newcomer may be ejected.

(d) Leaving the group. Ideally the issues that brought the member to therapy will no longer be pressing on leaving. The member discusses at length and negotiates with the group the appropriateness of leaving, and agrees a date which provides adequate time for the valuable work of the termination phase to be completed. Often the group does not want to lose a member, because this will change the pattern of relationships in the group.

When the conductor leaves, the decision has to be made whether the group should terminate, whether there should be an overlap of conductors, or whether she/he should leave before the next joins. In deciding whether the group should continue, the balance and potential strength of the group has to be considered, as well as the need of the members for further therapy. If the group is to continue, it must have the strength to express the feelings of disappointment, sadness, rage and pleasure which arise as the conductor's leaving is mourned.

Therapeutic activity
This aspect of the conductor's task is not confined to interpretation, but involves interventions such as asking questions, focusing the group on a topic, making comments and clarifying issues. These activities lead to the group and individual members gaining insight. *Interpretations* are important, but should only be given when the insight fails to emerge from the group. They are made about both the total situation, and about specific transference phenomena. Interpretations may be given in stages: in the example that follows the defence is first interpreted, which leads to an increase in anxiety, then the hidden feelings emerge as the resistance is interpreted again. The clinical example is a shortened account of one group session, and illustrates the conductor's *orientation* to the total group situation, to the interactions of all its members, and demonstrates how some of the conductor's therapeutic activities are integrated.

(a) Clinical example

Group content	*Conductor's thoughts*
Brian tells a dream of staying in a friend's house where a large hole or tank in the bed separates him from the other man. A dangerous fish is swimming around and Brian must catch it. He hears it jump, catches it, and awakes. He had not reported the dream the previous week as the conductor was away.	Brian links this dream to the conductor and his absence, and presumably it also relates to the last group meeting. *Locating* the dream in this way makes the conductor wonder what did happen last week. In the dream Brian is taking responsibility, as he does in the group, making sure everyone is alright by

supporting subgrouping and post-groups. In the dream Brian maintains the *boundaries*! Brian finds it difficult to accept the conductor's authority and responsibility for the group.

The conductor asks: 'What does hearing Brian's dream make you think of?'

The conductor elects to *focus* the group's attention and helps the members produce their *associations* to the dream, and not their interpretations, which would be defensive and stop *free group association*. In the conductor's *orientation* the dream is treated as relating to the group as a whole.

Maurice talks of feeling guilty at having sexual feelings for his sister. Claire wonders why Brian recollects this dream now. Joanne is feeling furious with a relative who abused her sexually. Brian thinks the dream relates to his special relationship with Joanne. He also feels that now he can face issues from his childhood.

Themes about sexual relationships, special relationships and abuse by people you trust are emerging. Two weeks previously the group were discussing sexual relationships. The group is now discussing the breakdown of sexual boundaries in families, the *latent meaning* of which is a fear of this occurring in the group. Therefore, the group members protect themselves by not becoming involved in the group.

The conductor decides to *interpret* this *restrictive solution* which is expressed in the dream. he considers the 'fish' should not be interpreted, but left as a *symbol*.

The conductor speaks to the group: 'Perhaps now I'm here you can give up responsibility for catching the fish.'

The men appear more relaxed, and the women more tense.

Claire leaves the room. On her return the conductor raises the issue: 'You feel less tense now you've returned?'

Claire's leaving is an example of *acting out* at the boundary. What feelings are being avoided? The members constantly take feelings out of the group with their post-groups. Now it is happening in the session.

Angrily Claire denies the relevance of her leaving. She is not tense. She begins to choke and starts crying. She claims people turn away from her, or would if they knew what she had done.

Joanne is relieved someone else feels like she does, confused with feelings of anger and shame. She appears distraught.

The hidden feelings are revealed, and Joanne *resonates* with the shame and anger

The conductor decides to make a *transference* link speaking to Joanne, and through her to the group, as she is expressing the group's rage as well as her own. (Note her association to the dream.)

The conductor links the feelings expressed about him in the present, with the past: 'I chose to be elsewhere last week, do other things – like your parents – and then you are abused.'

Joanne describes the abused becoming the abusers, and begins to reflect on her destructive anger which she controls by distancing herself from others. She describes finally understanding the basis of her self-destructive behaviour.

Joanne is thinking about her anger and not just expressing it because she feels *contained* within the group, the conductor having established the *boundaries*.

Referring back to Maurice's disclosure of incestuous fantasies, Lindsey says she has not spoken as she sees too much of herself in Maurice.

Through *mirroring*, Lindsey sees herself in Maurice and then, accepts having sexual feelings for the first time in her life.

Co-therapy

Bion and Ezriel both used observers who sat outside the circle of the group, and did not participate verbally. Group analysts favour co-therapy as an invaluable way to learn and gain confidence in conducting; but with the more experienced conductor, the group is often better off with one conductor, or one who is clearly in charge.

It takes time learning to work together, and it is often helpful if the therapists have similar levels of experience. Benefits of co-leadership include: co-therapists will understand the group differently, thus transference may be clarified; material is less likely to be ignored because of the conductor's counter-transference or defensive posture resulting from unresolved unconscious conflicts; and mistakes are more likely to be corrected. There is the companionship in what can be a very lonely job, and the opportunity to learn about the group and about oneself.

The role of group members

The new member is starting on a journey of exploration, not knowing what will be discovered, or who will be there. Joining an established group disturbs old members as well, as the structure, culture and patterns of relationships in the group alter in response to the change.

The member's task is to communicate verbally in the group in a way that the others can understand. There is a sharing with, and responding to, each other. Despite the anxiety and pressure that arises members should attempt to communicate the thoughts and ideas that occur to them, whether or not they appear to have a relationship to what others have been saying. Remarks about other members are welcome, and comments should not be censored as in normal social discourse. There is no set topic in the group, and members are responsible for raising issues, concerns and disappointments. Through freely expressing their thoughts, ideas and associations which arise in response to communications in the group, *free group association* becomes established.

The aim of the group is not that one member is centre stage with others offering understanding, but for there to be a free exchange of associations and ideas. The member is actively involved in therapy, taking responsibility for the group and the development of understanding, both in self and others. As the group matures the members become steadily more involved in the sharing of ideas, providing support, offering insight and interpretations. The member becomes caught up in the transpersonal processes of the group matrix, resonating to other members, and open to the ideas that emerge.

Group material is treated as confidential, as each member develops respect and trust in the other members as together they begin to take risks in the way they interact.

Major life decisions should be discussed in the group, as they may be a creative solution to problems, but they may also be a playing out of a member's compulsive need to recreate destructive patterns of behaviour, or be a defence against further analysis occurring.

Group development over time

Members are naturally anxious on entering a new situation with unknown people, and a conductor from whom much is expected, but this anxiety starts to dissipate as members begin to interact.

In the *formative phase* of the group the structure and boundaries of the group are challenged as members reduce their anxiety by behaving as they do in other interpersonal relationships. Both the authority of the group and the conductor is challenged, personal autonomy is threatened, greed and envy of others is aroused, and there are fears and wishes for intimacy. Strong emotions are excited, anger is expressed, and feelings of guilt emerge. As the boundaries of the group become established, a setting develops where members may reflect on themselves and become involved with others.

Within a few sessions the group establishes a pattern of interacting, a group culture, and enters the *established phase*. Under its own momentum the group moves from being leader-centred and egocentric, to group-centred and altruistic. There is a continuous interchange of giving and taking, being close and withdrawing, loving and hating, phases of resistance followed by a freeing up and more open communication. Important issues arise again and again, each time occurring at a deeper level as communication increases.

The focal conflict model explains one aspect of the cyclical patterns that occur in groups. If a session ends with a restrictive solution which reduces anxiety, defences will not be reinforced between sessions, and members will approach the next session more willing to take risks, and a facilitating solution is more likely to emerge.

During the *termination phase* there is a speeding up of the group process. Termination may involve one or two members, or the whole group. Ideally the termination date has been mutually agreed, and once arranged it should not be altered. As the anger and sadness is expressed the opportunity arises to reappraise the group experience, consider what has and has not been gained, and reflect on how the experience could have been different with the understanding the members now possess.

Mechanisms of change

In the group, change often precedes insight, though both are necessary for persistent therapeutic change to occur. A member joins a group with a 'problem' (Garland, 1982), but the group is an alternative system to the family where the 'problem' or pathology originated. The impetus for change is invested in the individual in group analysis, and it is the 'problem' that motivates the individual to join the group. As the 'problem' is disclosed, the individual becomes part of the group, receiving sympathy, understanding, support, advice, hope, a sense of not being alone with this difficulty; but these phenomena, though important in the development of the group, do not induce change, and do not make the problem disappear. It is when the member gives up focusing on the 'problem', and becomes involved in the ongoing life and process of the group, and caught up in the interactions of this new situation, that change occurs. The 'problem' becomes less central as the member becomes actively involved with others.

This involvement enables the group members to observe in the group situation the transactional patterns that moulded them, and led to the development of their neurotic patterns of relating to others. Through the analysis of the relationships that develop in the group, the understanding of the transference and the role of projective identification, the individual gains insight. The change becomes fixed as the individual and the group move towards gaining insight, mutual understanding and experimentation with new and creative ways of being.

It is within the matrix of the group as it slowly develops that maturation and individuation occur. The group member learns to create and use life experiences for personal growth. There is a richness and variety in the relationships established, and a sensitivity to others and their particular level of maturity (Pines, 1985).

In individual therapy, there is a focusing on how the problem developed, and an exploration and uncovering of its roots. Foulkes (1964) contrasted the 'vertical' analysis of individual therapy with the 'horizontal' analysis of group therapy, in which the focus is on lateral communication and the here and now interactions of the group. Transference neurosis (the recreation of the original relationship problems in the present therapeutic situation) develops in group analysis just as in individual therapy, but resolution is not solely by interpretation; it is by the opportunities provided in the group to recognize and relate to others. Through the establishment of firm boundaries, relationships totally uncoupled from outside emerge. The situation for free and open communication is established, where speech may occur which is free from the consequences and fears that blocked expression in the original family system.

Typical problems and their resolution

Issues which arise as the group proceeds
The initial phase establishes the pattern and culture both for that session and for the group as a whole. Careful planning and selection, followed by activity orientated to establishing a therapeutic group culture early on is important. But there is always the first time the conductor is faced with a particular issue which challenges the maintenance of a therapeutic group culture. Then it is important for the conductor to hold onto some basic guidelines:

  (i) maintain a sense of safety in the group;
 (ii) avoid the collapse of the group;
(iii) establish and maintain norms that facilitate work;
(iv) use events for the benefit of the group as a whole and for individuals in the group;
 (v) avoid doing harm; and
(vi) recognize and correct errors (Whitaker, 1985b).

Questions to and requests of the conductor
It is conceivable not to answer a direct question, but in some groups this will appear cold and rejecting. It is essential to understand why this person wants to know this fact, now. What is the meaning of this question at a group level, what will the group do with this material? It is not the function of the conductor to be a real person and give comfort to the members of the group – hopefully they will find that in each other. The conductor is there to help them look at the nature of their intrapsychic structure and interpersonal functioning. A response such as 'I can certainly answer that question but . . .' or an uninformative confirmation, followed by a request that they explore it, may be appropriate. There is always a part of the group that wishes to function on the dependency basic assumption, or establish a restrictive solution, and it is easy to be seduced into supporting this.

Information and advice
At times there are requests for information about group members from other professionals. The conductor should raise these in the group, redefining the issues as a group problem. Requests for advice should be treated likewise, naming or analysing the defence or restrictive solution inherent in this. The conductor is an expert, but in this situation an expert group analyst.

Individual sessions
Requests for individual sessions should be discussed in the group. The need often disappears and the secret is expressed as the group responds to the person's anxiety. Individual sessions may reassure the conductor, but the authority of the group is undermined.

Emergencies
Sometimes the conductor cannot wait for the group to raise an issue. If a dire emergency arises, such as a member becoming suicidal, the issue must be addressed directly:

> Jane turns on Brian as an intellectualizing . . . Joanne leaps out of her chair wanting to ring Jane's neck.

Conflict creates drama and excitement, stirs up emotions and is necessary to some degree in order for the group to be therapeutic. Violence, and the threat of it, interferes with open communication; it is the group's responsibility to contain such behaviour. If the conductor attempts to resolve these issues, then the special attention one member receives arouses jealousy, guilt at being special, and more attacks.

The conductor's responsibility is to keep the group functioning. This creates the opportunity to understand the meaning of the behaviour in the context in which it is occurring. Psychotic behaviour in a group is treated likewise. What is being stated is in response to this member being in this situation. Understanding behaviour and communication rather than just responding to them is often a totally new and mutative experience for group members.

Behaviour that threatens the group structure

Good preparation reduces *dropping out*, but it is essential to be sensitive to the struggles of the individual early on.

Flight from the group occurs when the person is suddenly threatened, often having actively resisted expressing something in the group. The tension becomes unbearable, and leaving seems the only solution. Sometimes an individual session will enable a member to rejoin the group.

The group should be informed in advance of *absences*. It cannot function with an inconsistent membership, because trust in others is undermined. Unplanned absences may be a way of coping with excessive anxiety, and are a restrictive solution both for the individual and group. The nature of the unresolved conflict should be explored.

Out of group meetings should be reported to the group. The pre-group, and post-group meetings may become part of the group culture. The questions, then, are: what is the group trying to resolve without the conductor, and what aggressive, or other unresolved feelings are being expressed?

Sometimes a new member will *monopolize* the group in a first or early session, disclosing information, establishing relationships which are premature and inappropriate to the level of group development. Often such people drop out, so it is helpful to intervene. Sometimes the group allows someone to monopolize the session while others sit back and watch. It is important to understand why this is happening. Is it an expression of anxiety? Is there a fear of confronting the monopolizer?

Silence

The silent individual, though possibly very much part of the group, will only gain by identification with others, and vicarious learning. Why the person is not talking needs to be understood. Thus the resistances and defences of a member who talks for the first time when the conductor is away are located in the relationship of that member with the conductor.

A silent group may be productively reflective, or responding appropriately to what is going on. But what is the group communicating by being silent? Is the silence out of fear of the conductor, who has perhaps made a plunging interpretation? Is it a vengeful silence or a defensive silence?

The conductor should assess how long the silence actually is, rather than how long it feels, and will normally wait for a member to break it. Exceptions to this will be if the group is becoming excessively anxious, or if it is actively avoiding an issue, which the conductor has to raise. One way is to speculate out loud on why one considers the silence is occurring.

Limitations of the approach

The analytic group is not shaped through following principles laid down by the leader, as are more structured group therapies (Pines, 1985). The approach is inappropriate when treatment is aimed at the removal of specific symptoms, or the group has a specific task such as increasing efficiency. Group analytic therapy does not directly attempt to change the outside environment of the patient, provide help or advice, offer social support and companionship, maintain the family structure, or provide a panacea for unhappiness.

The analytic group is unstructured, and it is through the exploration and self-organizational capacities of the group members that the group evolves. If a member considers the group to be relatively unimportant in comparison with the family or another group, that member will not freely share in the development of the group and gain from its potential.

As in psychoanalytic therapy, the individual is actively involved in understanding the meaning of symptoms and behaviour, and in exploring disowned aspects of the self and of relationships. The understanding gained in the therapeutic experience is reinforced as it makes sense of other experiences and, then, this knowledge becomes integrated into the individual (Brown and Pedder, 1979). Group analysis differs from psychoanalytic therapy in that the focus is more on the group and social situation, and emphasizes the interpsychic function of defence mechanisms, and how they change the environment, whereas individual therapy emphasizes the intrapsychic function of defence mechanisms, and how they change the individual. Regression is limited in the group situation; the member cannot establish a primitive two-person relationship with the conductor, as others have to be taken into account, and the conductor is more peripheral than the therapist in individual therapy. In the group there is not the same potential to reach back through the transference trauma to the situation that existed before the original trauma (Winnicott, 1965). The specific dependency needs of the individual may not be met by the group, and the group conductor is not necessarily in a position to respond to the individual, adequately meeting these needs at the appropriate time. People whose difficulties are rooted in early childhood may be more appropriately treated by individual therapy. Those who have been deprived early on may experience the group as yet another depriving experience, where sharing the therapist feels like rejection.

Primitive defence mechanisms such as projection, with the associated phenomenon of splitting, are difficult to analyse in the group, and their actions may be more easily revealed to the individual through interpretation of the transference in individual therapy, than through analysis of boundary issues in the group.

Often the interchange in the group makes the well-defended member aware of repressed conflicts, but group analysis is not appropriate when discussion of the presenting problem would inhibit the group. The medium of the group is verbal communication; adequate intelligence, and the ability to understand and to join in the development of a common language is necessary for group analysis to occur.

Typical qualities of effective leaders

The analytic attitude involves a love of truth even when unpalatable. The conductor listens without immediately categorizing the information to fit a preconceived pattern, and has an open mind to understand all that is being said.

The conductor's authority and power stems from the projection of the group. This power is not used to coerce members, or for the conductor's own gratification, but for the benefit of the group. The conductor does not have a mission to fulfil, or an inappropriate need to help people, but is someone who respects people, delights in them as they achieve their potential, and is knowledgeable of the numerous ways people find fulfilment.

As themes arise in the group, the conductor as part of the group is involved and resonates to them. At times, feelings about these themes are overwhelming. The conductor maintains an analytic stance, understanding these issues through reflection, supervision, personal therapy, and discussion with co-therapists. Occasionally, it will be appropriate to disclose them in the group.

The inexperienced conductor may try to be perfect. It is important that the therapeutic group experiences helplessness, hopelessness and despair while still feeling safe. This involves the conductor admitting to limitations, and not attempting to be the omnipotent father of the group.

These qualities will lead the conductor to gain understanding through personal therapy, the study of theory, supervision and observation of others. The reward is the privilege of being part of a living, developing group of people, a participant in the drama of life.

REFERENCES

Bion, W. R. (1961). *Experiences in Groups*. London, Tavistock.
Brown, D. (1985). Bion and Foulkes: basic assumptions and beyond. *In* M. Pines (ed.), *Bion and Group Psychotherapy*. London, Routledge and Kegan Paul.
Brown, D. and Pedder, J. (1979). *Introduction to Psychotherapy: An Outline of Psychodynamic Principles and Practice*. London, Tavistock.
Durkin, H. E. (1974). Current problems of group therapy in historical context. *In* L. R. Wolberg, M. L. Aronson and A. R. Wolberg. (eds), *Group Therapy: 1974, An Overview*. New York, Stratton Intercontinental Medical Book Corp.
Ezriel, H. (1952). Notes on psychoanalytic group therapy II: interpretation and research. *Psychiatry* **15**: 119–126.
Ezriel, H. (1973). Psychoanalytic group therapy. *In* L. R. Wolberg and E. K. Schwarz (eds), *Group Therapy: 1973, An Overview*. New York, Stratton Intercontinental Medical Book Corp.
Foulkes, S. H. (1938). Book review on Norbert Elias. *International Journal of Psychoanalysis* **19**: 263–265.
Foulkes, S. H. (1948). *Introduction to Group Analytic Psychotherapy*. London, Maresfield Reprints.
Foulkes, S. H. (1964). *Therapeutic Group Analysis*. London, George Allen & Unwin.
Foulkes, S. H. (1975). *Group Analytic Psychotherapy: Method & Principles*. London, Gordon and Breach.
French, T. (1952). *The Integration of Behavior: Basic Postulates*. Chicago, University of Chicago Press.
Garland, C. (1982). Group analysis: taking the non-problem seriously. *Group Analysis* **15** (1): 4–14.
Glatzer, H. T., Pines, M., Wong, N. and Kauff, P. F. (1983). Review and preview of psychoanalytic theory in group psychotherapy. *International Journal of Group Psychotherapy* **33** (2): 151–198.
James, D. C. (1984). Bion's "containing" and Winnicott's "holding" in the context of the group matrix. *International Journal of Group Psychotherapy* **34** (2): 201–213.
Kauff, P. F. (1979). Diversity in analytic group psychotherapy: the relationship between theoretical concepts & technique. *International Journal of Group Psychotherapy* **29** (1): 51–65.
Main, T. F. (1946). The hospital as a therapeutic institution. *Bulletin of the Menninger Clinic* **10**: 66–70.
Malan, D. H., Balfour, F. H. G., Hood, V. G. and Shooter, A. M. N. (1976). Group psychotherapy. A long-term follow-up study. *Archives of General Psychiatry* **33**: 1303–1315.
de Mare, P. (1975). The politics of large groups. *In* L. Kreeger (ed.) *The Large Group: Dynamics and Therapy*. London, Constable.
Pines, M. (1985). Psychic development in the group analytic situation. *Group* **9** (1): 24–37.
Schindler, W. (1966). The role of the mother in group psychotherapy. *International Journal of Group Psychotherapy* **16**: 198–202.

Stock, D. A. and Thelen, H. A. (1966). *Emotional Dynamics and Group Culture.* New York, New York University Press.

Sutherland, J. D. (1985). Bion revisited: group dynamics and group psychotherapy. *In* M. Pines (ed.), *Bion and Group Psychotherapy.* London, Routledge and Kegan Paul.

Trist, E. (1985). Working with Bion in the 1940's: the group decade. *In* M. Pines (ed.), *Bion and Group Psychotherapy.* London, Routledge and Kegan Paul.

Whitaker, D. S. (1985a). Some Connections Between a Group Analytic and a Group Focal Conflict Perspective on Group Psychotherapy. Presented to the American Group Psychotherapy Association, New York, 1985.

Whitaker, D. S. (1985b). *Using Groups to Help People.* London, Routledge and Kegan Paul.

Whitaker, D. S. and Lieberman, M. A. (1964). *Psychotherapy Through the Group Process.* New York, Atherton Press.

Winnicott, D. W. (1965). *The Maturational Processes and the Facilitating Environment.* London, Hogarth Press.

Wolf, A. and Schwartz, E. K. (1962). *Psychoanalysis in Groups.* New York, Grune and Stratton.

CHAPTER 3

INTERPERSONAL GROUP THERAPY

Bernard Ratigan and Mark Aveline

HISTORICAL CONTEXT AND DEVELOPMENT IN BRITAIN

The origins of interpersonal group psychotherapy lie in an amalgam of German existential philosophy, American self-psychology and British analytic theory. Its practice is focused on what happens between people and how these interactions may be used to facilitate desired changes in maladaptive patterns of relationships. While the personal histories of members are important, the work of the group is primarily with the here-and-now interactions within the sessions. Fundamentally, the approach is ahistorical. The group is both a laboratory where the form of interactions reveals the nature of the members' difficulties and a workshop where new resolutions may be achieved and practised.

The central concern of psychoanalysis has been with intrapsychic processes; thus, the exploration of them characterizes the practice of psychoanalytic psychotherapy and analytically inspired group therapy. In contrast, and at much the same period as when Freud was elucidating the workings of the unconscious, existential philosophers in Germany were exploring the ways in which humans define their own existence – their *dasein* or being in the world – and through this, find meaning in their life. Freud took a deterministic view; biology and the psychosocial environment of the first 5 years of life are the determinants of the adult character. The existential position stresses the responsibility that the person has for their actions and affirms freedom of choice in each life (Yalom, 1980).

Existential ideas found some acceptance in North America with its ethic of self-reliance, autonomy and industry. There it combined with another German import – the future-directed, individual psychology of Adler, as developed in the cultural theories of Karen Horney. Horney was interested in the consequences for the individual of his behaviour, and described characteristic patterns of relationships in which people move towards, away and against or more fruitfully with others.

The interpersonal school of psychiatry began with Harry Stack Sullivan, whose publications in the late 1940s located the concept of personality in the interpersonal arena. How we see ourselves is the summation of how others have appraised us, he declared. Another strand – the ahistorical element – was contributed by Kurt Lewin, a social psychologist and a founder of vector psychology. People define themselves through the assumptions that they hold; when the same assumptions are held by others, the field of forces so created restricts change. The training group (T-group), an educative forum originated in the National Training Laboratories at Bethel, USA, in the 1940s–1950s, provided an environment for change by bringing together groups of strangers who were encouraged not to define themselves by a restatement of past roles but rather to explore the reality of their interaction within the T-group.

Many of the ideas that make up the interpersonal approach found expression in the humanistic and later in the encounter movement that swept North America in the 1960s and Britain in the early 1970s. Carl Rogers was a spokesman for there being a potential for growth in each person which could be released once a sufficiently facilitative psychological environment was created and perceived by that person. The power differential between therapist and patient virtually disappeared as the two met as equals in a true meeting, the encounter of the movement that grew to meet the deficit of alienated modern life. In Martin Buber's phrase, the healthy human relationship was 'I – Thou', not 'I – It' (see Chapter 9).

Formal small group therapy in Britain has been powerfully influenced by psychoanalytic object-relations ideas and in particular those of splitting, projection and part-object. The notion of the group being moved as a whole by unconscious shared processes provides a way of understanding the phenomena of the group as a whole and of the individual in the group; it complements the above described member-centred focus on responsibility and encounter. The British writers Ezriel, Bion, Foulkes, Whittaker and Lieberman have made their contributions, some of which have become formalized in the group analytic school of the Institue of Group Analysis in London (see Chapter 2).

The interpersonal approach is in common use in Britain but has little formal recognition. Yalom, the Stanford psychotherapist, exemplifies the key elements of the approach in his masterly text book, now in its third edition (Yalom, 1985). The approach shares some concepts with group analysis, and is similarly concerned with improving personal relationships. The interest in meaning and language when considering the interpersonal acts of the group goes far beyond a behavioural analysis. Unlike the spectator role in gestalt therapy and psychodrama, the group is the vehicle for change and its good functioning is given prime importance by the leader.

UNDERLYING ASSUMPTIONS

Theoretical underpinnings

Interpersonal group psychotherapy takes as its focus what happens between people – the actions, reactions and characteristic patterns of interaction that constrain the individual in his interpersonal life and for which help in modifying is being sought in the group. A fundamental assertion of the approach is that each person constructs an individual, inner-world which is continuously being reconstructed through interactions with others and which determines that person's view of himself and others and affects what may be expected from others. A sufficiently secure assumptive world allows the validity of the model to be checked out and updated with significant others; a fear-ridden or rigid assumptive world leads that person to avoid or not attend to experiences which would suggest that revisions are necessary (Frank, 1974). The therapy group brings the individual face to face with how others are as people and how inner assumptions powerfully determine the patterns of interaction that develop. That confrontation is fundamental to the process of change which lies dormant at the inception of an interpersonal group.

In contrast to psychodynamically derived group psychotherapies, the interpersonal approach emphasises five concepts explicated in existential philosophy and psychology: (1) Human actions are not predetermined; freedom is part of the human condition. (2) The corollary of this is the importance of choice in human life and (3) taking responsibility for one's actions. (4) Death is inevitable; but the nothingness of this can give meaning to life. (5) We are each engaged in a creative search for individual patterns that will give meaning to our existence. Writers such as Heidegger and Sartre have provided the philosophical and literary underpinnings for a psychology articulating these important, but often ignored, givens of human existence. Recognition of these by the leader gives a distinctive cast to the interpersonal group.

The existential concepts of responsibility, freedom and choice in
interpersonal group therapy
Existential thought provides three important concepts for interpersonal

group psychotherapy – responsibility, freedom and choice. Judged against the background of the dominant current Anglo-Saxon intellectual ideology of positivism, such concepts often appear dangerously woolly and more at home in left-bank cafés in Paris. They try to capture important ideas about human existence, which are difficult to quantify in the categories currently fashionable in scientific circles. Existential philosophy emphasizes the significance for individuals of taking as much responsibility or control of their own lives as possible; it is the obverse of the idea that people are victims of internal or external forces. It challenges the belief that biology, history, society, God or 'nerves' are the all powerful determinants of a person's life. Thus, it is distinguishable from philosophical, psychological and sociological theories which see human beings as objects rather than subjects, as recipients rather than as authors, to an important degree, of their own realities (Yalom, 1980). Reality, this approach suggests, is socially constructed (Berger and Luckmann, 1967).

The approach provides a clinical context where group members can move from being trapped in a personal world view in which they are passive victims of cruel circumstance to a self-formed one where they can take more responsibility for their lives, relationships, symptoms and difficulties. The central therapeutic effect is not just an intellectual appreciation of an active world view but a lived experience in the group of enlarged freedom through experiences of new personal acts or refraining from maladaptive acts. This is not an absolute freedom but a tension towards a greater freedom and range of choices in human existence: a relative freedom within the context of a person's circumstances.

If the concepts of freedom and responsibility seem abstract, choice (the third concept), derived from existential thought, is more concrete. Human beings constantly exercise choice in their lives; their actions form their empirical reality, and reinforce value systems. However, the tendency of the human condition is not to want to shoulder responsibility for personal choice. In the group, members can come to see how, in that social microcosm, they are continually exercising choices which define their present being and predicate their future. For example, the very act of speaking or not can be seen as a simple example of the exercise of choice rather than a given, immutable fact (see pp. 53–7). The group can help show members the nature of their choices and identify characteristic, maladaptive interpersonal patterns; the group invites reflection on the desirability of the choices now made explicit and 'owned' by the individual, a process which prepares the ground for changing maladaptive choice patterns. From the microcosm of the group, the similar macrocosm of the member's personal and social worlds becomes clear. Hopefully, members will be able to exercise and experience responsibility and choice in the context of an extended sense of personal freedom.

The contribution of interpersonal theory

At the heart of interpersonal theory lies the concept of the self. William James' theory of the self makes an important distinction between the 'I' and the 'Me'. The 'I' is the pure ego of the individual while the 'Me' is the social self – that which is known to others. This was important for psychotherapy because it anticipated both role theory and object-relations theory. James (1890) believed that a person has as many social selves as there are individuals to recognize him and carry an image of him in their mind. The therapy group engages with and identifies the social self that a member offers. It encourages members to move into some of their other unexpressed selves and make them their own.

Lewin (1936) provided a useful analysis of the psychological space each person occupies. His field theory of vectors held that events are determined by forces acting on them in the immediate field rather than by forces at a distance.

The tenet that causation is a contemporary process has created some controversy in psychotherapy. Defending the importance of this, Ezriel (1956) argued that the unconscious structures the analyst uncovers in working with the patient are active in the present and are not necessarily replicas of past realities and reactions. Interpersonal group therapy draws upon Lewin's concept of promoting change by 'unfreezing' the person from the restrictive assumptions that they have held and others in their social world have come to hold about them by providing a new, unprejudiced psychological space for exploration, experiment, rehearsal and acquisition of new selves.

The third of the major figures in interpersonal theory was Harry Stack Sullivan (1953). His theory of interpersonal relations held that human experience consists of interactions or transactions between people. He held that an individual's history influences every moment of his life, because it provides a dynamic structure and definition of his experiences. Anxiety basically arises from threats to the individual's self-esteem; these threats are defended against by characteristic security operations. He took issue with Freud's idea that the basic structure of the personality was immutably laid down during the earliest years of life and argued for a period ending at adulthood, depending partly on the sociocultural conditions, and partly on the idiosyncracies of each person.

His theorem of reciprocal emotion states that integration in an interpersonal situation is a reciprocal process in which (1) complementary needs are resolved or aggravated; (2) reciprocal patterns of activity are developed or disintegrated; and (3) foresight or satisfaction, or rebuff, of similar needs is facilitated (Sullivan, 1953). These Delphic statements appear to mean (1) each person encourages others into certain role relationships, and (2) relationships are strengthened when needs are met and disintegrate when they are not. The interpersonal group shows to members how they are the architects of their interpersonal 'fate'. In Sullivan's view there are always more similarities rather than differences between people. Interpersonal group therapy seeks to show how individual sufferers may shed some of their pain and rejoin the mainstream. In this they are helped by one another and by the leader who is a participant observer and never just a mirror of the group process.

The contribution of analytic concepts applied to the process of the group
When the members of a group come together they begin a journey. If it is to be successful they need to be able to talk about themselves, their feelings, fears and worries, and about the other people in the group. From the outset the group will take on some of the characteristics of an individual being. Just as individuals distort and avoid, so do groups. The fears and reactions held in common move the group as a whole and this is the group process. The leader needs to be able to see this process at work and show the group members what is happening. If the process can be turned to good account it will lead to greater openness and sharing.

We have found the formulation of Ezriel (1950), a Tavistock analyst, helpful (see also Chapter 2). This formulation can be applied to individual as well as group processes. The group takes up a *required relationship* with the leader (or with the members in our extension of Ezriel's work) which safeguards them from being in the *avoided relationship* for fear that that would provoke the *calamitous relationship*. A clinical example may make clear this complex concept.

After some weeks in a therapy group, a 25-year-old mental health professional began missing sessions and turning up late when he did attend. He was black, articulate, and slightly physically handicapped. The leader noted that the atmosphere was tense when the man was present and relaxed in his absence. The group showed false friendliness with the man so as not to confront him with his behaviour (the *required relationship*). The leader confronted the group with what they collectively were doing. It became clear that the man's knowledge of group therapy, his blackness, his combative verbal style and his physical handicap all contributed to a sense of relief when he was absent. The group avoided facing the negative feelings about this man (the *avoided relationship*). As the leader persisted with the exploration of the group process aspects, some resolution was achieved; fears subsided that the group would disintegrate (the *calamitous relationship*) if the man was challenged and retaliated in anger or if the group faced unwanted feelings of racial prejudice.

The analytic perspective also shows other ways in which unconscious processes enter into the happenings of the group (see next section).

Key concepts

In being themselves in the group, members demonstrate their characteristic maladaptive interpersonal patterns. How these patterns are handled is what determines whether or not the group experience is therapeutic. Many elements (concepts) contribute to the therapeutic whole. In the group, members have the opportunity to gain *insight* into how they function with regard to others.

To derive benefit the member needs to have an *openness to being moved* both by the interactions with others and in himself in his personal and world view. It may well require more than verbal assent or protestations of openness for the member actually to be at this stage in their life. It is necessary for the member to be able and willing to assume *responsibility* for their own participation in the learning experience of the group. This means that they need to have a notion of themselves as agents, however minor, of their own destiny and not merely passive victims of biological, historical, social, religious or family forces. The experience of being in the group will help the member reveal his or her *assumptive world* (Frank, 1974), the accumulated set of inherited and acquired ways of looking at the world which profoundly affects a person's behaviour and relationships with other human beings.

In the group, members do not merely talk about their difficulties, they demonstrate them. Attending to the *here-and-now* interactions within the session is a characteristic feature of interpersonal groups. Members often find this focus difficult to cope with initially. What is experienced by the group in the shared present has an immediacy and accessibility which has a powerful potential to be therapeutic and is often frightening. It is a demonstration of the interpersonal difficulties and the start of a way forward toward the resolution of these difficulties. The ahistorical emphasis is dominant and while, as in other forms of group therapy, the exploration of the origin of difficulties does take place, it is not necessary for change.

The major exchanges and activities within the group are *disclosure, feedback, acceptance and risk taking*. *Disclosures* are of two main types: 'secrets' from the past and the present outside the group which the discloser judges to be determining their behaviour and, secondly, information about the feelings being experienced in the here and now. The *Johari window* provides a facilitative model (Luft, 1966; see Fig. 3.1).

Disclosure dismantles the *façade* that each presents to the other. The act of disclosing is almost universally accompanied by the release of emotional tension and the sense of a burden being lifted, unless the disclosure generates an attack. *Feedback* illuminates *blind spots*, aspects of the self that are obvious to others but not known to the self. In the process of feedback, information is transferred between members with the emphasis on accuracy

Figure 3.1 The Johari Window

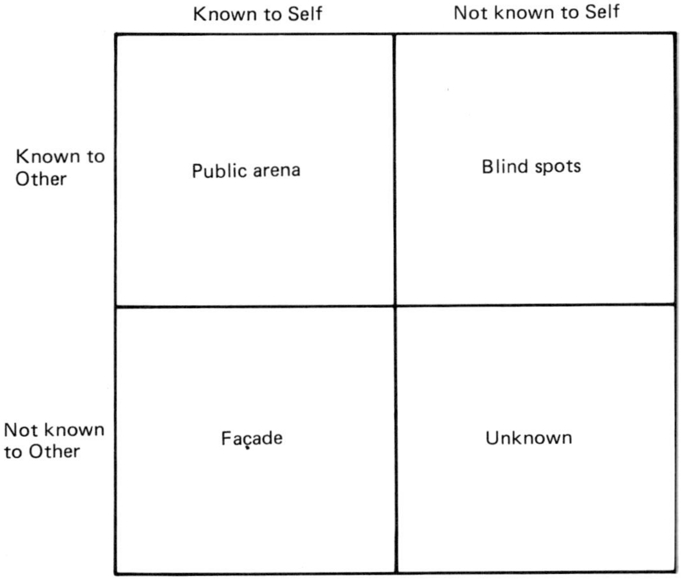

	Known to Self	Not known to Self
Known to Other	Public arena	Blind spots
Not known to Other	Façade	Unknown

and ownership. The person giving the feedback is encouraged to acknowledge that it is their own experience, and not claim universal authority for it, or exaggerate. Although many group members say that they are keen to receive feedback, they often find it hard to hear. It is particularly helpful in the resolution of oedipal difficulties, when the maturing person needs to be able to challenge authority figures, if members are able to give feedback to the leaders when they stand in that role in the transference. The concept of feedback is linked to that of *acceptance*. Feedback can be offered by one person to another: it need not be accepted. For it to be accepted, the timing has to be right and the recipient open and ready to hear. Feedback promotes the integration of buried parts of the self which have had to remain out of consciousness for fear of hurt or ridicule.

Underlying being able to use the group is the notion of *risk*, in that members have to put themselves to a greater or lesser degree in an exposed position. This may be just by being physically present but, if they are to derive maximum benefit, they have to take the risk of acting and especially of acting differently. This engagement will reveal the distortions that have brought the member to seek help through the exchange of group therapy.

Process refers to those unconscious elements which move the individual and affect the group as a whole. Individuals may, through the mechanism of *projection*, put into other group members and the leader archaic or otherwise inappropriate feelings and attitudes not fully based upon current experience. Likewise, in the process of *mirroring*, the member will have strong emotions about aspects of another's behaviour, words or actions which in fact represent aspects of their own personality. Often projection and mirroring are accompanied by *splitting*, which simplifies the complexity of human experience into two categories of good and bad. Similarly, the process of *scapegoating*, when the group blames a member for particular ills and tries to get rid of that person, suggests that the same hated aspects were present in other group members and being avoided. *Parataxic distortions*, the individual's proclivity to distort his perception of others, also provide valuable material which go to make up the work of the group. At times, the group will form a collective whole whose patterns make sense once the *required, avoided* and *calamitous* relationships are identified (Ezriel, 1952).

As the group develops over time, a certain ritual dramatic quality will emerge out of the regularity of time and place. It will soon develop a life and personality of its own. The mood will vary between sessions but a culture of shared norms, expectations and values will emerge. *Group cohesiveness* will develop, through which members will, to a greater or lesser degree, come to feel that they belong and this sets the stage for *interpersonal learning* (Bloch and Crouch, 1985; Yalom, 1985). A sense of group *solidarity* will be experienced which will counteract the feelings of alienation, isolation, individualism and fragmentation which the members will have hitherto experienced. One important component in this process is the sense of *being of assistance* to others in the group; this process is a vital element of the interpersonal group. Often members will report that what helped them in the group was not the contributions of the leader, however well intentioned, but the realization of all being in the same boat and that they had something to give to another human being. A sense of *koinonia* or fellowship will emerge.

There comes for each person in a group special moments when something has to be said or done. One of the Greek words for time, *kairos*, expresses better than our English word how this is the right or acceptable moment (Kelman, 1969). This is linked with the concept of *catharsis* which means the expression of strong emotion associated with stressful situations or memories.

The group can provide a *corrective emotional experience* in which earlier damage to a person can be worked through and, to some extent, repaired (Alexander and French, 1946; Frank, 1974). It provides a safe place where the *reflective loop* of doing, then looking back on what was done and understanding it, can be repeatedly entered upon. Finally, the group can provide a framework for individuals to grapple with finding *meaning* in their own existence and difficulties.

PRACTICE

Change requires courage. A person joining and staying in a group gives up temporarily and perhaps abandons altogether the notion that they are self-sufficient and do not need help. Coming to terms with these losses is often difficult (Wolff, 1977); by temporarily giving up the idea that they are coping, the stage is set for work in the group which will enable them to develop a more realistic and solidly based life. Groups are threatening; they evoke all kinds of fears and fantasies. In the group, members do not just talk about their difficulties but demonstrate them to the other group members, to the leader and, eventually, to themselves. The member is asked to do that which is most difficult and to say those things which cause them so much pain.

Generally, in a group meeting weekly for 1½ hours, it takes weeks or months for members to learn how to engage productively with the group. Significant personal change usually becomes apparent after 9–15 months membership.

The goals of the group

The goal of the group is to create a temporary social world in which therapeutic learning can take place. Each individual has his own goal of resolving certain recurrent interpersonal difficulties. The leader has the goal of enabling the members to change and supporting the group while the group members act as facilitators of that change; the leader fosters a climate in which enactments of interpersonal difficulties happen and helps the group and individuals to identify what is happening.

The leader has the goal of identifying when the member or group is ready for work and needs to be able to create sufficient tension to bring the person or the group to the point of readiness for work so that insight and change can occur, while knowing that there is a narrow divide between risking too much and not risking enough. At the outset the leader must be willing to make a judgement that, with help, the potential member will, in time, be able to make use of the group.

Inclusion and exclusion factors
It is only necessary that potential members be able to understand and withstand the group process and that they are able, perhaps with some help, to construe their difficulties in interpersonal terms. This means that they have recurrent difficulties in their patterns of relationships which are not purely intrapsychic and are potentially observable phenomena.

Those who should be excluded are the brain-damaged, the fragile, those who are not yet ready for a group and need the intimacy of the one-to-one therapeutic relationship first and those who somatize completely. Additionally, those who deny the psychological basis of their difficulties are not good candidates for group membership. Those who recognize the role of the psychological but who waver in their recognition may be included provided that they do not comprise the majority of the group.

The role of the leader

Selection and preparation
Careful selection and preparation help to make successful groups. It is important that, as far as possible, all members receive the same information and preparation for group membership. Boundary matters such as time, length, frequency of sessions, breaks and vacations are thoroughly rehearsed with each potential member. Commitment to the work of the group is important and questions of attendance and punctuality can be usefully discussed in the preparation session(s). The risk of drop-out may be reduced by anticipating with each member the interpersonal situations that may be specifically difficult for them; these often include intimacy, disclosure and the expression of strong feelings. If autonomy is a problem for a member, it is wise, perhaps, to insist that they come to the sessions under their own steam. Likewise, the all important question of confidentiality needs discussion. The usual rule of no contact outside the group, and it is to be reported if it does happen, should be mentioned.

Many potential members have only a very vague idea as to what constitutes 'work' in the group. Careful checking with potential members will reveal what they think the group is for. It always pays to explain the ground rules of expressing what is being felt, especially if it is difficult to do so, and attending even when reluctant, and acknowledging this to the group. These injunctions are simple to state but, of course, touch on the heart of learning in a group. It is especially important to keep clarifying the potential members' unrealistic expectations because of the strangeness of group therapy for most people: for many, groups equal sociability, and therapy means being told what is wrong with one and what the solutions are.

It is useful to send a written statement of what is on offer when a place in the group is offered. This acts as a tangible record of the orientation session and can be a useful check-list for the member of what their responsibilities are (Bloch, 1979).

In an ongoing group the leader may choose to let a member, once accepted and thoroughly prepared, meet with volunteer group members before joining, and have a few recent group reports if available to help them orientate themselves.

The work of the leader

An important function of the leader is to identify the particular conflicts that are most likely to cause difficulties with group members and to construct a balanced group. Ideally, the group should contain members with a heterogeneous range of personality styles and a more or less homogeneous level of interpersonal functioning. A variety of personalities is important because otherwise reinforcement of maladaptive personal styles may occur, such as schizoid avoidance of intimacy, and a group culture can develop which is antipathetic to change. Sometimes a change of membership may be necessary to break the collusive maladaptive culture.

The leader as a facilitator of interpersonal transactions is neither passive nor claims the centre stage but will be both observer and reflector of what is going on in the group. This latter role obviously has echoes of the psychoanalytic perspective. The leader also models helpful group behaviour to the members and in this the perspective is linked with social learning theory (Bandura, 1971, 1977). In the interpersonal group, there is a special emphasis on language (see below) with members being encouraged to speak for themselves and in the first person. The leader models respectful attention, giving full weight to what is being disclosed.

Technique

The beginning phase of the group is the most active time for the leader; he has to maintain the group and encourage it to develop helpful norms. If that work is done well, the leader can fade increasingly into a background role leaving the active work to group members. His role continues as an observer and a model of openness to learning, as boundary setter and the person who may have to bring difficult topics into the open. Prompting the group to look at the significance of breaks and endings will almost certainly fall to the leader in the first instance.

In interpersonal group therapy, the major functions of the leader are to:

   (i)   establish and sustain the group boundaries (selection and preparation of members, the group room, receiving apologies, etc.);
  (ii) model and maintain a therapeutic group culture;
 (iii) provide an understanding of the events of the session;
  (iv) note and reward member gains;
   (v) encourage members taking responsibility for their actions;
  (vi) predict (and possibly prevent) undesirable developments;
 (vii) involve silent members;

(viii) increase cohesiveness (by underlining similarities and caring in the group); and

(ix) provide hope for members (it helps members to realize that the group is an orderly process and that the leader has some coherent sense of the group's long-term development).

One distinctive elective way of supplementing these functions is by sending a written group summary to all members after each meeting (Yalom *et al.*, 1975). The summary, a personal non-authoritative account by the leader, gives a second opportunity to live the session and enhances its therapeutic impact; group norms are further shaped and it is possible for the leader to add afterthoughts or highlight change. Finally the summary fills the gaps for the absent member.

When summaries are used, they are as much a part of the dynamic processes of the group as are the sessions themselves, as this vignette illustrates. In a training group the leader omitted the name of one member from the seating plan in the summary of the sixth session. In the next session, no mention was made of the omission but the omitted person seemed distressed and annoyed and was not participating actively. Finally, one of the members asked him what was the matter. He replied with a torrent of abuse directed at the leader and then subsided into tears as he told the group of his incredulity on receiving the summary and finding himself omitted. During the ensuing days he had tried to pretend to himself that it did not matter but he became depressed and agitated at the thought of attending the next session. Throughout his life he had doubts about whether or not he mattered to people. He had seen the leader as a good figure until the omission, which he had experienced as an annihilation. During the remainder of the session, he was able to set about working on his feelings of isolation and this resonated with other members who talked about their own fears of being 'destroyed'. For many sessions afterwards members were preoccupied with the annihilation theme. Most of the group also admitted that on receiving the written summary they always anxiously scanned it for references to themselves. The leader should note how members react to the summaries because this illustrates their interpersonal sensitivities (Aveline, 1986).

Co-leadership

It is always more useful to have two leaders, preferably of differing genders. Besides providing support for each other, two leaders can adopt varying degrees of involvement and detachment; for example, if one leader is under attack by the group, the co-leader can help the group to examine what they are doing. Having a man and a woman leader often stimulates the exploration of sexual and parental conflicts.

Language, responsibility and group membership

The existential heritage of interpersonal group therapy places great emphasis on members being helped to take responsibility for their own lives.

As in all forms of therapy, close attention to the language group members use when speaking about themselves and others can be a productive source of material for the therapist. The words used can reveal, at first hand, how members see themselves and their position in the world. Often, they will speak about themselves as 'you', perhaps finding it difficult to say 'I'. This can lead to difficulties in trying to understand what the person is talking about but, more importantly, may indicate an attempt to distance themselves from the emotional reality of their situation. To speak in the first person is to own one's experience. The leader encourages this, not as a rule but as a facilitative group norm. Indeed, the ability increasingly to speak for themselves, and an increase in clarity of a group member's language, are good indices of movement toward health and positive change. The ego or sense of self is being strengthened and this is demonstrated through the words used to describe the self.

Micro-analysis of the language of group members can reveal how they approach the question of taking responsibility for their own actions. Phrases such as 'You have to, don't you?' or 'You don't have any choice, do you?' signifies an evasion of responsibility or a self-justification for seeing themselves as passive actors in their life (Schafer, 1983). By the gentle, persistent noting of such language the leader can encourage, firstly, an increased awareness and, secondly, an atmosphere in which members can begin to take responsibility and 'own' their behaviour and feelings through their language. The sequence might go as follows:

> You have to, don't you?
> I have to, don't I?
> I have to!
> I choose to.
> I choose not to.

Similarly, it is important for members to speak concretely about themselves and their experiences. Often the pronoun 'it' is used in such a way that the listener is left unclear about the speaker's meaning. Getting the group member to spell out exactly what 'it' is, is a basic interpersonal technique. The pronouns become nouns and the speaker is not only understood more clearly but they come to understand themselves better.

People come to therapy dissatisfied with the person that they are and feeling that in some sense, however tenuous, that they have a different person within them that they could possibly become. In the group they can actually begin to speak about and, in so doing, articulate the kind of person they want to be or the kind of things they want to do.

All the communications, both spoken and unspoken, are the subject of enquiry in the group. The meaning of the interactions that occur need to be decoded into what they say about how the person is and how they see themselves. The leader attends to gesture movement and posture as well as to the words spoken. The flow between members is another text to be understood – the kindnesses shown, the rage worked through, the ganging up and the acceptance.

The role of group members

Being in a group helps reduce isolation. Those seeking psychotherapeutic help commonly believe that their misery and suffering is unique. Of course, to the solipsist, it is. While not denying that an individual's experience is unique, his shared experience within the group powerfully demonstrates to members that they are not alone in their pain and that pain and suffering are part of the human condition. In this way groups stand against much in contemporary Western culture which plays down suffering or marginalizes it as individual weakness. By speaking of one's own pain and hurt in the group, the members encourage each other to share and, temporarily at least, help carry one another's burdens. The 'telling' also helps put the individual's suffering into some kind of context. Much pain and suffering is endured in our society because of the fear of loss of face and for the want of someone trustworthy to talk to. The group invites self-disclosure.

The group fosters tolerance. The leader can model this to those for whom it is a foreign language. In the early stages of the group, it is hard for members to understand that unconscious processes operate within the sessions and as such are part of the field of enquiry in the context of the exchanges. In their unconscious processes, both the individual and the group participate. For example, in projection, unacceptable parts of the self are discovered and put into others. Often in the process of mirroring, the member will attack this part of himself in the other before, usually with the help of the leader or another group member, coming to recognize that this is something for him to consider in himself. Similarly, the group may want to get rid of part of themselves, for example anger, by scapegoating this quality in a member who, to some degree possesses it. Such magical actions need to be confronted by the leader.

Humour is important. To laugh is therapeutic and life is sometimes so dreadful and unfair that all that is left is laughter at the comedy of human existence. Laughter also helps counteract the dreadful gloom that can beset groups where all may be vying for the position of the saddest or most put-upon person (Bloch *et al.*, 1983). Laughter with someone rather than at them and laughter that comes out of shared experience is helpful. The leader needs to identify laughter which is (a) defensive and indicates that work is being avoided or (b) demeaning, which suggests that someone in the group is being scapegoated.

For many group members one of the greatest benefits of being in a group is the simple pleasure of being together with others and feeling safe – perhaps for the first time in their lives – a truly corrective emotional experience (Alexander and French, 1946).

It is the task of group members to be physically present and emotionally available for the events of each session. By being there and willing to work, the solidarity of the group is built up. Presence is shown by being open to what is going on in the group, by being willing to speak of their own feelings and thoughts especially in the here-and-now of the group. It is especially important to speak that which is most hard to say when it is experienced. Attendance is essential. A quorum is necessary to ensure that work can take place. Sometimes group members with a history of earlier damage and unreliable or inconsistent relationships (including so-called helping ones) will find it hard to attend regularly or be on time (and in so doing they will demonstrate their difficulties). When these matters are raised, earlier hurts can be remembered, explored and faced. It may be through feeling let down, hurt or perhaps relieved at an absence or latecomer that a group member can come to recognize parts of their own biography or present experience that can be worked at and through.

In a group focusing on the interpersonal dimension all group members become peer therapists; all must refine their powers of observation and release their potential to be more than they were. Disclosures and feedback advance that end. In helping others, the helper realizes his or her own skills and capacity and, in so doing, builds a stronger sense of self. The power asymmetry of the leader–member relationship can be somewhat redressed. Each can take their turn at helping, being the leader or, in the Indian sense of guru, being the person that another can learn from. In such a situation group members have to face losing their previous belief that they were helpless, hopeless or incompetent. To be told by a group member that what one said or did was helpful is much more potent than being given 'feedback' by a therapist 'paid to say nice things'. Over time a group member can gradually regain (or even learn for the first time) competence in the simple tasks of being.

Group development over time

The natural history of the interpersonal psychotherapy group has three stages: a beginning, a middle and an end. Different factors emerge as being important at different stages in the life of the group; for example, at the start and for many weeks, it is important for the group to build collaborative norms. It may well be necessary for individuals to hold back on what seem like very pressing, personal disclosures until a sufficiently safe atmosphere of trust has been built. Confrontations, similarly, are often a more productive feature of a mature group which has the resources to handle them creatively.

The beginning, characterized by both hope and fear, sees the establishment of a therapeutic alliance between individual members and between them and the leaders. In this stage the members settle down, thrash around trying to make sense of the chaos they experience, and try and discover the 'rules' of the group. They also start to show each other and the leaders their difficulties. Much of the talk is of topics far removed from the here-and-now experiences of the group and, therefore, are safe. The leader is at his most active in this phase (see pp. 53–7).

By the time the transition to the middle section takes place the focus will be more, but not exclusively, on the here-and-now. This section is much concerned with *keeping* the focus on the transactions in the group. The focus will often slip away but the group itself will soon know this and experience these deviations increasingly as 'not working'. The thrust of the work will be in clarifying the distortions, risking saying what seemed impossible to say at the outset, in trying out new ways of being, in realizing that some things cannot be changed but can be accepted.

As the group comes to face its end, much important work remains to be done. But as with all human relationships the group must end. The leader will have kept the ending in focus. Members will face, to a degree, the universal questions of death, the inevitability of mortality, the many unresolved griefs in their lives, the fact that all ambitions can never be realized and that of the hopes that they brought to the group only some can be achieved; they will recognize how far they have come and what the group, the members and the leaders have meant to them.

Out of the experience, strength and individual potential will have been mobilized. Members will go forward alone to try new paths but carry with them the shared experience of having in an important way transcended their previous being and of having been more the person they sensed they could be. Thus, each ending is a new beginning.

Duration
Groups may be open or closed but, to get maximum benefit, the group of members should ideally meet for 1½ hours weekly for at least 9 months and preferably for up to 18 months or more. In our experience, an average duration of 12 months seems necessary, especially for patient groups in order to allow for the full range of interpersonal difficulties to emerge and be worked on with any degree of lasting benefit.

Mechanisms of change

Change takes place in an interpersonal group in two overlapping and alternating stages. In the first, the group members come to see themselves more fully. In the second, through a lived experience of being different within and without the group, they move towards the person that they might be if they were less fearful and conflicted. Yalom (1985), in an experimental study of 20 patients with good outcome following interpersonal group therapy (mean duration 15 months, range 8–22 months), showed that they valued in particular the interest of others, the catharsis of voicing feelings, and the sense of belonging. Top of 60 rank-ordered statements came 'Discovering and accepting previously unknown parts of myself', 'Being able to say what was bothering me instead of holding it in', and 'Other members honestly telling me what they think of me'. Replica studies show that promoting interaction among group members is a key therapeutic factor (Rohrbaugh and Bartels, 1975; Marcowitz and Smith, 1983). The selected statements refer to what Yalom termed *interpersonal learning* within the *social microcosm* of the group; interpersonal learning has two elements, input and output, and these correspond to feedback and disclosure in the Johari window described on page 49.

The group provides a sustaining structure in which the individual can take risks – the risk of discovering the contradictory and hidden aspects of themselves, the risk of venturing into new ways of being.

Typical problems and their resolution

Three examples of members presenting their problematic interpersonal selves in the group are given, the difficulties that this creates for the group is illustrated and an indication is shown of how this may be resolved creatively by the group with the help of the leader.

A pattern of playing safe resolved by disclosure and risk-taking
John always arrived in the group room at the precise time of starting. As the end approached he frequently looked at his watch which he had pro-grammed to bleep at the moment of escape. When the other group members eventually tackled him about his time keeping he denied that it was important. The observation was repeated in the following weeks. Finally, he blurted out that he did not want anything to do with the other group members who were clearly sick or they would not be in the group and anyway he did not have time to spend on inconsequential talk. Another member pointed out that she had seen him walking round the perimeter of the building before the starting time looking very tense. John immediately denied this. The quiet disclosure of another group member of her fears of

coming, of her sleeplessness the night before and of being seen coming into the building opened the way for John to tell the group that he was always frightened of arriving early because he did not know whether or not the leader would be present, and he was terrified of what the other members might get up to and say without the leader being present. So it was safer to arrive spot on time.

Recognizing and then exploring the significance of the simple act of arriving on time initiated change. In the months that followed John began to recognize that he had the potential to risk arriving early and 'just chat and mess about'. He did not need the protection of the adult/parent/leader. He linked his clock watching to the agonized days he used to spend in anticipation of his father's promised, but usually cancelled, visits and to the hopelessness and self-hatred he experienced subsequently. *This had many resonances for other group members.*

John became a valued cornerstone of the group. His interpersonal interactions became much freer and outside the group his relationship with his father became more equal. He experienced a new freedom to express himself with peers and authority figures which was the antithesis of his previous fearful assumption that safety lay in never stepping out of line.

*Self-hate hidden by inconsequential chat and resolved by
peer-acceptance*
Jean began most sessions by inconsequentially talking about matters outside the group. She usually had a tearful look about her but her wall of words usually stopped any interventions by either the group members or the leader. At first, the members of the group followed her lead and took the opportunity to engage in similar talk. The result was always the same: the chat went on and on and ended in that embarrassed silence that indicated that the group was not working. Gradually, the members of the group pointed out the pattern she initiated (and with which they colluded).

As the group progressed, Jean's chattering became less, though it never ceased completely. She gradually learned that the other group members did care about her but she always remained cynical about the motives of the leader. The group helped by allowing her to display her difficulties. The endless chattering hid the tears. The tears were for her feelings of profound hopelessness and lack of self-worth. She felt that she deserved nothing but she had begun to learn how to make a relationship both with the group and her boyfriend. She was able to make a world that fitted her better.

Rejection invited but averted by the action of the leader
Nicholas looked much older than his age suggested and dressed in ill-fitting, too elderly clothes. In his life, he felt he was an outcast. His family's

professional standard of living, his nationality and his religion were at variance with the context in which he grew up.

In the group he adopted a stand-offish, cynical attitude. His physical posture betrayed a withdrawn avoidance: no eye contact, arms folded, usually leaning back. What comments he did make were hostile and dismissive of others' difficulties. He gradually became very isolated and somewhat the object of other group members' fear and dislike. The group began to resemble the world he feared and was, perhaps, instrumental in creating it. As the group developed he stood still.

After about 6 months, a member of the group quietly asked him why he had joined and why he kept attending as he seemed not to contribute very much. Nicholas was hardly able to speak as a torrent of highly critical feedback came forth from many of the other group members. The leader felt that it was very important to protect him from the primitive and destructive forces in operation at this juncture, while preserving the importance of giving feedback. The leader encouraged the group to share with Nicholas how his behaviour affected them. He was also loudly told how much he was admired for still coming to the sessions in spite of his obvious discomfort. This illustrates the importance of members speaking for themselves, not assuming what is in the other's mind, and represents an important group norm for members.

Over the following sessions Nicholas was able to begin telling his story of how he had become such a brittle cynical person. He spoke of how he had acquired his defensiveness because he always felt an outsider and was frightened of opening his mouth lest his accent betray him. The family itself had developed a culture of silence in which none of the members ever discussed the difficulties they experienced in living. Nicholas can be seen as an example of how a person's assumptive world was formed and maintained and the quite powerful counter-experience needed to alter it.

Limitations of the approach

The chief limitation of the interpersonal approach to group psychotherapy is that it does not provide much space for individual exploration of severe psychological trauma. Although interpersonal group therapy emphasizes the power of the group as an agent of change and healing it does require that members are developmentally ready for the experience. This means, therefore that it is inappropriate for those who are overly frightened of social settings and have not reached the psychological stage of seeing that other people exist as whole persons and not just as part-objects. Thus the narcissistic person or those who can only relate to part-objects will find it very hard to engage usefully in the group.

Similarly, the person who wants or needs a technological, structural method, such as is found in behavioural group therapies like social skills and assertiveness training, will not find the interpersonal approach appropriate. Neither will those who want to engage in an extensive exploration of themselves: they would find person-centred or analytic groups or individual therapy more useful. While references to early life inevitably occur in any kind of group, the focus in the interpersonal approach is more on the here-and-now of current functioning than on the understanding of infancy and childhood. It is fundamentally ahistorical.

There is no neat matching of group therapy treatments to the variety of human problems. A more useful way is to see them addressing different aspects of personal functioning. It is the purpose of the interpersonal approach to focus on helping members live differently with others; this is its priority.

Typical qualities of effective leaders

In contrast with more analytic ways of working, in the interpersonal approach the effective leader occupies a more involved position – but not so much as in leader-centred modalities such as gestalt, psychodrama, and behavioural groups. Clearly, the effective leader needs to be able to observe and give feedback, comment in a professional way on the group processes and their own part in them but, perhaps more importantly, they need to be able to model the qualities of effective group membership. These can be summarized as openness, willingness to change, to take risks and be relatively undefended. The effective leader has, in addition, a belief that others can change and that, furthermore this change comes about through the collaborative effort of members and leaders.

The effective leader does not believe that all the potency for change lies within him or herself, but can see the potential of and in the group for effecting change. He or she can be comfortable with their leadership role changing, perhaps quite dramatically and almost, but never completely, withering away. Although the role might start off rather formally, it will soften as the group matures; this can usually be noted in the way the leader moves from being called Dr Y or Ms Z to first names, rather like a good parent will be able to adjust to their offspring moving from childhood through adolescence to adulthood.

Finally, the effective leader is not unbending in his approach but recognizes that both he and the other group members are, as is often said, 'all in the same boat'. To take the maritime metaphor a little further, the leader is rather like the skipper of a yacht who would not be going very far without the crew which, in turn, needs a skilled and experienced captain.

REFERENCES

Alexander, F. and French, T. (1946). *Psychoanalytic Therapy: Principles and Applications*. New York, Ronald Press.

Aveline, M. (1986). The use of written reports in a brief group psychotherapy training. *International Journal of Group Psychotherapy* **36** (3): 477–82.

Bandura, A. (1971). Psychotherapy based upon modeling principles. In A. E. Bergin and S. L. Garfield (eds), *Handbook of Psychotherapy and Behavior Change*. New York, John Wiley.

Bandura, A. (1977). *Social Learning Theory*. Englewood Cliffs, NJ, Prentice-Hall.

Berger, P. L. and Luckmann, T. (1967). *The Social Construction of Knowledge: A Treatise in the Sociology of Knowledge*. London, Allen Lane.

Bloch, S. (1979). Assessment of patients for psychotherapy. *British Journal of Psychiatry* **135**: 193–208.

Bloch, S. and Crouch, E. (1985). *Therapeutic Factors in Group Psychotherapy*. Oxford, Oxford University Press.

Bloch, S., Browning, S. and McGrath, G. (1983). Humour in group psychotherapy. *British Journal of Medical Psychology* **56**: 89–97.

Ezriel, H. (1950). A psychoanalytic approach to group treatment. *British Journal of Medical Psychology* **23**: 57–74.

Ezriel, H. (1952). Notes on psychoanalytic group therapy: II. Interpretation and research. *Psychiatry* **15**: 119–26.

Ezriel, H. (1956). Experimentation within the psychotherapy session. *The British Journal for the Philosophy of Science* **7**: 29–48.

Frank, J. D. (1974). *Persuasion and Healing*, revised edition. New York, Schocken Books.

James, W. (1890). *The Principles of Psychology*, 2 vols. New York; Holt.

Kelman, H. C. (1969). Kairos: the auspicious moment. *American Journal of Psychoanalysis* **29**: 59–83.

Lewin, K. (1936). *Principles of Topological Psychology*. New York, McGraw-Hill.

Luft, J. (1966). *Group Processes: An Introduction to Group Dynamics*. Palo Alto, California, National Press.

Marcowitz, R. J. and Smith, J. E. (1983). Patients' perceptions of curative factors in short-term group psychotherapy. *International Journal of Group Psychotherapy* **33**: 21–39.

Rohrbaugh, M. and Bartels, B. D. (1975). Participants' perceptions of 'curative factors' in therapy and growth groups. *Small Group Behavior* **6**: 430–56.

Schafer, R. (1983). *The Analytic Attitude*. London, Hogarth Press.

Sullivan, H. S. (1953). *The Interpersonal Theory of Psychiatry*. London, W. W. Norton.

Wolff, H. H. (1977). Loss: a central theme in psychotherapy. *British Journal of Medical Psychology* **50**: 11–19.

Yalom, I. D. (1980). *Existential Psychotherapy*. New York, Basic Books.

Yalom, I. D. (1985). *The Theory and Practice of Group Psychotherapy*, 3rd edition. New York, Basic Books.

Yalom, I. D., Brown, S. and Bloch, S. (1975). The written summary as a group psychotherapy technique. *Archives of General Psychiatry* **32**: 605–13.

CHAPTER 4

GESTALT GROUP THERAPY

Barrie Hinksman

HISTORICAL CONTEXT AND DEVELOPMENT IN BRITAIN

Gestalt therapy was developed over a period of three decades by Laura and Frederick Perls. Friedrich Salomon Perls (later 'Fritz') was a young Jewish neuropsychiatrist from Berlin who, in 1926, had entered psychoanalysis with Karen Horney. It was on Karen Horney's advice that Fritz Perls left Berlin to work with Kurt Goldstein who was doing pioneering work with the brain-damaged, based in part on the gestalt psychology of Wolfgang Köhler. Perls continued his personal therapy with a number of prominent psychoanalysts and then himself trained as an analyst.

His move to work with Goldstein in Frankfurt was pivotal in that he changed the focus of his work and also met the woman he was to marry and with whom he developed gestalt therapy. However, this was during the period of National Socialism in Germany and in 1933 the Perls fled – separately – meeting up again in the Netherlands, and then emigrating to South Africa.

On arrival in that country they set up in practice as analysts and were quickly successful. In 1940, Fritz Perls wrote his first book, *Ego, Hunger and Aggression: A Revision of Freud's Theory and Method* (Perls, 1947). In seven years, he had developed his thinking and practice to the point where he was ready to oppose some of the tenets and assumptions of psychoanalysis. In his book, Perls criticized Freud for his over-emphasis on things past and focused instead on current phenomena; he promoted experience in the place of analysis; he challenged the usefulness of focusing on the transference between patient and analyst and, instead, paid attention to projection as a normal function.

He still saw himself as a psychoanalyst but one who, like Adler or Sullivan, had a contribution to make which did not merely extend the received orthodoxy of the International Congresses of Psychoanalysis. His book shows clearly the influences of his analysts and teachers, especially that of Wilhelm Reich with his emphasis on the body. It is Reich's influence more than any which supported Perls' interest in hunger and aggression. Hunger, he argued, outranks even sex in the hierarchy of motivating needs. He also took a novel step by linking hunger with aggression in normal daily functioning and made them central to his therapeutic approach.

In 1946, Perls went ahead of his family to New York City where he worked for the next 10 years. Here Perls sought out, as he had done in Germany and South Africa, the artistic community. He had a passion for design, for theatre, films and literature and for the people who made these things their lives. He met Paul Goodman, an acknowledged leader of the artistic and intellectual new wave, and when Laura arrived in 1947 Goodman became her patient. Goodman and Ralph Hefferline were both members of a distinguished training group led by Fritz and Laura Perls in what became in 1952 the New York Institute for Gestalt Therapy. With Fritz Perls, they wrote the definitive *Gestalt Therapy: Excitement and Growth in the Human Personality* (Perls *et al.*, 1951).

Gestalt therapy had developed as a mode of individual therapy. During the New York period, it became a mode of therapy and training in groups. Köhler's basic model of perception centred on the way in which people distinguish figure from ground in an otherwise meaningless sea of perceptual data. In gestalt group therapy, the individual becomes, at certain points, a figure in the ground of the whole group, the focus of attention. That individual will focus on (i.e. make figure from ground) some particular issue or interest. That focus may well involve interaction with another group member or the leader. Participation in – or even observation of – these events shows that, in the process of differentiation, energy flows from the ground (in this case the group) into the figure (the individual member). It is for this reason that group members often report and display new attitudes, feelings and behaviours on the strength of someone else's work in their group.

The New York Institute was the first gestalt institute in the USA and was part of a wider developmental movement in psychology in the 1950s. There was a growing professional and lay public ready to listen to Perls and Goodman as they toured the country. In the early 1960s Perls was involved with others at the Esalen Institute in California, and it is at this point that the rapid importation of gestalt to Britain began. Many British people working in the fields of education, psychology and psychotherapy were excited by the 'human potential movement' then under way in the USA. Esalen drew them to learn and also offered models for the 'growth centres' of Europe, including Quaesitor in London. Quaesitor first offered gestalt as a contribution to the personal development of its professional and lay clients: later it offered therapy and training.

By the late 1960s there was a small number of psychotherapists in Britain with some experience of the gestalt mode which they had acquired in the USA. The growth centres brought together a much larger number who had a similar professional interest, and there was also a small number of gestalt therapists and trainers from the USA who wanted to work in Britain and other European countries. A number of such people came together in 1973 to found the London Gestalt Centre (LGC) which had a life-span of about 10 years before being overtaken by other organizations. The principal trainer at LGC was Dr Larry (Ischa) Bloomberg, and LGC invited other well-known gestaltists (including Laura Perls) to contribute to its training programmes. Bloomberg later developed the Gestalt Training Service (GTS) which now operates in a number of European countries including Britain. People who had trained with LGC and/or GTS later formed their own therapy and training organizations. Thus Scotland has the Scottish Association for Gestalt Education, England the English Gestalt Institute, and several European cities, regions and countries their own such resources.

Fritz Perls died in 1970, but the work that he and Laura began is still growing rapidly, and nowhere more so than in Britain.

UNDERLYING ASSUMPTIONS

Theoretical underpinnings

Gestalt therapy is therapy through *contact* and gestalt group therapy is that activity which promotes awareness through contact in the group context. The theoretical possibilities are endless: what happens in practice is that the group focuses on one member or on one issue in an exchange between two members. This focus is, in the terminology of gestalt psychology, *figure* or *foreground*, distinguished from the rest of the possibilities which are, for the time being *(back)ground*. The act of focusing is technically described as *gestalt formation*; it is the fundamental process which creates meaning and in which we engage during much of our waking and sleeping lives. When the therapy group (or some of its members) focus on some aspect of a member's behaviour, that behavioural feature becomes the meaningful meeting point between them and the individual member. The contact thus established promotes an awareness in the individual of her behaviour. Such awareness is the stuff of gestalt group therapy; it engenders that sense of heightened interest and excitement that is a characteristic of gestalt groups,. And it is the springboard for whatever changes the group members make in their therapy.

In gestalt usage, awareness must be distinguished from that self-consciousness which is the mark of insight. It differs, for example, in the way that one may either be aware of the sun shining on one's skin as one works in the garden or that one may generate images of oneself bending over the plants, seeing oneself under the hot sun. In the therapy group, the leader is working to promote the awareness of each member in the confident expectation that, when that member is ready to assimilate the awareness, changes will result more or less spontaneously. These changes will be examples of growth in the personality of that group member. The mechanisms of such change are self-regulatory, although the group member may well require a good deal of support and assistance from the leader and other members to undertake a development which has for many years been inhibited by fear. But the key to that eventual change is awareness, a unitary experience of doer and deed, of subject and the contacted other. Insight, on the other hand, does not promote this unitary experience nor realize its psychic potential, but rather represents ego function seeking to manipulate and adjust ego function.

To make sense of this last statement, we must consider the gestalt theory of the *self*. For present purposes we shall confine our attention to three sub-systems of this self; id, ego and personality. *Id* represents that powerhouse (almost always out of awareness) from which comes the excitement and energy of our drives and needs, that which must be satisfied. Id process is autonomously aggressive, goal-orientated (e.g. sexual desire) and responsive (e.g. anger). Because id process is so often impeded by repression, it may sometimes be observable only in unaware gestures or verbal slips. And yet it is not always moving: thus the confluence (see p. 71) which precedes contact may be understood as id process at rest.

When in the group two members engage with each other, it is through the agency of their *ego* function. It is ego function which forms figures from the ground, which identifies some possibilities and rejects others. If you are in a patisserie, it is your ego function that identifies almond slice and alienates or rejects cream horn. And it is your ego function that then proceeds to orientate and manipulate (a complex movement which is both mental and physical) the desired morsel to bring it into yet more intimate contact on the way to assimilation. Healthy ego function is characteristically deliberate and also spontaneous, in the sense of being creative and innovative.

The outcomes of a person's ego function will be apparent through her *personality*, because it is personality which has integrated the learning from previous contact experiences. Aspects of personality include, for example, our social roles; once we had painstakingly to experiment and learn these, but now we can think of them as roles, i.e. complex sets of behaviours which require no thought. We may well act quite autonomously in our various roles, and autonomy is a characteristic of personality but, by virtue of being in a role, we are *ipso facto* not spontaneous but predictable. Another window to personality is in our self-presentation as in, for example, our choice of clothes. People get used to seeing me in the kind of clothes I wear: if I suddenly change my mode of dress, I surprise them. More significantly, I feel different in myself, because the transition from, say, casual dress to a suit brings out some other aspect of myself. And if I find that my wardrobe is quite unsuitable for me – I want other colours, textures and lines in my dress – I can take it that my ego function has operated in such a way that part of my personality is no longer appropriate and new structures are on their way.

These new structures will quickly become established – part of who I am. This is a relatively trivial example but the principle holds good in other instances. If, for example, I have grown up in a single-sex environment and then find myself pitched into a mixed-sex environment, I have nothing in my personality to cope with such novelty. My ego function will have to deal with that, but in the meantime I must cope with what is, in effect, a hole in my personality. To do this I shall use whatever material comes to hand to fill the hole. I might have been taught (introjected) that the opposite sex is bad and to be avoided and thus I have to fill the hole in my personality with this introjected material. As a recipe for a fulfilling life, it may not look promising, but it meets my emergency needs. If I appear in your therapy group, it will not take you many minutes to work out that there is something in my personality that requires therapeutic attention. How and why that has come to be will not immediately be apparent to you (or to me, of course); but because personality is so transparent, you will know where to look. Changes in personality are the proof of the pudding in a gestalt theapy group: they may be a long time coming after the initial awareness of the hole or the maladaptation, but they are apparent to all when they happen.

Key concepts

To understand something of what happens in a gestalt therapy group, it is necessary to understand a little more of what gestaltists mean by *contact*. Contact is a function of the boundary between the organism and its environment – including, therefore, other organisms. This boundary is permeable and capable of permitting a flow (which may be regulated and modified). In the case of an individual, the flow includes sensing and expressing, ingesting and eliminating, active manipulation of the environment and passive reception or manipulation from the environment. The notion of contact applies both in the literal sense of touch as well as in the extended sense of sight or the more derived senses of physical proximity or affective warmth. Contact occurs in the therapy group simply by virtue of people being in the same room at the same time and being able to see and hear each other. But within this overarching contact we may discern smaller units or gestalten, as in the example when members focus particularly on some interaction between two others: within the global experience of contact, there is this smaller experience of contact.

   That contact is regulated (i.e. has certain stages) is apparent when one considers our contact with the environment in the matter of food. First, we experience a feeling of hunger and begin to look around for suitable food. The emergence of an impulse from id process (in this case, the sense of hunger) precedes contact and is sometimes called *pre-contact*. Another way to think of it is to regard the sense of hunger as figure against the ground of the body with its myriad other but undefined possibilities. Next, we prepare the food and ourselves to eat it, mobilizing our interest and energies: this is *fore-contact*. The tasting stage is accomplished by a complex series of physical manipulations whereby the food reaches our tongues inside our mouths: this stage is called *contact* (sometimes *full contact*). If all is well (e.g. if we like what we have in our mouths) we begin to bite and chew, grinding the food before swallowing it. This stage (*final contact*) involves that deconstruction of the food which is necessary if it is to be assimilated, and that process continues in our stomachs. It may be said that the food is, in any ordinary sense, inside us, and yet the interaction of organism and environment at the contact boundary continues in the digestive tract. The satisfaction of the final contact stage is felt as a full stomach, with hunger sated; all that remains is for that awareness to fade into *post-contact*, an experience completed.

   One can define other experiences of contact in the same manner – for example, a meeting with a fellow member in a gestalt therapy group. What is taken in and digested is, of course, the experience of meeting the other rather than the person herself! The model holds good whether the meeting is an amicable one or an angry one. And it is also the case that within the overall *gestalt* (unit of experience) of such a meeting there will be a number of smaller gestalten, e.g. opening up, discussing and finishing various topics of conversation. In each of these, the same process may take place as an item of interest arises, becomes figure in the ground of all the possible interests, leading in some cases from fore-contact to contact, final contact and post-contact. Or else the excitement in that subject may never get past the fore-contact stage, as in the case of our small talk.

   The contact process is stressed here because it is the foundation of any theory of gestalt therapy. Indeed, properly understood, one could say with Perls *et al.* (1951) that 'psychology studies the operation of the contact-boundary in the organism/environment field' (p. 275). Everything else –

understanding, for example, anxiety, neurosis or psychosis – depends on this fundamental concept.

However, life is not a series of simple experiences of contact and we must now consider some of the ways in which this process may be modified. To do so, we must describe, from a gestalt perspective, the mechanisms of confluence, introjection, projection, retroflection, egotism, reaction formation and sublimation.

Confluence is an antithesis of contact, and describes a state of non-awareness. This may be healthy, as in the normal state of our internal organs which only hurt when we are sick, or as in the common assumptions of our social relationships which may not come to light unless challenged by other people. In the gestalt therapy group, there will be many examples of normal and neurotic confluence. Normal confluence may be seen between two interesting experiences, as when a member has finished saying something, goes into a relaxed lull and then experiences a surge of excitement as some new need or interest emerges. That pre-impulse lull is confluence. Neurotic confluence is very evident in the behaviour of members with hysterical personality patterns. Such people may have all kinds of things they want to do or say in the group but have either an apparent difficulty knowing which to start with, or else a difficulty which they mask with random spontaneity or compulsive behaviour. In other words, they cannot satisfactorily form clear figures in the ground of their possibilities; either the figures will not emerge clearly, or the background will not fade satisfactorily, and what follows is an experience like walking in fog, or hearing particles of speech, or having glimpses of images or just feeling blank.

Introjection describes both the way a hungry infant might feed ('throwing it down') and also the way in which readers of psychological books may swallow wholesale what the authors present to them. The same term also describes the way we take in from our environment even less tangible things, e.g. parental attitudes to money or health. Our capacity to introject is vital; liquid food is one example, and so are important instructions such as 'don't take sweets from strangers'. However, most of us have a legacy of introjected material which can impede satisfying contact with our current environment. It is as though we have a piece of an older environment lodged within us: thus it may be our parents' or teachers' energy or interest which 'responds' in our adult relationships. An obvious example of this would be when a person pulls away from an otherwise pleasurable sexual encounter solely on the basis that 'it's wrong'. Nor is introjection to be thought of as a past event; when a group member habitually 'gives place' or 'gives way' to others, we are witnessing introjection and we may spot the physical swallowing that often accompanies this activity.

Likewise, *projection* describes a healthy and necessary function which can support contact as well as, in neurosis, sabotage it. The term projection indicates how we identify, ostensibly in other people, aspects of ourselves of which we may be unaware or which we may disown. These aspects could be socially inconvenient (e.g. lustful desires) or socially respectable (e.g. warm-heartedness). Often what we project is an introject. A good illustration of this is the way in which one member of a therapy group might project on to fellow members her introjected rules of behaviour: this might become apparent in an episode of blaming as in 'you shouldn't do what you're doing' (= you're bad because you break my parents' rules for me). Projections are also the basis for, to take another instance in the same group, compassion: how else can we imagine what suffering must be like for another member unless we are able to fantasize that we are that person?

The mechanism of *retroflection* is similarly socially useful. If the group leader becomes irritated with one of the members, she may choose to contain that annoyance instead of giving vent to it. Her aim is to maintain contact with the group member rather than to alienate her. The leader is demonstrating ordinary patience. That is achieved by a variety of means, chief of which is the use of energy to still the muscles which would have been employed in the expression (jaws, throat, hands, shoulders). That leader is turning her expressive energy back on herself (retroflecting), and thus avoiding one contact in favour of another. Habitual behaviour of this sort (as may be seen in a compulsively mild-mannered group member) is neurotic and uncontactful. People who habitually retroflect their emotional expression are likely to adopt a characteristic posture and gestures – the motor components of their interrupted contacts.

There are yet other ways in which contact in the gestalt group may be modified. For example, it may be that, week after week, one of the members turns up, joins in conversations with others, asks questions of the leader and generally participates, but yet seems uninvolved. What is missing is not quantity of participation but rather something in the quality; one never quite meets or reaches the heart of the other. Put on the spot, such a group member may have stories to tell of similar feedback: she is willing to take part but cannot 'commit' herself or 'express' herself in the ways that others do. There is indeed something missing; it is the follow through of the contact process to the point of letting go in final contact. 'Letting go' difficulties are the hallmark of *egotism* – so-called because it is one's ego function of choosing and rejecting which is figure in the ground of contacting, rather than the contacted other. Thus the group member who cannot bring herself to express what she feels is inevitably more concerned with herself than with her peer for whom she feels so much (anger, love, envy, fear). Healthy egotism, however, is an asset; the group leader has, one hopes, a sufficient degree of that. If she has not, she will have given little or no thought to the constitution of her therapy group, to the practical arrangements, to monitoring the growth of its members or any of the planning details before launching into such an important undertaking.

When people first enter a gestalt therapy group, they may be so anxious as to be difficult to approach, although they may be unaware of their anxiety. One member, for instance, may invite an approach from the leader by some very marked piece of non-verbal behaviour: but when the leader tells the member what she has noticed and that she looks uncomfortable, the member may blush, glare and then deny that she feels any such thing. The leader may wonder why a member of this therapy group should make such an obvious denial. The briefest reflection shows that there is no point in arguing the case; the member is adamant and, to judge by her colour, her upper thoracic breathing and the great gulp she gave when addressed, she is in a *reaction formation*. What happened was that the leader upset the member's rather precarious equilibrium in which unknown excitements (fear, grief, rage, love) had been held in check by some internal inhibiting action. The leader's intervention was too much; the repressed material threatened to break into awareness and overwhelm her. In one (attacking rather than defending) move, the group member denied her feelings and the anxiety they provoked, fended off the leader, produced a repressive amnesia (so that she genuinely cannot recall the feelings or the anxiety she momentarily felt) and is left (projectively) with the distinct feeling that she has been picked upon by the group leader. Gestaltists commonly work with such reaction formations, for they are very common in daily life, as well as recognizing the more common use of the term to describe fixed character traits (as in a group member whose forbidden sexual interests are masked by a fixed trait of prudishness).

In the same therapy group the leader will not have to look far to find examples of what people do if they are not obliged to set up such fixed reaction formations. For example, it may be that a man in the group has grown up with two conflicting impulses: one is to have sexual relations with boys, and the other a strong system of introjects which serves to remind him of the need to save young children from such attentions. Instead of the road of total denial this man has chosen a career running holidays for deprived city children in which his own childlike longings and his desire for children's company may be amply fulfilled. So far as sexual gratification is concerned, he has found in his work an effective *sublimation* through which he, the children and the community all profit.

Gestalt therapy began with the Perls' in South Africa as an activity involving two people at a time in a consulting room. By the time the Perls' had settled in New York City, they and their trainees were working with groups – of trainee therapists and of patients. In gestalt groups, the focus for the therapist and indeed the members is the whole *gestalt, the figure seen against the whole ground*. For example, if one of the women in the group becomes angry with one of the men, she will quickly arrive at the nub of her resentment – it is the man's offhand way that he always arrives late that becomes the figure in the ground. It makes her so angry, because it gives her the feeling that she is unimportant to him. He blusters a little and then ostentatiously switches off, at which she becomes first enraged and then sunk in despair. The leader meanwhile has not intervened and does not do so until the woman weeps and looks at her. The leader asks what she is experiencing and the woman tells her: the leader cannot and does not try to deliver her from her despair. Time passes and all are quiet. Later the woman speaks again, this time to the leader: 'What can I do to change him?' 'Nothing', comes the answer. There are more tears from a number of people who seem deeply affected by what is going on. Later the woman tells of experiences with her father whom she loved and who, in his offhand way, loved her. That offhandedness had been the problem and all her childhood and adolescence she has sought to change herself in order to effect some change in him. The only outcome had been her despair.

Now there is a way in which this woman's pain is displayed as the pain of part, at least, of the group. And the man's (as yet unacknowledged) pain at being found wanting is also the pain of part, at least, of the group; it is the figure waiting to be discovered in the ground. The group contains enough fathers and daughters for everyone to be involved in his or her own way, explicitly or implicitly. The events of that session involve events outside the group, absent people, the original traumatic experiences, and current events with present people including, of course, the group leader. This depth and spread comes from the gestalt assumption that what we study in psychology is activity at the contact boundary in the organism/environment field: that *activity promotes awareness*, and that *awareness leads where it leads*. The leader may not try to force awareness in any direction: that destroys it and organic growth cannot then occur. People make the connections they need as they work in therapy, and what starts as apparently one individual's hang-up about time-keeping grows into a group event with far-reaching implications.

Gestalt therapy group leaders may, however, work explicitly with the *group process* as a focus. An example of this may be found where the group has an unaware 'conspiracy' (what Bion calls the 'basic assumption of dependence' – Bion, 1961, pp. 77 *et seq.*) to get depressed and act in a gloomy fashion. This manipulation, it may well turn out, was 'designed' to give a strong message to the leader that she is not doing enough. People like strong leaders who will tell them what's what and make them feel better, and any leader neglecting these duties may well be punished by such passive aggression. Here the leader must confront the group and its process as a group: it will not be long before one or more of the members breaks ranks and engages with the leader so that the whole event may be unpacked and its important messages of fear, frustration, anger and hurt be clearly expressed, heard, argued and, by one means or another, answered.

It will be clear from what has already been said that gestalt therapy is therapy of the *whole person*. Perls owed to Reich more than to any other teacher and therapist his clear awareness of the unity of mind, body and spirit. He took from Reich the assumption that neurosis is as much a motor (i.e. skeleto-muscular) matter as it is psychological. Thus gestalt group therapists are trained to pay close attention to such matters as breathing, posture, gesture, and other physical behaviours. Sometimes such activity simply serves to inform the therapist of what is happening (e.g. the visible swallowing of introjection, the rapid and high breathing of anxiety). At other times, the leader may seek to promote the group member's awareness of her body behaviour, e.g. a retroflective movement forward of shoulders to collapse the chest and a movement downwards of the chin as a person pulls back from an angry encounter. Much gestalt *bodywork* is done in this 'hands off' way. At other times, the leader may adopt a 'hands on' approach. There are many ways in which this may be done. For example, where it seems that the group member maintains much tension in her jaws and throat and is thus inhibited from making any sounds to express her distress, the leader may gently hold her throat and ask her to let the tension go into her (the leader's) hand. She might, on the other hand, encourage the member to open wide her mouth and to stretch her habitually tight jaw muscles, thus relaxing the inhibition and opening up the possibility of making sound to express her emotion.

Finally, in this selection of key concepts, it is important to note that one of the implications of activity at the *contact boundary* is that the boundary belongs neither to one party nor to the other but *represents the locus of meeting*. At that boundary, group members and leader meet. The traffic at the boundary is *bi-directional*, and both parties will be changed in the experience. One way to understand this proposition is to look at it as a dialectical proposition. For example, a group member presents a thesis about life, namely that people are rotten. The leader presents an antithesis – not necessarily in words – which confronts the thesis and contradicts it. In the end, a synthesis emerges: both have shifted their ground. The member's experience of contact with the leader confounds her thesis – some people at least are good to meet, and some are not. The leader too is changed. What psychotherapist does not know the sobering feeling that comes from meeting someone to whom all the important others have been rotten – and yet somehow the person seeks to adapt and, at the least, survive?

PRACTICE

The goals of the group

People usually join a gestalt therapy group because they wish to live more fulfilling or less painful lives. It is the operating assumptions of the leader and the members which ensure that the tactical goals of such a group are distinctively those of a gestalt group. Whether or not the explicit language of contact process is used, the therapeutic work is aimed at bringing into awareness the interruptive modifications of contact which members employ as the life of the group develops. Because they are the same people in the group, at work and at home, they are likely to reproduce their maladaptive behaviour as agenda in the group. As awareness grows, so group members are able to experiment with new behaviours in which they are more able to choose how they initiate and respond.

Gestalt therapy is a widely applicable therapeutic approach. Because it is contact therapy, it is of prime importance that members have some willingness to be in contact (sometimes referred to as response-ability). Thus, where there is no motivation to change, gestalt is unlikely to be of use to the clients. Nevertheless, there are some interesting examples of the effective use of gestalt therapy in apparently unpromising settings, e.g. by social workers caring for young people in residential care, and by psychologists working with persons imprisoned for serious crimes. Fundamentally, the clients are the people who determine whether or not they have the motivation to change.

Gestalt therapists working without a (technically) 'secure' environment are unlikely to work with people whose psychotic behaviour is florid or violent. Nor, given the yardstick of (some) response-ability, are they likely to work with people whose behaviour is grossly psychopathic.

Practice in setting up groups varies widely. Most gestalt therapists run one or more groups each year, each with 8–12 members, meeting once a week, and, in total, amounting to some 40 sessions in the year. Many practitioners close the membership of their groups, whereas others are prepared to have a rolling membership. Other practitioners prefer to work with greater intensity in a series of weekend workshops: here again, membership may be closed or rolling.

The role of the leader

Gestalt groups commonly have one leader, although there are occasions when two may work together (e.g. a man and a woman focusing on parent-related issues), or the leader may have a trainee. Although leadership styles vary with personal temperament, culture and race, there is much commonality in their roles. For example, leaders of gestalt groups are directive; they devise experiments for members to carry out in the group.

The leader (the singular here should be taken to include one or more – and 'she' in this connection should be read to include 'he') is likely to begin the first session by discovering more of what each member wants from membership of the group. This involves a simple dialogue with each member in turn and other members who want to join in. At this stage of fore-contact, members are assessing one another and the leader. This initial meeting is an anxious time for most new groups, and the leader's task (as throughout the group's life) is to keep some balance between support of the members and frustration or confrontation (which can itself be supportive) of their games and manipulations. Thus the leader will not try to remove the normal concerns and tensions endemic in the formative stages of the group's life, but will support and encourage members who want to deal with such concerns by getting to know others.

As the group deals with its initial concerns, so it moves from fore-contact into contact. Again the leader's task is to 'stay with' the process of the group, being directive in the sense of keeping members focused on individual and group processes, but not directing in the sense of telling them how that process ought to be. Leaders encourage members to deal with 'what is' rather than worry about how things ought to be.

It is usually at this stage of contact that members bring forward some of the problems and difficulties which have brought them into therapy. The leader, again, sticks with the process – in this case the process of having problems and of defining oneself in terms of problems ('I have an impossible marriage/boss/mother'). By focusing on the process, she will help a member to undo her confluence with her problem and to feel for herself its manipulative power in the group. She can, for example, command attention and even assent that her life cannot be other than it is. The leader frustrates the confluence and promotes contact. She may do this very simply, as in 'Don't tell me the problem (a symptom of your confluence); tell me your solution (risk being contactful)'. Such a confrontation can prompt the member into announcing the missing solution, although, of course, this approach is one of those spur-of-the-moment interventions which demonstrates a general principle: it should not be used as a technique. Technique is something of a bogey word for gestaltists because it implies a fixed pattern of responses, whereas the essence of the gestalt approach is that spark of originality which is the mark of healthy ego function and lively id process.

Another and more obvious way to respond to the member with her problem is to offer her feedback. This can be contactful in that it may constitute an antithesis to her unaware neurotic thesis. Suppose, for example, that her problem is her sick husband. The leader may break the confluence around the problem by feedback such as 'you sound very sad when you speak of his illness', so that the group member's sadness becomes figure for her. It may be that the simple recognition of her sadness may lead that person to some expression of grief or resentment which will begin to free her to live her own life more satisfactorily. She may have to recognize that there is nothing she can do about her husband's illness, but that the illness need not diminish her own vitality. Technically, we might say that she has learned to undo her introjection of her husband and his illness as the important figure in the ground of her life.

Working in this way requires of the leader both deliberateness (the willingness to frustrate the woman with the sick husband) and, at the same time, spontaneity. These two, taken together, are marks of healthy ego function, and underlie the characteristic 'transparency' of gestalt therapists. Gestalt is a way of life and cannot be switched off at the end of a working day. Thus, if the leader is angry with a group member, contemptuous of her or sexually attracted to her, then these are factors in the field and may well become figures in the ground of the group. For example, it is common for group members to work on their relationship with the leader and, as in other therapies, for this relationship to be woven through with transference material. It is also axiomatic in gestalt practice that, where there is transference, there is also counter-transference. Thus the work on relationships with the leader will actively involve both parties. To take one example: a group members tries very hard to be a 'good' group member and gets upset when her (compulsive compliant) 'good' behaviour does not earn her obvious favour. Plainly it would be both unkind and unhelpful for the leader to lambast the group member for that. She is who she is and that is how she has made her way in the world: now she has brought herself into this group because, at some level, she knows she cannot keep going in the same old way. Her 'job' is to get on and be herself, and the more so the better. The leader's 'job' is to bring her manipulations into the member's awareness so that she can experience what she does as she does it. But the leader is also a human being and may find that such manipulation fills her with contempt: she will do her client no good by masking her own responses and there is also a limit as to how much she can retroflect without damaging her own well-being. She may well move to frustrate the member with a firm: 'I feel like the teacher in your class at school', or even, if she knows her well enough: 'Will you stop sucking up to me'. And if the member persists, the leader will confront her yet more firmly. At some stage, the two of them will discuss ways of meeting that are more mutually satisfying. The member will probably not enjoy the earlier parts of this experience, but she will have no room for confusion, nor need she feel condemned just because some of her behaviour irks others.

The leader who has a grandiose sense of her powers may well neglect to look after herself, and introject the needs of her group, making them primary. That is to ignore the whole gestalt of the group which, of course, includes her, and that ignorance is a recipe for illness and for compulsive work, relying on techniques.

A gestalt group leader is a powerful and charismatic figure, but one whose power empowers the members. To illustrate, let us consider the case of a group member whose current difficulty is defined as 'a lack of confidence in groups'. The leader will want to know how that problem is actualized in the group 'here and now'. The member responds from her confluence, 'I don't know.' The leader confronts the confluence: 'Take a look around this group: with whom do you experience this lack of confidence?' The member, feeling both a little anxious and yet supported by the leader, looks around the group: she identifies two people with whom she has this experience. Next the leader invites her to identify one or more people with whom she has an opposite experience. The member goes on to talk to the confidence-inspiring people and, as she does so, begins to identify how they seem to her to be people who give her permission, who smile at her in ways she finds encouraging. When, at the leader's suggestion, she turns to those with whom she experiences her lack of confidence, she does much the same, i.e. she projects her internal world (her introjects) on to them. These projections are of those introjects she picked up as a child about the badness of showing off. These conversations are more distressing for her and as she attributes these negative criticisms to her fellows she relives her hurt and her anger at being shut up and shut down by her parents when she was a bright little girl. At the point where she can begin to distinguish between her fellow group members and the introjected parts of her parents, the leader will probably set up a dialogue between her (the suppressed bright girl with all her anger and hurt) and one or both of her parents. The most common way of setting up such a dialogue is to use an empty chair in the group to represent the absent parent; this has the added advantage that the group member may later occupy that chair and respond as though she were herself the parent. She is now in a more powerful position than she was originally; her anger can be expressed in a way that can undo the oppression of past formative relationships. When she is ready to do so, she can destroy that internalized oppression, perhaps by a verbal rejection or maybe by some physical expression of tears or hitting (always some safe object such as a cushion). Now she can begin to experiment with being a bright and confident person in the contemporary group.

Two caveats should be entered with such an example. The first is that it is quite deliberately an abstract creation. Real people move through such powerful experiences of excitement, destruction and growth in the personality in a less ordered fashion. The second caveat is that the example of change can be misconstrued as not so much powerful as violent. Such deconstruction and growth may require and may unleash large amounts of emotion (that depends more upon the group member than upon the leader). People who are used to a 'talking therapy' will, at first, find this disturbs their expectations of therapy groups. Emotion is the fuel that drives us and is, by definition, powerful. As the work proceeds in the group, it does so out of the members' own id, own needs and drives; this is the leader's focus. If that is the case, the group member is unlikely to get herself into positions which are fundamentally untenable for her: that may happen if the leader is not working contactfully, e.g. if she intervenes with her own plans for the client, or else offers her confusing interpretations of what is going on.

In our example, it is clear that the leader is quite definitely leading. It is also clear that the other members are working; they co-operate actively with the leader by encouraging the unconfident member's projections, or they may get involved on their own behalf, triggered by the interactions in the group. The leader's task is to keep enough focus (one piece of work at a time) so that members are able to function and not become unnecessarily confused.

The leader has the primary responsibility for keeping the group's boundaries (e.g. of time, task, place, membership). She maintains the shifting equilibrium of frustration and support of the group and its individual members. She diagnoses as she works and theorizes about what is happening. Her diagnosing and her theorizing are articulated primarily in terms of activity at the contact boundary and she will pay attention to those aspects of the self (e.g. id, ego, personality) with which she is working. She will usually be willing to offer her diagnoses and her terminology in discussion with group members and indeed to share skills with group members.

The primary criterion for interventions by leaders is the promotion of contact, and the types of interventions which they make stem from that consideration. Leaders may make statements, ask questions, whisper, shout, touch or not touch group members; almost anything is possible as a means of contactful communication. The corollary also holds: they do not, for example, offer interpretations of their own or others' behaviour, because that tends to promote understanding in place of awareness. None of the interventions a leader may make is of itself contactful; it depends on the context and the spirit in which the intervention is made. For example, the leader may reach out to hold another who is weeping and in so doing could interrupt a necessary process of grieving; in such a case, it would be more contactful to leave the other an uninterrupted opportunity to cry. On the other hand, she might place a hand on the back of an angry group member and palpably support someone who would otherwise be unable to express a scary emotion.

The leader will at times be quiet, letting the process of the group unfold, and at other times be quite active. Let us illustrate what a leader might actively do: she might suggest that a group member (a) address her remarks to one other rather than the whole group, (b) 'talk to' an absent or dead father rather than ruminate about him, (c) concentrate on getting her breathing back into her abdomen rather than her upper thorax, (d) enrol others in the cast of her dream as she proceeds to re-enact it, and (e) practise saying 'No' to the others instead of her usual compliant behaviour. And, of course, it really does not matter whether or not the member acts promptly and efficiently on such suggestions. The leader is not teaching techniques to be followed but is devising experiments in contact. Where the members dare not, cannot or will not carry them out, the leader and other members shift their focus to whatever new behaviour (panic, anger, blankness, etc.) has become evident. Thus there can be no failure in such a group – only new awareness.

Any rules or techniques about touch, asking questions or any other interventions represent a loss of ego function which militates against contactful and effective gestalt work.

The role of group members

The group members inevitably serve many of the functions of members of any human group. For example, each will project on to others, creating around her a re-run of her family of origin, her work colleagues and so forth. These projections are an important part of the interaction and the spring of much of the work that is done. Group peers are also important in confronting and frustrating and in supporting others in their contact. At any time, some may be doing the frustrating and others the supporting. The means of support are various and it may be enough simply to be able to see a supportive person, to know she is there, or it may be important to be touched by her.

Members participate both actively and vicariously. Well-led groups are likely, for most of the time, to have lots of participative energy. The authors of gestalt therapy (Perls *et al.*, 1951) pointed out that clients are not cured by therapists but move from needing the catalytic action of the therapist to becoming autocatalytic. One could express that simply by saying that group members can be regarded as gestalt therapy trainees. And if, as often happens, the members want themselves to participate as 'therapists' in the group setting, then so be it – provided, of course, they can find themselves a client!

Members are encouraged to offer feedback to each other. Some of the most useful feedback comes from the unbidden, impulsive comments made while a piece of work is proceeding, as when two members are having a very patient discussion and a third person explodes with the irritation that they have avoided.

A more vicarious participation is also common. For example, it often happens that, as one member works on an important dream, others feel moved. They are moved not only in the conventional sense of being emotionally stimulated, but also in the sense of becoming newly aware. For example, in the earlier example, it may be that the woman is not the only person in the group who finds she has no confidence. Such awareness may prompt a second member to follow the first and work through her own difficulties, or it may be the case that the first woman's work triggers a spontaneous change in the second who finds that her difficulties dissolve.

Group development over time

Gestalt groups go through the same processes as all small groups and are subject to the same difficulties. Thus, for example, one may expect to find in a gestalt group what Bion (1961) called 'basic assumption behaviour'. Or, if one thinks of Gibb's (Bradford *et al.*, 1964) theories, the normal concerns he defines – of membership, decision, productivity and organiz- ation – are found in gestalt groups. What distinguishes the gestalt group is that the focus of group process (as well as individual process) is explicit: it is ground or context for whatever else goes on. And what is unique to the gestalt group is that the process is experienced and conceptualized as contact process. For example, the stage of initial formation of the group is defined as fore-contact, and at that stage the group may cling to its initial confluence and avoid the excitement of gestalt formation, e.g. avoid paying attention to the other members and then risking the next step.

If, however, the group members are open to meeting each other, i.e. move into fore-contact, they will quickly arrive at the 'norming' stage where, however unawarely, they sort out their rules and procedures which are designed to make life safe enough. This stage involves shared introjects, e.g. 'What we have to do is . . .' Thus they develop norms of operation which apply to them all: and, if they are unacceptable to an individual member, that person will probably introject the norms of the group as her own – at least for the time being. Confluence with such norms is inevitable and even useful as a basis for experimenting with new behaviours. Of course, some norms may prove unhelpful in the long run. For example, a group may become confluent with a norm about 'being helpful'. This introject has the effect of stylizing or fixating the behaviour of the group by defining it as a 'helpful' group. To bring the introject into awareness is to break the confluence of the members in that area and, to that extent, to threaten the cohesion of the group. Members may variously find this upsetting or liberating.

The leader knows that much of the group's self-support rests in its confluence with certain norms and, in confronting the 'be helpful' introject, will have an eye to the balance of frustration and support. One way to do this would be to check with members whether or not they are willing to experiment with breaking their rule, and to suggest that they assess the outcomes of the experiment.

The gestalt group is a flux of construction, deconstruction and reconstruction. Alliances come and go, norms are constantly being challenged, trust is made, broken and re-made, people fight and flee from each other – and all this occurs within boundaries which are ultimately firmly held by the leader.

There is no ideal life-span for a gestalt therapy group, although one should certainly think in terms of months or years rather than weeks. Therapy groups should be distinguished from self-experience groups which are usually brief (e.g. 10 weekly sessions or 4 weekends): these are often very therapeutic for their participants, but one would not refer to such a short-term group a patient requiring group psychotherapy. An exception to this may occur if the leaders of such groups can continue to work with the referred patients in ongoing groups when that proves necessary.

Mechanisms of change

The fundamental mechanism of change in a gestalt therapy group is that of awareness engendered by contact. Therapeutic change is effected by work through the personality, touching both ego and id processes. The therapist's task (and the therapeutic agent is not always the group leader) is to promote contact with the group member in what she is doing. Her impulses, inhibitions, avoidances, etc. (e.g. her modifications of the contact process) will gradually come into awareness. That is to say, the group member will experience herself doing what has been automatic or compulsive: she may at that point find she has choices which bring different results, and thus be enabled to shape her life differently. In practice, this usually means working over the same modifications of contact several times before there is sufficient awareness for change to be possible. Sometimes, however, the change is so spontaneous that the person changes first and only later becomes aware that she is different.

The type of change varies corresponding to the type of modification of contact. There is usually a discernible progression in the deconstruction of a neurosis through a number of such modifications, e.g. from reaction formation, back through the repression to egotism, retroflection, projection, introjection to the original impulse emerging from the confluence of the id process. To give an example: a group member (a) becomes markedly anxious; (b) identifies the two principal components of the anxiety, e.g.

her rising anger at a man in the group, alloyed with her introjected rule that she should be charitable to her neighbours; (c) explores the introject and its source in her lay-preacher father; (d) unloads the stored resentment of years of internalized oppression from that father; (e) re-assesses the introject and discovers that she cannot unlearn it; (f) finds a more creative adjustment to her introject, e.g. by tempering it with ' . . . provided he's not a pain'; and (g) expressing whatever feelings are currently directed at the man in the group.

Such work promotes more creative adjustment in that some of the ego function lost in her old modifications is restored and she is able to function more flexibly with men; it will lead, in the post-contact phase, to a lasting change in her personality, visible in her attitudes to men. This is a simple example; where people's self-systems are more severely disturbed, i.e. where they have had to generate more interruptive contact modifications, it is more difficult for them to become more functionally self-regulating and not to need therapeutic intervention.

Typical problems and their resolution

Problems which occur in a gestalt therapy group are conceived of as modifications or interruptions of contact. Thus, if the leader is uncontactful in the matter of boundaries, e.g. pays no attention to absences from the group, late arrivals, slowness to pay fees, then she should not be surprised if the group process shows symptoms of disaffection, low morale and unwillingness to take risks. It is often the case that group members are unwilling to make contactful initiatives; for example, they may prefer simply to chat. This might be because they are aware of an impending and feared conflict between two of their peers; or perhaps this week's reluctance is a carry over from a previous meeting. This kind of behaviour (often termed 'resistance') is interesting because it is precisely the material with which the gestalt group leader works; it becomes figure in the ground of the group. The leader who fails to treat this avoidance as the new figure, the interesting agenda, is likely to become angry with the group or else to switch into another reaction formation such as exaggerated patience. To criticize group members for their resistance (instead of treating the resistance as what is there is to contact) is to prove the gestalt dictum that resistance is a reaction formation of the therapist. When the leader turns to confront the resistance she will begin to hear of the members' mixture of fear and anger leading to painful anxiety, and thus the group moves from its reluctance back to work.

There is another problem area which can present difficulties for the leader. As group and leader become increasingly used to each other, their areas of confluence are apt to increase: that is to say, the awareness that comes from clearly defined activity at the contact boundary becomes hazy. One example of this can be seen in a group where the positive transference relationship of group members to the leader is so strong that, in effect, the group exists to lionize the leader and to admire her skills and power. The leader is, by definition, likely not to spot much of this confluence, and only dissension from a group member, or the intervention of a supervisor, will be able to break up that confluence. In practice, both are likely to happen, although inexperienced or frightened leaders may be unaware of seeking to perpetuate such confluence.

Limitations of the approach

Gestalt group therapy is contact therapy and requires that group members be prepared to learn from their experience. Therefore, gestalt is not an indicated mode for people who have little capacity for meeting others and learning from them. Such people may be able to learn from some other types of group experience. And, if there are special conditions where, for example, social workers, managers or nurses are told to be in a 'support group', gestalt group leaders are unlikely to be very helpful. They cannot work effectively in such dependence-sustaining positions. Such exceptions apart, it is the case that gestalt group therapy is a powerful mode with applications in a large variety of circumstances (see Fagan and Shepherd, 1970; Kempler, 1974).

Typical qualities of effective leaders

The prime quality of an effective gestalt group leader is what the literature terms 'contact-ability'. By this is meant a ready sensibility of activity at the contact boundary. In plain terms, the leader is in the business of meeting others. Thus a great curiosity about people (even nosiness) is important as the leader looks for areas in which the interests of leader and members meet. Into this meeting may come any of the range of experiences which both parties have: thus poetry or sport, gardening or politics may form the ground from which figures emerge as the focus of meeting. Whatever the leader is or has experienced is thus potentially there in the contact and the broader her interests and experience the more capacity she has for meeting others.

Human beings cannot be split into mind, body and spirit. Contact-ability includes an attentive interest in people's bodies – their posture, breathing, movement and looks. It is also important for the leader to have a strong feeling for language, including the language of id process as evidenced in verbal slips, sighs, swearing and choice of vocabulary.

The effective leader is thoroughly grounded in the theory of gestalt group therapy. In the oscillating attention at the contact boundary, as the leader's focus moves from the group to herself and back again, she will usually have a clear idea of what the process is in which they are presently involved. The theoretical structures will be well-integrated in her personality and thus second nature; if they are not so, then they will be introjects to which she must refer as she works (i.e. she will be consciously interpreting and will, to that extent, not be contactfully in the process of the meeting). In a creative moment, however, she may – at some prompting of her id process – do something quite surprising to both the group members and herself. These surprise moments are also part of effective leadership, a species of serendipity.

From the examples that have been offered in this chapter, it will be clear that what the leader offers is herself, as much of herself as she is willing and able to offer in a meeting with others. She knows that this meeting will change both her and the others, that neither party will emerge the same afterwards. That requires both a certain courage and a willingness to be changed. She should be a person who has plumbed the depths of her own neuroses in her personal therapy and ongoing supervision, and has made more creative adaptations as a consequence. Many of the limitations on her work will become familiar to her as her own limitations as a person. These will lead her spontaneously to change and to seek support, as in supervision, to promote further her own growth. Her own inhibitions and fixations will be challenged consistently if she is working contactfully. Thus her religious or political beliefs are likely to be confronted; any inhibitions she has about, for example, expression of feelings of anger or sexual attraction will come sharply into focus in the course of her work. In terms of self-structure, she should be self aware (id), autonomous (ego) and responsible (personality).

She will find other people very different to herself. She will have learned to let other people be, and not to be too ready to decide how they should be different.

Finally, the effective leader is an uncommonly exciting and stimulating person, and a person who proceeds in a self-authenticating way out of her own power. But she is not a paragon of all the psychological virtues: rather she is a person palpably engaged in her own journey in life who is ready to meet others whose quest may, for a time, touch her own.

REFERENCES

Bion, W. R. (1961). *Experiences in Groups and Other Papers*. London, Tavistock.
Bradford, L. P., Gibb, J. R. and Benne, K. D. (eds) (1964). *T-Group Theory and Laboratory Method*. New York, Wiley.

Fagan, J. and Shepherd, I. L. (eds) (1970). *Gestalt Therapy Now*. Harmonds-worth, Penguin Books.

Kempler, W. (1974). *Principles of Gestalt Family Therapy*. Costa Mesa, California, The Kempler Institute.

Perls, F. S. (1947). *Ego, Hunger and Aggression*. London, Allen and Unwin.

Perls, F. S., Hefferline, R. F. and Goodman, P. (1951). *Gestalt Therapy: Excitement and Growth in the Human Personality*. Harmondsworth, Penguin Books.

CHAPTER 5

PSYCHODRAMA GROUP THERAPY

Martin H. Davies

HISTORICAL CONTEXT AND DEVELOPMENT IN BRITAIN

Of all the contemporary approaches to human emotional growth and healing which lay claim to the title 'Group Therapy', psychodrama was undoubtedly well ahead of the field. Its originator, J. L. Moreno, first used the term Group Psychotherapy in 1932 and about the same time he developed the techniques of sociometry, demonstrating how human groups spontaneously and unconsciously establish an internal structure of roles and relationships which underlies their external characteristics (Anderson, 1974). The experiments in which he encouraged individuals to work on their emotional problems by acting them through in a controlled and supportive group setting had begun some 10 years earlier. They were the outcome of a natural marriage of his life-long enthusiastic commitment to the creative arts, in particular poetry, philosophy and the theatre, with an equally powerful determination to study social behaviour objectively. Although many other therapies have subsequently incorporated role playing or similar dramatic techniques in their repertoires, psychodrama alone is firmly rooted in Moreno's distinctive view of mankind's social nature, from which it grew and without which it would not survive as a coherent system of theory and practice.

What then is this distinctive view? It is one which emphasizes our species' innate creative drive, the urge to explore and experience life in the immediacy of the present. First apparent in the imaginative play of children, this spontaneity continues to express itself in every creative act we perform, in our thoughts, words and deeds. But as humans we can only develop and make sense of ourselves through our communion with other humans. We are the products of both our behaviour towards the people in our world and their responses to us on which we rely to validate our perception of us and them. So the fullest expression of our creative energy depends as much on others as on ourselves.

Born in 1892 of Sephardic Jewish parents in Bucharest, Moreno lived from the age of 4 years in Vienna where he attended university, studying mathematics and philosophy from 1910 to 1912 before enrolling in the Medical School. Even as a student he was impressed by the capacity of children to respond variedly and creatively when they acted the stories he told them. Later he initiated discussion groups among the prostitutes of the 'red light' district of the city and noted how these groups exhibited autonomy and structure, and how the collective dynamic interacted with the individuals' needs for self-expression and recognition.

On qualifying as a doctor in 1917, Moreno found himself for 3 years in charge of patients in a refugee camp during which his informal observations of group structure led him to suggest to the authorities that these principles should be used actively in organizing the community. Between 1921 and 1923 he worked with a group of young actors in Vienna using improvization to dramatize current events. In this 'Theatre of Spontaneity' it soon became obvious that without a script and detailed direction the players were expressing more and more of their own personalities. The step from this to playing themselves was the start of psychodrama. In 1925 Moreno took up residence in the USA, demonstrating his methods to the public in the Impromptu Theatre which he established at New York City and also applying them to the benefit of the deprived and maladjusted in state institutions. His classic work *Who Shall Survive? Foundations of Sociometry, Group Psychotherapy and Psychodrama*, was published in 1934, the Moreno Sanitorium at Beacon, New York was set up in 1936, and in 1937 *Sociometry*, the first journal in the field, was published. By this stage the techniques and format of psychodrama, as it has since been practised, were already well developed and in the 1940s and 1950s they were widely used in psychiatric, educational and corrective establishments throughout the USA where the American Society of Group Psychotherapy and Psychodrama provides a long established base for professional training in and development of the method.

It was, however, less well accepted in Europe, least of all in Britain. A few pioneering therapists, for example Maxwell Jones, embraced it, but generally the talking group firmly based on classical Freudian psychoanalytic principles held sway. Since about 1970, perhaps stimulated by the spread of Sensitivity Training, Transactional Analysis, Gestalt Therapy and Family Therapy, in which many of its ideas and methods have been rediscovered, there has been a resurgence of interest in psychodrama. But it is still only being used in a relatively small number of centres in Britain. For this there are probably several reasons including not only the emotional and physical demands which psychodrama makes on the therapist but also persistent misunderstanding of what it is and what it attempts.

When Moreno first experimented with psychodrama he was participating in regular sessions with the same actors and audience, the members of his 'Theatre of Spontaneity'. Later in New York he began to invite members of the public to join in on the spur of the moment and without any serious preparation or follow-up to the experience. Although this still happens at demonstrations of the medium, at short workshops or conferences for professional workers, there has been criticism of this use of psychodrama which does not seem to be sensitive to the possible countertherapeutic effects of suddenly exposing people to feelings and experiences which they normally avoid and may not have consciously intended to explore.

If the uncovered emotions are not adequately worked through, it is possible that those involved in the session may leave with a disturbed sense of having been 'seduced' into embarrassing self-revelations and a determination not to have anything more to do with psychodrama. Although such consequences may have been exaggerated, they are not to be lightly dismissed. Moreno's own charismatic presence and confidence in the method set an example which less gifted disciples have often mistakenly tried to emulate.

Psychodrama group therapy represents an attempt to combine an understanding of the group process and the need to allow this to develop spontaneously with the powerful facilitative techniques of psychodrama. This is likely to remain a controversial issue. But it must be acknowledged that for all but the least emotionally disturbed a slow, supportive and sustained group approach is the only one which enables deep-seated and painful issues to be tackled realistically.

The emergence of a British Psychodrama Association in the last 3 years owes much to the Holwell Centre established in Devon in 1974 by Marcia Karp. This has provided a nucleus of soundly trained practitioners whose work in various centres throughout the country has helped to educate their professional colleagues and counter their understandable suspicions and misconceptions. The appearance of Dramatherapy, a less intensive though overlapping system of training and treatment, may also have contributed to this slow development (Davies, 1987).

UNDERLYING ASSUMPTIONS

Theoretical underpinnings

Ideally our mutual appreciation of each other should be empathically accurate, what Moreno called 'tele' (Greenberg, 1974), a direct and uncontaminated sympathetic encounter between two persons. In practice it is more generally dominated and distorted by our previous experiences and imagined expectations of the future. The functioning form I assume as I react at a given moment to a specific situation involving other people or objects is my role in that situation. Role is the basic unit of social interaction. My sense of self or personal identity emerges from the many roles I find myself enacting from moment to moment. These roles are not all at a similar stage of development. Each faces a counterpart role which will also be evolving, not necessarily in harmony with mine. The totality of my roles and most important their internal and external relationships constitute my observable ego, personality or self-system.

This is therefore an interpersonal psychology which does not postulate an elaborate unconscious mind though it does recognize in our behaviour unacknowledged residues of previous encounters and a range of roles which as yet only exist in fantasy, what Moreno, to stress their unrealized potential importance, called 'surplus reality'. It also implies a continuing active testing through our meetings of what Kelly (1955) later labelled personal constructs. Action in Moreno's scheme is considered a more powerful and developmentally more primitive force than verbalization in shaping our behaviour. So it is logical that attempts to resolve role conflicts or frustrations should be more effective if they are approached through active experiment rather than discussion alone. The theory in acknowledging the influence of group structure on the roles it permits its members also presaged modern Systems Theory, whose concepts and techniques share some common ground with it.

In the simplest terms the application of psychodrama to a problematic situation assumes that it is likely to (i) increase mutual rapport, (ii) encourage the release of suppressed painful emotions, and (iii) allow participants to test out avoided or unconsidered roles in safer conditions. All three effects should make for a more balanced and objective perception of self and others, a greater warmth in relationships and a freeing of spontaneous creative energy previously blocked by fear, grief, anger, suspicion and avoidance of the unknown consequences of unfamiliar roles. This is to be achieved by facilitating a cohesive trusting and confiding group atmosphere within which members can recreate their subjective world, sharing their experiences past, present and future, exchanging roles with important others in their lives and discovering how unexplored alternative scenarios actually affect them when translated into a more concrete reality.

As with most forms of psychotherapy the application of objective observation to measure and compare complicated spontaneous social transactions has been relatively disappointing. Conduit (1986), in a review of research into psychodrama found that only a handful of controlled outcome studies have been performed (Harrow, 1951; Slawson, 1965;

Kipper and Giladi, 1978). These findings demonstrated little evidence of attitude change but did show a reduction of situational anxiety comparable to that produced by systematic desensitization. There has, however, been some interesting process research. Kreitler and Kreitler (1968) compared the behaviour of psychiatric patients in the scenes they played with accounts of their comparable daily behaviour in the wards. This indicated that they did act in character in the psychodrama and offers some defence to the accusation that psychodramatically elicited acts and emotions may be untypical of the subject.

Key concepts

Spontaneity

Conduit ends his review by suggesting that it may well be unrealistic to investigate an essentially qualitative activity by the quantitative methods of the scientist. In order to understand this point we need to look more closely at Moreno's underlying philosophy and the development of its principal concepts. Spontaneity is defined as the condition in which an individual responds with adequate effectiveness to a new situation or with a new response to an old one. The word comes from the Latin *sua sponte* meaning freely, of one's own accord. Although the response has quantifiable features – its intensity, variety, novelty and so on – Moreno concluded early in his studies that spontaneity could not itself be treated as if it were the equivalent of physical energy. A person does not have a specific amount available to be depleted by repeated demands. He or she is not obviously diminished by displaying it. But it is the essential condition of flexible adaptation and growth, the matrix of the creative activity which it catalyses.

Cultural conserve

Spontaneity gives birth to the definitive object, act, speech or thought whose form once created is now fixed, separated off from the original creative state which generated it. Collectively the products of our spontaneous activity constitute the 'cultural conserve', the accumulated framework of predictable artefacts to which we can return repeatedly for safety, security and inspiration. It includes all those things which preserve the values of a particular culture, books, buildings, music, rituals and customs. Our limited nature demands this structured system of conserved elements. In its absence we would have to create spontaneously for the same situations every day. Continuous unrestricted spontaneity would make superhuman demands upon us. Instead we find ourselves in a fluctuating interplay between these opposing tendencies. Pathological spontaneity, often a reaction to an over-restrictive cultural conserve, leads to disintegrated behaviour. Excessive conservation places a dead hand upon us, stifling individuality, originality and adaptiveness, eventually provoking an equally extreme counter-reaction.

Role

'Role is the functioning form the individual assumes in the specific moment he reacts to a specific situation in which other people or objects are involved' (Moreno, 1964, p. 4). It must be emphasized that role is the unit of culture. The individual's personality is in effect the sum total of the roles that individual plays, ranging from the most superficial, such as a customer in a shop, to the most profound, such as that of parent, child or lover.

Cultural atom

The cultural atom is this total range of roles.

> Every individual – just as he has at all times a set of friends and a set of enemies – has a range of roles in which he sees himself and faces a range of counter-roles in which he sees others around him. They are in various stages of development. The tangible aspects of what is known as 'ego' are the roles in which he operates, with the pattern of the role-relations around an individual as their focus. We consider roles and relationships between roles as the most significant development within any specific culture (Moreno, 1964, pp. 5–6).

Co-unconscious states

This term describes an implicit sharing of thoughts and feelings distinct from the Freudian individual unconscious mind or the Jungian collective unconscious. Individuals whose cultural atoms interlock – families, teams, working groups – share an awareness of each others' roles which is manifested in their behaviour even though they cannot express it consciously in words. This awareness is often a positive and advantageous attribute benefiting individual and group. But when it involves gross inequalities or contradictory perceptions of roles, the co-unconscious may be the source of major tension and conflict which interfere with the functioning of the group and its members.

Thus we remain unaware of many of our feelings about the roles we are playing and the strains placed upon us by their disequilibrium. Suppose, for example, that a couple who have lived together in apparently reasonable harmony for a period begin to irritate each other, to argue and to quarrel. Often they cannot conceptualize the basis of their differences. Nor does the most skilled and sensitive counselling increase their effective insight. But persuade them to re-enact what occurs between them and soon, once they have the confidence to take this risk, they will begin to discover all kinds of feelings in themselves and their partner of which they had previously been ignorant.

Mental catharsis

This brings us to what I would suggest is the most central and important concept in psychodrama, 'mental catharsis' (Moreno, 1940). Just as understanding of role has been hampered by focusing on only one of its aspects – internal, external, philosophical, psychological, sociological, anthropological or political (Holland, 1977) – so also have the nature and implications of mental catharsis. The word means literally purging. It was first employed in this context by the ancient Greek philosopher Aristotle to describe the pleasurable emotional relief experienced by the audience witnessing the powerful tragic or comic scenes simulated in the theatre. The spectator identifies with the feelings portrayed so vividly by the actors. That is to say that they not only remind him of parallel experiences of his own but also evoke in him the old emotions which are somehow now re-experienced in a form which makes them more tolerable and even strangely enjoyable. No doubt this remains one of the chief attractions of drama as an entertainment. It allows us to taste what might be in real life repelling experiences vicariously and safely. But catharsis need not only be passive and symbolic. It can be active and personal. In the psychodrama when the audience share what they know to be the real and personal world of another, the intensity and observable spontaneity of what occurs become a potent catalyst of emotional insight and change. It is truly active catharsis. But how does it differ from any other therapy which helps us to express intense emotions arising from a traumatic event or unresolved role conflict? Only in that drama recreates much more of the experience than talking and writing about it and that by its exploration in action the spontaneity generated appears to facilitate a more realistic acceptance of what seemed intolerable and its assimilation into a more effective adjustment of role relations.

In other words, active mental catharsis is not merely the release of 'bad' feelings, the draining of a psychic abscess. This was the kind of model proposed by Freud and Breuer in their first attempts to expose the sources of neurosis under the influence of hypnotic suggestion. But when it proved erratic and unpredictable in its effects they abandoned it in favour of free association and interpretation of transference.

The behavioural model of *in vivo* desensitization has a closer resemblance to catharsis. Sustained willing re-exposure to the event which caused a distressing loss of personal equilibrium allows the initial pain to attenuate. But catharsis also includes other strong emotions; the rising anxiety as the avoided re-enactment is approached and a positive sense of freedom when it has been survived. Moreover, it appears to include to a varying extent a reorganization of role relations indicated by changes of attitude and feeling towards important others. There is obviously no benefit in rehearsing over and over the old conserved stereotyped emotions and situations but there is something to be gained from re-entering the predicament with encouragement to expose oneself to all its possibilities, many of which may never even have been contemplated.

A better analogy is the use of controlled explosions to relieve pressure building up along fault lines in the earth's crust. Movement is not prevented nor precisely predicted but whatever the new alignment the other alternative, increasing strain and eventual seismic catastrophe, is bound to be worse. Except that in the role conflict the 'charges' are already in position. The difficulty is how to find and fire them. No claim is made that every unhappy life can be changed. We live in an often hostile environment. We form attachments only to lose them. Our achievements are transitory and our bodies frail. Yet we seem to be programmed to continue to struggle for affection, meaning and survival. This is the true drama of human existence. Psychodrama accepts this and then strives to stretch and share our separate individual parts in it as far as it can, allowing us to flesh out our dreams and nightmares and by experiencing them live more completely.

Instruments of psychodrama

   (i) *The director and protagonist*:   the person who conducts the psychodrama is called the director, as in the theatre, for it is his task to guide the enactment of the protagonist, the one who seeks to explore his cultural atom in this way.
   (ii) *The audience*:   the group who watch and share in the experience constitute the audience.
   (iii) *Auxiliary egos*:   those members or therapeutic aides filling the counter roles are called the auxiliary egos.
   (iv) *The stage*:   the area in which the action occurs is the stage.

When the psychodrama is produced in a real living situation with the actual people involved then that is the stage. This is, of course, rarely possible and so the psychodrama theatre was devised, a circular platform with two surrounding stepped lower levels by which to ascend to it, a small auditorium, a 'Juliet' box and some simple lighting equipment. But any room of reasonable size and acoustic quality will suffice.

Contrary to expectation protagonists usually find it easier to act through scenes of their personal world on stage than in more ordinary surroundings. Its structure embodies and enhances the shift into a dimension in which fantasy and imagination can be legitimately brought into play. While remaining responsible for their behaviour, they do not feel so acutely accountable for its consequences and can thus act more spontaneously, free to test out their surplus reality.

Role reversal

The protagonist 'role reverses' when he exchanges places with the auxiliary ego, assumes his or her role and expresses his or her emotions in the interaction between them. This can help to warm up the auxiliary into the role but, more importantly, it can be used at points of strong emotion to help the protagonst acquire a more empathic appreciation of the situation of the person in the counter role.

Doubling

An auxiliary 'doubles' for the protagonist by taking up a position alongside him or her, assuming his or her posture, expression and words. The double may speak for the protagonist, emphasizing his or her feelings or helping him or her to clarify the thoughts and emotions which are struggling to emerge as the psychodrama develops. Skilled doubling enables the protagonist to move into sensitive areas of his or her experience while feeling safe and supported.

Mirroring

The director instructs an auxiliary to 'mirror' the protagonist by taking his place in the psychodrama and repeating the scene which has just been enacted. The protagonist stands with the director or sits in the audience and observes how he has portrayed himself and the significant others in his psychodrama.

PRACTICE

The goals of the group

As I have already indicated in the first section of this chapter, psychodrama has been used to provide a one-off therapeutic experience. My own view is that this is of limited value and can even be dangerous in all but the most expert of hands. The psychologically well-defended tend to deflect the real purpose of the psychodrama by 'play acting' and the more sensitive tend to take fright, avoiding further exposure to the method. I believe that in general useful work with serious clients requires a closed group structure with sessions of about 2 hours duration held on a regular weekly schedule over a period of at least several months and sometimes 2 or more years.

The group members' goals are to develop a trusting and confidential relationship with each other and their leader within which they can discuss and act through the various important roles in their lives. In doing so they hope to achieve a fuller and warmer understanding of the important 'others' with whom they share their cultural atoms, to express old and avoided feelings and to acquire a more effective and fulfilling range of roles.

This usually necessitates a therapeutic contract committing patients and therapist to their regular meetings, and these should take place in a suitably sized and sound-proofed room effectively free from unexpected interruptions.

A number of therapists (e.g. Elefthery, 1975; Schutzenberger, 1975; Marrone, 1979) have adopted this approach in which the gradual and natural development of the group process is always given priority over efforts to elicit cathartic material from individual protagonists. Thus more than one session may be devoted to working through the products of a single psychodrama which often includes projections and transferences presently alive within the group, although their full significance is partly disguised behind the figures played by the auxiliaries. Such an intensive group will meet regularly over many months and, while direct interpretation is avoided, the changes in the participants' attitudes and insight make it obvious that they have successfully been tackling deep-seated and painful consequences of their past experiences.

Powell (1986) has convincingly demonstrated that the insights and cathartic experiences of a psychodrama group can be perfectly well understood in the terms and concepts of object-relations theory. The auxiliaries enable the protagonists to project upon them their internal objects, good and bad, and to work through the associated conflicts which have been kept from resolution by compulsive repetition of the self-defeating emotions and actions which serve to perpetuate them.

It would, however, seem impossible to employ psychodramatic and group analytical methods of therapy simultaneously. The goals of the psycho-drama leader are (i) to facilitate an open, self-disclosing, warm, spontaneous group interaction, which requires that he must himself provide a model of such behaviour (ii) to guide discussion towards a psychodramatic expression rather than further discussion, and (iii) to discourage interpretation and encourage positive mutual identification of shared experiences and roles. This is patently a contrasting approach to that of the 'low profile' opaque, detached analytical group leader whose method is aimed at reducing external behavioural cues and thus maximizing transference behaviour which can then be the more readily identified and interpreted.

In psychodrama group therapy the method is consistently psychodramatic. The leader observes the development of group defences, of transference feelings of group members towards one another and himself, but relies on the psychodramatic action to express them and allow the exploration of more positive and balanced role relations. Thus individual and group dynamics can be discerned in the psychodrama at one and the same time.

For example, a man enacting a scene depicting his battles with a loved and hated sibling may choose as his auxiliary a group member with whom a parallel conflict is apparent in the therapeutic setting. In the role reversals and doublings other members may share in the exposure of these real but painful feelings and by their identification gain relief, insight and some resolution of their own role conflicts. That this theme emerges at this point in the process of group development is no accident. It coincides with other indications of rivalry in the group. By encouraging them to work in this way each protagonist carries the momentum of the group dynamics forwards, the individual's theme resonating with the relationship pattern which the group is displaying at each stage of its progress.

The director may occasionally choose to work more like a gestalt therapist, focusing almost exlusively on a series of protagonists, striving to expose internal conflict and paying less attention to the group as a whole. This approach has often aroused critical comment, particularly from analytically trained therapists who argue that it is too confronting, that even when it succeeds in breaching the individual's ego defences it does not resolve the underlying conflicts and, thus, after a period of severe emotional discomfort, the old problems will remain, possibly still more resistant to change. That this can happen is undeniable.

Nevertheless, such an approach can be perfectly effective given the appropriate setting. For example, in a day or residential therapy unit where there is a continuing programme of group work and readily available staff support, it may be used quite deliberately to encourage an individual to look more closely at some specific aspect of behaviour which is manifesting itself strikingly and regularly. Whereas in the opposite situation of a person lacking in social support, possibly in the midst of an emotional crisis but not receiving skilled counselling, this kind of sudden assault on the emotions would be irresponsible.

The same principles of selection apply as in other intensive therapies, avoiding clients whose psychological and emotional limitations make self-confrontation difficult. The overtly psychotic, the grossly immature or impulsive, the rigidly obsessional or histrionic should normally not be considered for a group which it is hoped will do intensive therapeutic work. This does not mean that more superficial role playing exercises are also excluded. In fact, it is often easier for the less articulate and sophisticated to express themselves through action rather than words. Simple insights, social skills and confidence building can be acquired through group activities such as team games, masks, puppets and extemporized plays. This represents a shift in 'symbolic distance' from the high level of self-exposure of pure psychodrama to a lower one in which, nevertheless, new ways of seeing oneself and others do emerge, albeit more slowly and gradually.

Yalom (1975) has reviewed the effect of group composition on outcome. There seem to be two important types of influence, those favouring group cohesion and those which stimulate interaction. It has been claimed that a group with much in common will cohere rapidly but later lack the variety of experience to offer each other anything new. This has led to attempts to form groups from various selected personality types and diagnostic categories. Disappointingly this approach has not met with much success. Some 'demographic' heterogeneity, a reasonable range of age, sex and social background, does help, but generally it is the self-generated willingness of the group members to commit themselves to meet regularly and involve themselves with each others' cares that is crucial. Indeed such is the range of individual personality that a group of fairly similar individuals will eventually identify enough points of contrast between them to allow cathartic role conflicts to surface. So it is with psychodrama groups (Aveline, 1984). Provided that there is the motivation, success seems to depend most of all on the growth of group cohesion, trust and frankness.

The role of the leader (and co-leader)

The role of the leader, in this case the director, is to be therapist, analyst and producer, all simultaneously but in varying proportions according to the specific needs of the therapeutic situation at each point in the session.[1] He must encourage the participants to interact with sufficient freedom and spontaneity for one of them to come forward and present some facet of himself for psychodramatic enactment. He must then, like a theatrical producer, give practical instructions as to how the psychodrama can be set in motion and during the action make interventions which consistently support the protagonist in his efforts to bring out and clarify the significant emotions and events under scrutiny. Throughout all this he must also keep an eye on the reactions of the other group members, auxiliaries and audience and, when the psychodrama concludes, lead the 'feedback' to the protagonist.

The typical session takes place in three phases. Action is preceded by a period in which the director 'warms up' the group, facilitating a safe, open, confiding interaction from which hopefully a member will focus on some specific aspect of his own situation and agree to work on it. The type of warm-up and selection of the protagonist depends on the context in which

---

[1] Interested readers who wish to study the techniques of psychodrama in more detail could do well to look at Moreno's original writings. For a more concise handbook, Blatner's *Acting-In* (1973) can be recommended. *Psychodrama: Theory & Therapy*, edited by Greenberg (1974) covers a wider range of topics with contributions by Moreno himself and attempts to place psychodrama in its full social and historical setting.

the meeting takes place. In a well-established group the members will require little direction. When the session is part of the programme in a therapeutic community, day centre or residential unit there may be a deliberate decision to encourage specific members to use the time to look more closely at issues which are already presenting themselves in their interactions with each other. Conversely, when psychodrama is used in a training workshop for therapists, counsellors or educators and the exercise is strictly limited in time, then a more contrived warm-up may be justified, for example asking each participant to discuss what he might offer for psychodramatic exploration and then choosing a protagonist democratically from among the volunteers. This is not without its dangers because in any unselected group there can be quite disturbed individuals who bring with them emotional material too difficult for the others to tolerate at this point, or a person who uses histrionic behaviour to avoid more genuine but denied feelings can seduce the therapist into a superficial and unproductive psychodrama. The experienced director is often able to detect such tendencies and allow another person to be protagonist, but it is not always easy.

While some intuitive acumen is necessary, it is not enough in itself. The director should be prepared to take time to obtain a fuller picture of each group member against which to make a more rational appraisal of the appropriateness of the occasion for him to be protagonist. In a long-term group there is no need to hurry and it is often wise in the earlier meetings to avoid a potential protagonist who is very 'wound up' in favour of one who has a less obviously intense emotional presentation. In this way the group is not plunged too suddenly into highly personal and sensitive revelations. At the same time the 'rejected' protagonist is often able to use the other person's psychodrama and feedback to ventilate his feelings without the stress of entering the exposed position of protagonist. When the group has cohered it becomes easier to let the emotional priorities of the group members lead the way.

Although the director does literally direct the psychodrama, the aim is always to follow the spontaneous cues given by the protagonist. For example, the subject who emerges as a willing protagonist from the warming-up of the group may only have a vague idea of the kind of scene he or she is about to present to the rest. Perhaps it is some discomforting interaction with a parent, marriage partner, close friend or offspring.

As the director walks around the acting area with the protagonist, they discuss the background circumstances in more detail. A picture of the relationship, of its history, of the other important actors in the protagonist's social atom, and of details of daily life gradually become manifest. Thus the protagonist warms up into the situation and the director begins to get some sense of the subject's personal world. The protagonist is only then offered the possibility of presenting some relevant part of it in psychodramatic form. Although the director makes his suggestions clearly and positively, the subject is left in no doubt that they arise specifically from the information he or she has given and that there is no compulsion to try any of them. If it is suggested that it would be helpful to confront the other person represented by an auxiliary, the protagonist may be unwilling to risk the possibly unpleasant things he or she has left unsaid. But it might be more acceptable to replay another recent encounter between them. Once this is under way, the increased vividness and spontaneity will probably allow the avoided feelings to come out. In the absence of criticisms and feeling adequately supported, the protagonist will then be ready to explore them further. By moving gradually from scene to scene in this way, it is possible to enter deeply into the subject's 'surplus reality' without the help of other techniques.

Great care is taken to elicit as much detail as possible from the protagonist both in describing the setting and briefing the auxiliaries in their roles. In this way a more spontaneous recapture of the original experience is likely to occur. Or if it is a future event which is to be examined, the protagonist's imagined preconceptions can emerge more freely and clearly. Only when the director is satisfied that the protagonist is fully prepared does he or she suggest that the action should begin.

When it does begin, the authenticity of the action is carefully checked with the protagonist who may be asked to reverse roles with the auxiliaries to demonstrate exactly how they are to act and talk. In this way they are further warmed-up into a more accurate projection of the protagonist's subjective world. This in turn gains greater reality in its presentation and evokes from the protagonist still more spontaneity. As soon as the enactment has 'come to life' for the participants, the director can reduce his or her interventions and allow the picture to unfold until it reaches a climax or begins to fade or falter. At these points more specific interventions can be made, employing role reversal to help the protagonist feel how it must be in the other person's 'shoes' or asking other members of the group to speak as the protagonist's 'double', expressing possible concealed or incompletely acknowledged thoughts and emotions. The protagonist may even be requested to join the audience to observe the scene replayed with another in his or her role, presenting a living 'mirror' of the psychodrama.

At a suitable moment the director draws the action to a close, leads the protagonist back into the circle and begins the final phase of the psycho-drama.

Having checked that the protagonist is ready to proceed the director now asks each of the auxiliaries to describe what emotions and thoughts they have experienced in their roles. This is very important and should not be rushed. Auxiliaries often become deeply affected by the emotions of the psychodrama and must be allowed to complete their own catharsis. They are then firmly reminded that they are out of role and that they can join with the rest of the group in a sharing of feelings and the discussion which is to follow. When the protagonist has had time to absorb their comments and respond, the director invites contributions from everyone. These should be addressed directly to the protagonist in person and should focus on the group member's own feelings evoked by the psychodrama. They might well be memories of similar situations and relationships in his or her life and they may identify with one of the auxiliaries' roles more than the protagonist's. But the emphasis is on the sharing of personal emotion. Interpretations, psychological theorizing and questioning of the protagonist are actively discouraged. Only after the protagonist has had ample opportunity to consider and discuss each shared emotional experience does the director allow the discussion to become more general. In this way the cathartic effects of the psychodrama can continue into this 'feedback', often triggering a helpful release of emotion in the sharing group member as well as the protagonist.

Closure of the session occurs when the director is satisfied that all have had sufficient opportunity to share and may be achieved in one of several ways. If a strong positive caring mood between members has resulted, a spontaneous physical demonstration of sympathetic feeling by hugging and shaking hands is not unusual. A more equivocal outcome may be handled by asking each member to make a closing comment. For example, the director may tell the protagonist what he has gained personally from the psychodrama and ask the others to follow suit, or the group might be requested to consider possible protagonists for the following session. Because of the 'chain' reaction triggered by a psychodrama there are usually other members ready to take their turn. If they cannot easily risk themselves at the outset of a session it may help them to talk about it now when they are well 'warmed up'.

The title 'director' indicates quite explicitly the active guiding, controlling and encouraging functions of the therapist. He or she has to 'warm-up' the participants and 'produce' the psychodrama. This demands alert empathic attention, not only to the protagonist's behaviour but also to that of the audience and for much of the time of the auxiliaries as well. For this reason a 'co-director' is desirable, some might say essential, if the director is to do full justice to the three roles of producer, therapist and analyst which are required. The co-director should have had appropriate training. This will include experience as a protagonist and auxiliary in a teaching group led by a skilled director. Qualification as a co-director is regarded in some centres of training as a stage in the progression to becoming a certified director.

While the director is concentrating on producing the psychodrama, the co-director may observe hints of underlying emotions which had escaped the director's notice. These can be highlighted by sensitive 'doubling' for the protagonist. As the co-director stands close beside the protagonist, places a hand on his or her shoulder and speaks in sympathy with incompletely expressed feelings, the director takes note of this new information and, if it is empathically accurate, the protagonist may have the courage to elaborate on it further. If the director does not wish to interrupt the flow of the psychodrama the co-director will, of course, defer this and wait to see if the same indications recur. He or she may, however, remain close to the protagonist, acting as a supportive 'double'. This allows the director to stand further back from the action and be less at risk of over-identifying with the protagonist. By adding to the director's therapeutic and analytical powers the co-director frees his or her attention to fill the role of producer more effectively. But this must depend on the two therapists having close rapport and understanding.

Sometimes the intensity of the emotions arising out of the psychodrama is such that other members of the group begin to feel overwhelmed by reminders of their own situation. Here again the co-director is often able to see what is happening before the director and, by supportive 'doubling', help the person to cope until the opportunity to share these feelings is available. This acts at the same time as a signal to the director who also has the choice of bringing the new potential protagonist into the action in some way or of drawing the psychodrama to an earlier finish so that the sharing can begin while the cathartic effect is greatest.

Other observations by the co-director do not gain expression during the psychodrama itself. They may be of a kind which can be best conveyed through the same sharing of feelings in which the audience participate. On the other hand, they are often guesses about things which have yet to come into the open. Accordingly, the therapists must make sure that they have time together after the session to exchange their thoughts and impressions, particularly of those points at which suppressed experiences or emotions might have come close to manifesting themselves, checking whether the protagonist might need to be actively directed towards these areas or whether the pace was too 'hot' and a slower and less direct approach is necessary. This discussion is also an opportunity to consider the reactions of the other members and observe how the dynamic development of the group has been demonstrated through the session, possibly even to anticipate the direction of future sessions.

To illustrate some of the points made in this section of the chapter the following semi-fictitious description of a typical session may be of help to the reader.

The setting
The group consisting of seven members have been meeting weekly on the same evening at the psychotherapy clinic for 6 weeks. They have already revealed quite a lot about themselves but their psychodramas, though

leading to much lively discussion, have not yet touched off any powerful emotions. Tonight's protagonist, Mary, a married woman in her early 30s, sought help because of an aching in her head for which no physical cause could be found. She has talked before of her mother who seems to continue to dominate her life even now that she is married and has her own home.

The warm-up
The director begins the warm-up feeling low in energy, having spent the afternoon in a tedious and frustrating committee meeting. He decides he must now warm himself up. He sets the chairs in a circle, empties ashtrays, opens a window to clear the air, joking with the first arrivals about the smokey atmosphere. Mary is the last to come, looking slightly flushed. The protagonist of the last session discusses how he has felt during the week and there is some further sharing of feelings by the group. But soon Mary begins to talk. Her mother has done it again, interfering with her plans, criticizing her decision to move house even though this is a sensible action to take. The group attend closely to her. The director senses that they are involved and willing for her to use the session. He moves over and sits by her. Would she like to work on this issue? 'Yes. It has always been the same with mother!' Always? As long as Mary can remember she was not allowed to mix with the children of the street. Mother seemed to be wrapped up in father. Mary must fit in with their routines. The director invites Mary to 'walk and talk'. They stroll around the stage. Mary remembers how her mother never showed her much physical affection, rarely hugging or kissing her when they met or parted. Can she remember a particular example? After some thought she does. Where exactly was it? She describes the house. She was going away for the weekend to a relative. She was about 12 years old. She gives more details. The director asks her to show the group the physical layout, the position of the doors and windows, the colour of the walls and floor covering, the furnishings. How does it feel? Mary chooses her auxiliaries, her mother and father, telling each of them what they look like, how they talk, think and behave. Mother is breezy, offhand, businesslike. Father is quiet, meek, absorbed in his work. The director notes that she has selected the two members of the group who might well have some similarities to the auxiliary egos. The director asks Mary to begin her psychodrama.

The psychodrama
Mary has her things packed for the weekend. She describes how her mother insisted on checking everything. The director tells her to 'show us'. She reverses roles with the 'mother' auxiliary and adopts a nagging strident tone, wagging her finger. The auxiliary follows suit. Mary looks awkward. 'Mother' continues in the same vein. Mary flushes and clenches her fists. The director asks another group member to be her double. The double

stands, like Mary, stiffly. Mary responds to 'Mother's' query 'Have you remembered your wash things?' with a muttered 'Yes'. The double amplifies this with a louder 'Yes of course', followed by 'I wish you'd stop going on at me'. Mary begins to breathe hard. She suddenly shouts out at her 'mother' to leave her alone, grabs her bag and walks towards the door, but halts uncertainly. The director asks what she is feeling. She describes conflicting feelings. Part of her just wants to go angrily, the other wants her mother to acknowledge her. He asks her to face the door and express her anger. She does vehemently. He asks her to face her 'mother'. She does so silently. The director asks her what happens now and she begins to shout at her 'mother'. 'Mother' responds coldly and deflatingly. Mary says she feels like hitting her and 'mother' is given a cushion to hold in front of her and Mary hits it. Suddenly she weeps and clings to 'Mother'. Behind her anger it is her feeling of being unloved that hurts. 'Mother' admits she didn't realize this. 'Father', who has had no real part to play, joins them in a threefold embrace. After a while the director suggests that they rejoin the circle and takes his place by Mary.

The feedback

The director checks that Mary is ready to begin the feedback. 'Mother' is asked how she felt in her role. She describes how anxious she always felt to keep the world at bay, how she felt she had to be the support of her husband and that she could not risk her child getting our of her control in case some disaster struck. She felt this strongly in the psychodrama but was then quite shocked and overwhelmed at her 'daughter's' anger. When she had finished the director firmly instructs her that she is out of role and can later contribute as herself.

'Father' has less to say. He felt weak and ignored by 'wife' and 'daughter'. He too was upset at the anger of his daughter but admitted that he felt some anger too, but could not side with her against his 'wife'.

When 'father' has been deroled, Mary replies. She is more relaxed now. She says that her most painful experience was doubting that her parents really cared for her and she had been sure that if she showed her feelings she would be rejected instantly. Other members of the group now share their own experiences with Mary. Everyone seems to find something that strikes a chord with the subject of the psychodrama. The auxiliary 'mother' says that she was surprised how like her own present relationship with her teenage daughter it was. She feels she has learned from this and thanks Mary. Eventually all have contributed. The director asks Mary if she would like to say something to the group members before closing. She tells them how apprehensive she had felt about playing her psychodrama but how good it felt and that she appreciates their encouragement. She is due to telephone her real mother this week and wonders what it will feel like.

Epilogue

At the next meeting of the group Mary reports that she has felt much more unwound. She laughingly relates that she did telephone her mother and was amazed how much less hostile and critical she seemed! Mary worked on her relationship with her mother in later sessions. Her 'ache' gradually disappeared and when the group dispersed after a year of sessions she felt well and was being much more assertive and confident.

The role of group members

We have already distinguished between two situations, the classical psychodrama in which trained therapeutic aides act as auxiliary egos and the audience varies in composition from session to session, as opposed to the psychodrama therapy group in which a small number of subjects meet regularly and themselves become the auxiliaries as they take it in turn to be protagonists. In the first there is no developing group process. The audience, like the chorus in the ancient Greek theatre, represent public opinion, reacting spontaneously to the drama and providing a sounding board for the protagonist. Simultaneously, they are helped by the protagonist to see themselves in the common denominators of the human predicament enacted in the psychodrama.

Foulkes and Anthony (1965) suggested that the unstructured psychotherapy group works very like this and paid tribute to Moreno's creative exploitation of dramatic action as a method of therapy. The interaction between the actors and audience is paralleled by that between the active and passive members of the group. The unresolved conflicts of the group are channelled through a spokesman so that they can 'know' what they dare not admit to themselves. As a conflict finds expression in the interaction between the group and this member or the director, the recreated feelings can be evaluated and integrated more successfully again. But resolution of conflicts requires repeated exposure in order to overcome that tendency to 'inertia' which Freud labelled 'repetition compulsion'.

In the psychodrama group this process is made explicit, in fact becoming the primary task of the group members. They will not only be the audience but take it in turns to be the protagonist, auxiliary ego or double. They will also be encouraged to make spontaneous 'doubles' and to share their own personal experience with the protagonist in the 'feedback'. The director models for them a strongly sympathetic and warm involvement. Because they are encouraged to work in this way a trusting and supportive atmosphere is generated and maintained. Without this it would not be possible to take the risk of personal exposure which the method requires.

For this reason the director never 'interprets' and, if group members confront one another with some negative aspect of themselves, will often ask the challenger to describe what part of their own feelings prompts this reaction. In other words, the approach to emotional conflict is always via positive identifications.

This does not mean that negative feelings are ignored, but if they can be allowed to emerge within the psychodramatic action the group members are not going to be able to use them so defensively, splitting good and bad feelings and projecting the bad while holding on to the good.

Likewise the director does not interpret the group dynamics. There are times when the group's defences inhibit them. This is a cyclical trend, resistance often following a period of active therapeutic work and self-revelation and vice versa. Subgrouping, scapegoating, negative transference towards the director and other defences can frequently be discerned. If the leader waits patiently, a protagonist will emerge whose psychodrama allows the group defence to be worked through in the guise of an aspect of the protagonist's world. For example, the feeling that the therapist has too much power or is not caring may be represented in an interaction with a parental figure, subgrouping may be symbolized in sibling or neighbour rivalries and disputes, and so on. I have no doubt that psychodrama and verbal psychotherapy have much more in common than at first appears. In both the group members are ultimately the source of the spontaneous encounters which generate new insights and allow old feelings to dissipate. This honest mutual exchange of real emotion matters more than the technical virtuosity of the therapist.

Group development over time

In the earlier meetings of the group the process of 'getting acquainted' dominates. This is also the phase during which the leader is demonstrating how he or she works. The pattern of warm-up discussion, psychodrama and feedback is followed regularly. During these sessions the action may be quite brief or deal with events in a relatively 'safe' or superficial way. A meeting with friends, an outing to relatives, a school parents' evening, a problem with the car, all kinds of current commonplace situations are possibilities. This phase parallels the kind of 'temperature testing' which verbal groups exhibit in their initial encounters.

As the group coheres and the level of trust and warmth increases more sensitive and personal themes begin to appear. Protagonists associate current situations with parallels in the past. Again there is a clear similarity to the verbal analytical situation as formative experiences are reconstructed and worked through. At this stage the more personal material excites powerful identification in other group members. The sharing of emotion in the feedback may extend into a second session and new protagonists emerge to work through their own psychodramas stimulated by what they have shared. Alternatively, one member may embark on a series of psychodramas, recapitulating events which reach eventually back to early childhood. At the same time the group begins to acquire some of the therapist's skills, becoming more alert to each other's feelings, doubling more perceptively and using the auxiliary roles with increasing insight and courage.

After periods of greater therapeutic activity there may be sudden pauses in which the group becomes quieter and protagonists are slower to come forward. There may be a group defence of the kind described in the preceding section, but often it is almost as though the group have to pause, temporarily exhausting their capacity for cathartic emotional release, needing perhaps to allow the experience to be integrated more fully before moving on to newer areas.

Well-established groups learn to look at their 'surplus reality', projecting themselves in psychodrama into the future or acting through their dreams and fantasies. They can continue to work constructively through many hours and the point at which they eventually are ripe to disband is not very predictable. The group's natural life-span varies but is rarely less than 1 year and some groups go on for several years. I consider that it is helpful to make an initial contract to meet for a specified number of sessions and to renegotiate this agreement at the end of that time. Even if all the members agree to disperse at the same stage there is always a need to provide some sessions to act out the feelings of loss and separation. A follow-up meeting 6 months or 1 year later has also proved valuable to the therapist and the group.

Mechanisms of change

Research evidence for demonstrable measurable change of behaviour resulting from psychodrama is difficult to obtain, not because change does not occur but because the methods of measurement appropriate to such a complex endeavour are necessarily very involved and difficult to put into practice. Conduit (1986) argues that a more useful approach would be to examine specific aspects of the process which might more easily be systematically varied in order to assess their contribution to the effect of the whole therapeutic activity.

Thus we assume that psychodrama enables individuals to express thoughts and feelings more fully and effectively. One specific technique aimed at this goal is doubling. S. Goldstein (1967) and J. Goldstein (1971) showed clearly and in a controlled trial that doubling significantly increases the verbal output of group members.

Mental catharsis, the process in which avoided emotions and attitudes are expressed in psychodramatic action is believed to reduce the intensity of the avoided feeling and lead to modified attitudes in its sphere of influences.

Conduit quotes Logan (1971), who demonstrated in a controlled study that cathartic release of aggressive attitudes did indeed modify the extrapunitive behaviour of his subjects.

Role reversal should increase the ability of the person who reverses to accept compromise and to be more tolerant of the other person concerned. Here Conduit refers to the findings of Johnson (1971), who asked his subjects to take sides in an imaginary court case and subsequently plead the case of the opposing side. In fact the outcome appeared to depend on the rigidity of the initial stances taken. If there was some, even small, acceptance of a valid alternative view, compromise was effected. But if the initial positions were mutually exclusive the role reversals reinforced the contradictory attitudes of the adversaries. This suggests that the use of role reversal in therapy requires an accurate appreciation by the therapist of the underlying emotional trend of the protagonist's utterances and that if these are misjudged then the technique could be anti-therapeutic.

I have already emphasized that much of the therapeutic process in psychodrama could be attributed to the warm, supportive group atmosphere in which members are gently but firmly encouraged to face and follow through their adverse experiences of life. Equally it can be seen in psychodynamic terms to be a means of externalizing primitive internal images, representations of hostile parents, etc., and thus reintegrating them at a more adult and realistic level of development.

I would suggest that this is perfectly compatible with the role theory of personality, emphasizing as it does the persistence of infantile roles into adult life and their significance in later problems of adjustment. In my own experience this is borne out by the reports of protagonists who have benefited from intensive cathartic experiences of this kind.

Typical problems and their resolution

The strengths of this therapeutic medium are also the source of its difficulties. If the group fails to 'warm-up' and the director finds that there is not enough spontaneity generated to produce a willing protagonist, he or she may be tempted to 'pull out the stops' in order to get a performance. This may work once or twice but as the group becomes more apprehensive they will be more resistant and soon begin to opt out of the activity. It is better to allow the group to develop its own pace, often staying with relatively superficial scenes at first, until it becomes apparent that they are comfortable working in this, to them, novel way.

There is always the danger of seeking a 'performance' which might impress all involved but be totally removed from the objective realities of the protagonist's world. Psychodrama is not play acting. To expose oneself in action is felt to be extremely threatening even by the most confident. The aim here is not to emulate the skills of the professional actor. Psychodrama is usually more effective when the struggle for honest expression of real feelings is being won. At these moments, despite the stumbling and hesitation, the whole group can be seen to attend with the utmost seriousness and concern to what is emerging. Often a tiny glimpse of deeply felt emotion is enough to trigger reverberating identifications throughout the group and lead on to a prolonged and productive 'feedback'. Conversely, when a cohesive group has achieved a high level of trust and is working creatively the director is able to initiate more elaborate scenes which do indeed possess a quality of excitement and a complexity as stimulating as a theatrical production. But that is not the primary goal.

Achieving and maintaining conditions of mutual respect and consideration with and between the group members, professional humility and patience are therefore even more important than in the less active and directive group therapies. I will consider this and other aspects of the therapist's functions in the final section of the chapter.

If the group becomes completely 'blocked' after a number of meetings it can help to get them to present an 'action sociogram', rather like the 'sculpting' of family therapy. Each member is asked to place all the group in positions which physically represent their relationships with one another. This rapidly shows what form the group resistance is taking, whether there is an isolated member, subgrouping, competition with the director, and so on. They can then be invited to change the sociogram to what they would prefer. This exercise often resolves the conflict and allows new protagonists to present themselves.

For example, one member, who had always found difficulty integrating into social groups, was an 'isolate' in every member's 'sculpt' including her own. As they became increasingly aware of this the others addressed her, expressing their concern at her exclusion but voicing the anxiety they felt in her presence, the suspicions that her outwardly aloof appearance was in fact a rejection of them. From this beginning she began to describe her difficulty communicating with people and went on to enact a poignant scene from her adolescence with which most of the group identified. In subsequent sessions she became noticeably more outgoing and involved, and the group continued to encourage her to share their feelings.

The problem of catalysing spontaneity is matched by the difficulty of controlling it once it is present. The director should not hesitate to move quickly into the group sharing and 'feedback' after a few minutes of action if there has been a genuine cathartic release of feelings. This is particularly true when the content of the psychodrama has deeply touched others who also need to demonstrate their own emotions. The help of a sensitive co-director is invaluable in this respect.

I have no doubt that failure to allow individuals to 'derole' and to complete their cathartic experience, at least to the point where they can leave the session with some sense of emotional relief, is a much more common error than is realized. When it is obvious that a member is strongly affected, steps should be taken to offer further contact and support over the next 24 hours, including even the opportunity to telephone the leader or other members of the group.

At the practical level the enterprise can be wrecked by unsuitable conditions. The sessions must have a minimum of 1½ hours and preferably 2 hours duration. The room must be of adequate dimensions, reasonably sound-proofed and regularly available. If there is no time for the 'feedback' the group may become anxious and frustrated. If there are not predictable surroundings and especially if group members are constantly distracted or interrupted it is not surprising that they find the process difficult.

Finally, the director should beware of 'saboteurs' who refer, perhaps again an expression of some unconscious hostility, clients who are too disturbed or have been falsely led to believe that they are being asked to attend some kind of drama class. If the director falls into this trap it is likely that the group will go badly and the use of psychodrama be unfairly blamed for this.

These seem self-evident points, but in many institutions, whether or not by conscious intention, at least one of these difficulties is likely to present itself if the therapist does not clearly and firmly specify what is required.

Limitations of the approach

Particular caution should be exercised in using the psychodramatic approach with social systems. In family therapy the ongoing nature of the treatment, the opportunity for immediate comment and the more intimate and longstanding nature of the network make it a particularly useful catalyst. But in larger systems whose stability requires that the members adhere to well-defined and predictable roles, vertical and horizontal, the introduction of an unaccustomed degree of self-revelation can expose unacknowledged hostilities, resentments and rivalries which some otherwise effective members are too vulnerable to tolerate. Also, it is all too easy for the sessions to be used manipulatively to attack absent members of the system, reinforcing prejudices and paranoid group defences.

For example, a disaffected set of staff members may subtly lead the psychodrama into becoming an assault on a senior member who is not present. The parodied caricature is enthusiastically savaged, all the irrational projected hatred is reinforced and, worst of all, their victim invariably learns of what has been done with inevitable damage to working relationships. So it is wise to restrict the use of psychodrama to a less personal level. For example, a sociodrama, in which representatives of whole groups, management and workers, doctors and nurses, debate their roles, can be healthily productive.

Psychodrama is not a panacaea. It requires a greater amount of risk taking than less active psychotherapies and for a proportion of individuals it is better to stick to more traditional group therapy.

Typical qualities of effective leaders

Finally, the personality and training of the director must be considered. Psychodrama needs a relatively uncommon blend of extraversion and sensitivity. It demands much energy, theatrical as well as therapeutic skills, and an ability to 'think on one's feet'.

Polansky and Harkins (1969), commenting on the lack of widespread use of psychodrama in psychiatric practice, commend it as an effective method but list several reasons for its limited practice, all to do with the demands upon the therapist. The first is the therapist's own need for a better developed general theory of personality on which to ground the techniques. Secondly, it calls for an outgoing, confronting style incompatible with the character defences of many skilled individual therapists. The high level of activity, inventivenes and 'controlled flamboyance' required is not given to many. Finally, the degree of spontaneity necessarily involved exposes the therapist to intensive group scrutiny which only the most resilient and tough personality can tolerate for long without discomfort.

While I would agree that these explanations are generally correct I have found that the 'hybrid' psychodrama therapy group with its gentler pace and attention to the group process does not require so much innovative talent or histrionic virtuosity. It does require a thorough grounding in group dynamics and practical training in the specific techniques of psychodrama itself.

Generally, psychodrama is at its most effective when the action is conveying the subject's memories and dreams as realistically and concretely as possible. If the director can make the protagonist feel safe enough to do this then no more elaborate techniques may be required. But if not, then the most ingenious manoeuvres will fail to have any impact. The aim is always to help the protagonist to expand his or her experience by living out the potential range of roles whose absent or partial expression is causing frustration and pain. It is the director's responsibility to help the group create a sufficiently 'safe' setting in which to do so, to encourage by example a respectful, confiding, warm and open pattern of interaction and, while striving for spontaneity, always to contain the outcome, setting clear limits and protecting protagonists when the group process leans towards pathological spontaneity or hurtful defensive projections.

CONCLUSION

Psychodrama is clearly a potent method of exploring human relationships and learning how to achieve more satisfying and effective roles in life. It is an approach of which even the uninitiated can quickly make sense. In an era of more rapid and immediate communication, in which the written and spoken word are largely superseded by action and the visual, life-like presentations of the film and video screen, it should have a natural appeal. Whether the recent growth in interest reflects these trends is a matter for speculation, but it is in tune with the spirit of the age in which we now live.

However, psychotherapy is much dominated by fashion and we can never be certain whether psychodrama is merely 'back in vogue'. I hope not. It is a rewarding way of working if it is taken as seriously as the inventor intended. I believe it will continue to gain acceptance and to inform and enhance our other psychotherapeutic endeavours.

REFERENCES

Anderson, W. (1974). J. L. Moreno and the origins of psychodrama: a biographical sketch. *In* J. A. Greenberg (ed.), *Psychodrama, Theory and Therapy*. New York, Behavioral Publications.

Aveline, M. (1984). Comparison of psychodrama and group psychotherapy for treatment of hospitalised patients. Paper presented to the Society for Psychotherapy Research Conference, 19 May 1984. Ravenscar, North Yorks.

Blatner, H. A. (1973). *Acting – in: Practical Applications of Psychodramatic Methods*. New York, Springer.

Conduit, E. (1986). Process research in psychodrama. *Journal of the British Psychodrama Association* **1** (2), 38–45.

Davies, M. H. (1987). Dramatherapy and psychodrama. *In* S. Jennings (ed.) *Dramatherapy in Theory and Practice*. Beckenham, Kent, Croom Helm.

Elefthery, D. (1975) Psychodrama group therapy. In G. M. Gazda (ed.), *Basic Approaches to Group Psychotherapy and Group Counseling*, 2nd edition. Springfield, Illinois, Thomas.

Foulkes, S. H. and Anthony, E. J. (1965). *Group Psychotherapy: The Psychoanalytic Approach*, 2nd edition. Harmondsworth, Penguin Books.

Goldstein, J. (1971). Investigation of doubling as a technique for involving severely withdrawn patients in group psychotherapy. *Journal of Consulting and Clinical Psychology* **37**, 155–62.

Goldstein, S. (1967). The effect of "doubling" on involvement in group psychotherapy as measured by number and duration of patient utterances. *Psychotherapy: Theory, Research and Practice* **4**, 57–60.

Greenberg, I. A. (ed.) (1974). *Psychodrama, Theory and Therapy*. New York, Behavioral Publications.

Harrow, G. S. (1951). Effects of psychodrama group therapy on role behavior of schizophrenic patients. *Group Psychotherapy* 3, 316–20.

Holland, R. (1977). *Self and Social Context*. London, Macmillan.

Johnson, D. W. (1971). Use of role-reversal in inter-group competition. *Journal of Personality and Social Psychology* 7, 135.

Kelly, G. A. (1955). *The Psychology of Personal Constructs*, Vols 1 and 2. New York, Norton.

Kipper, D. and Giladi, D. A. (1978). The effectiveness of structured psychodrama and systematic desensitization in reducing test-anxiety. *Journal of Counseling Psychology*, 25, 499–505.

Kreitler, H. and Kreitler, S. (1968). Validation of psychodramatic behaviour against behaviour in life. *British Journal of Medical Psychology* 41, 185–92.

Logan, J. C. (1971). Use of psychodrama and sociodrama in reducing negro aggression. *Group Psychotherapy and Psychodrama* 24, 138–49.

Marrone, M. (1979). An approach to analytical psychodrama. *Dramatherapy* 3 (1), 21–3.

Moreno, J. L. (1940). Mental catharsis and the psychodrama. *Sociometry* 3 (1), 209–44.

Moreno, J. L. (1964). *Psychodrama*, Vol. 1. New York, Beacon.

Polansky, N. A. and Harkins, E. B. (1969). Psychodrama as an element in hospital treatment. *Psychiatry* 32, 74–87.

Powell, A. (1986). Object relations in the psychodramatic Group. *Group Analysis* 19 (2), 125–33.

Schutzenberger, A. A. (1975). Psychodrama creativity and group process. *In* S. Jennings (ed.), *Creative Therapy*. London, Pitman.

Slawson, P. F. (1965). Psychodrama as a treatment for hospitalised patients: a controlled study. *American Journal of Psychiatry* 122, 530–33.

Yalom, I. D. (1975). *The Theory and Practice of Group Psychotherapy*. New York, Basic Books.

CHAPTER 6

COGNITIVE-BEHAVIOURAL GROUP THERAPY

Waseem Alladin

INTRODUCTION

There are different forms of cognitive-behavioural therapies. However, the focus here will be on Beck's cognitive therapy, anxiety management training and assertion training, all of which have been developed as individual therapies and their application to a group format has been largely a matter of cost-effectiveness, especially when trained cognitive-behavioural therapists are scarce.

Cognitive-behavioural group therapy (CBGT) has several specific goals (see pp. 124–5). However, CBGT also has a number of broad goals which may be described as follows. First, to provide a safe social milieu for participants to facilitate disclosure of problems and engage in experimenting with different behaviour patterns. Secondly, to encourage social interaction so that participants may have feedback from others to test their own impressions of themselves. Thirdly, to help participants to learn methods of behavioural and cognitive change (e.g. a problem-solving method so that they may monitor their own behaviour and learn to be more efficient and systematic in problem-solving). Finally, to help demedicalize the problems of living and introduce cognitive-behavioural models of understanding maladaptive behavioural and cognitive patterns.

HISTORICAL CONTEXT AND DEVELOPMENT IN BRITAIN

Cognitive-behavioural approaches to individual therapy are well-established in Britain. However, cognitive-behavioural approaches to group therapy are of fairly recent origin, with published accounts first occurring in the 1960s and 1970s.

The transfer of a specific type of individual cognitive-behavioural therapy to a group setting is really individual therapy done in a group. Therapy done *with* individuals in a group but not *by* the group, is strictly speaking not group therapy. However, this is the most common form of CBGT. Thus, for example, individuals with social difficulty may be offered social skills training in a group format.

Cognitive-behavioural group therapists place more emphasis on individual rather than on group processes. Behaviour therapy and psychodynamic psychotherapy have important differences. For example, the focus on cognitions and feelings and the emphasis on catharsis and self-understanding based on insight is not regarded as sufficient for behavioural change by behaviour therapists. This difference has blurred with the advent of cognitive-behavioural therapy which focuses on cognitions to understand affect and change behaviour. In the early days of behaviour therapy, the effectiveness of the therapy was attributed to the potency of the techniques. However, as behaviour therapy developed, there was increasing recognition of the importance of the therapeutic relationship.

On the other hand, in cognitive therapy the importance of the therapeutic relationship has been recognized right from the beginning (cf. Beck *et al.*, 1979). Cognitive therapy also shares some similarities with psychodynamic psychotherapy in that it focuses on cognitions – what happens 'inside' the head is regarded as of crucial importance. How one thinks about something determines how one feels about it and, then, acts. Nevertheless, the emphasis in cognitive therapy is not on understanding the interaction between the therapist and the client in-depth, since the focus is problem-centred, not process-oriented (cf. Hollon and Shaw, 1979).

In contrast, behaviour therapy is based on one or more of the following paradigms from experimental psychology: classical (Pavlovian) conditioning, operant (Skinnerian) conditioning and observational learning (Bandura).

In classical conditioning learning is said to occur because of the pairing of a neutral stimulus (e.g. the sound of a bell) with an unconditioned stimulus or UCS (e.g. food), which by itself naturally evokes a particular response (e.g. salivation occurs naturally at the presence of food but not at the sound of a bell). After classical conditioning, the neutral stimulus (sound of the bell) now acquires the property of the UCS and produces salivation.

In operant conditioning, learning is said to occur by reinforcing a particular behaviour. For example, a therapist who listens attentively to a client is likely to increase self-disclosure.

Observational learning or modelling refers to learning which occurs by imitating or copying the behaviour of another person. For example, an anxious person may be afraid to engage in a particular behaviour, fearing negative consequences. The modelling by another person engaging in the same behaviour without negative consequences occurring can encourage the anxious person into engaging in the feared behaviour.

Traditionally, behaviour therapy focused on patterns of reward and punishment and ignored the person, that is what happened 'in the head'. It soon became apparent that this did not reflect the complexity of clinical problems. Thus what was happening 'inside' the head (thinking) began to be regarded as equally important. Bandura (1969) is generally credited for introducing imitation learning or modelling into behaviour therapy, because he regarded operant conditioning procedures as inefficient and impractical for teaching complex skills. Bandura's social learning theory emphasized the prominent roles played by vicarious, symbolic and self-regulatory processes in psychological functioning; it explains human behaviour in terms of a continuous reciprocal interaction between cognitive, behavioural and environmental determinants.

The 1970s was marked by the introduction of cognitive approaches to behavioural theory and therapy. Aaron Beck, Albert Ellis and Donald Meichenbaum are the major figures associated with cognitive therapy, rational-emotive therapy and cognitive-behaviour modification respectively. However, there were those who felt that this was a step in the wrong direction (e.g. Ledwidge, 1978). Behaviour therapy had rejected private mental events, introspection was suspect but cognitive therapy was seeking to bring this back! It was also argued that cognitive therapy was merely attaching different labels to behavioural concepts, a case of old wine in new bottles. However, cognitive approaches have now been integrated into behaviour therapy resulting in cognitive-behaviour therapy.

The first published account of CBGT was in the area of depression by Hollon and Shaw (1979). The major reason for this development seems to be so that more clients could be treated than in individual therapy. Earlier, Rush and Watkins (1981) compared the group format with individual therapy to see if there were any advantages of the group format over individual therapy. They tentatively concluded that CBGT appears to be less effective than individual cognitive-behaviour therapy for depression. However, Hollon and Shaw (1979) caution that this may be due to the greater drop-out rate in CBGT.

Several British contributors have made major contributions to the theory, research and practice of behaviour therapy (e.g. Eysenck, Rachman, Marks, Mathews, Gelder) and more recently, to cognitive-behaviour therapy (e.g. Dryden, Teasdale, Williams, Gilbert, Willner) but there is no British text devoted to CBGT. However, British clinicians and researchers have been, and continue to be, involved in running groups and workshops in diverse areas of cognitive-behaviour therapy (Jupp and Dudley, 1984;

Tarrier and Main, 1986). Self-help groups which draw upon cognitive-behaviour therapy are increasingly popular. The main forms of CBGT which are widely practised are (1) social skills training which may include assertion training, communication and problem-solving skills training; and (2) anxiety management training.

Social skills training (SST) is particularly strongly represented by British academics, researchers and clinicians. Michael Argyle (1967) and Peter Trower (1984) are two pioneering contributors, recognized for the motor skill model of social skills and for developing a radical, cognitive approach to social skills, respectively. Sue Spence, Geoff Shepherd, Owen Hargie and Adrian Furnham, among others, have made important contributions. Assertion training is regarded as a subset of SST.

Anxiety management training (AMT), though widely practised, is not associated with any particular contributor, though Isaac Marks at the Institute of Psychiatry in the University of London helped develop the first behavioural psychotherapy course for psychiatric nurses which brought into being specialist nurse behaviour therapists.

UNDERLYING ASSUMPTIONS

Theoretical underpinnings

CBGT draws upon four paradigms: classical conditioning, operant conditioning and social learning theory, all of which assume that maladaptive behaviours are learned in the same way any behaviour is learned and therefore can be unlearned. The fourth paradigm is that of cognitive theory which assumes that dysfunctional or maladaptive thinking patterns lead to maladaptive behaviours and emotional disorders (e.g. anxiety and depression).

One main focus of CBGT is behaviour itself. It is the observable which can be recorded and monitored. This is also important in evaluation, which is an essential part of therapy. In cognitive therapy, the focus is on cognition or thinking which is recorded and monitored by the client introspecting and thinking aloud. Thinking is 'measured' by counting the number of negative thoughts a client has about a particular issue at a particular moment.

The historical determinants of current maladaptive behaviour are not regarded as important, the focus being on the here and now. In other words, the search for 'root causes' is not seen as important in treating maladaptive behaviours and dysfunctional cognitions. Thus one can ask every necessary question, but 'why' questions are discouraged. Knowing why a particular maladaptive behaviour occurs is often not sufficient to change it, and may not be necessary either for the treatment plan.

Cognitive-behavioural assessment proceeds by asking 'what' questions. For example, what is the problem, 'what are the antecedents and consequences of a particular behaviour or cognition'? It may also involve questions of frequency, intensity and duration. This helps to provide a baseline from which improvement or deterioration may be judged. Clients are often trained to keep records (in the form of diaries) of target behaviours and cognitions.

A thorough functional analysis which considers the antecedents and consequences of maladaptive behaviours and dysfunctional thinking is an essential part of cognitive-behavioural assessment. The aim is not to search for causes (which may prove elusive) but rather to identify maintaining factors which can then be undermined.

Target problems are explicitly defined and treatment goals are expressed objectively in specific terms, in the interest of greater clarity and to enable the therapist to be more precise in interventions and facilitate replication by others. Though CBGT focuses on behaviours and cognitions, often behavioural change is the main criterion for treatment outcome. Self-reports and multiple baseline measures may be used in evaluation. Generalization is explicitly facilitated by homework assignments, recognizing that what happens outside the group is equally, if not more, important than what happens in the group. This contrasts sharply with other psychotherapy groups.

Cognitive-behaviour therapists reject the view that people behave and think the way they do because of stable personality traits. Most cognitive-behaviour therapists today follow an interactionist position (cf. Bandura, 1977) which suggests that behaviour is a function of internal predispositions and external situations. For example, a shy person who suffers a rebuff after making a request may not only stop making requests (avoidance behaviour) but may also think negatively ('I'm not worthy of being helped'). This is not due to some inadequacy or defect of the personality itself but probably due to a combination of low self-esteem, a failure experience and possibly a pre-existing depressed mood.

Cognitive therapy regards cognitions, not behaviour, as the primary focus. Nevertheless, the goal of cognitive therapy is to change behaviour by changing maladaptive cognitions (see Beck *et al.*, 1979; Ellis and Harper, 1976; Dryden, 1984, for expositions of the theoretical underpinnings of cognitive therapy and rational-emotive therapy, respectively).

In cognitive therapy, the assumption is that cognitions – one's thinking and beliefs – mediate or determine one's behaviour. For example, a depressed person is unlikely to take the initiative in applying for a job, because in the depressed state the person's thinking is likely to be dysfunctional: 'I'm no good. I won't get the job. It's a waste of time applying.' Thus, by changing cognitions or beliefs, one may then get the person to engage in behaviour likely to lead to success. Put simply, change what people think and you can change what they do.

Key concepts

Cognitive-behaviour therapists have a wide repertoire of concepts to draw upon. The following describe some of the key concepts and is not intended to be exhaustive. Cognitive-behaviour therapists often use some combination of the following concepts which are weaved into CBGT.

(a) Reinforcement. This is used to strengthen behaviour through rewarding the consequences. In other words, to encourage a person to engage in a particular behaviour, it is necessary to arrange the situation so that the consequences of doing so are pleasant for the person. Cognitive-behaviour therapists therefore take pains to construct situations so that success is practically guaranteed by getting the client to break down a task into smaller steps or identifying subgoals in a major goal, and, then, suggesting ways in which the client may go about achieving the subgoals.

(b) Shaping. This is rewarding rough approximations to a desired behaviour until the response becomes the desired outcome. For example, a client who comes across as aggressive is 'shaped down' gradually by focusing on one behaviour at a time.

(c) Modelling. This is learning by imitation or observing the behaviour of another. For example, the cognitive-behaviour therapist may help an anxious person, who has difficulty in making small talk with a stranger, by modelling an interaction which the client can then imitate.

(d) Role play. This is regularly used to help participants adopt different roles. Role play may involve the client playing a particular role in a difficult situation in the safety of the group in which there is support and constructive comment for improvement. The client is allowed to make mistakes which will not be so hazardous to self-esteem since the situation is not 'real' but a role play.

(e) Role reversal. This is essentially a role play in which the client reverses his or her role and adopts the role of some other person – often a significant other such as a spouse or an employer. Role reversal helps clients adopt the perspective of the other and to see themselves as they seem to others. It may be less threatening than role playing oneself; the distancing can help the client become more detached and hopefully adopt a less defensive attitude towards conflict situations. Through observing what is happening, the

therapist gains some idea of the client's interpersonal environment. Finally, role reversal may encourage greater interpersonal flexibility.

(f) Behavioural problem-solving.   This involves a number of discrete steps. First, the particular behaviour of interest is specified in concrete terms. Secondly, the task is broken down into smaller more manageable steps. Thirdly, the short-term, medium-term and long-terms goals are delineated, as desired. Fourthly, learning is facilitated by using behavioural learning principles such as reinforcement and shaping. Finally, the learned behaviour is reinforced (rewarded) so that it is maintained.

(g) Functional analysis.   This refers to a systematic analysis of the antecedents and consequences of a particular behaviour. A functional analysis serves to identify the function(s) a particular behaviour serves, using the ABC format which stands for A (Antecedents), B (Behaviour) and C (Consequences). The consequence of a particular behaviour may be rewarding or punitive or even ignored. For example, suppose Jane is fed up being submissive (antecedents) and decides to assert herself (behaviour) at work with male colleagues. She is then put down (consequences) by remarks that she is an aggressive bitch. This punishing consequence of behaving assertively may lead to an inhibition of further assertive behaviour. On the other hand, if the same assertive behaviour is rewarded by social approval and admiration as might occur in a CBGT, this will encourage Jane to behave assertively again in that situation.

Negative cognitions and false logic
Beck's cognitive theory (Beck *et al.*, 1979) holds that depression and anxiety are the result of distorted thinking which are maintained by negative cognitions and false logic. Negative cognitions or thinking refers to the distorted interpretations of reality which are said to characterize those who are depressed or anxious. For example, a depressed person is said to regard one mistake or disappointment as total failure. So failure in one job interview results in such negative cognitions as 'I'm no good. I'm a failure. I'll never get another job.' Beck's theory postulates that depressed people have a negative view of their self, of the world and of the future, which Beck terms 'the negative cognitive triad', and holds to be responsible for the symptoms of depression. For Beck, the negative cognitive triad is maintained by several forms of false logic or 'errors of logic', which are defined as follows.

(a) Arbitrary inference.   This is drawing an arbitrary conclusion in the absence of evidence to support the conclusion or even when the evidence is apparently opposite to the conclusion reached. For example, the person in the above job interview example may have been commended for his or her

interview performance but fail to recognize that the successful candidate may have been more experienced and conclude that he or she is no good, a failure and will never get another job.

(b) Selective abstraction.   Selective abstraction is focusing on one particular negative item taken out of context and then viewing the whole experience or situation on the basis of that one particular item. A depressed woman may focus on her husband's remark that the toast was not to his liking and conclude, therefore, that he does not love her anymore.

(c) Overgeneralization.   This is making a general rule on the basis of one or more isolated incidents and applying it indiscriminately to all situations. The depressed person in the interview example may go on to conclude that he or she is a useless spouse, a failure as a parent and so on.

(d) Magnification (making a mountain out of a molehill) and *minimization* (dismissing or downplaying the magnitude of the positive aspects of one's experience). In the interview example, magnification occurs when the depressed person regards one failure at one interview to mean failure in everything. Minimization in the same case refers to the depressed person's tendency to reject the interview panel's commendation of his or her strong points or even dismiss it as insignificant.

(e) Personalization.   This is the tendency to make personal some external event that has no such connection. A depressed man may conclude that his wife burnt the toast because he is 'not good enough as a husband' and that some past behaviour of his must be the cause of her burning the toast, refusing to consider that it may simply be an accident on her part.

(f) Absolutistic, dichotomous thinking.   Is the tendency to categorize all experiences in two extreme categories. Life is either wonderful or terrible. The depressed person's tendency is to focus on the negative categories. Apparently, this black-and-white thinking does not recognize an intermediate position.

Cognitive restructuring
This involves the views that (a) emotional responses are mediated by our beliefs and thoughts and (b) dysfunctional emotional responses can be changed by challenging our maladaptive beliefs and thoughts and restructuring them into more adaptive ones. For example, a client may hold the belief that if he behaved assertively, others would stop liking him. The client is taught to examine the evidence for and against this belief and challenge it by asking a series of questions such as: 'What is the evidence', 'How can I be

so sure', 'Is there another way of thinking about it?', and so on. Finally, the client is asked to experiment and test out his belief that others would stop liking him by recording the consequences of behaving assertively.

The Therapeutic conditions necessary for change
Though cognitive-behaviour therapists may not describe themselves as person-centred, they, nevertheless, implicitly (as is evident in references to patients as clients) or explicitly (see Beck *et al.*, 1979) acknowledge the importance of the therapist–client relationship. Carl Rogers (1957) identified what he regarded as the necessary and sufficient conditions for change. Because most cognitive-behaviour therapists regard these conditions as being 'facilitative' or helpful but not sufficient for change, only the necessary conditions will be considered here.

(a) Empathy. This is the ability to experience another's world as if it were one's own without ever losing that 'as if' quality, that is retaining one's separateness from that person. Empathy is feeling *with* a person, whereas sympathy is feeling *for* the person. Empathy leads to the feeling that 'somebody else understands' even though one's problems may be unique. It can also lead to the recognition that others also have similar difficulties and increases closeness and cohesion in a group.

(b) Warmth or 'unconditional positive regard'. This is about valuing another person for what he or she is, warts and all. Warmth helps to build trust and makes clients feel safe to speak their minds, i.e. it facilitates self-disclosure.

(c) Genuineness or authenticity. This is coming across as 'real' or human. A group therapist who makes clients feel that he or she is superhuman and infallible is unlikely to inspire hope. Genuineness is also about being open in communication. Genuineness on the part of group leaders encourages clients to be open in their communication so that they do not have to conceal their true feelings and thoughts from others.

PRACTICE

By joining a CBGT group, participants are indicating a recognition of their need to change and a commitment to help themselves. Basically, the cognitive-behavioural group therapist is an educator who takes the roles of teacher, participant, observer, coach and confronter. Participants will be taught to take responsibility for themselves, decide what they would like to change and what goals they wish to achieve. The task of the therapist is to show them how to go about it.

Group leaders need to have an understanding of group processes so that they can facilitate the development of the group and identify obstacles to communication. The ventilation of feelings is not encouraged because CBGT is problem-centred. Nevertheless, some attention will be paid to the ventilation of feelings to ensure that therapy is not hindered. The Rogerian therapeutic conditions of empathy, warmth and genuineness, are used to facilitate the work of the group.

Significant personality change (though it may occur) is not an explicit goal. The explicit goal is to change cognitions and behaviours. CBGT is a short-term therapy and on-going groups lasting more than 1 year are not consistent with the philosophy of CBGT. Typically, a CBGT group with 15 members meets weekly for a 1½–2 hour session for 10–12 weeks. However, it is not uncommon for a CBGT group to continue for some 20 sessions. The membership of CBGT groups may either be open or closed. Some groups are theme-centred (e.g. assertion training, cognitive therapy for depression) and others may have a more general focus as in the typical CBGT, where the participants have mixed problems.

To give adequate individual attention, a CBGT group should have more than one leader. In a group with mixed problems, it is important to have more than one leader because with the diversity of problems too much will be happening for a single leader to fully comprehend it. The leader of a CBGT group, unlike in interpersonal group psychotherapy for example, plays an active role in steering the group towards predetermined goals and often is centre-stage. However, a highly experienced leader may be able to manage alone a homogeneous group of depressed people. But, even this can prove too much since the leader has to be active for a good part of the time. If it is impossible to secure a co-leader, then a compromise would be to work with a smaller group, as in interpersonal group psychotherapy.

The goals of the group

In CBGT each client is encouraged to identify his or her own goals within a cognitive-behavioural framework. Though there are common overall goals for a particular group, clients may have unique goals. Whereas it may be acceptable in other group psychotherapies for clients to have goals such as 'coping with life' or 'achieving happiness in relationships', in CBGT clients are asked to make their goals more specific and divide them into short-term and long-term goals. For example, clients may say that they cannot cope with life because of frequent arguments with their spouse. Thus, a goal here could be to learn to deal effectively with marital conflict and the clients would be helped to identify specific issues so that they could work on them one at a time. The specific goals of CBGT may be seen as follows.

(i) To teach clients anxiety management techniques. All clients have the potential to benefit from being relaxed, a state which encourages them to be more receptive to the therapy. It is often (but not always) found that relaxation reduces anxiety levels (cf. Wolpe, 1958). In cases where it does not, cognitive techniques (e.g. cognitive restructuring) appear to be an effective way of producing mental relaxation.

(ii) To teach or improve clients' social skills, hopefully leading to increased interpersonal effectiveness. Supportive relationships are important for people and can have a buffering effect against anxiety and depression.

(iii) To reduce or eliminate distressing anxiety and depression by teaching cognitive-behavioural techniques so that clients may recognize that interpretations of their interpersonal reality are not necessarily synonymous with that reality itself but may be prone to distortion. Clients are taught to identify thoughts and beliefs which may be mediating their distress and how to test and modify them.

All participants are offered an initial individual assessment to ascertain their suitability for CBGT. Potentially, individuals who do not meet the exclusion criteria are likely candidates for CBGT.

Exclusion criteria

Clients likely to be disruptive by virtue of their existing psychological states (e.g. those who are excessively emotionally labile, floridly psychotic) and those who have an overinvestment in medicalizing their problems are excluded, as are clients for whom secondary gain is a major issue. Brain-damaged individuals are not necessarily excluded unless their comprehension or capacity for learning is impaired or likely to retard the group.

Some clients may have been in individual cognitive-behaviour therapy and may subsequently be offered CBGT, especially if they have significant social difficulties.

Finally, some people may have complex problems which may require both an individual and a group therapeutic setting.

The role of the leader and co-leader

As noted above, CBGT can be led by a single leader, but in practice, however, it is better to have a co-leader, preferably of the opposite sex. This has several advantages:

(i) The presence of leaders of both sexes helps mirror social reality. A single leader may be competent and caring but a male and female therapist can each model behaviours from their different perspectives.

(ii) Because the group leader is active and directive in providing structure and support to a whole group, this is often very exhausting for a single therapist.

(iii) Two leaders can display more variety in their therapeutic styles, thus helping participants learn that there is more than one appropriate way of responding.

(iv) Two leaders can also model disagreement for participants who may thereby be encouraged to realize that therapists too are human and that disagreements are not necessarily destructive.

 (v) Two leaders can take turns to contribute equally and thereby help reduce stereotyping masculine or feminine behaviours.

(vi) Two leaders can share out tasks and help each other so that, while one leader makes a presentation, for example, the other may monitor the reactions of participants and encourage the 'silent ones' to be more forthcoming.

Pre-group preparation
On selection, participants are thoroughly briefed with regard to the administrative aspects of the group. Thus, they may be provided with a handout which details such matters as the venue, duration and frequency of sessions. Participants are given some idea of what to expect but no mention is made of role plays which often raises considerable anxiety. This seems better handled during the first meeting of the group when the issue of confidentiality is also stressed. The author is wary of giving too much detail about the group because this may increase anxiety levels even more. For example, some participants have preconceived notions about what may or may not help them. It is only as the group sessions unfold that 'the penny may begin to drop'; detailed advance knowledge of the contents of all the sessions may result in premature termination or selective attendance at group sessions.

Participants' anxieties about the group and their role in it are elicited and attempts made to alleviate them. For example, it is stressed that members are free to participate as much or as little as they wish and at their own pace. Paradoxically, this reduces performance anxiety and encourages more participation. However, a commitment to attend regularly is required. Unlike other therapy groups, there is no explicit requirement of no contact outside the group. On the contrary, contact as a group, especially after the group proper is over, is sometimes encouraged so that participants can meet on a self-help basis. Participants are, however, advised not to meet on a pair basis or socially until they have resolved their own difficulties so that there is no pathological pairing.

The work of the leader
A major role of the group leader is as an educator who will be didactic at times. The group leaders are there not only to facilitate the attainment of goals of the group but also to teach clients cognitive-behavioural techniques of anxiety management, assertion training and coping with depression.

Several functions of the leaders have already been outlined above. In addition, the leaders need to ensure that group cohesion is facilitated. This can be encouraged by starting with a few 'warm-up' exercises during which participants (including the leaders) introduce themselves and may engage in some light-hearted activity to reduce initial anxieties. For example, a non-threatening exercise is to get participants to introduce each other in pairs and exchange compliments, with the group leaders joining in.

Although group processes may not be used as a major therapeutic vehicle, the leaders should be aware of the basic concepts such as resistance, transference, collusion, and so on. Some cognitive-behavioural therapists may then go on to make some intervention to resolve these obstacles. However, cognitive-behavioural therapists tend to stay task-focused and not all have the training to deal with these issues. Nevertheless, an understanding of the developmental stages of the group is valuable if maximum benefit is to be obtained. Leaders need to ensure that more vocal participants do not monopolize the group by allowing (but not pressurizing) everyone to participate in turn.

CBGT is a structured approach with predictable phases. However, a good leader is not rigid, balancing being flexible to individual needs without compromising the goals of the group. This may be facilitated by aiming to:

(i) Develop a working relationship with each participant by learning the names of all participants, addressing them by their preferred name and making links with the theme of the moment with the particular difficulties. Group leaders may give occasional talks but this is never a straight lecture because at appropriate points it is personalized.

(ii) Provide an overview of the entire group by providing a one page written outline giving some idea of the structure of the group (see p. 128) as shown in Table 6.1. This is introduced at the beginning of the group.

(iii) Outline the structure of each session verbally so that participants will know what to expect (see the structure description on pp. 133–4).

(iv) Use their experience with groups to mobilize hope, for example, by pointing out that participants in previous groups had similar difficulties but improved with CBGT.

(v) Ensure that participants are socially rewarded, for example by praise, which should be specific and genuine, and shaping inappropriate responses without rejecting them as wrong.

(vi) Provide a summary of the previous session and sum up each session of the current group.

(vii) Monitor non-verbal behaviour and act accordingly. For example, nervous laughter may indicate the need for anxiety reduction. The judicious use of humour may facilitate this.

Table 6.1 Overview of a cognitive-behavioural therapy group

Session	Main topics covered[a]
1	Relaxation training; coping with stress; the importance of homework
2	Applying behavioural concepts to everyday concerns; defining problems and setting goals; keeping diaries
3	The interrelationships between feelings, behaviours and thoughts, i.e. the ABC model
4	Applying cognitive concepts to everyday concerns; role play and role reversal
5	Assertion, aggression and non-assertion; completing questionnaires and rating scales
6	Assertion techniques: fogging; broken record; expressing positive and negative feelings
7	Applying behavioural concepts to individual problems
8	Applying cognitive concepts to individual problems
9	Putting it all together, i.e. a summary of the main points of all the previous sessions: 'What have you learned so far?'
10	Preparation for termination: 'All good things . . .'
11	Maintaining improvement; preventing relapse
12	Unfinished business. . . . Farewell . . . and follow-up details

[a] The concepts in these titles are explained briefly in simple language to participants

(viii) Help participants stay in the here-and-now especially when unproductive discussions of past histories and root causes surface.

The question arises as to what exactly do the leaders do. How are the exercises and techniques structured, e.g. role play? Further, how do leaders decide what to do with whom? Briefly, CBGT aims to teach all participants the same principles but the content of each exercise is tailored to suit individual needs. There are also other considerations which help the leaders make choices.

First, the assessment of need often decides whether a participant requires a particular intervention beyond that which the group already offers. Then there is the question of assessment of the particular source of difficulty for a particular client. For example, a client may have difficulty seeing another person's viewpoint. One way is to get the client to do a role reversal to highlight blind spots. Another way is to provide video feedback, but some people find this too threatening.

Cognitive-behavioural assertion training
There is little agreement about which particular procedures constitute assertion training (cf. Rimm and Masters, 1979). However, as Rimm and

Cunningham (1985) point out, assertive behaviour has three important characteristics:

(i) it is honest and open interpersonal behaviour involving the expression of feelings and thoughts;
(ii) it is socially appropriate behaviour; and
(iii) due consideration is given to the feelings and thoughts of others.

Any cognitive-behavioural technique incorporating the above characteristics may be used to help participants act assertively. The following are commonly used procedures: assessment, behavioural rehearsal (using role play and role reversal), coaching and modelling, feedback and the use of a hierarchy.

Assessment of need for assertion training is often done by the use of questionnaires and interviewing. There are several assertion inventories available (e.g. Rathus, 1973; Gambrill and Richey, 1975; Galassi *et al.*, 1974).

Using behavioural rehearsal a particular response is practised until it comes across as assertive. The client and therapist role-play relevant interpersonal situations. The therapist and group participants provide feedback recognizing that it is a matter of social judgement as to the appropriateness of any particular response.

An assertive response should not be seen as a case of all or none. The 'minimal effective response' is that behaviour which would ordinarily accomplish the client's goal with a minimum of effort and apparent negative emotion (cf. Rimm and Masters, 1979). Only if the minimal response fails should the client escalate the response. In other words, there is no need to use a hammer when a fly-swat would do. An example may clarify this point.

Jane was upset by the noisy late-night party next door. Her first response could be something like this:

> I wonder if you would turn down the music? I'm having trouble getting to sleep at this late hour (said in a firm but friendly tone of voice).

Should this response fail, then it can be stepped up with Jane eventually warning:

> Look, it's 1 a.m. and you have ignored my request. If you don't turn down the music in the next 5 minutes, I'll have to call the police.

Feedback is provided by the therapist and participants who are encouraged to offer constructive comments on each other's performance.

The use of a hierarchy (or 'graded task assignments') is not regarded as essential in assertion training (cf. Rimm and Masters, 1979). However, as in all forms of cognitive-behavioural therapy, it is important to start with the simple and less-anxiety provoking situations first and then move on to the

Table 6.2   Models of the development of social anxiety

| | Assumptions | | |
Model	Social skills	Problem areas	Possible interventions
Skill-deficit	Absent	Lack of appropriate learning experience or role models	Arrange opportunities, teach skills, provide modelling
Response-inhibition	Present but person-inhibited	Conditioned anxiety from past experiences, maladaptive beliefs, fear of negative consequences	Counter-conditioning (e.g. relaxation), cognitive restructuring, minimize negative consequences, encourage occasional risk-taking
Faulty-discrimina-tion	Present but used in-appro-priately	Misperceives situational cues, misinterprets verbal and/or non-verbal cues	Teach role rehearsal, help client consider multiple interpretations of behaviour, discourage mind-reading, encourage testing assumptions
Rational choice	Present but person chooses not to use skills	None	–

Adapted from Alagaratnam (1982).

more difficult since it keeps anxiety levels down and is a form of 'inoculating' against failure.

More recently, behavioural assertion training alone has been found to be inadequate because it assumed a primarily skill-deficit model: clients were deemed to be lacking skills, a case of not knowing what to do. However, a client may know what to do but simply feels too anxious to perform (response inhibition). Others, 'anxious performers', may engage in assertive behaviour but feel guilty about it and experience high anxiety. Behaving assertively all the time is inappropriate and the client should choose to behave assertively after considering the costs and benefits of doing so.

Synthesizing what has gone before, Table 6.2 depicts a practical model of assessment for social skills training. The skill-deficit model implies lack of skills. The response-inhibition model implies the presence of skills but inability to respond. The faulty-discrimination model suggests that though skills are present the person uses them inappropriately. These are more usefully conceptualized as different facets of a cognitive-behavioural model of social skills rather than being separate models.

There are two common ways of reducing social anxiety. One is relaxation, the other is cognitive restructuring.

Relaxation or Anxiety Management Training (AMT) typically involves the use of a set of exercises following the progressive relaxation originally devised by Jacobson (1938), which involves the tensing and relaxing of the muscles of the entire body progressively, typically starting from the head and ending with the toes. The use of pleasant imagery (e.g. picturing oneself relaxing on a sandy beach on a warm summer's day, dreaming away without a care in the world) helps to relax people who commonly report that their body is relaxed but not their mind. When progressive relaxation by itself is insufficient to produce deep relaxation, or when the client reports anxiety persisting, cognitive restructuring is indicated.

In AMT, the anxiety or discomfort level is measured by getting the clients to rate themselves using the Subjective Units of Discomfort Scale (SUDS) or a Visual Analogue Scale (VAS). SUDS is simply a mental scale from 0 (no anxiety) to 100 (unbearable anxiety) on which clients rate themselves. A VAS is similar but clients actually mark a point on a 10-cm line to indicate their anxiety level. The purpose is to monitor changes in tension levels.

The rationale for including relaxation training in CBGT is based on the observation that when people are tense they may not be able to think clearly and often get inhibited. Furthermore, anxious people may develop physical symptoms such as palpitations and sweaty palms. AMT can alleviate these symptoms which often distress participants who infer that there must be something wrong with them.

The role of group members

Although CBGT may be construed as having a large teaching component, group members are not passive. Group members are encouraged to:

(i) Adopt a psychological model of maladaptive behaviour and recognize that 'neurotic behaviour' is largely learned and can be unlearned using cognitive-behavioural techniques.

(ii) Recognize that it is not always necessary to search for root causes of maladaptive behaviour.

(iii) Recognize that maladaptive behaviours and cognitions may be modified by using cognitive-behavioural techniques.

(iv) Learn to apply a functional analysis.

(v) Learn to think for themselves.

(vi) Learn to do a simple cognitive-behavioural analysis, keep records and monitor their progress.
(vii) Learn to conduct simple cognitive-behavioural experiments to test the validity of their beliefs and assumptions.
(viii) Learn to feel comfortable with playing different roles.
(ix) Offer suggestions and take a peer–therapist role in coaching fellow participants.

Although CBGT leaders may not have explicit models such as the schema in Table 6.2, they nevertheless do follow implicitly some such model in practice to guide their decision-making.

A clinical example may clarify how participants may apply cognitive-behavioural techniques. Jane told the group she was convinced that her marriage was breaking down because 'only today my husband, John, came back from work in a bad mood yet again'. She had burnt the toast that morning and he did not finish his supper that evening, and was silent all day. She concluded: 'he doesn't love me anymore'.

Jane was asked to use cognitive techniques and to check out the inferences she had made as her homework assignment. In the following session, Jane reported that she recalled learning in the group that mind reading in relationships can lead to erroneous conclusions and, therefore, asked John: (i) what his moodiness was about; (ii) to explain his poor appetite; and (iii) explain his quiet behaviour.

John confessed that he had been told of his impending redundancy and wanted to spare her the worry. He apologized for being moody. Jane recalled a mini-lecture when she learned that depressed people may become asocial, lose their appetite and have poor concentration. Now she knew why he behaved out-of-character! His unfinished supper had no connection with the burnt toast. Jane had made an 'arbitrary inference' and jumped to the conclusion that he did not love her anymore (overgeneralization).

Group development over time

The natural history of a psychotherapy group is common to all therapy groups. Thus, as time progresses, cohesion in the group tends to increase as participants get to know each other better. In CBGT participants have less opportunities to get to know each other because the group is task-focused. However, the realization that others in the group also have similar hopes and fears confirms that they are not alone in their difficulties. This is known as the universality assumption (Yalom, 1985).

MacKenzie and Livesley (1983) describe a developmental model of brief group therapy and note that Tuckman (1965) summarized the stages of group development with the terms 'forming', 'storming', 'norming', and 'performing' to which others have added 'adjourning'.

In CBGT the stages of forming, storming, norming and performing are telescoped into a shorter time period. The group leaders have to facilitate this within the structure they have provided with a person-centred approach to the therapeutic relationship.

Four phases may be discerned in a CBGT group – preparation: collaboration, treatment, consolidation and termination (cf. Yost *et al.*, 1986). This pattern is strengthened by having a formal plan for the group (see Table 6.1) during its life and for each session. The following is an outline of a cognitive-behavioural group therapy session.

Introduction
This begins with a welcome to new members (if the group is open-ended). Then there is agenda-setting, which sets the structure for the session. This is done by the leaders but suggestions from participants are also incorporated, as appropriate. Next, all participants engage in warm-up exercises to break the ice and as a means of making the group less serious and more enjoyable. Feedback from participants is elicited and this may result in further agenda-setting or modification.

Homework review
The homework given in the previous session is reviewed by the group leaders, participants are encouraged to share their successes and guidance is offered for any problems encountered.

Mini-lectures (5–10 minutes)
One of the group leaders gives a talk on a particular area, e.g. on defining problems and identifying goals. The points made are demonstrated by the leaders and feedback from participants is again elicited. Then, an exercise is devised by the leaders on 'Defining problems and identifying goals' for participants to complete in the session, and the leaders offer guidance and clarification as necessary.

Discussion of individual concerns
There are two types of discussion. First, whole-group discussion is where everyone participates and, secondly, small-group discussion is where groups of three or so people discuss their individual concerns. Items of general interest to all are discussed at the whole-group discussion, whereas items of a more personal nature or only relevant to the small group are discussed in the privacy of the small group. Therapists provide modelling of any strategies suggested or to demonstrate a point. Participants then role play to test their understanding and acquire competence. Again, feedback is elicited. This is

followed by another exercise – 'Assignment of homework' – tailored to suit individual concerns.

Summary of session

The leaders summarize the session with the aid of a flip-chart. Participants comment briefly on 'What I found helpful' in that session and offer suggestions of topics which they would like covered in future sessions. There is a brief review of the next session by the leaders and the session ends with a positive self-statement exercise in which everyone says something positive about themselves to their neighbour, with the group ending on a positive note.

Agenda-setting, homework review, mini-lectures, assignment of home-work, participants' comments on what they found helpful and suggestions of topics are features unique to CBGT.

Mechanisms of change

Change in CBGT can be considered by focusing on the areas of skill acquisition, self-sufficiency and autonomy (cf. Yost *et al.*, 1986). Skill acquisition in particular targeted areas is easily observed. However, self-sufficiency and autonomy are rather global concepts. In CBGT it is therefore necessary to evaluate behavioural and cognitive change along several dimensions. In the behavioural domain there may be changes in the participant's repertoire, i.e. some new skill may be acquired. The fact that a participant is able to apply a functional analysis to problems demonstrates competence and application to other areas of his or her life confirms that generalization has occurred. In practice, this is not always the case. In the case of assertion, this is not surprising, because assertiveness is conceptual-ized as situationally-specific. Nevertheless, there are several studies which have demonstrated the efficacy of assertion groups and the procedures employed (cf. Rimm and Masters, 1979). Participants may also show improvement by demonstrating increased flexibility in the way they respond to interpersonal situations. In the cognitive domain, participants should be able to demonstrate the application of cognitive techniques, such as challenging dysfunctional cognitions, so that they begin to change mala-daptive beliefs.

Cognitive changes have often to be inferred and it is difficult to ascertain whether or not these changes are permanent. Typically, follow-up sessions some 6 months later are held to check if progress has been maintained.

The cognitive-behavioural group therapist's confidence that a participant has indeed improved would be strengthened if behavioural and cognitive changes can be demonstrated independently, e.g. that significant others confirm changes in clients that have also been reported by them.

Although most clinicians do not publish their evaluations of CBGT, the techniques they use appear to be supported by research and clinical trials. The effectiveness of the utilization of opportunities for group interaction through discussion, modelling and role playing has been demonstrated by Harris (1979). Lynn and Frauman (1985) found that group therapy models share a common feature: their therapeutic impact is augmented by the interactions, multiple relationships, and sense of 'togetherness' or cohesion that group processes facilitate. This suggests that in addition to the efficacy of any particular techniques used in CBGT, the group processes when properly used have an additive effect on therapy outcome.

Behaviour therapists would explain change in terms of a change in the patterns of reinforcement (rewards), the facilitation of new learning and/or the unlearning of maladaptive behaviours. However, cognitive-behavioural therapists would argue that changes in cognition tend to precede changes in behaviour, whereas strict behaviour therapists would argue that behavioural change produces changes in cognition. However, it is increasingly accepted that change in therapy is not unidirectional and no one modality is necessarily primary all the time, and that different methods can have the same effects, depending on one's theoretical orientation, a view in accord with this author's perspective.

Typical problems and their resolution

Before problem-solving can begin, it is necessary to elucidate the cognitive-behavioural model and correct the misapplication of a medical model to the problems of living. Some common issues follow.

'Why' questions

As in other groups, participants often tend to fall back into asking 'why' questions and recounting past histories. The leaders need to socialize participants into the cognitive-behavioural model and gently shape them into thinking in cognitive-behavioural terms. For example, instead of asking why he or she is overly anxious in the presence of the opposite sex, the participant will be encouraged to ask (1) what exactly is the problem (this encourages specifying what it is about the situation that is anxiety-provoking); (2) what are the antecedents to my anxiety in this situation (part of the functional analysis); and (3) are there some situations in which I do not feel anxious with the opposite sex? If so, which ones? (perhaps he or she has strengths in some areas and the anxiety may not be cross-situationally consistent). Depending on the responses to these questions, the leaders can then suggest procedures such as relaxation training, construct a role play situation, or model different ways of coping in that situation.

Anxiety about role playing
This is a very common problem which can be tackled by the leaders describing how uncomfortable they themselves felt when role playing for the first time. Following Wessler and Wessler (1980) I encourage overly anxious participants to deliberately perform *anxiously*, stressing that a good performance is not wanted. This reduces performance anxiety. Alternatively, or additionally, the production of anxiety in the session can be exploited for therapeutic demonstration. For example, the participant could be asked to verbalize his or her cognitions immediately before role playing, and the inferences tested.

Difficulties in responding assertively
Some people have great difficulty in responding assertively, having been reinforced for acting meekly all their lives. In such cases, they may be helped by the leaders deliberately asking them to go to the other extreme and to respond aggressively (in the safety of the group). They can then be 'shaped' down to respond assertively.

'I see what you're getting at, but I just can't bring myself to do it'
This problem relates to the possibility that the participant is too anxious and thus inhibited from putting into action a particular response. It may be due to maladaptive beliefs or fear of the consequences which may or may not be realistic. These factors need to be explored and anxieties allayed.

Termination of the group
The leaders should gauge the atmosphere in the group and, well before the end, prepare participants for termination, explaining that most people feel a sense of loss when the supportive group which showed care and understanding is coming to an end, and that such feelings are natural. However, this loss can be alleviated in part by offering a follow-up meeting, typically a couple of months later.

Limitations of the approach

The main limitations of CBGT is that the group processes are often not adequately exploited. Poor attention to group processes by leaders may result in inappropriate conclusions being reached about why certain participants have dropped out or failed to progress, contrary to expectation. Behavioural and cognitive-behavioural therapies are probably the most researched among psychotherapies, but this should not lull leaders into thinking that these approaches are necessarily superior or best for all clients.

For example, CBGT may not be the treatment of choice for a client whose major problem is essentially existential. Similarly, leaders should be cautious not to assume that negative cognitions are necessarily distortions. Cognitive-behaviour therapists are likely to advance further if they bear in mind the caution of Meichenbaum (1985, pp. 284–285):

> The field of psychotherapy is 'maturing' as it searches for an integrative perspective to understand how people change. Each psychotherapeutic approach described in this volume [*Contemporary Psychotherapies*] has been 'humbled' by the limited efficacy of its approach. As a result, many psychotherapists have turned to an integrated cognitive-behavioral approach as a way out of this morass. Cognitive-behavioral therapies are not a panacea, nor even a proven therapeutic approach, but they do offer a promising conceptualization for understanding and nurturing behavior change. Much research is now underway in order to determine whether this enthusiasm is justified.

Typical qualities of effective leaders

Typical qualities of effective leaders are, on the whole, the same as those for other psychotherapies. These are described by Aveline (Chapter 14, this volume) and Yalom (1985). In particular, cognitive-behavioural therapists should be able to:

(i) Demonstrate flexibility rather than rigidly follow a particular model or technique. In other words, the therapeutic techniques may need modifying to suit the client's particular difficulty.

(ii) Ensure that they have mastered the cognitive-behavioural model, understand its principles, appreciate its strengths and recognize its limitations. Only then can they do justice to their approach and, more importantly, do their best for their clients.

(iii) Cognitive-behavioural group therapists should ensure that they have regular supervision with peers.

(iv) Prepare process notes describing how they think change was effected in the group. Alternatively, or additionally, audio- or video-recordings (with the clients' consent) may be made of sample sessions or phases in the life of the group for discussion during supervision. Depending on memory alone is likely to prove inadequate and unreliable.

CONCLUSION

Cognitive-behavioural therapies have contributed a new methodology for assessing what was previously regarded as unreliable and invalid introspective accounts. The integration of behavioural insights derived from empirical work with clinical experience and the attention devoted to thoughts, beliefs and images is a significant advance for a group psychotherapy. Future developments could enhance the effectiveness of CBGT even more by attempting to integrate, within the cognitive-behavioural framework, the use of group processes, and by devoting more attention to the group as a whole and to exploring the interaction between the group and the individual. Finally, a possible integration of affect, behaviour and cognition (cf. Greenberg and Safran, 1984) may eventually produce a hybrid cognitive-behavioural group psychotherapy which marries the best of group psychotherapy (in the strict sense of the word) with the strengths of cognitive-behavioural therapy.

REFERENCES

Alagaratnam, W. J. (1982) Rethinking interpersonal communication research: methodological problems in the design and evaluation of social skills training programmes: suggestions for a multimodal approach. *In* S. J. Harrison, T. Keighley, P. Sissons and P. Walsh (eds), *Proceedings of the Royal College of Nursing Research Society's Annual Conference*, pp. 25–49. London, Royal College of Nursing.

Argyle, M. (1967). *The Psychology of Interpersonal Behaviour*, 1st edition. Harmondsworth, Penguin.

Bandura, A. (1969). *Principles of Behavior Modification*. New York, Holt, Rinehart and Winston.

Bandura, A. (1977). *Social Learning Theory*. Englewood Cliffs, NJ, Prentice-Hall.

Beck, A. T., Rush, A. J., Shaw, B. F. and Emery, G. (1979). *Cognitive Therapy for Depression*. New York, Guilford Press.

Dryden, W. (1984). *Rational-Emotive Therapy: Fundamentals and Innovations*. Beckenham, Kent, Croom Helm.

Ellis, A. and Harper, R. A. (1976). *A New Guide to Rational Living*. North Hollywood, Wilshire.

Galassi, J. P., Delo, J. S., Galassi, M. D. and Bastien, S. (1974). The College Self-Expression Scale: A measure of assertiveness. *Behavior Therapy* **5**, 165–71.

Gambrill, E. D. and Richey, C. A. (1975). An assertion inventory for use in assessment and research. *Behavior Therapy* **6**, 550–61.

Greenberg, L. S. and Safran, J. D. (1984). Integrating affect and cognition: a perspective on the process of therapeutic change. *Cognitive Therapy and Research* **8**, 559–78.

Harris, F. (1979). Behavioural approach to group therapy. *International Journal of Group Therapy* **29**, 453–470.

Hollon, S. D. and Shaw, B. F. (1979). Group cognitive therapy for depressed patients. *In* A. T. Beck, A. J. Rush, B. F. Shaw and G. Emery, *Cognitive Therapy of Depression*. pp. 238–53. New York, Guilford Press.

Jacobson, E. (1938). *Progressive Relaxation*. Chicago, University of Chicago Press.

Jupp, H. and Dudley, M. (1984). Group cognitive/anxiety management. *Journal of Advanced Nursing* **9**, 573–80.

Ledwidge, B. (1978). Cognitive behavior modification: A step in the wrong direction? *Psychological Bulletin* **85**, 353–375.

Lynn, S. J. and Frauman, D. (1985). Group psychotherapy. *In* S. J. Lynn and J. P. Garske (eds), *Contemporary Psychotherapies: Models and Methods*, pp. 419–58. Columbus, Ohio, Charles E. Merrill.

MacKenzie, K. R. and Livesley, W. J. (1983). A developmental model for brief group therapy. *In* R. R. Dies and K. R. MacKenzie (eds), *Advances in Group Psychotherapy, Monograph 1*, pp. 101–16. New York, International Universities Press.

Meichenbaum, D. (1985). Cognitive-behavioral therapies. *In* S. J. Lynn and J. P. Garske (eds), *Contemporary Psychotherapies; Models and Methods*, pp. 261–86. Columbus, Ohio, Charles E. Merrill.

Rathus, S. A. (1973). A 30-item schedule for assessing assertive behavior. *Behavior Therapy* **4**, 398–406.

Rimm, D. C. and Cunningham, H. M. (1985). Behavior therapies. *In* S. J. Lynn and J. P. Garske (eds), *Contemporary Psychotherapies: Models and Methods*, pp. 221–59. Columbus, Ohio, Charles E. Merrill.

Rimm, D. C. and Masters, J. C. (1979). *Behavior Therapy: Techniques and Empirical Findings*, 2nd edition. London, Academic Press.

Rogers, C. R. (1957). The necessary and sufficient conditions of therapeutic personality change. *Journal of Consulting Psychology*, **21**, 95–103.

Rush, A. J. and Watkins, J. T. (1981). Group versus individual cognitive therapy: A pilot study. *Cognitive Therapy and Research* **5**, 95–104.

Tarrier, N. and Main, C. J. (1986). Applied relaxation training for generalised anxiety and panic attacks. *British Journal of Psychiatry* **149**, 330–36.

Trower, P. (ed.) (1984). *Radical Approaches to Social Skills Training*. Beckenham, Kent, Croom Helm.

Tuckman, B. W. (1965). Developmental sequence in small groups. *Psychological Bulletin* **63**, 384–99.

Wessler, R. A. and Wessler, R. L. (1980). *The Principles and Practice of Rational-Emotive Therapy*. San Francisco, Jossey-Bass.

Wolpe, J. (1958). *Psychotherapy by Reciprocal Inhibition*. Stanford, Stanford University Press.

Yalom, I. D. (1985). *The Theory and Practice of Group Psychotherapy*, 3rd edition. New York, Basic Books.

Yost, E. B., Beutler, L. E., Corbishley, M. A. and Allender, J. R. (1986). *Group Cognitive Therapy: A Treatment Approach for Depressed Older Adults*. New York, Pergamon.

CHAPTER 7

A COMPARATIVE REVIEW OF SMALL GROUP THERAPIES

Mark Aveline and Windy Dryden

In this chapter, we bring out similarities and differences between the five approaches to small group psychotherapy described in Part 1. In preparing the review, we had five questions in mind. (1) Does the differing language of the contributors indicate fundamentally different conceptualizations of theoretical underpinnings, key concepts and purpose or a hidden commonality? (2) How are the therapeutic effects achieved and problematic situations overcome? (3) What are the roles of the leader and the members? (4) Are there specific indications or contraindications for each approach? (5) Can the personality characteristics of effective leaders in each mode be differentiated? These questions are considered in turn.

We hope that comparing approaches will facilitate the process of comprehension for the reader. Our review also raises questions of parsimony in language and evaluation of effectiveness which, in turn, could inform the shape of training. If the difference between approaches is one of appearance rather than substance, how may the essence be simply stated but without doing an injustice to the subtlety of the original conceptualizations? Alternatively, how may unique contributions in conceptualization be brought into sharp focus? At this stage, we can only make extrapolations from the terms used and the definitions given. Any conclusions would need to be refined by, for example, experienced practitioners presenting instances of actual practice to practitioners of other persuasions and debating with them what aspects were being attended to and how they might be named. The therapeutic significance of the refined concepts would, then, need to be evaluated. There is as yet only a weak association between hypothesized mechanisms of change and demonstrated effects. Here is a substantial challenge that will need to be faced if the field is to advance. Finally, these two steps of economical naming and evaluation should lead to more accurately focused training for therapies of greater refinement and effectiveness.

PURPOSE, THEORETICAL UNDERPINNINGS AND KEY CONCEPTS

We open this section with a consideration of purpose. Therapy groups are purposeful constructions which members join in the hope of deriving some special benefit for problems which have been framed, by and large, in interpersonal terms. When considering the form of an approach, the question of which is primary – theory or therapeutic purpose – is interesting. Freud, certainly, considered psychoanalysis to be, first, a connected body of observations about unconscious mental processes; secondly, a technique for investigating unconscious mental life and, only thirdly, a method of treatment for mental disturbances (Main, 1968). By requiring the contributors to state both their theory and practice, it becomes easier to see how in a particular approach the two interrelate and which aspects of group life are given relatively more or less attention.

There is a major overlap of purpose among the approaches. The group-analytic approach seeks to free the individual from intrapsychic conflicts and difficulties in interpersonal relationships; greater awareness of thoughts and feelings is sought and, ambitiously, it is hoped to realize the full potential of the individual for relationships. In the interpersonal group, the individual brings to the group as their personal agenda recurrent interpersonal difficulties and enacts them within it. The group forms a laboratory where these interactions can be identified and a workshop where new resolutions may be achieved and practised. A sense of meaning and purpose in life is strengthened through the exercise of responsibility and choice. In the gestalt group, members join because they wish to live more fulfilling or less painful lives. Maladaptive behaviours which are bolstered by interruptive modifications of contact are undermined by members working towards greater contact with themselves and with others. In psychodrama, extension of role is central with the group providing an arena in which spontaneous, creative experimentation can take place. By acting through the important roles that they and significant others in their cultural world take, fuller and warmer understanding of the roles and counter-roles is reached, old and avoided feelings are expressed, and a more effective and fulfilling range of roles is acquired. In contrast to the other approaches, the cognitive-behavioural group is much more goal-directed in its focus. The purpose is to modify specific problematic cognitions and behaviours put forward by the client; these may or may not have an interpersonal cast. The clients are taught how to manage feelings of anxiety, how to improve social skills which may have a secondary effect of improving interpersonal effectiveness, and how to use techniques for identifying, testing and modifying distress-inducing thoughts and beliefs.

At the core of the small group therapies lies a concern with, first, how a person relates to others – the patterns shown, the consequences, reinforcing elements and historical antecedents – and, secondly, their relationship to their own being – their selves, their roles, their intrapsychic conflicts and the unintegrated aspects of their character. These therapies differ in the emphasis given to these elements and the language used to describe the theory and key concepts; stemming from these differences is a significant variation in practice. While each approach is ultimately and fundamentally concerned with the individual and the problems that brought that person to the group, some will achieve their end through a greater attention to the group as a whole and some to the individual member.

If the therapies are arranged on a dimension that has group-focused on the right and individual-focused on the left, analytic groups take the right-hand position with interpersonal being next in line. Then comes gestalt, psychodrama and, finally, cognitive-behavioural. The 'conservative' position of the first two reflects their allegiance to the classic orthodoxy of group practice in making full use of group process and group interaction. The contributors on gestalt and psychodrama describe ways of working with individual members at any one time but stress the importance of the interrelationship between this and the group context and the shared experience of the membership in all its resonances and variations; they eschew forms of their approach that focus alone on the individual and neglect the history of the group from session to session; they deplore one-off, ill-considered applications of their method. In cognitive-behavioural therapy, a familiarity with group theory is advocated but little formal use is made of it except to foster group cohesiveness as a means of creating a temporary, or perhaps continuing, supportive social network.

We now turn to the theoretical underpinnings and key concepts. These reflect and inform the dominant concerns of the different approaches.

The unique contribution of the analytic groups is the framework that they provide for understanding unconscious processes that move the group as a whole; these insights are also explicitly utilized in the interpersonal approach and are there to be drawn upon by the psychodramatist. In the Tavistock model whose locus of attention is very much on the therapist, a common group tension prompts the group to display a required relationship with the leader for fear of the avoided and calamitous relationships in this tripartite formulation. In the interpersonal approach, this formulation is also applied to relationships between members. The formulation points to defensive manoeuvres based on fear. A more positive note and one which usefully adds to our understanding of the history of a group, how it comes to develop in a particular way and might change over time, is introduced by focal conflict theory. Here successive solutions to focal conflicts become the group history; the solutions may be restrictive in the group's avoidance of dealing with disturbing wishes and the associated anxiety and guilt or enabling when the conductor assists the group to engage in full discussion. Collusive restrictive patterns are recognized by interpersonal group therapists and are addressed as such by psychodramatists who wait for a protagonist to come forward who, unknowingly, will be the spokesman for the group anxiety and by gestaltists in the resistance to contact between members which becomes the figure in the ground for the group. With the exception of cognitive-behavioural therapy, all the approaches make use of psychoanalytic concepts such as transference or parataxic distortion, projection, splitting and mirroring.

How the approaches conceptualize the nature of their members' problems varies. Both the analytic, in its group analytic form, and gestalt approaches see them as communications. In the former, the individual is the nodal point within a network of communication. Symptoms are blocks to free communication and are expressed in symbolic disturbance which, initially, is unintelligible to both the member and fellow members. As the group works towards an ever more articulate form of communication, the manifest communication is translated and the latent meaning emerges. This is similar to the gestalt concepts of contact and confluence. Contact occurs at the boundary between one person and another. When the boundary is permeable, all stages of the contact process may be completed and the individual will be in a state of full awareness. The antithesis of contact is confluence and it is this state of non-awareness that the leader works on in order to return the member to the greater good of contact. Confluence may be maintained by processes whose terms are derived from psychoanalysis – introjection, projection, retroflection (= turning against the self) and reaction formation (= repression with somatic expression of repressed contents).

The gestalt leader is alert to manifestations of confluence, be they verbal or somatic, and makes these the figure or foreground against the many other possibilities that are for the time being in the (back)ground. The fluidity of focus between the innumerable gestalten that make up the gestalt of the group and the sense of the group as a whole and of the individual as a whole makes a valuable contribution to the practice of group therapy; it reminds the leader of the many possibilities and levels that are open to him and to the group.

In interpersonal and psychodrama group therapy, the members' problems are construed in terms of the selves or roles that they present to the group.

The member enacts his problematic self or selves in the group, his Dasein or being in the world, or selects from his cultural atom, the total range of his roles, the role that is his reaction to the specific situation he faces. In psychodrama theory, there is a reciprocal relationship between the role presented and the counter-roles faced. In interpersonal theory, this reciprocity is articulated in Sullivan's theorem of reciprocal emotion. In psychodrama, there is an elective opportunity to experiment with alternative roles and even with counter-roles, usually in present or past relationships external to the group. In the interpersonal group, James's concept of each person having as many social selves as there are individuals to recognize them, and Lewin's vector theory combine to justify the therapeutic provision of a new, unprejudiced psychological space in which to experiment with and move into unexpressed selves. Though operating at a simpler level of abstraction in its concern with behaviours, the behavioural learning theory concept of reinforcement and Beck's cognitive theory of false logic suggest ways in which restrictive selves or roles may be maintained; the information derived from these insights is ordered in cognitive and behavioural or functional analysis, the latter in the ABC format.

The philosophical underpinning in existentialism in the interpersonal group leads to a distinct emphasis on members taking responsibility for their actions, being authentic and exercising their freedom of choice, a feature of practice of gestalt group therapy too. This serious note is balanced by an emphasis on humour, an element shared with psychodrama and gestalt which, in turn, stress the vitalizing force of creativity and spontaneity.

All the small group therapies underline the importance in achieving therapeutic effects of attending to the here-and-now of what transpires in the group. The analytic group therapies, and to a lesser extent gestalt, also attend to the historical antecedents, whereas the rest are essentially ahistorical. The determinedly outward gaze of the cognitive-behavioural group towards the real-life problems of its members constitutes a distinctive feature. This is expressed in the problem-solving approach and the setting and review of homework assignments. Two particular strengths of this approach are the clarity with which problems are operationally defined and the way in which the definition, then, serves as a benchmark against the effects of pragmatically conceived treatments can be assessed.

In the 1950s and 1960s, Northrop Frye, a literary critic, developed a categorization scheme for literature which was applied by Schafer to psychoanalysis in his influential book on language (Schafer, 1976) and, subsequently, by Messer to psychoanalytic therapy and behaviour therapy. Four themes encompass the ways of seeing life's possibilities – the romantic, ironic, tragic and comic visions (Messer, 1986). The romantic vision sees the world as we would like it to be and life as an adventure in which the hero triumphs over darkness and transcends adversity; it idealizes the individual and prizes being natural. Humanistic therapies, quintessentially, subscribe to this vision, as does to a much lesser extent psychoanalysis. Psychoanalysis is deeply ironic in that it challenges our romantic illusions and, taking a position of relative detachment, stresses the inherent difficulties of human existence and the layered complexity of psychological life. In the tragic vision, happy endings are mistrusted and the limitations in life are accepted, not all potentialities are realizable; however, in contrast to the ironic perspective, the individual is fully and purposefully involved in his life. Psychoanalysis incorporates tragic aspects into its view, as does to a lesser extent rational-emotive therapy in its recognition of people's need to accept limitations and imperfections. Finally, in the comic vision, the trend is from bad situations to better and sometimes to best. The emphasis is on external, unfortunate situations which can be struggled with and overcome, rather than with discordant inner conflicts. Behaviour therapy takes this action-oriented view, as do the humanistic therapies to a lesser degree.

Applying the above thematic structure to the small group therapies, the following categorizations may be made. Analytic group therapies are predominantly tragic in their view with their emphasis on underlying, unconscious conflicts that have to be faced and come to terms with; it is also romantic in its belief that the full potential for human relationships can be achieved. The conductor is the spokesman for the ironic vision, because from a neutral position he seeks to help the group look below the surface. The interpersonal approach partakes strongly of the romantic and the tragic plus a leavening of the comic. In its humanism, the approach is hopeful about the individual and what that person may achieve with the help of the group, but its existential heritage confers a tragic realization of the inevitability of death and unfulfilled ambitions. Gestalt is more romantic and comic than tragic. The romantic vision is particularly seen in the transparent, open involvement of the gestalt leader in the happenings of the group. Psychodrama has the same visions, except that tragic and ironic views are present in the acceptance that a person's view of their life may become more, rather than less, complex as therapy proceeds and that there are no easy answers. Cognitive-behavioural therapy has a predominantly comic vision. Members can become more efficient in their problem-solving; where a person is coming from and what they are making of their life are unasked questions.

Thematic analysis indicates significant differences between the small group therapies. The visions summarize the differences in theory and key concepts but, in this context, they are also likely to reflect the personal visions of their portrayers. This raises two intriguing questions. The first is of the chicken and egg variety: does training shape personal visions or are therapists drawn to approaches that they are already in harmony with and, then, modify to reflect their individual bias? We suggest that the latter is the principal pattern. This important question is further explored in Chapter 14 where it is stated that training should help the therapist make explicit his model of help-giving, and examine how it may be integrated with the group situation and identify natural preferences that may obstruct his therapeutic role. The second question is one of pluralism. Schacht (1984) argues that we do not just discover what is inherent in nature but we invent our own categories and theories and view nature through them. From this point of view, all the foregoing concepts are partial and misleading if they are taken to represent the whole. Is it possible and, if possible, desirable for leaders to attempt to hold a comprehensive view? Since few comparative studies of the effectiveness of the group therapies, let alone the effectiveness of individual leaders, have been carried out, the question is presently unanswerable scientifically.

THERAPEUTIC EFFECTS AND PROBLEMATIC SITUATIONS

While the small group therapies differ in theory, the language of change is remarkably similar. The analytic therapies posit insight as a necessary element if change, which may have already occurred, is to become persistent. In contrast to the vertical or historical insight of psychoanalysis, insight in the group is horizontal, i.e. in the here-and-now of the group in the way in which the member's 'problem' blocks free communication. Change occurs when the individual gives up focusing on the 'problem' and enters into the ongoing life of the group; then maturation and individuation can occur. Both interpersonal and gestalt describe similar processes. In the former, the enactment of maladaptive relationship patterns (the 'problem') yields as the person takes the risk of being the person they might be if they were less fearful and conflicted. The change is initiated by disclosure and feedback, and consolidated by the lived experience of being different; the experience of being of assistance to others and being valued by them is particularly helpful. In the latter, change may proceed awareness, but awareness is what the group is about. The route to this goal is through the openness of contact.

Psychodrama shares the emphasis on experiment as a mechanism of change and subscribes, as do all the therapies, to the fundamental importance of being a member of a warm, supportive group, but adds to these two other concepts. Active catharsis allows the protagonist to express avoided feelings in the most vivid form and, in the spontaneity of the drama, catalyses insight and change for protagonist and audience alike. Role reversal may, but only may, increase tolerance of the other and the acceptance of compromise.

In the past, much argument has taken place in cognitive-behavioural circles over which comes first, change in behaviour or change in cognitions. Now it is recognized to be a two-way process. Participants may gain confidence through gaining competence in making their own functional assessment and successfully applying behavioural or cognitive principles to rehearsed, personally problematic situations in the group and outside in homework assignments; change is evaluated and consolidated through constructive appraisals of performance by the leader and other participants.

The difference in what constitutes a problematic situation for the leader in the small group therapies highlights the distinctive features of each. Boundary and process issues are dominant for the analytic group therapist; questions to the leader are not answered but explored, as is the significance of outside group meetings, demands for individual sessions and silence. In the interpersonal group, the chief problem is members completing to their own detriment their self-restrictive patterns of relationship. This is resolved through encounter, whose pace is well-judged; the leader supports and encourages member and peer disclosure and acceptance; the use of summaries underlines the open approach. The problems of psychodrama arise from the special features of the dramatic form and may either be a paucity of spontaneity or an over-abundance, the latter being difficult to contain productively. The director deals with paucity by allowing the group to develop its own pace or by mapping the dynamics of the group with a sculpt; the intensity of the drama requires intensive de-roling. Boundary issues of a different sort dominates gestalt; here what is made figure in the ground is any interruption in contact between members. Echoing the analytic theme, resolution does not come through merely identifying the interruption or resistance but through exploring beyond it to fears and conflicts. The techniques of cognitive-behavioural therapy contribute their special problems; the asking 'why am I like this?' tendency is discouraged, role-plays are made less anxiety-provocating by working up to them and over-assertive responses shaped down. The termination of the group is softened by reunions and informal continuation.

THE ROLES OF THE LEADER AND MEMBERS

It may be said that language defines our vision and regulates our actions. Compare the terms used to describe the leader. The analytic leader is the conductor who interprets the communications of the group and the social matrix, staying in the background as much as possible and working towards the group taking responsibility for itself. The role is austere and highly professional; it is not to give comfort or to be real – hopefully members will give this to each other. The interpersonal leader is seen as a facilitator of interpersonal transactions and as a fellow-traveller in the journey of life; taking an increasingly background role, he attends to the language, both verbal and physical, that is used in the group and its meaning. In the remaining approaches, the leader definitely leads. The gestalt leader frustrates confluence and promotes contact, may initiate technical procedures, is transparent and sees himself as being fully part of the group. [For the gestaltist, the word technique has negative connotations if it implies a routine response and an interruption of contact. However, it is the use of the technique that determines its value and action techniques may be beneficially used in many forms of psychotherapy (Aveline, 1979)]. For the leader in psychodrama, the role of director is prominent and responsible; analyst and producer are subsidiary roles. The director has the responsibility of selecting which protagonist to work with and then of following the spontaneous cues given by that person through each state of the drama to the very important endpoint of sharing with the audience and de-roling. The cognitive-behavioural therapist takes his stage as educator; he may be didactic, directive and evaluative; he promotes the acquisition of skills.

In cognitive-behavioural therapy, the role of the members is task-orientated; the tasks, themselves, may or may not be common to all. A uniformity of role unites the other approaches and is summed up in the gestalt term contact-ability. Interpersonally, members must be present and emotionally available. In psychodrama, members are engaged in exploring and understanding the cultural atoms of themselves and others. In the analytic group, the members are on a journey of exploration, not knowing what will be discovered or who else will be there.

INDICATIONS AND CONTRAINDICATIONS

Not surprisingly, convergence characterizes the selection criteria for membership. In essentially identical terms, the leader in the first four approaches looks for an ability in the member to understand and withstand the group process (in analytic terms, to have an observing ego), to construe difficulties in psychological or interpersonal terms, to be open to change, and to have sufficient self-generated willingness to commit themselves to meeting and to involving themselves in each other's cares. Cognitive-behaviourists look for the ability to formulate specified goals and to work with the techniques of relaxation training, social skills improvement and cognitive modification; they are more open to the possibility of combining group membership with individual therapy. No approach wants members who are unwilling conscripts. To varying degrees, all leaders place emphasis on careful pre-group preparation of new group members. It should be noted that, as detailed in Chapter 13, preparation for the role of member is one of the few consistently, positive factors in research studies on outcome.

Psychosis or severe personality disturbance of the paranoid, narcissistic, obsessional or impulsive kind tends to be an exclusion criterion, as does brain damage. The group format does not permit extensive exploration of individual dynamics and, for those that require this or are too fragile, one-to-one psychotherapy is to be preferred. The analytic therapist makes the valid points that those in crisis may at that time find the questioning of their defences in the group unhelpful and, perhaps reflecting the relative austerity of the approach, that socially isolated members without a supportive social network may find the rigour of the group hard to bear. However, it should be borne in mind that selection is not for groups in general but for a particular group; a seemingly unpromising prospective member may find a fruitful combination in one group and not in another.

PERSONALITY CHARACTERISTICS OF EFFECTIVE LEADERS

The enthusiasm of group leaders for their work shows in the descriptions of the personal qualities of effective leaders. This is well-stated by the analytic contributor when he writes of the privilege of being part of the group, a participant in the drama of life, respecting others and the many ways in which people find fulfilment in their lives, and delighting in them as they achieve their potential. The leader who can avoid falling into the trap of striving to be omnipotent or to be the source of all the fruitful happenings in the group is commended. All the approaches stress the importance of the leader being open to the feelings and events in the group, resonating to them, tapping into his own spontaneity, and having contact-ability.

The analytic leader derives his authority from the projections of the group which he then uses for the benefit of the group; this includes him demonstrating his analytic love of truth, even when unpalatable. In the interpersonal and gestalt, the effective leader acts as a model of good membership; he tries to be open, shows willingness to change, takes risks and is relatively undefended; he is in the business of meeting people as a fellow traveller. Stemming from the special techniques deployed in psychodrama and cognitive-behavioural therapy, these two approaches have extra requirements. Psychodrama requires an uncommon blend of extraversion and sensitivity, as well as energy and the ability to think on one's feet and to tolerate the scrutiny of the group in the prominent role of director. The cognitive-behaviourist must be flexible in modifying techniques to suit the needs of particular clients, and have a sustained commitment to evaluating what has been achieved. In all approaches, the effective leader has a thorough grounding in theory and refines his skills through supervision.

CONCLUSION

Our review indicates a divergence of language and structure between the small group therapies but a convergence of indications and, to a lesser extent, of purpose and effective leader qualities. In terms of therapeutic factors, it may well be that what the groups have in common is more important than what divides them. It is also likely that the actual practice of experienced leaders in different approaches is, special techniques apart, more similar than has been portrayed. This is a rich field for operational research.

REFERENCES

Aveline, M. O. (1979). Action techniques in psychotherapy. *British Journal of Hospital Medicine* **22**, 78–84.

Main, T. F. (1968). Psychoanalysis as a cross-bearing. *British Journal of Psychiatry* **114**, 501–507.

Messer, S. B. (1986). Eclecticism in psychotherapy: underlying assumptions, problems, and trade-offs. *In* J. C. Norcross (ed.), *Handbook of Eclectic Psychotherapy*, p. 379–97. New York, Brunner/Mazel.

Schacht, T. E. (1984). The varieties of integrative experience. *In* H. Arkowitz and S. B. Messer (eds), *Psychoanalytic Therapy and Behavior Therapy: Is Integration Possible?*, pp. 107–31. New York, Plenum Press.

Schafer, R. (1976). *A New Language for Psychoanalysis* London, Yale University Press.

PART 2

THE THERAPEUTIC VALUE OF OTHER GROUP APPROACHES

CHAPTER 8

THE THERAPEUTIC COMMUNITY

David Kennard

THE DEVELOPMENT OF THERAPEUTIC COMMUNITIES

Two developments, one in the first half of the nineteenth century, the other in the first half of the twentieth, anticipated some of the basic ideas of the therapeutic community. The first was moral treatment. This developed as a reaction against the conditions and treatment of the 'insane' in the eighteenth century. The principles of moral treatment included a belief in treating the mentally ill in a humane and dignified way, creating an intimate family-like atmosphere, and in the need for such qualities as kindness and tolerance in those responsible for their care. If we take such beliefs for granted today this was not always so. It its time, moral treatment was both radical and successful but, by the end of the last century, it faded with the rise of the large asylum and the shift towards a biological view of mental illness.

In 1913 an American called Homer Lane was invited to England to open a community for delinquent and disturbed adolescents. His use of self-government as the basis for running the community had a major impact on twentieth-century education. Among those directly influenced were A. S. Neill, George Lyward and David Wills. Wills developed Lane's ideas into 'Planned Environment Therapy', which included the principles that punishment should never be used to correct a child's behaviour, all relationships should be egalitarian and non-authoritarian, and therapy should be based on a loving, accepting relationship between child and adults. Today many communities and schools for disturbed children and adolescents – and also some for normal children – continue to be influenced by these principles.

Moral Treatment and Planned Environment Therapy show us that the idea of an egalitarian community in which change is brought about through caring personal relationships rather than the use of degradation, punishment or authority, has been a recurring theme in the history of society's response to its disturbed and deviant members.

The therapeutic community was first given its name in a short paper published in 1946 by Tom Main. In this Main described developments at Northfield Hospital in Birmingham, a military hospital in the Second World War, where a handful of psychoanalysts – of whom Main was one – had been working at the best way to overcome problems of low morale and inefficiency in the psychiatric wing of the hospital. Main's historic and still much quoted paper described this work as,

> an attempt to use a hospital not as an organisation run by doctors in the interests of their own greater technical efficiency, but as a community with the immediate aim of full participation of all its members in its daily life and the eventual aim of the resocialisation of the neurotic individual for life in ordinary society (Main, 1946, p. 67).

At the same time as the Northfield 'experiment' was in progress, a parallel development at a hospital in London was being pioneered by the man whose name was to become most closely identified with therapeutic communities – Maxwell Jones. A research physiologist by training, Jones had made the 'discovery' that patients with physiological symptoms of anxiety – and there were many during the war – were best helped by each other, in an atmosphere of open communication, reduced hierarchy, and daily structured discussions by the whole unit.

If these two developments could be reduced to a single phrase it would be 'patient involvement'. What both experiments were showing was that patients with psychiatric problems could be helped more fully when professionals were willing to be less hierarchical and patients were allowed to become involved in helping one another and in the hospital *as a community*.

Unusual circumstances of wartime England had given rise to the therapeutic community: the need to treat large numbers of psychiatric casualties, a climate of practical experimentation rather than tradition; hospitals placed in the care of non-hospital professions (psychoanalysts, researchers); and a focus on communal problems such as morale rather than on individual problems. Following the war, the creation of a National Health Service in 1948 'exposed the pitiful state of the chronic psychotics, legally imprisoned in the antiquated, dilapidated asylums' (Clark, 1977, p. 560). Interest in psychiatry, the harmful effects of institutional care and the dynamics of mental hospitals produced a spate of significant research in the 1950s and early 1960s (Stanton and Schwartz, 1954; Caudill, 1958; Barton, 1959; Rapaport, 1960; Menzies, 1960; Goffman, 1961). Socially and politically this was a period in which traditional authority and values were being challenged and replaced by more permissive, liberal ideas. In this climate of social change therapeutic communities became one of the standard bearers of new ideals within psychiatry. They were established in large psychiatric hospitals and in small specialized units, while therapeutic communities of different kinds were set up by ex-drug addicts in America and by protagonists of the anti-psychiatry movement in England. Although these communities differed from each other in important ways they could all be seen as part of a general movement away from paternal authority towards the ideal of the self-help community that characterized the 1960s.

By the mid-1970s it was being claimed by some that therapeutic communities had had their day. Manning, a social scientist who had made a particular study of them, suggested that therapeutic communities had followed the characteristic course of social movements: 'an early stage of unrest . . . an enthusiastic mobilization of popular appeal when the movement takes off; and a final stage of institutionalization (Manning, 1976, p. 277). David Clark, one of the movements pioneers, agreed: 'It is clear', he wrote,

> that the 'idea of the therapeutic community' as a revolutionary concept in psychiatry, in medicine and in intellectual and political thinking, has passed. . . . By the 1970's most psychiatrists were able to snuggle back into their nineteenth century identities and dismiss the therapeutic community as a 'fad that has passed'. Its days as a slogan and trail-breaking concept were over.

Yet, he added,

> The treatment method . . . remains (Clark, 1977, p. 562).

With the decline of its revolutionary aspect, the last 15 years have seen growing recognition of the therapeutic community as a treatment method used in a variety of settings. The Association of Therapeutic Communities was founded in 1972, the *International Journal of Therapeutic Communities* in 1980, and an accredited 1-year training course was launched jointly by the ATC and the Royal College of Nursing in 1986. With these developments the therapeutic community has gradually evolved from its earlier status as a radical movement to become an established method and theory of residential and day care.

THEORETICAL UNDERPINNINGS

The theoretical underpinnings of therapeutic communities derive from four main sources:

 (i) Psychoanalytic theory;
 (ii) Studies of small groups;
(iii) Studies of organizations and social systems, from both sociological and
        psychodynamic viewpoints; and
(iv) A systems view of mental illness.

Psychoanalytic theory

Although psychoanalysis is conducted in a one-to-one therapeutic situation,
many of its theories and concepts are relevant to other therapeutic contexts.
Those psychoanalysts who pioneered the therapeutic community adapted
their approach to a multi-person situation. In this chapter I will indicate
briefly some of the relevant theoretical concepts.

The creation of a free space within a structured boundary
Perhaps the most relevant aspect of psychoanalysis is not its theoretical
account of human behaviour, but this most basic aspect of the practice of
psychoanalysis. The patient is given a firm boundary of time (the beginning
and end of the session), place (like analyst's office), persons (the reliable
presence of the analyst) and task (to say whatever comes into his mind).
Within this bounded freedom, whatever the patient does or does not say can
be understood and interpreted as coming from the patient, determined by
his own thoughts and feelings. Extended to the therapeutic community, a
resident is faced with the structure of the community – the place, the staff
and other residents, the times of meetings, the various roles allocated to
people, the rules of the community. Within the limits set by this structure he
is free to participate in whichever way he chooses. He may talk. be silent,
attend meetings or avoid them, express himself in words or by actions. This
behaviour can then be understood and interpreted as coming from him, as
his response within and to the given structure. In therapeutic community
terminology this freedom is referred to as permissiveness.

   This concept provides an important theoretical distinction between a
therapeutic community and other more behavioural regimes. In the latter,
the aim of giving a resident a particular task would be to encourage his
behaviour to change in a desired direction. In a therapeutic community, the
aim of doing this would include creating a situation in which the resident's
true attitudes and feelings emerge.

   Example: A resident is given the job of helping another resident to
   prepare a meal for the community. He co-operates in a passive, bored
   way and allows some of the food to overcook. In a meeting the next day
   some members of the community complain about the food, and the
   resident's co-worker confronts him with not really trying. He replies that

he doesn't like having to play second fiddle to anyone and prefers to be able to do things on his own and in his own way. This leads on to a discussion of his general attitude towards other people.

Transference
Transference refers to the idea that the patient experiences feelings towards the therapist which belong to, and are transferred from, an earlier significant relationship. In a therapeutic community transference reactions may be experienced by a resident in a number of ways. An individual staff member or another resident may be seen as an authority figure, or imbued with the attributes of a mother or father, a brother or sister. These we may call 'two-person' transference situations. What may also occur is a transference response involving more than two people. A resident may perceive a relationship between herself and two or more others – say a staff member and another resident – in terms of an earlier set of relationships.

> *Example:* A female resident felt intensely jealous of a male patient who she felt was getting special attention from a female staff member. The situation recalled with intense vividness her feelings when an older sister to whom she had been very close had married and devoted her time to her husband.

In addition to these personal transference situations a resident may experience the community as a whole in terms of a 'transferred' relationship – e.g. as intrusive parents who want to pry into her thoughts, or as an ideal, caring family.

Defence mechanisms
Psychoanalytic theory postulates that it is human nature to seek to avoid emotional pain, such as may be caused by anger, loss, conflict or anxiety. Such pain is avoided by defence mechanisms, which are unconscious psychological techniques, acquired by all of us in childhood, for getting rid of painful feelings. A useful summary of the different types of defence mechanism is given by Brown and Pedder (1979).

Countertransference
This term refers to some of the feelings which the therapist experiences towards the patient, in particular to feelings provoked by the patient's transference towards the therapist. Thus, if the patient treats the therapist as if he were a wise, all-knowing parent, the therapist may find himself unconsciously fulfilling this role and feeling particularly competent and understanding towards the patient. The concept of countertransference has

been the subject of much debate in the psychoanalytic literature and definitions vary. In the context of therapeutic communities, it has particular relevance because staff members may experience a wide range of feelings towards residents, and they need to have some understanding of where these feelings originate from. I will return to this topic in relation to staff dynamics.

Theories of group functioning

These will not be considered in any detail and the reader is referred to other chapters for accounts of different theoretical approaches to group func- tioning. Among those which have relevance for therapeutic communities are Bion's formulation of a group's *basic assumptions*, Foulkes' conception of the *group matrix*, and the *changing role of the group conductor*, studies of *phases of group development*, the *impact of different leadership styles on groups*, and recent work on *therapeutic factors in group psychotherapy*.

Studies of organizations and social systems

These studies are relevant to therapeutic communities in a number of ways. At the risk of over-simplifying I will present them in terms of three basic findings. The interested reader is referred to original sources, and also to some useful summaries (Whiteley and Gordon, 1979; Roberts, 1980; Jones and Fowles, 1984).

Finding 1: Traditionally run institutions are harmful to patients'
social and psychological well-being
Many studies have exposed the effects of institutional life on long-term psychiatric patients. Two of the most influential have been Goffman's *Asylums* (1961) and Barton's *Institutional Neurosis* (1959). Goffman described from a sociological point of view the nature of life in what he termed a 'total institution', that is 'a place of residence and work where a large number of like-situated individuals, cut off from the wider society for an appreciable period of time, together lead an enclosed, formally administered round of life'. Among other things he drew attention to 'batch living' where 'each phase of the member's daily activity is carried on in the immediate company of a large batch of others, all of whom are treated alike and required to do the same thing together' (Goffman, 1961, p. 17). Barton, a psychiatrist, addressed the psychological consequences of living in such conditions and identified a disease which he termed 'institutional neurosis', the clinical features of which included apathy, lack of initiative, loss of interest in the outside world, submissiveness and resignation. These and other studies provided overwhelming evidence that the traditional ways of

running psychiatric hospitals should be replaced by ways which preserve patients' individuality and independence.

Finding 2: Staff behaviour and expectations have a powerful impact on patients' level of functioning

Several studies have examined the connection between staff behaviour and expectations and the behaviour of patients. One example is the work of Stanton and Schwartz (1954), who found that covert disagreements between staff in a mental hospital ward could result in a collective disturbance among the patients. More recently, Miller and Gwynne (1972), in their excellent study of residential institutions for the physically handicapped, have contrasted two sets of staff expectations regarding the potential of inmates to care for themselves. These they term the 'warehousing model' and the 'horticultural model'. In the former the staff see their primary task as prolonging physical life and pay little attention to the psychological needs of patients. In the latter they see their main task as developing residents' unfulfilled capacities. Not surprisingly, residents in institutions run on 'horticultural' lines were generally less dependent and more actively involved in running their own lives than residents in 'warehousing' institutions. The authors make the point that both models can be misapplied, and that both may represent an avoidance of patients' real needs for a mixture of dependence and independence. An interesting line of research by Caine *et al.* (1981) has shown that attitudes to treatment are related to other more fundamental attitudes such as conservatism and direction of interests, and that this is true both for staff and patients. This suggests that attitudes to treatment may be difficult to change and that treatment approaches such as the therapeutic community may be most effective when the selection of staff and patients take such attitudes into account.

Finding 3: The unconscious group dynamics within the staff team can have a powerful impact on individual staff members and on the organization as a whole

Unconscious mechanisms of defence against anxiety and conflict operate powerfully among groups of people faced with difficult, stressful responsibilities. Menzies' (1960) classic study of staff in a general hospital demonstrated how the allocation of tasks to junior staff was designed to protect them from becoming emotionally involved with patients, and therefore from all the concerns and anxieties that this might give rise to. Similarly, anxieties over assuming responsibility for decisions were avoided by passing responsibility up the hierarchy – an avoidance colluded in by both junior and senior nursing staff. Menzies identified a number of ways in which the social system of the hospital served as a defence against anxiety, but in so doing also robbed staff of the opportunity for more meaningful involvement in their work. Junior staff of high ability became disillusioned at the lack of freedom to make decisions. Thus the defence which worked at one level – protecting staff from anxiety – failed at another – losing able staff from the profession.

Whereas Menzies studied a large staff organization, Main (1957) studied the dynamics within a small, well-trained team of psychiatric nurses. He noticed how even within such a team certain dynamics may occur which impair staff functioning. These dynamics can centre around patients who come to be regarded as 'special' by the staff. Such a patient may split the staff into those who feel she is just playing up and needs a firm approach, and those who feel she is misjudged and misunderstood. Each side regards the others as misguided. When carried to extremes, this division may lead to a breakdown in communication between staff and even to staff resignations. Main's way of tackling these difficult situations was to set up a discussion group with nursing staff to enable them gradually to acknowledge and discuss these splits within the staff group.

In addition to impairing staff morale and working relationships, collective group processes may sometimes jeopardize the existence of an entire ward, unit or community. This can occur when the members of a community become so convinced of the correctness of their own approach that all criticism from outside is ignored. This process can act as a defence against acknowledging doubts, difficulties or internal conflicts within the community. Such idealization cannot last indefinitely and sooner or later it is resolved either in a constructive or destructive way for the community concerned. Hobson (1979) has described the stages in this process in terms of a 'therapeutic community disease'. Roberts (1980) has enumerated a range of destructive group processes which may occur in therapeutic communities.

Our awareness of these processes poses the question, are therapeutic communities potentially harmful? The answer is probably that any form of treatment that uses the spontaneous events arising in a community is using powerful forces that can have a negative as well as a positive effect. Awareness of their potential negative effects indicates that therapeutic communities are no longer idealized as the answer to all institutional problems. They generate their own problems which are now beginning to be better understood. Properly organized and run, however, therapeutic communities have demonstrated their effectiveness in the treatment of personality disorder (Whiteley, 1970; Copas *et al.*, 1984) behaviour disorder (Miles, 1969), chronic neurosis (Caine and Smail, 1969), drug dependency (Wilson, 1978; Wilson and Mandlebrote, 1985) and schizophrenia (Mosher *et al.*, 1975).

A short note on systems theory

Implicit in the therapeutic community, and in much of the literature cited above, is the idea that the individual members of a group, community or institution can be regarded as the connected parts of a system. In fact, a hierarchy of social systems can be seen as extending from the individual to his immediate family group, to the wider groups of which he is a member (school or workplace, neighbourhood, club, etc.) on to his membership of religious, class or ethnic groups and eventually the whole society to which he belongs. A number of significant concepts flow from this theory, one of which is the view that mental illness is located not primarily *within* an individual but in the network of relationships of which he is a part. For a useful, readable summary of systems theory applied to the therapeutic context, the reader is recommended to read Skynner (1976).

A systems view of mental illness

In the medical tradition, illness is seen as occurring within an individual – a defect or malfunction in some part of the individual's physical or mental apparatus. Individual therapies often maintain this view and attention is focused solely on the individual, or includes others simply as informants or supporters of the treatment regime. From a systems viewpoint, mental disorder is regarded primarily as a social or interpersonal phenomenon, occurring between a person and those with whom he relates. This view of mental illness has, perhaps, been most widely accepted in the field of family therapy (Minuchin, 1974; Skynner, 1976). It also underlies the work of Foulkes (1964), one of the early therapeutic community pioneers who subsequently developed the method of group analysis and whose ideas are well summarized by Pines (1983). Anticipating by some years the application of systems theory in psychiatry, Foulkes regarded the individual as fundamentally part of a social network, as closely linked with it as are the neurones in the individual's central nervous system. He used the image of a 'nodal point' to describe the position of the individual in a communicating network. The healthy individual receives and responds to communication in an open, non-distorting way as does the healthy neurone. By contrast, 'The neurotic position in its very nature is highly individualistic. It is group disruptive in essence for it is the result of an incompatibility between the individual and his original group' (quoted in Pines, 1983, p. 269).

To Foulkes the neurotic is someone who has become isolated from his social network, and the object of treatment is, therefore, to create a situation in which free, open communication can once again be established. Group therapy and therapeutic communities flow naturally from this view.

Foulkes' view of the way group therapy works is worth stating here: 'The deepest reason why patients can reinforce each other's normal reactions and wear down and correct each other's neurotic reactions is that collectively they constitute the very norm from which individually they deviate' (quoted in Pines, 1983, p. 271). Groups, when they are freely interacting (an important proviso) are healthier than their individual neurotic members. Through group participation the disturbed individual gradually moves from his isolated position and idiosyncratic norms towards the healthier, collective norm of the group. In this context, the main task of the group leader is to promote and maintain a group culture of free, and open communication.

ELEMENTS OF PRACTICE

Some definitions

The rest of this chapter deals with the practicalities of running and working in a therapeutic community. It may be helpful to begin by defining some common terms and principles. One source of misunderstanding can come from terms similar to 'therapeutic community', which itself is often used rather loosely. I shall try briefly to differentiate some of these terms.

'Community psychiatry' refers to the provision of psychiatric facilities within the communities where people live rather than in designed environments away from their homes. 'Social or milieu therapy' refers to the general use of the hospital environment and its activities as a mode of treatment, including a range of social and work activities designed to provide hospital patients with purposeful activity. 'Therapeutic community' refers to a residential or day-care setting (either hospital or non-hospital) in which the *group experience itself* becomes therapeutic for the clients involved.

Kennard (1983, pp. 6–7) has distinguished between 'four broad but distinct ways in which the term therapeutic community is used':

(i) Institutions for the chronic mentally ill which have introduced more active, caring regimes where the rights and dignity of inmates are recognized and respected. The role of the staff changes from being mainly custodial towards creating an atmosphere in which inmates are trusted and encouraged to take responsiblity and initiative.

(ii) Small, cohesive communities where therapeutic decisions and functions are shared by the whole community and status differences between staff and residents are greatly reduced though not abandoned. These are sometimes known as the Maxwell Jones type of community, after his influential work at the Henderson Hospital. Most therapeutic communities within the NHS, Social Services and therapeutic education are of this type.

(iii) Communities mainly concerned with the rehabilitation of drug addicts. Although similar to democratic-analytic communities, described in (ii) above in their use of peer group support and pressure, they differ in having a clear hierarchy or chain of command within the resident group, making explicit use of social rewards and sanctions, and often employing former addicts as staff members.

(iv) A range of alternatives to mental hospital, usually centring around a particular faith or philosophy of life, rejecting conventional labels such as 'patient', 'staff' and 'illness', and emphasizing the equality of all members. Such communities were associated with the anti-psychiatry movement of the 1960s. Communities which offer alternative asylum may, in practice, merge into alternative life-style communities.

Four guiding principles

In his sociological study of Henderson Hospital, Rapaport (1960) identified four ideological themes that characterized the beliefs of the unit's staff. These themes have since become widely quoted as guiding principles for therapeutic community workers.

(i) 'Democratization' refers to the view that each member of the community should share equally in the exercise of power in decision-making about community affairs – both therapeutic and administrative.

(ii) 'Permissiveness' refers to the belief that a therapeutic community should function with all its members tolerating from one another a wide degree of behaviour that might be distressing or seem deviant according to 'ordinary' norms. Ideally this should allow both for individuals freely to expose their behavioural difficulties and for others to react freely to this, so that the uses for both sides of social relationship patterns can be examined.

(iii) 'Reality-confrontation' refers to the belief that patients should be continuously presented with interpretations of their behaviour as it is seen by most others, in order to counteract tendencies to use massive denial, distortion, withdrawal or other mechanisms that interfere with the capacity to relate to others in the normal world.

(iv) 'Communalism' refers to the belief that a therapeutic community should be characterized by tight-knit sets of relationships, sharing of amenities, informality (e.g. use of first names) and freeing-up of communication.

The goals of a therapeutic community

These can be divided into those which concern the unit or institution as a whole and those which concern the individual patient, resident or client. The goals for a particular unit or institution usually have to do with making it a more effective therapeutic environment. In the much quoted sentence of Maxwell Jones, 'What distinguishes a therapeutic community from other comparable treatment centres is the way in which the institution's total resources, staff, and patients, and their relatives are self-consciously pooled in furthering treatment' (Jones, 1968, p. 85). From this point of view, the goals of a therapeutic community include:

   (i) Attempting to understand and resolve group tensions within the institution.
  (ii) Creating a more democratic structure, delegating power and responsibility down to ward or unit level.
 (iii) Fostering open communication between staff, and improving the flow of information upwards and downwards.
 (iv) Setting up regular meetings in which roles, relationships and attitudes are examined.
  (v) Maintaining staff learning and morale through continuing support, supervision and training.

For further discussion of this aspect of therapeutic community goals, the reader is recommended to read Clark (1965) and Ahlin (1981).

Regarding goals for the individual, Main wrote that a therapeutic community has 'the immediate aim of full participation of all its members in its daily life and the eventual aim of the resocialization of the neurotic individual for life in ordinary society' (Main, 1946, p. 67). While this still stands as a broad definition of goals, subsequent developments have seen therapeutic communities created for people with different needs and therefore pursuing different goals. A good example of this differentiation of goals is provided by Blake *et al.* (1984), who describe three levels or models of therapeutic community day care. These they term the resocializing (supportive) model, the re-educative model and the reconstructive model. Each caters for a different client group, ranging from those with chronic psychosis controlled by medication to those with personality disorders and chronic neuroses, and each pursues different tasks or goals. Between them, these models reflect a hierarchy of goals which may be summarized as follows:

   (i) Encouraging motivation and initiative, reducing dependency on services, breaking the re-admission cycle.

(ii) Enabling the individual to establish a sense of personal identity.
(iii) Enabling the individual to acquire a sense of responsibility for his behaviour and its effect on others.
(iv) Increasing self-awareness and self-understanding.
(v) Increasing social competence.

Selection
Many therapeutic communities conduct a selection procedure in which a potential new member spends a day or more in the community so that a mutual choice can be made about the candidate's suitability for admission. In general, suitability is likely to depend less on the particular symptoms of the individual and more on his attitudes towards treatment and helping relationships. Caine and Smail (1969) found that patients who benefited from a therapeutic community placed more emphasis on the importance of relationships formed within the hospital and less emphasis (when compared with those in conventional settings) on physical treatment, discipline and the power of staff. Smith *et al.* (1980), reviewing research on the outcome of therapeutic communities, concluded that therapeutic community treatment compared favourably with traditional psychiatric treatment for patients who already had some capacity for social involvement. Those who adopted the community ideology, participated actively and formed close relationships were those who improved.

From these studies, it seems likely that the following criteria are relevant to assessing suitability for treatment in a therapeutic community:

(i) Some initial capacity for social involvement.
(ii) Seeing personal relationships rather than drugs or impersonal techniques as the most valuable source of help.
(iii) Willingness to acknowledge and talk about emotional problems with other patients in a group setting.
(iv) Preferring informal, democratic staff-patient relationships.

Components of the programme

Although therapeutic communities vary a good deal in their clientele and goals, there are certain basic components which are necessary to create the dynamics of a therapeutic community.

Community meetings
These are at best held daily and at least once a week, and should involve all patient and staff members of the community. The community meeting is the

hub of a therapeutic community and has both an administrative and therapeutic function. Administratively, information and problems affecting the community as a whole can be shared and discussed. Therapeutically, meetings can explore recent events or disturbances in the community and the individuals concerned can be presented with the effects of their behaviour on others, with efforts to modify behaviour or attitudes through giving feedback, reality confrontation, and using the pressure of the patient's peer group to bring about change.

A third function of the community meeting, although less visible, is no less important. The meeting provides a sense of cohesion, togetherness or 'we-ness' for the members of the community. Even passive attendance allows the individual to experience himself as part of a community which has shared interests and concerns. Simply by being there each member becomes part of the communication network which is the prerequisite of treatment.

In practice, these different functions – administrative, therapeutic, cohesion building – may blend together, as shown in this example taken from Main (1975, pp. 84–5):

> A woman patient cautiously asked the group to formulate a view about behaviour at night in the corridors. . . . The group split into those who were and were not in favour of making rules. Ideas and arguments about designating 'quiet areas' arose. Respecting the rights of others and society's needs for defences against anarchy took the topic into abstract levels. . . . The original speaker and her request became ignored. Many grew silent. Eventually, an intervenor addressed the first speaker, and said surely, her's was not an academic question. What had happened at night to lead to the question? Could it be spoken about?
>
> Well, the speaker's child had been woken by 'people' talking on the corridor at 10 pm last night and it had taken an hour to get him to sleep. People? Could she mention names? Well, she didn't want to cause trouble. Others murmured their support of her keeping the issues anonymous. Now, several speakers declared their personal innocence and indignant sympathy for the mother. Eventually, a pressurizing silence arose as if in wait for a sinner to confess. The intervenor said if she had been one of the night-time talkers, she couldn't possibly say so now, because the group was somehow now making a Federal offence out of a bit of ordinary carelessness. She had herself sometimes forgotten to keep quiet outside a child's room and she couldn't promise to be perfect in future but she would try. Was it a hanging matter? One or two others said that they too had sometimes forgotten to be quiet in the corridors. Two patients said they thought it must have been them. They had forgotten about the child and hadn't realised it until this meeting. The mother smiled grimly and said she knew it was them but hadn't liked to say so (although she had met them that morning). She had been furious last night. There was some laughter and more apologies. Individuals had emerged. The group's heat about general moral issues vanished and discussion moved on to another topic, with members again in possession of themselves and relating to others.

A structured day
In addition to community meetings, the therapeutic community should

include a daily structure of activities which usually includes small group meetings, work activities, and other events/activities/groups designed to facilitate involvement and interaction. These can include, for example, special groups for newcomers or leavers, art therapy, psychodrama, family groups, patients' committees, etc. All these groups and activities provide opportunities for patients to become involved in the affairs of the community and to work on their own particular problems and difficulties. The existence of such a structured programme provides the necessary framework within which patients' difficulties in coping with every day relationships and situations are more likely to emerge than in an unstructured *laissez-faire* environment.

Roles and responsibilities

A range of roles should be available for patients to take on. These may vary, according to the capacities and readiness of the individual patients and also the community as a whole, from fairly simple domestic and self-catering tasks through to increasing levels of responsibility in the day-to-day running and management of the community. The demands and rewards of different roles provide opportunities for patients to practice different social skills, to gain feedback from others, and to learn about themselves. More will be said about patient roles below.

Informal relationships

Alongside the structured programme of activities, and the performance of roles, patients and staff are also able to get to know each other on an informal and equal basis. Coping with unstructured time and informal relationships provides additional opportunities for interpersonal learning. Important occurrences can be fed back into group meetings for discussion. The example of a community meeting quoted above demonstrates the way in which this may be done and the value of it for modifying feelings and attitudes.

Staff meetings

These are an essential part of the therapeutic community and usually fall into two types. *Staff reviews* take place after each community meeting and also after other groups and activities. They provide an opportunity for staff members to go over the events of the preceding group, to explore its underlying dynamics, to understand the roles of different participants – both staff and patients – and to provide mutual support between staff. *Sensitivity meetings*, as they are often called, usually take place once a week. These provide an opportunity for staff to focus on their own experiences and anxieties, to acknowledge tensions or difficulties within the staff group or in the therapeutic community as a whole and to attempt to understand and resolve these. Even if only partly successful, the commitment to such a process is essential if destructive processes which may occur (see above) are not to undermine staff morale and effectiveness.

Staff roles

The roles of the staff member of the therapeutic community can be described under three headings: (1) participating as a member of the community; (2) facilitating others' participation in the community – both patients and staff; (3) intervening in small and large group meetings. Only large groups will be considered here because the role of the small group leader is considered elsewhere in this book.

Participating as a member of the community
As well as being a therapist, the staff member is also a *member* of the therapeutic community, participating in informal social activities and relationships, e.g. helping to prepare a meal or dig the garden. In so doing, staff members can help to break down the therapist–patient barrier and reinforce the principles of democratization and communalism. Patients do not have to 'look up to' staff as superior beings but can see them as ordinary people, skilled, caring, but not super-competent or all-knowing. At the same time patients can learn to see themselves as potentially competent and skilful in doing certain things for themselves and others. There is no unbridgeable gap between the competencies of staff and patients.

In addition to demonstrating potential equality of competence, staff members also share many of their personal feelings and responses, both in informal social situations and in group meetings. They may acknowledge feelings of insecurity or anxiety, enabling patients to see that these are universal experiences not confined to people labelled as 'patients'. A common defence in many psychiatric settings is for staff to present themselves as free of personal problems while patients present themselves as lacking in any personal strengths. By showing themselves as human beings with both strengths and weaknesses, the staff allow patients to do the same. Again there is no unbridgeable gap between people who can understand and help others and people who need help and understanding.

This aspect of the staff role requires staff who have a personal preference for, and are comfortable with, natural intimate staff–patient interactions, rather than more formal, distant relations. There is, however, a limit to this breaking down of barriers and it is important that staff members recognize this. The purpose of the therapeutic community is a therapeutic one, and as in any form of therapy, the therapist needs to maintain a distinction between relationships which are intended to be therapeutic and relationships which are intended to meet his or her own personal needs. The informality of relationships in a therapeutic community can make this distinction a difficult one to maintain. This difficulty underlines the importance of honest self-analysis and feeding back information about relationships into the community.

Facilitating others' participation in the therapeutic community
This aspect of the staff members' role includes a number of elements.

(a) Modelling. Much of what has just been said can be seen as modelling desired behaviour. If staff members are open and honest about their own feelings, this can provide an example for patients to follow. Similarly, if staff show that they are willing to take risks, e.g. by trying to do something that they are not confident about (such as taking part in a football match), this makes it easier for others to take similar risks.

(b) Maintaining the structure and boundaries of the community. In order for a therapeutic community to function effectively, it is important that the structure of meetings, activities, decision-making processes, etc., are clearly maintained. If staff indulge in lateness, unexplained absences, or other behaviour inconsistent with the ethos of the community, then patients' behaviour can no longer be examined in relation to the community's norms and expectations because these will have become unclear. From this point of view, working in a therapeutic community demands a high level of commitment and self-discipline on the part of its staff.

(c) Allowing others to take responsibility. An important part of the staff's role is knowing when to take the lead and when to stand back and allow others to have a go. Activities may often be more efficient in the short term if led by the staff – but if the ultimate goal is to help others become more competent then this requires staff to tolerate inefficiency in the short term.

(d) Interpreting the meaning of behaviour. The activities and roles within a therapeutic community provide a framework within which patients' emotional difficulties often emerge through their behaviour. For example, failure to carry out an agreed task may express a patient's difficulty in relating with others. Enabling the patient to acknowledge and explore this is one of the key therapeutic tasks of the community. At moments of crisis, a special meeting may be called so that those involved can share their feelings

and give feedback to one another. Often the work of interpreting the meaning of a particular piece of behaviour can be undertaken by the patients themselves. At other times this may need to be done by staff members.

(e) Awareness of potential destructive processes. The powerful group forces operating within a therapeutic community can have destructive as well as beneficial consequences. Staff need to be aware of these, especially in the way they may affect particular individuals. One of the most common risks is that of scapegoating, where a particular individual is singled out as the source of the community's current difficulties. 'If it weren't for him', people say, 'everyone here would be a lot happier.' While such a person may have a talent for attracting such rejection it is likely that they are displaying behaviour or attitudes that others have also experienced. It is important that staff recognize such group processes and enable people to acknowledge those aspects of themselves that they are projecting into the scapegoat.

(f) Explaining the therapeutic community rationale. Although a therapeutic community is best understood by living in one, it is important that those whose contact with it is brief (e.g. visitors, students, patients' relatives, other professionals involved with a patient, administrators) are helped to make sense of what they see. First impressions can often be disquieting, especially to those accustomed to more traditional treatment settings. An insular attitude on the part of staff is likely to render the therapeutic community's task more difficult by alienating outsiders. Some early therapeutic communities paid the price for this insular attitude and were closed partly because administrators would not support their innovative procedures. Today, therapeutic communities seem to have learned the lesson, and many excel in good public relations.

Skills of intervention in community meetings

The functions of community meetings (see above) and the dynamics of large groups require a somewhat different approach to that of the small group facilitator. In the example of a community meeting given earlier, the helpful intervention was not a direct interpretation of behaviour, nor a confrontation of those members who had been thoughtless, but simply a sharing of ordinary human fallibility. The combination of ordinariness (rather than cleverness) and self-disclosure rather than focusing on others enabled people to come forward who might otherwise have stayed silent.

Large, unstructured group meetings readily produce in their members feelings of frustration, ineptitude, fears of looking foolish or that 'something awful' will happen. Feelings and opinions can easily become polarized into 'us' and 'them'. These dynamics, and their underlying mechanisms, are well described by Main (1975, p. 57–86) in the chapter from which the example has been taken. In the writer's own experience, every large group meeting repeats a journey from anxious anonymity towards regaining a sense of one's personal identity through the recognition that others are individuals very like oneself. Such a journey may be facilitated or impeded by the interventions made by individuals. The frequent use of questions, interpretations, advice, etc., tend to emphasize the separateness of the speaker and thereby to reinforce the sense of isolation which members feel. A particular trap described by Main is what he calls 'Nobel-Prize' thinking, which stems from the belief that any utterance must be supremely wise and clever if it is to be made in such a large group. In reality, it is the ordinary every day thoughts which reduce the sense of distance and isolation and enable others to begin contributing. Once a large group meeting is 'on its way' and members are contributing freely and spontaneously, then other processes – feedback, confrontations, interpretations – may be used to good effect.

Residents' roles[1]

Residents in a therapeutic community have a number of potential roles. These can be divided into those which belong to all residents, and those which are allocated to individuals. Underlying these various roles is the more fundamental one of becoming an active, involved participant in the life of the community. In the following breakdown of different roles I have drawn on the work of Reda (1985) and Manor (1982).

Roles common to all residents
Residents may be seen as having three basic roles

(a) Therapeutic role. All residents are expected to discuss their problems and feelings and also to discuss other members' problems and to give feedback about each others' behaviour. Often, residents may be in a better position than staff to interpret or confront a fellow resident's behaviour

---

[1] The terms 'patient', 'resident' and 'client', are used interchangeably in this chapter. Preference for one term or another tends to vary between settings and also according to the significance attached to the implications of different terms. Many feel that the term 'patient' implies a passive subordinate role and prefer the term 'resident'. In the writer's view, the terms are what you make of them. Patients can be active or passive, residents can be independent or patronized.

because of their capacity to identify with that resident. Open and honest expression of feelings is perhaps the most basic expectation of the resident's role.

(b) Socializing role. Residents are expected to socialize with other community members outside group meetings and to participate in social gatherings. The introduction and drawing in of new or relatively isolated residents is seen very much as a task of residents rather than staff. In this way it is residents who play the major role in passing on the norms and values of the community.

(c) Decision making role. All residents have the right to vote or express opinions on a range of issues. These can include activities on the unit, dealing with rule breaking and acting-out behaviour, selecting new admissions and considering a resident's readiness for leaving. By taking part in such decisions residents can acquire a greater sense of social responsibility, and that they have to accept the consequences of a decision. Delegating decisions to residents does not mean that staff abdicate their own responsibilities. It is for staff to judge whether the community will benefit, or at least not suffer from a particular decision, and that the residents who made it will gain some learning experience as a result.

Roles allocated to individual residents

A variety of tasks are allocated to individual residents, often by a vote at a community meeting. Some of these tasks involve an element of leadership, such as chairing the community meeting, organizing sport activities, acting as a workshop leader or ward representative, etc. Other tasks involve carrying out 'service' jobs such as cooking, cleaning, shopping, etc. Manor (1977) has suggested that the most useful roles are those which he terms 'creative posts', such as ward representatives or workshop leader, which attract positive reward when tasks are accomplished for the community or a fellow patient has been helped.

Group development over time

Phases of group development are probably most easily observed in small closed groups which begin and end with the same members. Therapeutic communities consist of a large number of patients and staff, and are open in the sense that there is a continual turnover of both, although slower in the case of staff than patients. This means that at any given time individuals will be at different stages in their relationships within the community, and no overall sequence of beginning, middle and end stages may be observed. However, in his study of Henderson Hospital, Rapaport (1960) reported a recurring oscillation between equilibrium and disorganization. Although stated as an hypothesis rather than a reliable finding, a number of subsequent studies have tended to confirm his description (Trauer, 1983). Of particular interest is the changing role of the staff according to the needs of each phase and the reader is recommended to read the original account (Rapaport, 1960, pp. 134–42). A brief summary of the four phases will be given here.

During the first phase the patients are behaving in accordance with the expectations and ideals of the community. There is little deviant behaviour and the staff feel confident to delegate responsibilities and adopt a permissive attitude. The atmosphere is a relaxed one that fosters trust. This is the phase of relative equilibrium. In the second phase the more 'constructive' patients are discharged and replaced by new patients with disruptive tendencies. Because the climate is still one of permissive tolerance, acting-out is permitted and tension begins to rise. Not to be out-done, older patients may also begin to act-out. Increasing tension leads to increasing anxiety and defensiveness. This is manifested in falling attendance at groups, less participation, more guarded communication. The atmosphere is one of the increasing inhibition and distrust.

In the third phase tension reaches a point where something must be done to safeguard both individuals and the community itself. Typically, the turning point is an event which so threatens the unit (e.g. external complaints about residents' behaviour, an attempted suicide in the unit) that the staff feel it necessary and justified to suspend the norms of democratization and permissiveness. They invoke their latent authority to discharge or transfer patients judged to be untreatable or in need of more 'medical' care. Following this 'pruning' process the fourth phase is one of rebuilding the norms of the community. The staff and remaining patients may feel guilty for the authoritarian measures taken and for the acting-out that made them necessary. Wishing to repair the damage everyone works hard to re-establish an atmosphere that will again allow permissiveness and democratization to be used. As constructive patients begin to speak up and participation improves the first phase is gradually regained.

Mechanisms of change

Despite a fairly large literature over the last 40 years describing various processes in a therapeutic community, our understanding of the mechanisms of change – how the therapeutic community works – has received relatively little attention. The one finding which has emerged most clearly is that participation leads to improvement. In their review of research into the outcome of therapeutic communities, Smith *et al.*, concluded that:

> Therapeutic community treatment appears to compare favourably with tradi-
> tional psychiatric treatment, at least for those patients who already have some
> capacity for social involvement. Those patients who adopt the community
> ideology, participate actively in the community, and form close relationships, are
> those who improve (Smith *et al.*, 1980, p. 128).

What is less clear is how this process works. How exactly does participation lead to improvement? Manor (1982) has suggested that for certain patients taking a particular role, e.g. Community Chairman, can be an effective way of changing a patient's self-image. Responding to others' expectations and feedback, the patient receives confirmation of hitherto untested aspects of his personality – e.g. being able to take responsiblity, exercise power, show caring for others. In the words of a former Henderson patient: 'Bit by bit, almost grudgingly, the fact dawned on me I wasn't surrounded by forty sticks of furniture but by Jim, Gary, Jane. . . . I cared for them. . . . I had helped them' (Mahony, 1979, p. 85). This mechanism of change is explicitly sought in the hierarchical ex-addict communities, where residents are encouraged to assume responsible roles on an 'act as if' basis. The assumption is that by acting in a responsible or caring way, the appropriate changes in feeling, attitude and self-concept will follow. It seems likely that while this can be a powerful mechanism for change it does not necessarily work for all residents. Those who reject the norms of the community are unlikely to benefit in this way.

A widely used approach to studying the mechanisms of change in group therapy has been the concept of therapeutic factors (Yalom, 1975). This approach has only recently begun to be applied to therapeutic communities. Using a method devised by Bloch *et al.* (1979). Whiteley and Collis (1987) asked residents to describe what had been the 'most important event' in their treatment during the preceding week. The results suggest that two types of event – those classified as 'learning from interpersonal action' and 'self-understanding' – appear to be equally important in out-patient groups and a therapeutic community. Nor surprisingly, events classified as 'acceptance by others' emerge as particularly important to new residents in a therapeutic community. Perhaps the most revealing finding was that only half the most important events took place in formal group meetings. The rest occurred in informal social situations with other residents or a mixed group of residents and staff.

Whiteley and Collis note that the therapeutic community 'has similarities with those methods of family therapy in which group meetings at spaced intervals allow the participants to work on the problems outside the formal group, in the system of the family.' They conclude that:

what the therapeutic community has to offer, which circumscribed group therapy does not, is the opportunity to put into practice the insights or realisations gained in therapy and to experiment with new roles and modes of coping in an accepting and understanding social system (Whiteley and Collis, 1987, pp. 11–12).

In addition to understanding how individuals change, any complete account of how therapeutic communities work must also include the way in which the norms of the community are maintained. The goals of a therapeutic community are directed not only towards the resocialization of its individual members, but also to the preservation of the community as a positive, therapeutic environment.

Almond *et al.* (1969) have proposed a model of change which takes this into account. Following a detailed research study they concluded that two parallel processes occur in a therapeutic community. One is the socialization of the new members into the community, leading to behaviour change and ultimately to clinical improvement. The second is the process of what they call 'acculturation' in which patients accept the values of the community, emphasizing openness, responsibility and joining in. They argue that this value change is not necessary to a patient's individual improvement but is necessary to the maintenance of the community's cohesion and effectiveness. It is because they have acquired the community's values that older residents play an active part in drawing in and socializing new members.

A similar model has been suggested by Clark (1967), in which patients initially become involved in social activities and dyadic relationships, move on to adopt a favourable attitude towards the unit, and then become fully involved in the formal group meetings which leads to improvement. This model is consistent with Whiteley and Collis's finding that for new members the most important events are those which indicate acceptance by the community (through social activities and dyadic relationships), whereas for older residents the most important events are those which derive from full involvement in the community.

Schematically, the models of change outlined above may be combined as shown in Fig. 8.1.

Typical problems and their solution

The sections above dealing with destructive processes and oscillations give a general idea of the naturally occurring problems which are part of the therapeutic community process. In this section I would like to give more concrete examples of problems and how they may be tackled. It should be noted that apparently different problems may arise because of certain dynamics operating in a community at a particular time. For example,

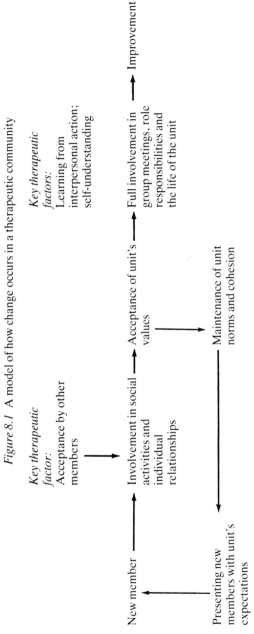

Figure 8.1 A model of how change occurs in a therapeutic community

during a phase of disintegration the weakening of the community's sustaining culture may be associated with a number of different problems. During such a phase the resolution of problems may call for different measures than during periods when the community is functioning well. Having made this general point let me describe three common problem areas.

Leadership, communication and morale within the staff team

Problems in these areas are by no means unique to therapeutic communities, but may be heightened because of the greater demands placed on the staff – both emotional and organizational – when compared with more conventional settings. Therapeutic communities require leaders, but leaders who are sensitive to the needs of the community and can adjust their leadership style accordingly. Democratic, non-directive leadership is appropriate when the community is functioning well and staff and residents are able to share responsibilities in a constructive way. Even when anxieties are raised, democratic leadership may allow community members to work this through and find solutions to problems. Authoritative, containing leadership is appropriate when anxiety is such that individuals' effectiveness at solving problems has been severely reduced, or when serious incidents of acting out are being ignored. Being capable of both styles of leadership, and judging which to use when, it not an easy task. A therapeutic community, particularly in its formative stages, may run into problems when staff leaders cling to either the authoritative or democratic model regardless of the state of the community.

An example of the first situation is when the doctor on a therapeutic community ward insists on seeing patients individually or continues to make unilateral decisions regarding treatment, or when a senior nurse issues a written instruction to staff after a complaint is made by a visitor. In both cases the staff leader, anxious about discharging her responsibilities properly and about potential (or actual) criticism from colleagues or superiors, fails to trust and use the group process within the staff. Sometimes the leaders do not attend staff meetings regularly, so that the staff's frustration and the leader's isolation increase over time. The answer to this situation is more obvious than it is easy. Unless staff leaders attend staff meetings and decision making is shared among the staff group, or delegated by mutual agreement, a therapeutic community will be one in name only. It may also be necessary for other staff members to examine their own attitudes towards decision making, which they may have avoided. If, however, repeated attempts to involve staff leaders in staff groups fail, it is likely either that the individual(s) concerned, or the system within which they operate, are unable to tolerate a therapeutic community, and a wider reappraisal of objectives is needed.

In the second situation the staff leaders may be committed to therapeutic community principles, so much so that all matters are decided by the community. While the community is functioning responsibly all is well and cohesion and morale are high. But the desire to preserve this sense of cohesion and harmony may lead to a denial of difficulties or problems, or the failure to question an unwise decision. In this situation the leaders may be failing in their job of ensuring that the community survives, and survives as an effective therapeutic community. Examples of such situations can include the decision to give responsibility to an untrustworthy resident, failing to challenge persistent lateness, ignoring indications that a staff member or resident may be abusing drugs or alcohol, not following up complaints from outside that residents have been seen breaking the law or behaving anti-socially.

Avoidance of areas of potential disagreement or conflict within the community may be associated with a tendency on the part of the staff team, and especially on the part of its leaders to 'idealize' their community. Hobson (1979) has described this as the 'therapeutic community disease' in which members see their way as 'right', and any outside criticism as arising from ignorance or envy. Unchecked, the course of this 'disease' can lead eventually to disillusion or catastrophe when events force staff members to recognize that the community has fallen short of its ideal. This can be an extremely painful realization, the more so the greater the preceding idealization. Such a scenario may be avoided if the staff, particularly staff leaders, can sustain honest self-analysis of their attitudes and feelings, can recognize and discuss splits and disagreements within the staff group, and can sanction appropriate shifts in leadership style when processes within or outside the community pose serious threats to its work.

In addition to a whole unit being threatened by idealization, individual staff members may also suffer as a consequence of excessive idealism and commitment. Valuable in moderate measure, overcommitment may lead to undernourishment of the staff members' own needs, and eventually to what has been called 'staff burn out'. Long-term therapeutic community staff must learn to care for themselves as well as their clients, a point made by Meinrath and Roberts (1982) in their well-titled paper, 'On being a good enough staff member'.

Clique formation and pairing
Therapeutic communities give rise naturally to a range of informal pairings and sub-groups. When these are 'fed back' into the community and openly discussed they can provide opportunities for sharing and learning that are an

integral part of therapy. New or vulnerable members may seek to create exclusive relationships in order to protect themselves from what they perceive as threatening scrutiny and pressure by the community. When a community is functioning well such fears can be sensitively handled by more experienced patients. Rapaport provides an illuminating example of this:

> A newly arrived homosexual patient suddenly announced to a few of his wardmates that he could not tolerate the Unit any longer and planned to leave immediately, refusing to give his reasons or to discuss his feelings with anyone. A day before his departure, one of the ward leaders (a fellow patient) approached him and said that his decision to leave would upset and discourage others in the ward, as he was so generally liked. After discussing the possible effects of his departure, he confided to the leader that he had fallen in love with another male patient and was reluctant to speak about it for fear of being rejected by this patient and by the entire community. His fear had mounted to the point where he could not even tolerate the thought of discussing his problem at the community meeting or with the patient he was fond of. The leader promised that he would not make the situation public without his consent. However, he asked the homosexual patient whether he objected to his discussing the matter with the other involved and then, if he agreed, to bring the matter before the group. After successfully completing his mission as an intermediary, the leader spoke about the affair at the community meeting the following day. Here it was handled sympathetically and served to encourage other patients who had experienced (or were experiencing) similar problems to speak up. The reaction of the group enabled the fearful patient to talk about his feelings and remain in the Unit. It also facilitated the handling of ward problems created by homosexual attachments (Rapaport, 1960, pp. 156–7).

An important point to note about this example is that the patient was not forced or bullied into conforming at once to community norms regarding openness, but was enabled to get there by the sympathetic encouragement of someone he could trust and who showed he respected the patient's concerns about rejection. Therapeutic communities, in their enthusiasm (and idealization) can sometimes become insensitive to anxieties about rejection or humiliation that new members may face. While maintaining a sensitive approach, it is equally important not to collude with such anxieties to the extent of offering assurances of confidentiality, a position which inexperienced staff members sometimes adopt in the belief that in this way they can help an anxious patient who is afraid of taking his problem to the group. Such collusion usually occurs when the staff member shares some of the patient's anxiety about the community. The example above, and the earlier one of a community meeting, both demonstrate how a sensitive, supportive intervention can lead an individual through his or her fears into a frank discussion of shared feelings and problems with the rest of the community.

Relationships with the outside community
No therapeutic community is an island. All operate within a context which

includes neighbours, other professionals, an organizational hierarchy patients' families and, slightly further removed, the media, politicians and 'public opinion'. Each of these groups is likely to hold certain preconceptions about psychiatric patients, those who work with them, and what is proper in staff–patient relationships. Such preconceptions often differ sharply from therapeutic community values and practice, where patient and staff roles overlap and a wide range of feelings and behaviour are tolerated. This renders them vulnerable to misunderstanding, criticism and fantasies of improper, bizarre or dangerous goings on.

It is not perhaps surprising that, faced with the day-to-day problems within the community itself, staff may choose to turn their backs on a puzzled and potentially hostile outside world. In this situation any event which attracts outside publicity – a suicide, damage to property, complaints of ill-treatment – can easily lead to misinformed criticism or protests. A series of incidents may even lead to demands for closure of the unit. In order to avoid or survive these potential threats to its work and survival, it is necessary that a therapeutic community maintain a realistic awareness of itself as part of wider networks – professional, organizational, social. Energy needs to be put in to setting up and maintaining open communication with all those who have a legitimate concern with the impact of the unit on its patients, its staff, its neighbours, its parent organization and on the wider community. In practice this task may be undertaken mainly by the unit's leaders, who stand on the boundary between the therapeutic community and the outside networks and who have to represent the needs and concerns of each to the other.

Limitations of therapeutic communities

The limitations of therapeutic communites are largely a matter of organizational constraints and staff skills and attitudes (Kennard, 1979). Both of these will set limits on the extent to which therapeutic community methods can be used. The 'parent' organization must be able to allocate permanent, suitably qualified or experienced staff, and must be willing to allow them sufficient autonomy and independence to develop their own working arrangements. While it may be unrealistic, and unnecessary, for all staff to have had relevant training, unless key staff members have a clear understanding of the underlying principles there is a risk that early enthusiasm will lead to dogmatic insistence on particular rules or techniques, or alternatively that doubt and uncertainty will lead to demoralization and return to safer, more traditional roies.

Once in progress, therapeutic communities can be fairly robust in the sense that they can be adapted to meet the needs of different client groups, as indicated on page 164. Even patients who are unlikely to benefit because of their limited capacity for social involvement – for example, mentally handicapped or chronically institutionalized individuals – may still be best cared for in a supportive, communal setting in which staff allow feelings to be openly expressed and share responsibilities in a flexible way. Perhaps the most important limitation in terms of patient characteristics are the personal expectations and preferences that individuals bring to their treatment. Those who require and seek a solely medical/physical solution to their problems, those who can tolerate a confiding relationship with only one therapist, those who cannot accept equal relations between staff and patients and require a hierarchical order, will be likely to avoid or have minimum contact with a therapeutic community.

The future of therapeutic communities

The last 15 years have seen a decline in the number of therapeutic communities in psychiatric hospitals and, at the same time, an increase in their use outside hospitals – in day hospitals, social services and voluntary sector hostels, day centres, etc. This change is reflected in, among other things, the membership of the Association of Therapeutic Communities. Originally, almost exclusively hospital-based, the membership is now evenly split between hospital and non-hospital workers. The decline of therapeutic communities in psychiatric hospitals can be attributed to a number of factors. These include a return to more traditional psychiatric roles, focusing on individuals in isolation from their social environment; the growing autonomy and separation of the different professions within psychiatry making real collaboration harder to achieve; and the introduction of business style management into the NHS which has often been implemented in a style incompatible with participative decision making. It is an interesting observation that, at its best, the new approach to management echoes the therapeutic community's emphasis on allowing patient participation in responsible decision making.

At the present time there are some signs of a revival of interest in therapeutic community methods in psychiatric hospitals, especially among nursing staff. The setting up of a 1-year training course jointly by the Association of Therapeutic Communities and the Royal College of Nursing may stimulate this development in the coming years. However, it is likely that therapeutic communities will never again be predominantly hospital-based, and will find their greatest future use in local residential and day units for people with a range of psychiatric and behaviour problems. In addition, the movement of patients, staff and resources out of hospitals into the community has led to the setting up of numerous community health teams. These have brought with them many of the issues of staff–staff and staff–patient relationships that were the original stimulus to creating therapeutic communities. Staff working in these settings will, I believe, continue to require an understanding of the issues dealt with in this chapter if they are to function effectively as teams in the community.

REFERENCES

Ahlin, G. (1981). A model for institutional development towards therapeutic community. *Group Analysis* **14**, 57–63.

Almond, R., Keniston, K. and Boltax, S. (1969). Milieu therapeutic process. *Archives of General Psychiatry* **21**, 431–42.

Barton, R. (1959). *Institutional Neurosis*. Bristol, Wright.

Blake, R., Millard, D. W. and Roberts, J. P. (1984). Therapeutic community principles in an integrated Local Authority Community Mental Health Service. *International Journal of Therapeutic Communities* **5** (4), 243–73.

Bloch, S., Reibstein, J., Crouch, E., Holroyd, P. and Themen, J. (1979). A method for the study of therapeutic factors in group psychotherapy. *British Journal of Psychiatry* **134**, 257–63.

Brown, D. and Pedder, J. (1979). *Introduction to Psychotherapy*. London, Tavistock.

Caine, T. M. and Smail, D. J. (1969). *The Treatment of Mental Illness: Science, Faith and the Therapeutic Personality*. London, University of London Press.

Caine, T. M., Wijesinghe, O. B. A. and Winter, D. A. (1981). *Personal Styles in Neurosis*. London, Routledge and Kegan Paul.

Caudill, W. A. (1958). *The Psychiatric Hospital as a Small Society*. Cambridge, MA, Harvard University Press.

Clark, A. W. (1967). Patient participation and improvement in a therapeutic community. *Human Relations* **21**, 85–95.

Clark, D. H. (1965). The therapeutic community – concept, practice and future. *British Journal of Psychiatry* **111**, 947–54.

Clark, D. H. (1977). The therapeutic community. *British Journal of Psychiatry* **131**, 553–64.

Copas, J. B., O'Brien, M., Roberts, J. and Whiteley, J. S. (1984). Treatment outcome in personality disorder: the effect of social, psychological and behavioural variables. *Personality and Individual Differences* **5**, 565–73.

Foulkes, S. H. (1964). *Therapeutic Group Analysis*. London, George Allen and Unwin.

Goffman, E. (1961). *Asylums*. Harmondsworth, Penguin.

Hobson, R. F. (1979). The messianic community. *In* R. D. Hinshelwood and N. Manning (eds), *Therapeutic Communities – Reflections and Progress*. pp. 231–344, London, Routledge and Kegan Paul.

Jones, K. and Fowles, A. J. (1984). *Ideas on Institutions*. London, Routledge and Kegan Paul.

Jones, M. (1968). *Social Psychiatry in Practice*. Harmondsworth, Penguin.

Kennard, D. (1979). Limiting factors: the setting, the staff, the patients. *In* R. D. Hinshelwood and N. Manning (eds), *Therapeutic Communities – Reflections and Progress*, pp. 181–93, London, Routledge and Kegan Paul.

Kennard, D. (1983). *An Introduction to Therapeutic Communities*. London, Routledge and Kegan Paul.

Mahony, N. (1979). My stay and change at the Henderson Therapeutic Community.

In R. D. Hinshelwood and N. Manning (eds), *Therapeutic Communities – Reflections and Progress*, pp. 76–87, London, Routledge and Kegan Paul.

Main, T. F. (1946). The hospital as a therapeutic institution. *Bulletin of the Menninger Clinic* **10**, 66–70.

Main, T. F. (1957). The ailment. *British Journal of Medical Psychology* **30**, 129–45.

Main, T. F. (1975). Some psychodynamics of large groups. *In* L. Kreeger (ed.), *The Large Group* pp. 57–86, London, Constable.

Manning, N. (1976). What happened to the therapeutic community? *In* K. Jones and S. Baldwin (eds), *Yearbook of Social Policy 1975*. London, Routledge and Kegan Paul.

Manor, O. (1977). Social roles and behaviour change. Unpublished thesis, quoted in Whiteley and Gordon (1979, p. 117).

Manor, O. (1982). The looking glass effect of self-management in a therapeutic community. *International Journal of Therapeutic Communities* **3** (3), 138–54.

Meinrath, M. and Roberts, J. P. (1982). On being a good enough staff member. *International Journal of Therapeutic Communities* **3** (1), 7–14.

Menzies, I. (1960). A case study of the functioning of social systems as a defence against anxiety. *Human Relations* **13**, 95–121.

Miles, A. (1969). Changes in the attitudes to authority of patients with behavioural disorders in a therapeutic community. *British Journal of Psychiatry* **115**, 1049–57.

Miller, E. J. and Gwynne, G. V. (1972). *A Life Apart*. London, Tavistock.

Minuchin, S. (1974). *Families and Family Therapy*. London, Tavistock.

Mosher, L. R., Mann, A. and Matthews, S. M. (1975). Soteria: evolution of a home-based treatment for schizophrenia. *American Journal of Orthopsychiatry* **45**, 455–67.

Pines, M. (1983). The contribution of S. H. Foulkes to group therapy. *In* M. Pines (ed.), *The Evolution of Group Analysis*, pp. 265–85, London, Routledge and Kegan Paul.

Rapaport, R. N. (1960). *Community as Doctor*. London, Tavistock.

Reda, S. M. (1985). Patients' perceptions of their roles in therapeutic communities. Unpublished M. Phil, thesis, Manchester Polytechnic.

Roberts, J. P. (1980). Destructive processes in a therapeutic community. *International Journal of Therapeutic Communities* **1** (3), 159–70.

Skynner, A. C. R. (1976). *One Flesh: Separate Persons*. London, Constable.

Smith, P. B., Wood, H. and Smale, G. G. (1980). The usefulness of groups in clinical settings. *In* P. B. Smith (ed.), *Small Groups and Personal Change*. pp. 106–53 London, Methuen.

Stanton, A. and Schwartz, M. (1954). *The Mental Hospital*. New York, Basic Books.

Trauer, T. (1983). A study of collective disturbed behaviour among psychiatric patients. *British Journal of Clinical Psychology* **22** (4), 265–75.

Whiteley, J. S. (1970). The response of psychopaths to a therapeutic community. *British Journal of Psychiatry* **116**, 517–29.

Whiteley, J. S. and Collis, M. (1987). The therapeutic factors in group psychotherapy applied to the therapeutic community. *International Journal of Therapeutic Communities* **8**, 21–32.

Whiteley, J. S. and Gordon, J. (1979). *Group Approaches in Psychiatry*. London, Routledge and Kegan Paul.

Wilson, S. (1978). The effect of treatment in a therapeutic community on intravenous drug abuse. *British Journal of Addictions* **73**, 407–411.

Wilson, S. and Mandlebrote, B. M. (1985). Reconviction rates of drug dependent patients treated in a residential therapeutic community: 10 year follow up. *British Medical Journal* **291**, 105.

Yalom, I. (1975). *The Theory and Practice of Group Psychotherapy*, 2nd edition. New York, Basic Books.

CHAPTER 9

THE PERSON-CENTRED APPROACH TO LARGE GROUPS

Brian Thorne

FROM NON-DIRECTIVE THERAPY TO PERSON-CENTRED LEARNING COMMUNITIES

From 1938 until 1950 the late Carl Rogers was discovering what it might mean to relate to another person in a way which was truly helpful and effective. He dedicated himself to the experience and the understanding of the one-to-one therapeutic relationship and emerged from this period with the conviction, tested repeatedly in experience, that what mattered was the facilitative climate that the counsellor or therapist could create for his client who could then be trusted to develop in life-enhancing ways. Since that time, Rogers frequently reiterated this belief that constructive personality growth and change can only occur when the client is both aware of and experiences a special psychological climate in the relationship. Furthermore, this climate does not spring from the therapist's knowledge or his intellectual training or from techniques learned in some particular school of thought. The conditions which characterize the creative therapeutic relationship are feelings and attitudes which must be experienced by the therapist and recognized by the client if they are to prove effective. These feelings and attitudes which Rogers deemed essential for creative personality growth are now well known. The therapist, he believed, must be genuine in the relationship, that is to say, properly in touch with his own feelings and thoughts and capable of expressing them when appropriate, he must be unconditionally accepting of his client and he must show a sensitive empathic understanding of the client's feelings and personal meanings. When these 'core conditions' are present in a therapeutic relationship then,

Rogers discovered, creative movement will take place. This is a position from which he never deviated, although the theory has been both refined and elaborated over the years in the light of experience and research both by Rogers himself and by other person-centred (a fairly recent label) practitioners.

Carl Rogers encountered individual human beings in his consulting room and gradually discovered that his work as a clinician had profound implications for human relationships in general. Although he professed to be astonished at the way in which the person-centred approach has now permeated so many areas of human activity, it is clear that almost from the outset Rogers believed that if he could discover even one essential truth about the relationship between two people he would inevitably have something important to say in a whole range of other human arenas. Significantly, Rogers was also the kind of man who was highly motivated to exercise influence and, in the latter part of his life, he showed an astonishing determination both through his involvement in countless workshops and seminars throughout the world and through his voluminous writings to bring the insights first culled from individual psychotherapy to bear upon a whole range of human situations.

The movement out of the consulting room was publicly registered with the appearance in 1961 of *On Becoming a Person*, where Rogers clearly demonstrates the application of his work as a therapist to human relationships in general. This book had an instant appeal to people outside the professional circles of psychology and mental health and it continues to have a profound impact on many contemporary readers who find articulated in its pages thoughts and feelings of which they have been dimly aware but which they have never been able clearly to formulate. It was during the 1960s, following the publication of *On Becoming a Person*, that the focus of Rogers' professional activity shifted from the one-to-one relationship to the small group. The era of the so-called 'encounter group' had arrived. As early as the late 1940s Rogers had used the group setting as a primary context for the training of counsellors, but the encounter group had different objectives and attracted a far wider spectrum of participants. Essentially it offered the opportunity to a participant both for self-exploration and for providing sensitive support to other members of the group (usually of about 8–15 persons) who also wished to develop their self-understanding and their capacities for relating more creatively to others. The role of the group leader (usually known as 'the facilitator') is to engage in the process in such a way that an atmosphere or climate is established in which members can gradually exhibit towards each other the qualities of genuineness, acceptance and empathic understanding which characterize the effective therapeutic relationship. The facilitator eschews the role of the expert or the consultant and if he does his work effectively his behaviour and involvement may well become indistinguishable from that of other group members.

During the 1960s the encounter group movement swept the United States and many strange and bizarre events were reported in both the professional and popular press. Rogers and his colleagues were horrified at many of the developments and especially at the emergence of manipulatory and gimmicky 'techniques' which were perpetrated by untrained and unskilled group leaders who seemed launched on irresponsible and potentially dangerous power trips. With the proliferation of groups and with the ubiquitous use of the word 'encounter' it was difficult to preserve both the integrity and the credibility of the person-centred model but, during this period, Rogers and his associates nevertheless discovered that their experience in individual therapy was confirmed and further enhanced by what happened in small groups when they were facilitated by experienced person-centred practitioners. The belief in the innate wisdom and re-sourcefulness of the individual, once he or she is offered a relationship in which acceptance, genuineness and empathy are present, was mirrored by a growing trust in the capacity of a small group to discover its own wisdom and resourcefulness for meeting the needs of its members, given the presence of the same qualities in the overall 'climate' of the group's interactions. In the same way that an individual could be trusted to find the way forward to a more creative way of being so, too, could the small group be relied upon to evolve a more satisfying approach to its group life – provided always that the 'core conditions' were established and cultivated.

It was in the context of the so-called La Jolla Programme, established in the latter half of the 1960s by associates of Rogers in order to provide learning opportunities for the development of facilitative skills, that for the first time the staff experimented with the notion of the community meeting at which all the participants in a training programme (some 100 or so people) could meet frequently together. Even if total institutions could not be transformed overnight, it seemed appropriate to discover whether or not a temporary community of some size could create for itself a climate where the core conditions were powerfully present. Rogers himself commented on this experiment in hopeful terms in his book *Encounter Groups* which appeared in 1970:

> Last year the staff [of the La Jolla Programme] experimented with the concept of the community meeting – frequent and intensive meetings for the entire community of participants, a development which it was felt would have particular application to their back-home settings. This proved definitely successful (Rogers, 1970, p. 153).

The large group experience was launched and, in the years following, commanded an increasing amount of Rogers' time and energy. By the mid-1970s the man who had begun his career as the non-directive counsellor in a one-to-one relationship was increasingly to be found sitting patiently in the midst of large groups of people, often of different nationalities and cultures. What is more he displayed the same kind of faith in the potential of such a heterogeneous community as he had formerly shown in an individual client.

BACKGROUND TO THE LARGE GROUP APPROACH

Although with hindsight it seems that the gradual movement from the one-to-one relationship to the large group was simply a logical and inevitable progression, this would be to under-rate, I believe, the strong and initially unostentatious thread running through Rogers' work which has justifiably been labelled political. For Rogers, the individual human being is innately good and creative and can be relied upon to move in a positive direction as long as the right conditions for growth are provided. The enemy, clearly, is 'society', which has somehow managed to produce pressures and constraints and to invent organizations and institutions which, far from encouraging the growth of human beings, actually stunt and cripple them. The source of such mismanagement was never fully explored by Rogers, but clearly he would have little sympathy with such notions as 'original sin' or the 'glorious flaw' which might seem to indicate that men and women are *not* innately good and forward-moving. Instead he tended to focus on *the abuse of power* and saw this as the primary cause for much human misery. Human beings, when they are afraid or feel threatened, resort to defensive or aggressive postures in order to preserve their own shaky security. Such measures tend to increase the aura of fear, and certainly do nothing to develop increased understanding within and between people. Differences are automatically seen as divisive and dangerous and are, therefore, not open to exploration and negotiation. Instead they are more likely to result in power struggles and conflicts where one side or faction attempts to dominate the other. The political animal in Rogers strove consistently to attack this process whereby differences lead inexorably to mistrust and hostility. It was his goal, which he pursued with great single-mindedness, to create large group learning situations where individuals have the chance to experience a totally different outcome.

DEVELOPMENTS IN BRITAIN

In the spring of 1974 Dave Mearns, a young psychologist from Glasgow, had recently returned from a year's study with Rogers as a Visiting Fellow at the Center for Studies of the Person in La Jolla. At the same time Charles (Chuck)

Devonshire, a close associate of Rogers and founder of the Center for Cross-Cultural Communication, was in the early stages of what could appropriately be called a 'mission to Europe'. It was thanks to the initiative of these two men that in the following year a Facilitator Development Institute (FDI) was established in Britain (whose four co-directors were Mearns, Devonshire, Elke Lambers, a Dutch person-centred therapist, and myself) which had as its aim the creation of residential summer workshops on the person-centred approach to groups. The first such workshop took place in Glasgow in August 1975 and similar workshops have occurred every summer since then in various parts of the country. In each case a primary task has been to create a learning community where individuals can experience the large group as an environment conducive to personal and professional development. Over the years some 500 people have participated in the workshops (including many from countries other than Britain) and there seems to be no lack of people still coming forward to take part in what is a unique and intensive opportunity to learn about the person-centred approach and its many different aspects. The recently established Person-Centred Network has drawn on the experience of FDI (Britain) in the conduct of its large group activities and both the Group Relations Training Association and the Association for Humanistic Psychology have explored the large group through 'person-centred' eyes. There is in Britain no other organization as yet, however, regularly offering the kind of experience afforded by the FDI summer workshops.

THE AIMS OF THE LARGE GROUP EXPERIENCE

The fundamental aim of the the FDI Workshop (and of similar person-centred large group experiences) is to provide an environment where the maximum learning can take place for every participant. Emphasis is placed in the advertising brochure on the interrelatedness of personal and professional development and the workshop is presented as an opportunity for participants, who are drawn principally but not exclusively from the helping professions, to find strength and support for both their personal and professional lives through the exploration of new ways of working and being together. It is made clear that the staff members do not see it as their responsibility to plan the workshop beyond its initial stages and that what happens during the week will be the outcome of a community design, created to meet the initial and emerging needs and interests of all participants, including the staff. At the same time the staff members indicate in the publicity material that they have particular interests and experience which they will be willing to share with participants. The person-centred philosophy of trust in the individual's capacity for development and for taking responsibility for his or her own learning is spelt out as clearly as possible. In short, the expressed aim of the workshop is to enable individual participants, given the over-arching philosophy of the person-centred approach and the different experience and competencies of the staff members, to discover and explore their own needs and to create both an environment and a structure where those needs can be met. In the event, the kind of programme which evolves usually includes a number of large group or community meetings, smaller encounter groups and a number of options or workshops around specific themes. In no way, however, is the week pre-planned by the staff nor do they seek to push the participants in a particular direction. The invitation to share in a community design is an authentic one and, on occasions, has resulted in unusual and unexpected structures which could not possibly have been foreseen.

The person-centred approach is concerned with the development of attitudes and the large group experience clearly provides a powerful context for attitude change and formation. The attitudes in question are those which have been shown to be *facilitative* of positive changes in clients and others and one way of looking at the FDI large group experience is to focus on the essential meaning of the Institute's own name. What does it actually entail to be in the business of developing *facilitators?* How can people be 'trained' to develop an unconditional regard for each other? How can they be encouraged to be more honest and authentic so that their outward behaviour and utterances are in correspondence with their inner thoughts and feelings? How can they be enabled to understand another individual from that person's own frame of reference and then communicate their understanding with clarity and sensitivity? In short, how can a large group become an effective context for individuals to learn how to be more accepting, congruent and empathic?

A common and conventional educational approach is to focus mainly on the cognitive component in learning. In this model students are likely to read books, listen to lectures and write about their growing knowledge in essays and examinations. Such a model is unlikely to be effective in the development of attitudes for it tackles only one component (the cognitive) in attitude formation and pays little attention to the affective (feelings) and behavioural components. Attitudes are only likely to be affected if people prove totally involved as thinking, feeling and behaving persons. The implications for the large group experience are well summarized by Dave Mearns and Elke Lambers in an article contributed to *Self and Society* in 1976:

> . . . our philosophy . . . in our workshops is to emphasise experiential learning
> involving the thinking, feeling and behaviour of the participant. We try to create
> an environment in which the participants will be fully involved as persons not as

'students' or 'trainees'. A vitally important aspect of this environment is that participants are encouraged *to take responsibility for themselves* and for what happens during the programme. There is considerable *freedom* for them to design a programme which they consider worthwhile. The individual participant is encouraged to express his wishes and to endeavour to have them met in the context of the wishes of others (Mearns and Lambers, 1976, p. 11).

From the outset participants in the FDI Workshops have been encouraged to take part in on-going participative research into the process and effectiveness of the events. In the early years John McLeod, at that time a doctoral research student at Edinburgh University, acted as researcher to FDI and his doctoral thesis presented in 1977 draws extensively on his involvement with the summer workshops. He continued to perform an important research function for the Institute for many years subsequently and discusses his research methodology in a chapter co-authored with Dave Mearns which appears in a later symposium on the person-centred approach published in America (Mearns and McLeod, 1984). McLeod believes that research which attempts to explore complex and often shifting subjective experience can only be undertaken by a researcher who is himself known and trusted by the subjects of the research. He was, therefore, fully participant in the workshops and openly discussed his research objectives with the workshop members. He invited them to keep journals throughout the events and to share these or parts of them with him subsequently. In this way those participants (and they were many) who agreed to co-operate in the research were enabled to have a close and confidential relationship with the researcher and witnessed his own struggles to make sense of his experience. Both the journal material and the letters and other information which were passed to the researcher were, therefore, offered within the context of a trusted relationship and to someone who was himself fully participant in the process which he was seeking to elucidate.

McLeod's doctoral thesis explores in some depth the FDI Workshops of 1975 and 1976 and, among other things, he examines the expectations of participants prior to their involvement in the workshop experience. It is evident that for most of them there was indeed the expectation of learning which would embrace both the personal and the professional. It is also clear that many hoped for opportunities to work at a feeling level and to experiment with their interpersonal behaviour. Although there were wide differences when participants attempted to elaborate their expectations, there was a common hope that close relationships would be possible and that there would be an involvement of the total person. Such expectations were, in fact, justifiable and McLeod comments:

> Finally, members' expectations – of forming 'intimate' relationships, undergoing personal learning and change, talking about personal problems and so on – were generally fulfilled. As one participant wrote: 'If people come they will work to get what they came for' (McLeod, 1977, p. 269).

PREPARING FOR THE LARGE GROUP: THE ROLE OF STAFF AS CONVENORS

In much that has been written about the large group experience both by Rogers himself and by his close associate John Wood, considerable emphasis is placed on the significance of the preparatory stages before the group itself actually assembles (i.e. Rogers, 1977; Wood, 1984). What may seem, for example, like mere administrative issues, turn out to have important implications and the dynamics within the staff group are shown to have particular relevance to the large group's subsequent evolution. The British experience confirms these findings.

An FDI Workshop begins, in an important sense, with the composition and publication of the advertising brochure. The staff struggle with its compilation so that nothing appears that is not fully acceptable to everyone. This usually means much hard work and several re-draftings before the brochure is fully and accurately expressive, not only of the workshop's aims but also of the personal interests and preoccupations of each staff member. Even at this early stage the staff group is modelling the kind of co-operative and responsive way of being together which encourages the expression of personal differences in the interests of arriving at a satisfactory group decision.

Financial issues are also of great significance at this point. Staff members' desire or need to ensure at least a reasonable financial return for their work and commitment has to be balanced against the fact that many likely participants will have limited financial resources, especially if they are students or working outside the conventional structures. A number of strategies have been adopted over the years to ease this dilemma including differential payments for those who are self-financing and those supported by agencies or organizations, an invitation to wealthy participants to pay more than the workshop fee, the establishing of a bursary or scholarship fund, the acceptance of payment by instalments, and so on. Scholarships are awarded to anyone who asks for them and each individual is asked to determine the size of his or her own scholarship up to a maximum of 50% of the participation fee. Although the FDI staff have never adopted the method devised by Rogers and his colleagues of allowing all participants to determine their own fee (having been given basic data about accommodation and tutorial costs). I believe it is true to say that no applicant for an FDI Workshop place has had to withdraw because of financial difficulties. Certainly many students and several unemployed people have taken part.

Once the brochure has been published and distributed (usually some 8–10 months before the event) a period of correspondence begins which intensifies as the workshop draws nearer. Every attempt is made to personalize this process. Those who register or enquire about the workshop receive individualized replies and great care is taken to ensure that a warm and responsive attitude is conveyed by the tone and content of letters or telephone calls. Only at the last stage when joining instructions and information are sent out to the participants do we resort to a 'packaged' communication and even then a scribbled note or post-script will often add a personal touch. These may seem to be trivial points but there is no doubt that for some participants such attentive behaviour conveys an attitude of respect and caring which does much both to reinforce the tone of the brochure and to provide evidence of its genuineness.

The importance of the staff meeting immediately prior to large group workshops cannot be overestimated. At least a whole day needs to be allotted for this purpose and, in the case of particularly large workshops where the staff may number as many as 20 people 3–4 days is not excessive. The FDI team has been small (usually no more than six) and the members well-known to each other. Nevertheless, the profound significance of the pre-workshop staff meeting has been proved on every occasion. It is not simply an opportunity for attending to last-minute administrative details, although clearly this often has to be done. Much more important is the quality of the relating which the staff members can achieve in this comparatively short time. They attempt to create an environment in which it is possible to listen to each other, to express important feelings and to share hopes and fears about the forthcoming workshop. Frequently the meeting gives rise to interpersonal issues which have to be addressed or to the discovery that a particular theme seems to be a shared preoccupation, even if there is little agreement on its precise nature let alone its resolution. What is aimed at is a preparedness to live in-depth with each other and a willingness to be honest, open and supportive even when confrontation has to be risked. In brief, the major task of the staff group during this preliminary time together is to be themselves. Rogers and his associates have described the process in the following terms:

> . . . we spend time together, before the workshop convenes, so that insofar as we are capable:
> We can be fully open to each other, and later to the whole group;
> We can explore new and unknown areas of our various life styles;
> We are truly acceptant of our own differences;
> We are open to the new learnings we will receive from our fresh
> inward feelings, from the group and from each other, all stimulated by the group experience (Villas-Boas Bowen *et al.*, 1978).

BEGINNINGS

By the time the first participants appear the staff group, if all has gone well, are feeling relaxed with each other and open to experience. They are 'tuned up' for what is to follow. The reception of people as they arrive now engages their whole attention. It is very easy at this stage for the staff to take on a kind of proprietary air as if they are the real 'owners' of the workshop and the other participants merely temporary tenants. Every effort is therefore made to convey the message that the workshop 'belongs' to everyone and is not something being 'put on' by the staff group. Early arrivals, for example, may be quickly incorporated into the reception team and may find themselves escorting other participants to their rooms or conveying information about facilities. Other participants may take charge of the polaroid cameras and assume the task of persuading workshop members to have their photographs taken in order to aid identification in the early stages of the workshop. When these photographs are subsequently displayed the staff members' pictures will not be placed apart but will be mixed up with all the others. These details of behaviour are not part of an elaborate plot on the part of the staff to deny or reject their roles, nor do they stem from a laid-down set of procedures which the staff feel obliged to follow. It is in no sense 'policy' to suggest that early arrivals help with the organization but it tends to happen because of the *attitude* adopted by the staff towards participants. Indeed, much of what goes on in these early stages is the outcome of the staff's desire to communicate that they wish to be attentive and responsible *to* participants but have no desire to be responsible *for* them or to arrange their lives during the workshop.

When the community assembles for the first time, usually within an hour or so of the end of the registration period, the tension is high. Over the years the FDI summer workshop group has ranged in size from 25 to over 80 but even when the *numbers* have been relatively small the group at the outset will appear enormous to many of the participants. For some, the sense of being overwhelmed and of the sheer impossibility of relating to what appears an amorphous mass will be predominant. Their initial reaction will be one of fear and even of an urgent desire to escape. A staff member will usually be the first to speak and who this shall be will probably have been decided by the staff group prior to the meeting. Nobody, however, will know what the particular facilitator is going to say and it is unlikely that even he or she will know until the words have been uttered. The chances are, however, that what is said will be a mixture of feeling and expectation:

> I feel very nervous but at the same time excited now that we're all together. I've no idea what we're in for but I hope we shall be able to make something good of this week together. I'm Dave, by the way, in case there are some of you who haven't identified me yet.

Such a statement is saying many things. It gives high priority to feelings, it is hopeful, it refutes any notion of staff prescience or omnipotence, it points to the corporate responsibility of the group and it indicates a desire to be known as a person. It is likely to be followed by silence but in some way it will have sown the seeds for what is to follow. The likelihood is that in a first meeting of this kind the ensuing process will actually seem haphazard and fragmented. Several people may speak, expectations and fears may be voiced, there may even be some tentative self-disclosure but there will be little sense of coherence or continuity. The task of the staff members will be to remain attentive to everyone in the room and to attempt, as far as is possible, to hear fully what is said and to acknowledge it, especially in cases where an individual's contribution seems in danger of disappearing into the black hole of silence which a large group can so easily create. It is unlikely to be helpful if the staff find themselves adopting a high profile in these early stages, but at the same time they must feel free to express strong feelings if and when they experience them. In short, they will be attempting to be real and they will be doing all they can to show that they value the contributions of others, especially when these appear confused or negative or seem destined to sink without trace. Perhaps more than anything else they will be attempting to listen and to maintain this listening attitude in a group where the fears and expectations of the majority make this an acutely difficult activity. They will be listening, however, not only to the contributions of others but also to the changing and probably chaotic flow of experience taking place within themselves. It is exhausting and demanding work.

DEVELOPMENT OF THE LARGE GROUP

In a large group which reaches a creative state a number of stages in its development are generally discernible. Clearly not every group does achieve such a state and there are many occasions when large groups seem to attain few capacities beyond those of a crowd or collective. The creative state (if it is reached) is characterized chiefly by the ability of the members to be both autonomous and co-operative. Initially, it is of overriding importance that participants experience their own validity and significance. If they feel that they are mere cogs in a machine or pawns in some elaborate and incomprehensible game they will not be able to attach value to the community as a whole. Instead, they will see it as threatening, a kind of prison where they are without identity. Much of what occurs in the early stages of a workshop can therefore be seen as attempts by individuals to discover if they can be autonomous without being rejected or ostracized by the community. Such attempts will take various forms but commonly some participants will become angry at what they see as a lack of effectiveness on the part of the staff, others will give expression to feelings of confusion or frustration and others again may register their disapproval by absenting themselves from group meetings or leaving in the middle of sessions. During this period it is important that the staff members seek to respect and to understand the feelings and behaviour of those participants who test out their autonomy in this way without, however, denying feelings of hurt or irritation which, as staff members, they themselves may be experiencing. The residential setting provides many additional contexts in which the feelings of individuals can be acknowledged and explored and staff members will often find themselves drawn into or seeking exchanges at meals or in the bar.

Most often the need of individuals to feel valued and significant as persons results in an early request for the large group to split up into smaller groups. This development serves to focus on the comparative fragility of the large group, and there are usually those who oppose the movement into smaller units because they fear that the community will not survive such fragmentation. Such people are expressing a care and concern for the total community and act as a counterbalance to those whose main need at this early stage is to find a place where they can feel a sense of security. It is these 'community carers' who usually ensure that, if the large group does break up into smaller units, a time is established at which the whole community can come together again to review its position.

It is not always easy for the large group to decide *how* to divide itself into smaller units and often there is a period of pain and struggle as various permutations are suggested and rejected. The role of the staff members can again become the focus of attention and much discussion will often centre around whether or not each smaller group shall have a staff member as its facilitator. Frequently, a number of small groups will be formed, some of which will have staff members while others opt to be 'leaderless'.

Whether the large group splits into small groups or whether, as in exceptional cases, it remains as a total community, the next stage of development is critical if a creative state is ultimately to be achieved. I have come to think of this part of the process as the search for mutuality or the quest for intimacy. Within the context of a small group, especially if it is ably facilitated, most participants in the workshop will quickly discover a sense of belonging and of acceptance. This in itself, however, is insufficient if the total community is to make significant advances. Participants need to know not only that they are acceptable but also that they can contribute significantly to the well-being of others. In short, they must experience themselves as givers as well as receivers. This achievement of mutuality or intimacy can happen in a variety of ways. Often it will take place within the small group as group members establish strong bonds and experience their interdependency. Sometimes, though, it will happen on the periphery of the workshop, in the bar or walking in the grounds. As always the example of the staff members is powerfully influential at this stage. If they are self-sufficient and appear to be omnicompetent they are unlikely to encourage the quest for mutuality. If, on the other hand, they show themselves to be vulnerable as well as resourceful, willing to relate in depth rather than remaining aloof or distant, then the move towards mutuality within the community is likely to be hastened.

It is my belief that once the majority of participants in the workshop have experienced at least the beginnings of mutality there is a strong likelihood that the large group itself will undergo a transformation. People will begin to listen to each other with greatly increased attentiveness, and individuals will be bold enough to express their needs or to offer their ideas without being undermined if these are not immediately taken up. The large group will begin to have confidence in its capacity to make decisions and will be willing to experiment with a variety of structures, both formal and informal. This confidence springs, I believe, from an increasing willingness on the part of the workshop members to be changed by experience. Having found a modicum of security and having discovered that they are important to at least one other person, the participants are eager to take risks and to trust that the large group will provide an environment for growth. There is often a much greater degree of self-disclosure and the increased attentiveness leads to intimate exchanges and sometimes to considerable physical contact. Gradually the large group seems to shrink in size and is no longer threatening to its members. Instead they begin to perceive that this previously unwieldy community has its own patterns and that they have a contribution to make to its own life. At one and the same time there is a realization of corporate identity and of individual uniqueness. When the large group attains, however momentarily, this supremely creative state the ancient problem of the one and the many melts away.

Not all groups, of course, attain such a creative state or do so only fleetingly. For some participants the anger and frustration with the workshop staff may persist for many days and when this happens there is little chance of forward movement until the feelings have been fully expressed and acknowledged. There are times when the staff may have to work hard at enabling this anger to emerge or when they may feel it necessary to explain that their reluctance or refusal to impose a plan of action on the workshop springs from a deep respect for the needs and resources of the group as a whole and not from indifference or some underlying urge to manipulate through inaction. Particular difficulties can arise when the workshop membership contains a number of participants who have been 'sent' by their organizations or institutions. Such people have come under authority rather than through personal motivation and are therefore ill-prepared for the struggle to achieve personal autonomy. They are resentful of the authority which has placed them in a situation where there is apparently no authority and, as a result, can rapidly become not only angry but highly confused. Such individuals are often helped by the preparedness of staff members or other participants to spend lengthy periods of time with them outside group meetings in order to discover whether or not they can identify goals and objectives for themselves which they can pursue during the workshop without reference to the stated or assumed objectives of the employing organization which originally sent them. Such one-to-one explorations often involve deep ethical issues about the moral rightness of a member of the helping professions seeking to satisfy his or her own needs and longings while the employer is footing the bill.

The atmosphere of intimacy and closeness which is increasingly generated as the community develops is itself a stumbling block for some participants. Often the desire for intimacy is accompanied by a fear that to take the risks involved in opening up to others will mean a confrontation with deeply buried feelings which will then prove intolerable. Here again, when there are several such people in a workshop, the facilitators may have to be highly sensitive to their needs and fears and must be willingly available to respond to them in private session if need be. Often, of course, such persons are greatly assisted if they are fortunate enough to belong to a caring small group which is patiently responsive to their fears and anxieties. In most instances the final realization that nobody is going to *coerce* them to be more intimate or self-revealing than they wish proves to be the key to alleviating their fear. What is more, this realization often engenders the very openness which had previously seemed so threatening.

In many ways an FDI Workshop is a space apart, for some a kind of 'magic island', and for most at the very least a place where different conditions prevail to those under which they normally live. The problem of re-entry is therefore a major one for almost all participants and the return home is sometimes far from easy. McLeod's (1977) research reveals the agony for some participants of attempting to share with spouses or intimate friends and colleagues the learnings and experiences of the workshop. Often it is difficult to find appropriate language and, especially when the week has been powerfully creative, participants are shocked at the inability or unwillingness of their intimates to share their enthusiasm or understand and accept the changes which they have undergone. Some provision is made for responding to these re-entry problems by convening a follow-up to each workshop which takes place some 2–6 months after the original event. In most cases the organization of these follow-ups has been undertaken by workshop participants themselves who have usually arranged the appropriate venues. On average about 50% of the participants attend and most of the staff members. The follow-up event has usually taken the form of an intensive week-end, some of which is spent in the whole group and some in small groups. During the workshop itself it is common for the issue of re-entry to be raised during the closing days and groups have often been convened specifically to explore the kind of difficulties which participants are expecting or might encounter. In addition, net-working is encouraged and staff members make it clear that they are happy to respond to letters or even to arrange meetings with individuals if participants encounter grave difficulties on re-entry. For some years an informal *Newsletter* also circulated among former workshop members. Research on person-centred encounter groups undertaken by Rogers himself has indicated that a fair number of participants report a temporary change in behaviour which rapidly disappears (Rogers, 1970, p. 126). The aim of the FDI follow-up and of the net-working between individuals is to create opportunities for participants to capitalize on and reinforce learnings, whether these be in the personal or professional domains or, as is likely, in both.

MODES OF GROUP LEARNING

There is little doubt that large group experiences such as that offered by the FDI Workshops have about them a strong element of unpredictability. It is safe to assume that many factors contribute to this, not least the effects of setting, sunshine, the holiday spirit, romantic love and the composition of the group membership. Nevertheless, there are certain forms of group learning which commonly recur and deserve special comment.

Issues of power

Most large groups are notorious for their tendency to render individuals powerless. In a person-centred workshop, however, the large group can become the arena in which an individual feels *empowered* and this comes about through the conscious valuing of differences. First the staff members then others demonstrate by their behaviour that validating and empowering others is the facilitator's chief art. The person who feels himself respected and valued is then willing to put his or her skills and resources at the disposal of the community. People who are empowered are unlikely later to abuse their power. Many organizations and institutions would be transformed if they could capitalize on this simple truth.

Dealing with crisis

It is seldom that a workshop takes place without a crisis of some kind and frequently this will occur within the large group setting. Crises can take such forms as an apparently irreconcilable conflict between participants or bizarre behaviour which smells of psychosis. It is very common, too, for a member of the community to 'break down' and for there to be prolonged tearful episodes during a large group meeting. In most instances, the large group shows itself to be a remarkably healing environment when such incidents occur. The concentrated attention and concern of a large number of people creates a network of safety and the deep respect which is usually shown for the member's distress gradually turns the crisis into an opportunity for change and development. In everyday life the response to crisis is so often one of panic and of 'doing something'. The large group behaves differently. It contains the crisis and gives space and attention to the person or persons involved. It is in no hurry and is concerned not with solutions but with staying alongside until the crisis is defused. What is more, when the large group session ends, individuals are not left alone unless they wish to be. The community continues to care through those who elect to stay closely in contact with the person or persons who have undergone the crisis. Sometimes it may be staff members who provide this continuing support but, as a workshop proceeds, it is much more likely to be other participants. One of my own most powerful memories is of collapsing in the large group myself and of the way in which the group accepted my vulnerability and my inability to cope. I did not feel a less effective facilitator as a result.

Decision-making and planning

In the initial stages of a workshop the large group seems particularly inept at making decisions and formulating plans. The brochure's promise of a 'community design', created to meet the needs of all participants, seems far removed from the capabilities of an ill-organized and apprehensive crowd of bewildered people. Decisions are made on impulse, plans are drawn up by power groups or by forceful individuals. Gradually, however, as the quality of listening improves and as members feel valued and resourceful the process of decision-making and planning changes completely. Proposals are made or suggestions offered and these in turn are discussed, modified or perhaps opposed. Indeed, particular attention is given to individuals who have strong negative feelings, and this encourages those who may normally sit on their misgivings to speak up and register their disquiet. The decisions and plans which emerge from this often long and complex process are often beautifully crafted and take note of the desires and feelings of all members of the community, some of whom may well, of course, have undergone radical shifts of attitude during the process itself. This kind of decision-making goes beyond the normal structures of democracy and it is seldom that the large group resorts to head-counting or to calling for a vote. Occasionally, when the group members have achieved an exceptional degree of sensitivity and openness to each other there develops what John Wood has called a 'participatory intuition', which leads the whole community to adopt a course of action which is not consciously decided upon in the large group meeting but which evolves in each individual as a result of the group's previous interaction. Wood recounts how one day every member in the community woke up knowing that it was a holiday and that there would be no planned activities that day. Nobody had apparently made the decision and yet everybody knew (Wood, 1984, p. 307).

Transformation through awareness

Many of the participants at an FDI Workshop and at similar person-centred events are members of the helping professions and for them the workshop, whatever else it may be, can be a powerful training experience. Undoubtedly, depending on the structure and the content of the programme which evolves, such people will learn much of relevance to their professional activity. At the very least they will gain insight into the facilitation of small and large groups but they may learn much, too, about the person-centred approach to education and psychology and to institutional life. They will certainly undergo an intensive training in empathy development! None of these gains, however, can explain the radical shift in perception which has been reported by several participants and which seems to spring primarily from experience in the large group itself. It is difficult to avoid religious terminology in attempting to explain this shift. It seems that the heightened awareness which develops in the context of the intensive residential community leads to a fresh interpretation of reality for many participants. It is as if the large group both confirms and illuminates the uniqueness of individuals, while at the same time establishing beyond any shadow of doubt their inter-connectedness. Such a perception reveals a pattern behind the surface of things and therefore gives to individuals a sense of meaning and of belonging to an orderly creation which is both mysterious and supportive. When this transformation through heightened awareness comes about in a large group consisting of people from many different nations and cultures, there is the added excitement of glimpsing the essential unity of humanity which is currently obscured by warring power blocs and international strife.

EFFECTIVE LEADERSHIP IN THE LARGE GROUP

Most of this chapter tells of large groups which attain a high degree of creativity. It has been stressed that the leaders or facilitators of such groups need to be persons who are capable of embodying to a high degree the facilitative attitudes which are the cornerstone of the person-centred approach. The facilitator who cannot be congruent, even when this means revealing his or her own vulnerability and inadequacy, should not embark upon this kind of work, nor should persons who are not deeply accepting of their fellow human beings. What is more, the level and intensity of empathic listening and communicating which is required of the large group facilitator, especially in the early stages of the group's existence, is unlikely to be attained by someone who is not deeply involved in therapeutic work in the normal course of his or her professional life. The large group facilitator, in short, needs to be wise, experienced, self-aware and deeply self-accepting.

Having portrayed such a paragon it is important as a counterbalance to stress what is perhaps the most crucial attitude of all, namely humility. The facilitator needs to be totally free of the temptation to play the role of expert or teacher or, even worse, of psychological technician armed with a bag of manipulative 'techniques'. On the contrary, he or she enters the large group experience as a learner who is prepared to be with the group as a whole person. I have written here of 'successful' large groups, but their success has depended to a high degree on the willingness of the facilitators for the group to fail. Chuck Devonshire, himself the personification of the inspiring learner, has summed up the whole matter:

> When the facilitator allows a group to struggle freely with its own success or failure and joins in that struggle him or herself, it becomes increasingly clear that growth for persons depends upon their free interaction and not upon the super ability, skill or techniques of the 'expert' (Devonshire and Kremer, 1980, p. 16).

It will be clear that the task of the large group facilitator demands a somewhat formidable array of personal and professional qualities and, in the long run, the presence or absence of such qualities will determine the facilitator's effectiveness. There are, however, skills to be learned, not the least of these being the ability to distinguish between those times when it is appropriate for the facilitator to be self-effacing and those when an intervention is called for. Such skills are in no sense techniques. They evolve from the facilitator's growing capacity to remain congruent even in the most chaotic interactions and to be able to deploy that congruence in the interests, if need be, of one individual in a group of 100 – all this, however, without losing sight of the needs of the group as a whole even if such needs have to be left for the moment in the care of others. Large group facilitators need, therefore, to be experienced counsellors or therapists who are also practised in the facilitation of the small encounter group. Additionally, it is highly desirable that they have taken part as an ordinary participant in at least one residential large group experience before attempting to undertake a staff role. FDI has made it possible for a number of people to experience the role of co-facilitator as a form of additional apprenticeship for this work. A co-facilitator is a member of the staff team who is none the less using the workshop both to monitor closely the behaviour of other staff members and to receive help and feedback from them. Steps are also taken to ensure that co-facilitators do not find themselves overloaded with responsibilities during a workshop so that they are unable to reflect on their experience or lose touch with their own needs and limitations.

THE LARGE GROUP AS A TRAINING EXPERIENCE

Mention has already been made of the obvious benefits which are likely to be derived by members of the helping professions through participation in large group experiences such as those offered by the FDI residential workshops. In addition to the knowledge gained of the person-centred approach in its many different facets, however, there are perhaps other and deeper issues at stake. Essentially, participants in a large group experience of this kind come as persons rather than as professionals. And yet they often arrive weighed down by the burdens of their professional activity and by the ravages which their work may have wrought in their personal lives. Often they feel drained, tired and uncared for either by their professional superiors or by their spouses and families. For many such people the workshop becomes an oasis where they can take stock of their lives and reveal their own wounds and need for emotional nourishment. In this sense the workshop is often a powerful form of therapy for the helpers. It can also serve as a necessary warning for those who are, sometimes unwittingly, moving towards exhaustion and burn-out. Such a warning can often make a profound impact on the individuals involved. It tells them, before it is too late, that they, too, are persons of value and deserve just as much care and attention as they are wont to lavish on their clients.

Much suffering in the helping professions is caused by insensitive bureaucracy and authoritarian hierarchical structures. Such situations frequently demand assertive behaviour from the potential victims but there is little in the training of the helping professions which encourages such a response to the abuse of power by those in positions of authority. The FDI Workshop with its insistence on co-operative planning and on the unique importance of each individual presents a model which is non-hierarchical and non-authoritarian. For many it is an empowering experience which gives them the confidence and the energy on their return to do battle with insensitive authority and the courage not to be intimidated by apparently intractable structures. An indication of this kind of personal development is often provided during the workshop by the participant who for the first time in his or her life speaks with conviction to a group of over 50 people and finds that they listen and are even prepared to change their plans as a result.

In brief, organizations which encourage their members to participate in large group experiences of the kind described here should not be surprised if their employees return with a greatly heightened awareness of their own needs and a quiet determination to have those needs acknowledged and met. In many instances this may well entail a questioning of perhaps time-honoured administrative procedures and a refusal to accept structures which pay scant regard to individual needs and differences.

THERAPY OR A THERAPEUTIC EXPERIENCE?

It will be clear that the large group experience is for most of the participants a highly therapeutic event from which they derive benefit both personally and professionally. It should not, however, be seen as therapy. In the brochure of the FDI summer workshops it is clearly stated that those undergoing counselling or therapy should discuss participation with their therapist before applying (see Appendix). The reasons for this are many. In the first place, such an experience is by its nature unpredictable: distressed and highly vulnerable people may find its demands too great and its evolution frustrating or even damaging. Furthermore, if their needs for help and safety are disproportionate they are likely to hinder the kind of risk-taking in other participants who wish to extend the boundaries of their own self-awareness. Secondly, the presence of a number of manifest 'clients' can make it virtually impossible for those participants who are members of the helping professions to lay aside their professional roles and anxieties and to derive from the group the kind of nourishment and learning which comes from confronting themselves and others as persons without role expectations. Thirdly, it would be irresponsible of the staff members even to appear to be offering individual or group therapy when they are likely to be outnumbered by about 12 to 1 by the participants and where there can be no possibility of interviewing applicants prior to the group.

Clearly, from time to time, the large group experience throws up for participants conflicts and personal issues which require subsequent therapy. In such cases staff members do their utmost to ensure that the individuals in question are put in touch with therapists in their own locality and make a point of maintaining contact over the following months. Indeed, it seems likely that a small number of participants attend such events in order to precipitate a crisis which will then ensure that they are forced to seek the therapeutic help which they require. In this sense, therefore, the large group experience can be seen as a stepping stone to therapy for those who, whether consciously or unconsciously, have previously lacked either the courage or the insight to acknowledge the depth of their own needs.

SOCIETAL AND CROSS-CULTURAL IMPLICATIONS

From the outset the FDI summer workshops have attracted participants from countries other than Britain. They have also brought together members of many different helping professions and people of widely differing religious, philosophical and political viewpoints. Since 1978, when a large cross-cultural workshop was organized in Spain (shortly after Franco's death), the Center for Cross-Cultural Communication (founded by former FDI co-director Chuck Devonshire) has sponsored similar workshops annually in many different countries of the world, including Hungary. These events, too, have been facilitated in the person-centred tradition described in this chapter and have added immeasurably to an understanding of the processes involved (Devonshire and Kremer, 1980). Most importantly, they have shown repeatedly that large groups of almost unimaginable heterogeneity are capable, given the appropriate conditions, of finding ways of working constructively together which affirm individual experiences and respect human differences. In the FDI Workshops there have sometimes been as many as 10 different nations represented, but this pales into insignificance when contrasted with the 20 or more represented each year in the specifically cross-cultural events.

Our own country is currently more divided than it has been for many years. A period of economic recession has led to a mass of unemployed people and an increasing gap between North and South. The inner cities are often a tinder box where inter-racial feeling runs high. In the world at large, too, the divisions between nations and cultures are as wide as they have ever been and the nuclear threat does not diminish. The appalling scourge of the Aids virus has now focused attention on the urgent need to discover forms of relating intimately which, in the face of so grotesque a plague, do not further endanger our species.

In such a context, the need to discover ways of enabling individuals to transcend their differences of culture, education and upbringing becomes all the more critical. The temptation may well be to resort to authoritarian modes of control so that differences are not transcended but rather suppressed or stifled. Certainly the fear of the large group increases as conflicts become more overt and the challenge to authority grows. It is my belief, however, that the large group experiences which I have attempted to describe have within them the seeds of an approach to the pressing problems of our time which preserves a faith in the human spirit which is neither naive nor foolishly optimistic. What is more, if therapists profess to minister to the individual but fall silent on the needs of the world, I for one cannot help feeling that there is a dereliction of responsibility somewhere.

REFERENCES

Devonshire, C. M. and Kremer, J. W. (1980). *Toward a Person-Centred Resolution of Intercultural Conflicts*. Dortmund, Pädagogische Arbeitsstelle.

McLeod, J. A. (1977). A study, using personal accounts and participant observation, of two "growth" movements as social-psychological phenomena, with a discussion of the possibility of a Humanistic Science of Persons. Unpublished thesis, Edinburgh University.

Mearns, D. and Lambers, E. (1976). Facilitator Development Institute. *Self and Society* **4** (12), 9–12.

Mearns, D. and McLeod, J. (1984). A person-centered approach to research. *In* R. F. Levant and J. M. Shlien (eds), *Client-Centered Therapy and The Person-Centered Approach*. New York, Praeger.

Rogers, C. R. (1970). *Carl Rogers on Encounter Groups*. New York, Harper and Row.

Rogers, C. R. (1977). *On Personal Power*. New York, Delacorte Press.

Villas-Boas Bowen, M., Justyn, J., Kass, J., Miller, M., Rogers, C. R., Rogers, N. and Wood, J. K. (1978). Evolving aspects of person-centered workshop. *Self and Society* **6** (2), 43–9.

Wood, J. K. (1984). Communities for learning: a person-centered approach. *In* R. F. Levant and J. M. Shlien (eds) *Client-Centered Therapy and The Person-Centered Approach*. New York, Praeger.

APPENDIX: EXTRACTS FROM A CURRENT FDI BROCHURE

Facilitator Development Institute   Summer Workshop 1986

The Workshop

The workshop has a primary training function for those who are working with individuals or groups, and it also provides a context for personal growth and development. Because of its international nature it serves to foster cross-cultural as well as interpersonal communication. It is designed to provide an intensive learning experience in which the participants can discover their own and others' power and resources, find strength and support for their personal and professional lives and explore new ways of working with individuals and groups.

The basic philosophy of FDI is person-centred in the tradition of Dr. Carl Rogers. This approach is one in which there is trust in the individual's responsibility and capacity for development.

Only the initial steps of the workshop will be planned by the staff. The overall format will be a community design, created to meet the initial and emerging needs of all participants, including the staff. Each person shares the power to influence the course of the workshop. Group experiences, now spanning many years and many countries, lead us to trust that self-direction and collaborative decision-making in a climate where feelings and intellect are equally respected, contribute to constructive personal and social change. The workshop offers the possibility of experience in small groups and large community meetings. In addition, areas of exploration may develop around the interests of staff and participants, for example:

- Experience and theory of group facilitation
- Empathy development
- Person-centred approaches to psychotherapy
- Person-centred approaches in education
- Person-centred approaches in organisation and training
- Voice work and creativity

PARTICIPANTS

The Workshop has particular relevance for those working in education, counselling, research, social work, psychology, psychiatry, community work, management, the churches, the health professions, trade unions, and the armed services. Those taking part in the workshop are not, however, in any way restricted to these professions. Since the primary language of the workshop will be English, a working knowledge of that language is highly desirable. For this workshop an upper limit of 50 participants is envisaged.

TEAMS

Organisations and institutions are encouraged to send teams of participants to the workshop. This can be particularly valuable where the aim is team-building or where organisational innovation is being considered.

RESEARCH

Individual reflection and evaluation of the workshop experience has been characteristic of FDI in the past, primarily through journal keeping. The staff very much hope that this feature will be continued and that a new method of research may evolve during the summer workshop. It is the staff's experience and belief that participation in this way can contribute significantly to the individual's own understanding of the workshop experience. Members of the workshop are invited to keep their own private journals. Participants are under no obligation to contribute to any new research programme.

CONDITION FOR PARTICIPATION

An F.D.I. educational workshop is not a substitute for psychotherapy or counselling. Participants are in all ways taking part because of their own free will, and are fully responsible for themselves during the workshop. Those currently undergoing psychotherapy or counselling are required to discuss participation in the workshop with their therapist or counsellor.

Information about F.D.I. Summer Workshops and about F.D.I. Counsellor and Psychotherapy Training may be obtained from:
    The Administrator,
    Norwich Centre for Personal & Professional Development,
    7 Earlham Road,
    . NORWICH NR2 3RA.

CHAPTER 10

THE STUDY OF
ORGANIZATIONAL DYNAMICS

Eric J. Miller

INTRODUCTION

The 'human relations school' of organizational theorists had its origins in the 1930s with writers such as Mayo (1933) and Roethlisberger and Dickson (1939). The prevailing mechanistic models of organization, involving detailed division of labour and hierarchical control, based on 'scientific management', carried serious human costs. During and after the Second World War, which had been presented as a struggle between democracy and totalitarianism, awareness of these costs increased. Surely there must be effective forms of organization and management that also met human needs?

In the United States, up to the late 1950s and beyond, there was emphasis on participative styles of management (e.g. McGregor, 1960). In Britain, the Tavistock Institute of Human Relations (TIHR) was developing the concept of the *socio-technical system*. Research and experimentation, initially in coal-mining and textiles, demonstrated that, although work organization had to fit the technology, a given technical system did not predetermine a unique form of social organization: choices were available, some being more effective than others in meeting social and psychological needs. Moreover, technical systems themselves were not immutable. In design of work organization, therefore, the appropriate goal was *joint optimization* of the technical and social systems, of task and human needs (Trist and Bamforth 1951; Rice, 1958, 1963; Trist *et al.*, 1963; Trist, 1981). This concept led to many versions of *autonomous work groups*, based on the principle of self-management (Herbst, 1962). Most showed improvements both in job satisfaction and in productivity compared with the atomized forms of work organization that they replaced (Srivastva *et al.*, 1975).

Organizational development in the United States was strongly influenced by Maslow's hierarchy of human needs (Maslow, 1943). This was a contribution to the psychology of the individual. TIHR (which had been incorporated in 1947) had grown out of and remained closely linked with the Tavistock Clinic (Dicks, 1970), and hence brought a more psychoanalytic perspective to individual psychology. In addition, however, this perspective was also being applied to the study of groups. Wilfred Bion, who had been developing approaches to group therapy during the war years, was now confirming that underlying processes he had identified in such groups belonged not to the disturbances of patients but to characteristics of the group itself (Bion, 1946, 1947–51, 1961; Bion and Rickman, 1943). He noted the inherent tension between individuation and submergence in the group, which evokes emotional states that belong to a very early phase in the infant's development.

Practitioners in TIHR from the late 1940s onwards were therefore not only taking on board the Clinic's psychodynamic orientation but also extending Bion's conceptualization to the study of unconscious processes in workgroups and indeed of organizations. Thus Jaques postulated that: 'One of the primary cohesive elements binding individuals into institutionalized human association is that of defence against psychotic anxiety' (Jacques, 1953, p. 4; see also Wilson, 1951; Jaques, 1955). Following Jaques, the classic study of a hospital by Menzies analysed mechanisms used to defend nurses against conscious and unconscious anxieties evoked by the task (Menzies, 1960).

In 1957, TIHR also mounted the first of what came to be called the 'Leicester Conferences', which specifically focus on underlying processes in groups and organizations and which are the central theme of the rest of this chapter. The first section describes the Conference itself: its origins, development and current format. The second describes the concepts and assumptions that underpin the Conference and links them to the Institute's other work with organizations. The third relates to practice: the roles of members and staff, the Conference process and the nature of learning. It also examines some problems and limitations of the Conferences. Finally, the fourth section discusses dissemination and application.

THE LEICESTER CONFERENCE: ORIGINS AND DEVELOPMENT

The Leicester Conference is a 2-week residential conference, devoted to experiential learning about group and organizational behaviour, with a particular emphasis on the nature of authority and leadership. Its purpose is educational. The Conference usually brings together an international membership of 50–60 people drawn from a wide range of occupations and professions: industry and commerce, education, medical and social services, the voluntary sector, etc. The staff group of 10 or so is similarly diverse. Since 1957, the Conference has been held once and sometimes twice a year – over 40 altogether. All have been sponsored by the Group Relations Training Programme (GRTP) of TIHR, sometimes in co-sponsorship with other organizations. The first seven conferences were jointly sponsored by Leicester University, and almost all have been held at Leicester in one of the university's halls of residence.

The first Conference, entitled 'Exploration in Group Relations', was meticulously planned and documented (Trist and Sofer, 1959). It was the first British experiment with the 'laboratory method', which had been developed at Bethel, Maine, from 1947 onwards by the National Training Laboratories (NTL). This model of intensive experiential learning had sprung directly from the work of Kurt Lewin, whose group theories had strongly influenced the early Tavistock group. His Research Center in Group Dynamics and TIHR had jointly started the journal *Human Relations*, the first issue of which featured Lewin's last major paper (Lewin, 1947). Most of those involved in setting up TIHR – social scientists and psychodynamically oriented psychiatrists – had been using group approaches to tackle practical wartime problems. Some, for example, had created the War Office Selection Boards (Morris, 1949) and later the Civil Resettlement Units, which were transitional communities for returning prisoners-of-war (Curle, 1947; Curle and Trist, 1947; Wilson *et al.*, 1952), whereas others, Bion among them, were experimenting with therapeutic communities (Bion, 1946; Bridger, 1946, 1985; Sutherland, 1985; Trist, 1985). Given that history and the immediate post-war interests of TIHR already described, it was hardly surprising that the Tavistock Institute and Clinic were under pressure to mount a British version of Bethel.

Of the 45 participants in that first conference about a third were recruited from industry and the rest came mainly from education, social welfare and the probation and prison services. Overall, the evaluation was positive: a second conference was held in 1959, and three more in 1960–61.

In the earliest conferences the central event was the small *study group*, consisting of 9–12 members, a staff consultant and a staff observer. Its task was to study its own behaviour, as a group, in the here and now. The other main events were lectures ('social theory sessions') and *application groups*, which were intended between them to help members make sense of their study group experience and consider how it might be applied in their external roles. There were also plenary review sessions. This design was broadly similar to that at Bethel, though the equivalent Bethel group was larger – up to 20 members. Also the Leicester consultant's orientation was less person-centred: it addressed the dynamics of the group.

The 1959 Conference saw the experimental introduction of an *inter-group event*, in which members were asked to divide into groups and negotiate an agreement on how to use vacant slots in the programme. Consultants helped to interpret the inter-group dynamics (Higgin and Bridger, 1964).

In 1962 A. K. Rice took over direction of the conferences and introduced significant developments in design (cf. Rice, 1965). The first was the innovation of the *large group*. Its task was the same as for the small study group, but it included all the members (sometimes 70 or more) with two to four consultants. Secondly, the inter-group event was redefined as having a single task: the membership was to form itself into groups and to study their interrelatedness in the here and now. Thirdly, a second type of inter-group event (later called the *institutional event*) was introduced, in which the focus of study was the member–staff relationship within the conference institution as a whole. Finally, as a natural consequence of the increasing emphasis on experiential learning in the here and now, the lectures were reduced and eventually dropped. Plenary sessions and application groups were retained, and there was increasing use of interim *review groups*, to give members an opportunity to reflect on their experience in the here and now sessions.[1]

Despite subsequent theoretical and technical developments, the Leicester Conference model of today was essentially established by the time Rice died in 1969. Then, as now, a typical day's programme in the first week would comprise four 1½-hour sessions, with a break in the afternoon: Small Study Group (SSG) and Large Study Group (LSG) in the morning, and two sessions of Inter-Group (IG). In the second week, the Institutional Event (IE) would replace the IG, and towards the end there would be Application Group (AG) and Plenary (P) sessions. Some conferences also include the Very Small Study Group (VSSG) of five to seven members (see Gosling, 1981).

Thus the SSG has become only one of several settings for the study of the relatedness of individual, group and organization. The conference as a whole, comprising both members and staff, is designed as a temporary educational institution, which can be studied experientially as it forms, evolves and comes to an end.

---

[1] The 'single-task' model introduced by Rice, with its insistence on the study of the here and now, had some critics within TIHR. They believed it could be too threatening to some members and could inhibit learning rather than encourage it. Accordingly, Harold Bridger, who was centrally involved in the earlier Leicester Conferences and had introduced the inter-group experiment in 1959, has developed an alternative conference model, based on a 'two-task' design. In this, membership groups are given specific assignments *and* study the dynamics of the groups in tackling them. Bridger continues to organize these conferences through TIHR and in association with other institutions. That model, however, is outside the scope of this chapter.

It also became clear during the 1960s that 'group relations' was too broad and vague a description of what was being studied. To be sure, the focus of interpretation in the Leicester model has always been on the dynamic of the group as a whole, and not on individuals. In the early days (and I speak from painful personal memories) a trainee consultant would feel grateful to identify any group-as-a-whole dynamic at all. With experience, however, although the consultant may still feel lost at times, often there is an evident choice of interpretations that might be made. Rice recognized that the definition of the *primary task* of the conference as a whole and of the events within it was therefore important. In the early 1960s he was defining the primary task as 'to provide those who attend with opportunities to learn about leadership' (Rice, 1965, p. 5). He then redefined it more precisely in terms of exercise of authority. Recognition that there are choices in the definition of primary task and, therefore, in the focus of interpretation, enlarged the scope of conference design. Thus the late 1970s saw a new series of Leicester Conferences with the title 'Individual and Organization: the Politics of Relatedness'. These alternated with more 'traditional' conferences on the theme of 'Authority, Leadership and Organization', which still continue. In these, the primary task is defined in some such terms as this: 'to provide opportunities to study the exercise of authority in the context of inter-personal, inter-group and institutional relations within the Conference Institution'. The primary task of each event is defined in relation to that overall definition.

Nowadays, alternate conferences make special provision for members with previous Leicester (or similar) experience: in some sessions they work separately from 'first-timers', in others, jointly. Other conferences include a *training group*. The first such group was introduced in 1963. Initially this was designed to expand the pool of potential staff. It now has the broader aim of helping people to understand and practise the consultant role in group and organizational settings. Members of the training group have usually already taken part in at least two residential conferences.

CONCEPTS AND ASSUMPTIONS

I share with a number of colleagues, past and present, a continuing theoretical interest in the relatedness – the processes of mutual influence – between individual and group, group and group, and group and organization, and, beyond that, the relatedness of organization and community to wider social systems, to society itself. As Bion recognized, in all these forms of relatedness there is a potential tension. The individual needs groups in order to establish her/his identity, to find meaning in her/his existence, and to express different aspects of her/himself. Correspondingly, the group also needs the individual member for its own collective purposes – both to contribute to the group's task and also to participate in the processes through which the group acquires and maintains its own distinctive identity. But this process is one that often threatens individuality.

This theoretical perspective is central to the conceptualization of the conference model; and obviously the conferences themselves illuminate the theory. However, the primary task of the conferences is not to contribute to theory but to provide members with opportunities to learn about their own involvement in these dynamics. More generally, the aim is to enable 'the individual to develop greater maturity in understanding and managing the boundary between his own inner world and the realities of his external environment' (Miller, 1977, p. 44; cf. Miller and Rice, 1967, p. 269) – in other words, to become less of a captive of group and organizational processes.[2]

Such a formulation has important implications. What the individual experiences and learns is unique to her/him. It makes no sense to define what she/he 'ought to have learned': that phrase in itself implies dependence on an external authority. Other people, including staff consultants, may offer their views of a situation; but only the individual member is in a position to interpret, in the light of the role he/she has, what is happening around him/her and what is happening in her/his own inner world. Hence it is on the individual's own authority that she/he accepts what is valid for her/him and rejects what is not.

This, of course, is the model of conventional psychoanalysis. Contrary to popular belief, Freud's breakthroughs were achieved not by studying individuals in greater depth – that had proved sterile – but by extending the field of study to the two-person relationship, of analyst and analysed. Crucial here was his recognition and use of the transference. That is to say, the patient displaces and projects onto the shadowy figure of the analyst feelings that have little or nothing to do with the analyst as a person: instead, the analyst becomes the receptacle or object of, for example, the patient's early feelings about mother or father. The corollary is the countertransfer-ence – the feelings that the patient evokes in the analyst – who then has to distinguish how far she/he is responding as the patient's parents might have responded, and how far the patient is evoking feelings that belong to unresolved issues in the analyst's own past.

Leicester Conferences similarly assume that the behaviour of individuals and groups is affected by unconscious forces, and that attempts to elucidate these forces at the group and organizational levels will provide a worth-while learning process, through which individuals will be better able to exercise their own authority. Hence the concepts of transference and

[2] There is an obvious link here with TIHR's values in promoting autonomous work-groups.

countertransference are central to the staff's method of working. The staff consultant (again contrary to popular belief) is far from being a fly on the wall, observing group dynamics as if they were 'out there'. The consultant's relation to the member group is analogous to the analyst's: he/she is trying to understand and use as a basis for interpretation his/her relatedness to the group. Feelings are as important as observations. (The role of staff observer in study groups has been dropped because it tends to distort or dilute study of the transference.)

From psychoanalysis also, and in particular from Melanie Klein, is drawn a useful and relevant formulation of the process of infant development and its effects in adult life. She postulated (e.g. Klein, 1959) that the very young baby does not distinguish between inside and outside: it still lacks the 'ego function' that would enable it to separate its feelings from the causes of those feelings. What it feels about an object becomes an attribute of that object: this is the process of projection. The feelings are polarized: the infant's world, according to Klein, is made up of 'good objects' that it loves and seeks to preserve and of 'bad objects' that represent pain and frustration and that it seeks to destroy. But it has to learn that it is often the same object – for example, mother's breast – that is sometimes satisfying and sometimes frustrating. This awareness is the beginning of an ego function. The mature ego distinguishes between what is real in the outside world and what is projected from inside. However, those primitive processes of splitting and projection are never wholly overcome, and indeed they are constantly reactivated in adult life in relations, for example, between followers and leaders, between groups, and indeed between nations. (The transference, of course, is the special case of projection on to the analyst.) The picture that emerges is of the individual struggling to exercise his/her own authority and – to use a term to which we have given increasing currency – to manage her/himself in role (Lawrence and Miller, 1976; Lawrence, 1979).

We can now see that Bion, who was himself influenced by Klein, had made a breakthrough with the group, which was closely similar to Freud's with the individual: he focused on the group in relation to himself as consultant, using the transference and countertransference.

Bion's postulate is that at any given time the behaviour of the group can be analysed at two levels: it is a *sophisticated group* (or *work group*) met to perform some overt task and, at another level, it is at the same moment a *basic group*, covertly acting as a whole on a *basic assumption*, to which members contribute anonymously and in ways of which they are not consciously aware. The basic group constantly modifies – often detrimentally, sometimes positively – the goals and activities of the work group. Bion identified three such basic assumptions: fight/flight, dependency, and pairing. He argued that one function of the basic assumption prevailing at a particular moment is to exclude the emotions associated with the other two.

His theory was important not only in itself but in the developments it stimulated. Essentially, it helps us to focus on the group as a system and to recognize that the behaviour manifested by the group may not necessarily follow from the conscious intentions of its individual members. In larger groups and organizations, which are themselves differentiated formally or informally into various sub-systems, the notion of the two levels of activity has proved to be a useful heuristic tool, though the complexity of course is greater. For example, when the large study group (LSG) was introduced into the Leicester Conferences, it quickly became apparent that it was rare for any one of the three basic assumptions to pervade the group as a whole. Other dynamics were also operating. Rice felt that Bion's concepts described

> special cases which are most easily observed in small groups, because they are large enough to give power to an alternative leadership (i.e. an alternative to the consultant), and yet not so large as to provide support for more than one kind of powerful alternative leadership at any one time (Rice, 1969, p. 40).

Turquet (1974) began to elucidate the characteristic dynamics and myths of groups of different sizes: the pair, the triad, 5–6, 8–12+, 20–30, 50–80. He also explored in depth the threat to identity that is characteristic of the LSG experience (Turquet, 1975).

Leicester Conferences therefore use the psychoanalytic notion of transference in all the experiential events, as a way of elucidating the dynamics of the system under study (cf. Klein, 1977). The conference staff are always part of the dynamic.

The Leicester Conference, however, despite its debt to psychoanalytic thinking, is not in the business of therapy: it is an educational institution concerned with learning, not treatment. In part, the distinction is semantic – a matter of labelling. A significant shift in individual insight and functioning can occur through an intervention calling itself therapeutic, through an educational process, through a religious conversion, or indeed through a dramatic life-experience. But the distinction has to be asserted because different labels carry different meanings – and fantasies – which affect the dynamics. 'Therapy' implies illness and treatment; it evokes a fantasy of an institution in which members are patients and staff are responsible for treating them. This is hardly consistent with the notion of exercising personal authority and managing one's own learning.

In any case, psychoanalysis is only one part of the intellectual heritage of Leicester Conferences. Rice himself was not an analyst but (as I am) an organizational consultant. He, with some of his TIHR colleagues, had been much influenced in their thinking about work-groups as socio-technical systems by the concept of *open systems*, developed first by the biologist, von Bertalanffy (1950a,b); and he began to adapt it as a framework for analysing whole organizations (Rice, 1963, 1969, 1970; Miller and Rice, 1967; Miller,

1976). These organizations included the Leicester Conference itself (Rice, 1965). This concept makes it possible to look simultaneously at the relation between part and whole, between whole and environment. It also allows us to recognize that individual, sub-group, group and organization have similar *systemic* characteristics.

A key connecting concept is that of *boundary*. Any human system exists, and can only exist, through continuous interchange with its environment, whether of materials, people, information, ideas, values or fantasies. The boundary across which these 'commodities' flow in and out both separates the system from, and links it to, its environment: it marks a discontinuity between the task of that particular system and the tasks of the related systems with which it transacts. Because these relations are never stable and static, and because the behaviour and identity of the system are subject to continual renegotiation and redefinition, the system boundary is best conceived not as a line but as a region. That region is the location of those roles and activities that are concerned with mediating relations between inside and outside. In organizations and groups this is the function of leadership; in individuals it is the ego function. The health and indeed the survival of a system depends on an appropriate mix of insulation and permeability in the boundary region.

In Leicester Conferences it is a task of staff, who act collectively as management, to provide the boundary conditions – task, territory and time – within which all participants – members and staff themselves – can engage with the primary task of the conference. Much of the work of the conference is the examination of boundaries, within and among groups (especially between membership and staff), and between the group and wider system of the conference as a whole. Members may also explore their own boundaries, between person and role, and indeed between their individual inner and outer worlds.

The study groups are sometimes described as unstructured. This is erroneous. In relation to the task of the group there is a very simple structure with two roles – consultant (with the task of providing opportunities to learn) and member. As I noted earlier, the familiar structures of organizations are not only a means of getting the task performed but also provide members with defences against anxiety, including anxiety engendered by the task itself. In the minimal structure of, say, the LSG, it is postulated that we can see and experience dynamics that are present in all groups of similar size but rendered less visible by the conventional structures. This in turn provides evidence of the underlying anxieties that the structures defend against and contain.

It must be re-emphasized that staff, in their management role as well as in the consultant roles that they take up, are part of the conference as a system. The ways in which they struggle to manage their roles, much of the time in the presence of members, provide, for better or worse, a model for members struggling to manage their own.

PRACTICE

The role of director and staff

People invited to join the staff at Leicester have been members of at least two residential conferences and probably also of a training group, and obviously they have displayed some propensity for the work and interest in it. Beyond that, there are no specific qualifications. They may first have taken a staff role in a shorter conference, perhaps non-residential. Usually each staff group includes at least two – often more – staff from related institutions, in which case they will have had considerable staff experience in other conferences, often including directorship.

In the early conferences it was considered mandatory that study group consultants should be analysts or at least have had an extended analysis. By the early 1960s, with increasing demand for conferences, it became clear that insistence on this qualification would severely constrain growth and dissemination. There were other factors. Initial anxieties about individual disturbance had turned out to be exaggerated, so that clinical experience was not needed. Indeed, it could be a distraction from focusing on the group as a whole. Moreover, other events, besides the study groups, had been added and the task and boundaries were more clearly defined and held. And finally, experience with growing numbers of members showed that clinical training was not correlated with insight and learning. The fundamental qualification for consultancy seemed to be an ability to stick to the task and role. Accordingly, the early training groups included university teachers, managers from industry and prison governors among others.

Leicester Conference Directors have continued to be people with analytic experience, though not necessarily analysts; and indeed for the first 12 years there was a policy that the director role should *not* be taken by a psychiatrist. It was argued that under psychiatric leadership the membership would be more likely to produce 'patients' and that the stance of the conference might tilt away from the educational towards the therapeutic. By 1970, however, the model was firmly enough established to make that less of a risk.

The conference director is appointed by the sponsoring institution(s). The director is initially responsible for conference design and the appointment of staff. By accepting the invitation, staff members are individually confirming the director's authority; but, as indicated above, the staff group as a whole, including both consulting and administrative staff, are collectively the 'management'. Hence the authority of the director has to be confirmed by

Figure 10.1 The relation of the consultant to the group. m, individual member; M, member group; C, consultant. Reproduced from Miller (1977), with the permission of Macmillan Press Limited.

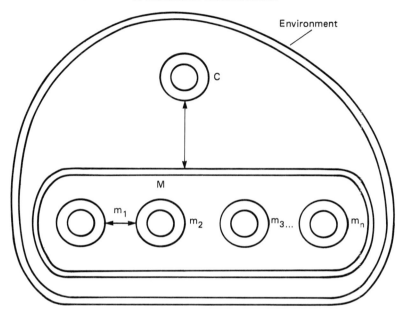

the staff group at their pre-conference meeting, and that authorization has to be kept under review as the conference proceeds. Once the conference has begun, *the staff group has the authority to replace the director*. If there is irreconcilable disagreement between the director and one or more staff members, then (s)he or they have to resign. Although in practice this has never happened it has nearly happened; and it is vital in a conference focused on authority that the authority of the director should always remain to some extent problematic. Transference of the membership – and indeed of staff – onto the director yields insight into the collusive processes through which organizational hierarchies in general are sustained.

At the conference itself, the director has overall responsibility, on behalf of the staff group, for boundary management – the external boundary, especially in relation to the hall of residence in which it is held; and internally, the boundary between staff and membership. Management of practical matters on these boundaries is delegated to the Conference Administrator(s). The director leads the work of staff in public, for example in plenary sessions, and in its own separate meetings. The director also takes a consultant role, usually in the LSG.

Figure 10.1 illustrates the systemic framework within which the staff consultant is working, and represents a small study group. Transactions among individual members, $m_1 - m_2$ are to be understood in terms of the relatedness of the member group and the consultant, $M - C$. That in turn implies some image or fantasy of the system as a whole that includes both M and C and of its relation to its environment. (In the LSG, C may be 2–4 consultants. The same basic model can be extended to the more complex situation in which m is a sub-group of members, M is the total membership of the group, and C is the staff of the conference.) A consultant's interpretation is essentially a working hypothesis about this set of systemic relations, drawing on his/her observations and internal feelings. To take a simple example, when in a SSG a silent member is being picked on by others, the consultant may feel and say that the attack is really on him for not contributing what the members want from him; further, he may feel that the attack is displaced because there is anxiety that if it were directed to the consultant it would be so violent as to destroy him and throw the group into anarchy; and beyond that again, that the small group has to be kept safe because the wider system – the conference at large – is felt to be evil and indiscriminately destructive. Ideally, therefore, the working hypothesis contains a 'because clause' – a possible explanation of why this dynamic is occurring. The consultant is not always able to offer such a 'because clause' immediately: he may have to make two or three intervening observations first. Always, however, the consultant is trying to use his experience of being pushed into this role or that in order to work at the task of the group – the study of its own behaviour, as a group, in the here and now. Comments on individual dynamics are avoided.

In taking up this interpretative role, the consultant is operating at the boundary of the system, trying to understand what is happening between the parts and the whole, and between the whole and its environment. One hopes that at times members will learn to take up this boundary perspective themselves.

Two other points may be made about consultant behaviour in experiential groups which sometimes causes puzzlement. First, she/he enters and leaves the group territory strictly according to the timetable. This predictability offers a form of security; it defines the time available and leaves the members with their authority to decide how to use it; and it enables the consultant to interpret the way they use it. Secondly, the contributions of the consultant are always so far as possible directed to the task: thus conventional social rituals, such as 'good mornings', which are not task-related, are eschewed.

In the review and application groups, which have a different task, the role of the consultant is correspondingly different: it tends to be less interpretative and more facilitative, and is occasionally even didactic, in that the consultant may offer conceptual frameworks to help members understand processes they have experienced.

The membership role

There are no specific qualifications for membership. Undeniably, some members find the conference stressful, and people going through emotional turmoil in their personal lives are probably not in the best state to make use of an intensive educational programme, but the decision has to be theirs – our assumption has to be that as managers and professionals with responsibility for the well-being of others, they must be capable of making such a decision. Sometimes we receive enquiries from organiz-ations about whether to send a particular manager to the conference – perhaps someone with relationship difficulties. Our response is that we do not provide treatment for such difficulties, and we recommend against *sending* anyone: learning is much more likely if the individual exercises his/her own authority to apply. The fee structure itself encourages two or more members from the same organization to attend together: experience shows that they are more likely to apply their learning effectively when they go back.

In the conference opening, the director may typically say: 'Staff are not here to teach in the conventional sense but to provide opportunities to learn. What you learn and the pace at which you learn are up to you.' There is a starting assumption that application to become a member implies some preparedness to engage in the task of the conference. Beyond that, the role of member is not defined. There is no compulsion to attend sessions on time, or at all. Taking up a membership role is left to the individual's authority.

The experience of being a member is nevertheless initially disconcerting. Members experience themselves as acting as individuals, yet the consultants persist in interpreting their behaviour as a function of the group as a whole (Miller, 1980). Whereas the individual is clear that she/he intended this, or did not intend that, the consultant seems perversely to focus instead on effects and consequences, and from these infers unconscious intentions at the level of the group. So quite basic, taken-for-granted assumptions about one's identity, one's sense of self, are being called into question; the boundary between self and other, which had seemed obvious. suddenly becomes problematic.

Although no individual counselling is given, the review and application groups allow members to tease out their experience in the various roles they are taking within the different events and to examine its relevance to the roles they have outside.

The conference process

Members and staff are participating in the construction, evolution and ending of a temporary institution. That applies at the level of the conference as a whole and also at the level of events within it – particularly the SSG and LSG which continue through most of the 2 weeks.

The early stage sees the sharing of prior expectations and fantasies. By the end of the second day most members have 'joined', in the sense of being caught up in the process, and a conference culture has begun to emerge. For example, the majority are strictly observing the time boundaries of sessions and the consultant role has become less alien. At the end of the first week there is a 36-hour break, during which most members leave Leicester for at least part of the time. 'Ordinary life' – life outside the conference – is often felt to be disorienting, particularly for members going back to their families. They have become much more involved than they had realized. Before the break there is anxiety: will others come back, will the consultant come back? Behind that of course is the basic question: will *I* come back? Commitment is tested. The second week tests what members thought they had learned in the first: it is a form of application. 'I've learned not to get caught like that again' – and then getting caught in just the same way; or carefully avoiding one landmine, only to tread on another. There are also of course the more positive experiences: for example, learning about group organization and representation from the inter-group event may prove useful in the institutional event which begins after the break. Then, as they come to the final sessions of SSG and LSG, and to the closing plenaries, staff and members are working at the processes of ending. This means sorting out some of the projections of the past 2 weeks and redrawing the boundary around oneself. Application sessions help in this by re-alerting members to their external roles.

There is another level of the conference process that needs to be mentioned. At various times during the fortnight most members find themselves immersed in and extracting themselves from unconscious dynamics. These seem strange, even bizarre, yet are not easily explained away. For example, in the IG and IE, when members form themselves into groups, often one of these begins to behave as a quasi-staff group; and it is not at all uncommon to discover that the configuration of such a group is identical to the staff group, both in overall size and in its gender and ethnic distribution. Or a set of members may erupt with violent feelings against some 'enemy', and then subsequently realize that they had been behaving quite irrationally and mindlessly.

Mechanisms of learning and change

This brings me to the nature of learning and what may be learned. As I have reiterated, the conference model assumes that authority for making use of the experience and learning from it lies firmly with the individual member. Outcomes are unpredictable. The nature of interpretation, the structure of the conference and the intensity of the 'social island' nevertheless combine to call existing assumptions into question and to generate new insights.

Experience suggests that three different kinds of learning are likely to occur. At the simplest level, members learn to identify and label some of the unfamiliar phenomena that they encounter. A second kind, going beyond this, is partly conceptual: the experience adds to the ways in which the individual classifies the world and his experience in it – particularly unconscious processes. Members often speak of conference learning as giving them another perspective on human behaviour, and that is often what they mean. They may, however, be referring to a third kind of learning, which implies not an *additional* perspective but a *different* perspective. There is a correspondence here to the three levels of learning postulated by Bateson (1973). Palmer (1979) draws on Bateson in an important paper on 'Learning and the Group Experience'. This third level, as he elegantly puts it, 'entails discovering a capacity to doubt the validity of perceptions which seem unquestionably true'. He goes on to say:

> This is something different from merely replacing one apperceptive habit by another, as might be the objective of behaviour therapy. . . . It is also something different from being knowledgeable about one's own character, in the manner of those who justify their behaviour with statements like: 'Well, you see, I am a very dependent (obsessional, paranoid, untidy) person.' The experience of Learning III is the experience of becoming responsible for one's dependence (obsessiveness, paranoia, untidiness) as something one is, and is doing (Palmer, 1979, p. 173).

These distinctions are important, but difficult to operationalize. 'Learning III' implies some degree of personality restructuring – a systemic change – of a kind which would be fully in line with the aims of the conference; but how likely is this to happen within the 2-week span? And how does one measure it?

In the absence of systematic research, I offer the following tentative conclusions:

(i) 'Level II' learning – the additional perspective – is a fairly common and obviously desirable outcome. Although the groundwork for it is laid by the conference, it becomes established only in the ensuing months – notably when a member identifies a process that is dynamically similar to one in which he was involved in the conference. It is helped if the member is returning to a setting where others already share that perspective.[3]

---

[3] Menninger (1972, 1985) gives an account of an attempt in one organization to bring about a significant cultural change by encouraging a substantial number – a critical mass – of its professional and administrative staff to attend Leicester Conferences and others based on a similar model. The second paper follows up the experience after some 10 years.

(ii) Level II learning is a necessary but not sufficient condition for Level III, which may be even more desirable, but is less common and more elusive. It is often, though by no means always, expressed in significant changes in the individual's work and personal life: for example, a career move, a job change, a change of partner. (Such moves, of course, are not in themselves to be taken as positive indicators: they may also be symptoms of avoiding confrontations that a Level III change might require.)

(iii) Statements made by members at the end of the conference are a poor guide to outcome. Scepticism tends to be a more positive indicator than enthusiasm or euphoria: it implies that they are still internally wrestling with their experience.

Problems and limitations

Notwithstanding the difficulties of evaluation, the continued demand for membership over a period of 30 years must represent some acknowledgment of its usefulness. Many organizations, based on experience from returning members, have encouraged others to attend, and there has been a continuing connection over many years. And very many individuals have come on the recommendation of colleagues and friends. All this is positive.

But the very fact that the Leicester Conference has become an established institution poses both a paradox and a problem. The paradox is that in its aims, as we have seen, the conference is subversive. It invites members to test and perhaps discard cherished assumptions, both as individuals and in their organizational roles. Accepted notions of 'reality' are thrown into disarray. Managements that encourage personnel to attend must presumably be either very enlightened (and indeed some are) or else, which is more worrying, confident that Leicester graduates will not be too much of a threat to the *status quo*. Our impression is that Level II learning can enable people to be more effective and to use their authority to test the boundaries of their roles, but without turning the world upside down. Assimilation of Level III learners tends to be more difficult: although some become skilful innovators, others seek out alternative settings for what they are aspiring to do.

The problem with becoming an established institution is a shift in the motivation of members. An increasing proportion enrol less with the intention of learning than in order to gain a form of accreditation. Some have connections with the institutions that run conferences based on the Leicester model and have already taken part in one or more of these: 'Leicester experience' may be necessary or at least helpful to progression to staff roles in these institutions. Also, there are various professional circles, especially in mental health, where attending (and surviving) a Leicester Conference has almost become a *rite de passage*, or carries some cachet. And beyond these two categories there are others who have been primed by previous members and have an idea in advance of what to expect. The proportion of 'naive' members, lacking in such external connections and in prior knowledge, has diminished. The *cognoscenti*, who outnumber them, tend to bring, in addition to their (at best) mixed motivations, some prefabricated defences: for example, trying to take up an observing, interpretative role as a way of avoiding involvement; using psychological jargon to outface the 'naive' members; trying to set up situations that will defend them against the uncertainties of the member role by demonstrating their competence in their external professional roles.

These defences put some technical demands on staff, but the structure and dynamic of the conference support the task, and the overwhelming majority of members find that they become involved – they 'join' – almost in spite of themselves. There is, however, a residual difficulty. There is a persistent myth that Leicester Conferences produce psychiatric casualties. It certainly produces disturbances; but so far as I can discover only three members have been admitted as psychiatric patients during or immediately following a conference. One was in the early 1960s. The second was a member who became disturbed during the mid-conference break and was taken to hospital by 'helpful' colleagues: we had some difficulty in getting him released for the final plenary session. In the most recent case the member discharged herself within 3 days and was fully competent during the rest of the conference. So the actual incidence of serious breakdown is extraordinarily low – of the order of 0.1%. The myth nevertheless persists, evidently in order to 'prove' how dangerous the experience is – which means: 'How clever I am to survive it.' Members of the so-called helping professions have an interest in producing casualties: by becoming care-givers, they can then reaffirm themselves in their professional roles. The staff response is to focus not on the individual but on the group dynamic: our working hypothesis is that any increase in the individual's disturbance is a product of projections from the group. Rigorous interpretation at the group level will almost invariably undo the projections. But the pressures to regard the disturbed individual as a patient are very seductive.

In almost every conference there is a tiny handful of members who are unable to use the experience. As indicated earlier, we have no way of identifying them in advance. If, as it seems, they are too defended to learn, all we can do is to respect their defences. Authority remains with the member.

DISSEMINATION AND APPLICATION
Development of other conference institutions

Alongside Leicester Conferences, TIHR's Group Relations Training Programme (GRTP) has regularly run shorter, theme-centred conferences, residential and non-residential – for example, on male–female working relationships (Gould, 1979), destructiveness and creativity, or interdependence and conflict – as well as series of weekly study groups, focusing on small group behaviour. The GRTP also has a long history of designing, running, directing and/or staffing training events for other organizations. In these the 'Leicester model' is a sometimes central, and sometimes much more marginal influence.

However, the staff of TIHR who have been involved in the Leicester Conferences over the years have never wanted to be exclusively or even mainly in the conference business. Indeed, continuing experience as practitioners was seen as a necessary condition for effectiveness in conference work. Yet, during the 1960s and early 1970s in particular, the national and international demand for 'group relations training' was such that there were pressures to devote more and more time to it. The TIHR response was to encourage and help other institutions in Britain and abroad to acquire their own capabilities to sponsor and staff events based on the Leicester approach. The earliest examples in the 1960s were, in England, the Grubb Institute of Behavioural Studies (formerly Christian Teamwork) and, in the United States, the Washington School of Psychiatry and the Yale University School of Medicine. In both cases, the TIHR co-sponsored a series of 'Leicester-type' conferences, initially providing the director and most staff, until the institutions were equipped to run the events themselves. Subsequently, there has been similar collaboration in other countries, including France (with the International Foundation for Social Innovation), India (the Indian Institute of Management, Calcutta) and most recently Israel. Meanwhile, the A. K. Rice Institute, which was separately incorporated in 1970 to develop conferences in the USA, where it now has a number of active regional affiliates, has itself engaged in a similar institution-building process in Sweden. Groups elsewhere – for example, Finland, Germany and Norway – have taken the initiative to run regular conferences themselves, using Leicester Conference 'graduates' to direct and staff them.

Organizational interventions

This international experience has confirmed that in temporary organizations such as the Leicester Conference the basic model offers an effective methodology of enquiry into underlying dynamics. How far is it directly applicable in ongoing organizations?

Sometimes there are requests to run a one-off experiential conference for, say, all the staff of a clinic or of a department in a company. Explicitly or implicitly, the prospective client system is hoping that this will unlock relationship difficulties and catalyse change. In my judgement the one-off conference can be more damaging than constructive, and should only be undertaken as part of a longer-term intervention within which the consultant(s) can take continuing professional responsibility to help the client work through the outcomes.

One such Tavistock intervention was with the US Dependents Schools (European Area), which provide education for children of American servicemen posted overseas. In this case, after initial work with the headquarters group, senior staff from all the schools were brought together for an intensive 5-day experiential event, which included some training on mutual consultation. This was followed by a 6-month application phase during which regional groups met regularly to support each other in using the conference experience to analyse and tackle problems in their own schools. Conference consultants were available for some of these sessions. The intervention concluded with another 3-day residential conference, which combined some additional experiential sessions with more practical review and forward planning.

Although this was generally seen as a productive experience, this type of 'in-house' intervention, like the one-off conference, carries an inherent tension: who is the client? In the regular Leicester Conference, the 'client' is assumed to be the individual member. Even though the fee may be paid by an employing organization, the presumption is that it is the member who applies, on his/her own authority, and correspondingly that it is for the member, not for the conference sponsors, to manage his/her accountability to the employer. How to report back is a common issue in application groups towards the end of the conference. In organizational interventions of the kind just described there are two clients: the organization *and* the individual participant. The tension arises from the subversiveness of the Leicester Conference approach, in that it is encouraging members to question the nature of authority and hence the ways in which they manage their role relationships to superiors, colleagues and subordinates in their own organizations. But in an 'in-house' application the organization, through its management, is also a client. Even though we may demand that membership should be voluntary, in reality individuals may feel under pressure to attend. Managers wanting to be 'equal' participants within the conference will be pushed towards mobilizing their external managerial roles. To the extent that they feel that the conference experience is a threat to their external authority, they are liable to be set up by the rest of the membership – perhaps to lead an attack on the conference staff – and so the boundary between membership roles and external roles becomes blurred. In such settings, it is a continuing technical problem for consulting staff to work at this inherent ambiguity and tension of the dual clients.

Another example was a seriously under-performing manufacturing company with just under 1000 employees, which was part of a large international group (see Miller, 1977; Khaleelee and Miller, 1985). It operated on two sites: one, near London, included the main factory and the head office; the other, in the Midlands – 100 miles away – contained a much smaller plant. This was the result of amalgamating two businesses, which had previously been competitors. What was now the main factory had belonged to a company that the group had purchased, while the Midlands factory was the residue of the group's own former subsidiary that made a similar product. Moreover, the sales force had been removed from the acquired company. And there had been other disruptive changes.

In this case the intervention began with a diagnostic survey of all employees. This revealed acute splits cutting across one another: between management and workers, between employees from the two previous enterprises, and between departments. Identification with the organization as a whole was notably absent. Boundaries had been fractured and partly disintegrated; employees had fallen back onto their individual boundaries in a culture of survival.

The consultants postulated that the fragmented boundaries needed to be reconstructed, and designed what came to be called the 'People Programme'. Its main feature was an extended version of a Leicester Conference for 120 managers, supervisors and specialists, with weekly small study groups, week-end inter-group events and finally weekly large groups, which exactly matched the need to work at the boundaries at three levels: the individual in role relationships, the department and other groupings in their inter-group relations, and the organization as a whole in relation to its environment. Meanwhile, consultancy was being provided to the top management group – which in this case was the primary client. A formal system of employee consultation was also set up.

Within a year, significant changes had occurred: the People Programme, instead of being run by the consultants, had been taken over by the participants; the training was being extended to other employees; the large group was still meeting weekly (and continued to do so for 3 years); task groups arose spontaneously to tackle pressing problems; inter-departmental coordination improved; the organization gained a new sense of identity; and manufacturing performance and profits went up dramatically.

The consultants, who had already been providing consultancy on request, not only to top management but to various other internal groups, including a joint trade union body, then negotiated a new contract. This established them as a quasi-independent Consulting Resource Group (CRG) with its own budget, and made it explicit that the organization as a whole – not management – was the client system. In addition to servicing internal groups, the CRG took on a new task, which was to try to elucidate the overall dynamics of the organization. This involved experimenting to see whether the methodology of, say, the large study group, could be extended to a group of nearly 1000, only a tiny proportion of whom could be present with the consultants at any one time. The common link was use of the transference. The CRG, like the group consultant in a conference, was both outside the organizational boundary and also part of a wider client–consultant system, and hence available for projections from the organization. The technique used was a weekly session, which anyone – manager or worker – was free to attend, in which the CRG members reviewed their work during the week with parts of the organization as a basis for formulating working hypotheses about the system as a whole. Evidence included their experience of being pulled in or pushed out, idealized or denigrated, homogenized or split, and so on, as well as observations of the pattern of projections among different groupings within the client system. Members of the organization present at the meetings were taken as representing a microcosm of the whole. They worked on these hypotheses and added their own preoccupations; and beyond that the consultants used the emerging interpretations directly and indirectly in their work with various groups in the ensuing week. In these ways the voice of CRG was 'heard' by a significant proportion of the organization and seemed to have some influence.

> The most overt evidence was in the growing number of individuals able to perceive organizational processes in which they were implicated and able also to act on their understanding by taking greater personal authority in their . . . roles (Khaleelee and Miller, 1985, pp. 363–4).

Beyond the organization

This experiment encouraged a group in the London-based organization, OPUS (an Organization for Promoting Understanding in Society), to try to extend and adapt the methodology to the study of societal dynamics, by explicitly setting out to use the microcosm to reflect the macrocosm (OPUS, 1980–86; Khaleelee and Miller, 1985; Miller, 1986a). As Rioch (1979) notes, conferences based on the Leicester model often mirror current societal phenomena. At present it appears that significant underlying themes can emerge in quite small groups that are given the task of examining their experience in their role as 'members of society'. Larger groups, of 30–40, may unconsciously enact, in vivid and painful ways, important societal processes. A recent example was an OPUS conference on 'Society and the Inner City', which belatedly realized that it had unconsciously reproduced, by creating an isolated sub-group, the very phenomena that it was discussing (Miller, 1986b).

CONCLUDING COMMENT

I have been concentrating here on applications of the conference model. However, this model is itself an application, for an educational task, of a conceptual framework evolved through and for TIHR's action research and consultancy with organizational clients, in which use of primary task and the open-system framework, and alertness to unconscious elements, have been pivotal. So also, of course, is the reflexive use of the consultant role. What the conference does is to apply a magnifying glass to the unconscious dynamics. In an organizational intervention too, as in a conference, the consultant is using his/her feelings to help to elucidate organizational dynamics; but the direct here-and-now interpretation is useful only in the relatively rare settings where clients (perhaps through Leicester-type experience) are attuned to that perspective. Organizational consultants have to formulate their insights in ways that the client can hear and use. Nevertheless, there is ample evidence (e.g. Richardson, 1973; Hausman, 1976; Levinson and Astrachan, 1976) that the member role and, still more, the consultant role at a Leicester Conference can be an invaluable developmental experience for the organizational consultant and others, including managers themselves, engaged in the management of change.

REFERENCES

Bateson, G. (1973). *Towards an Ecology of the Mind*. St. Albans, Paladin.
Bertalanffy, L. von (1950a). The theory of open systems in physics and biology. *Science* 3, 23–9.
Bertalanffy, L. von (1950b). An outline of general systems theory. *British Journal of the Philosophy of Science* 1, 134–65.
Bion, W. R. (1946). The leaderless group project. *Bulletin of the Menninger Clinic* 10(3), 77–81.
Bion, W. R. (1947–51). Experiences in groups: I–VI. *Human Relations* 1–4.
Bion, W. R. (1961). *Experiences in Groups and Other Papers*. London, Tavistock.
Bion, W. R. and Rickman, J. (1943). Intra-group tensions in therapy: their study as the task of the group. *Lancet* ii, 678–81.
Bridger, H. (1946). The Northfield Experiment. *Bulletin of the Menninger Clinic* 10(3), 71–6.
Bridger, H. (1985). Northfield revisited. *In* M. Pines (ed.), *Bion and Group Psychotherapy*, pp. 87–107. London, Routledge and Kegan Paul.
Curle, A. (1947). Transitional communities and social reconnection: a follow-up study of the civil resettlement of British prisoners of war, Part I. *Human Relations* 1, 42–68.
Curle, A. and Trist, E. L. (1947). Transitional communities and social reconnection: a follow-up study of the civil resettlement of British prisoners of war, Part II. *Human Relations* 1, 240–88.
Dicks, H. (1970). *50 Years of the Tavistock Clinic*. London, Routledge and Kegan Paul.
Gosling, R. (1981). A study of very small groups. *In* J. S. Grotstein (ed.), *Do I Dare Disturb the Universe? A Memorial to Dr. Wilfred Bion*, pp. 634–45. New York,

Aaronson. Reprinted in A. D. Colman and M. H. Geller (eds), *Group Relations Reader 2*. Washington, D.C., A. K. Rice Institute, 1985.

Gould, L. J. (1979). Men and women at work: a group relations conference on person and role. *In* W. G. Lawrence (ed.), *Exploring Individual and Organisational Boundaries*, pp. 111–21. Chichester, Wiley.

Hausman, W. (1976). The reorganization of a university department of psychiatry: a blueprint for change. *In* E. J. Miller (ed.), *Task and Organization*, pp. 309–26. London, Wiley.

Herbst, P. G. (1962). *Autonomous Group Functioning*. London, Tavistock.

Higgin, G. and Bridger, H. (1964). The psychodynamics of an intergroup experience. *Human Relations* 17, 391–446.

Jaques, E. (1953). On the dynamics of social structure. *Human Relations* 6, 3–24.

Jaques, E. (1955). Social systems as a defence against persecutory and depressive anxiety. *In* M. Klein, P. Heimann and R. E. Money Kyrle (eds), *New Directions in Psychoanalysis*, pp. 478–98. London, Tavistock.

Khaleelee, O. and Miller, E. J. (1985). Beyond the small group: society as an intelligible field of study. *In* M. Pines (ed.), *Bion and Group Psychotherapy*, pp. 354–85. London, Routledge and Kegan Paul.

Klein, E. B. (1977). Transference in training groups. *Journal of Personality and Social Systems* 1, 53–64.

Klein, M. (1959). Our adult world and its roots in infancy. *Human Relations* 12, 291–303. Reprinted in A. D. Colman and M. H. Geller (eds), *Group Relations Reader 2*. Washington, D.C., A. K. Rice Institute, 1985.

Lawrence, W. G. (1979). Introductory essay: exploring boundaries; A concept for today: managing oneself in role. *In* W. G. Lawrence (ed.), *Exploring Individual and Organisational Boundaries*, pp. 1–19; 235–49. Chichester, Wiley.

Lawrence, W. G. and Miller, E. J. (1976). Epilogue. *In* E. J. Miller (ed.), *Task and Organization*, pp. 361–6. Chichester, Wiley.

Levinson, D. and Astrachan, B. (1976). Entry into the mental health centre: a problem in organizational boundary regulation. *In* E. J. Miller (ed.), *Task and Organization*, pp. 217–34. Chichester, Wiley.

Lewin, K. (1947). Frontiers in group dynamics, Parts I and II. *Human Relations* 1, 5–41; 2, 143–53.

Maslow, A. H. (1943). A theory of human motivation. *Psychological Review* 50, 370–96.

Mayo, E. (1933). *The Human Problems of an Industrial Civilization*. New York, Macmillan.

McGregor, D. (1960). *The Human Side of Enterprise*. New York, McGraw Hill.

Menninger, R. W. (1972). The impact of group relations conferences on organizational growth, *International Journal of Group Psychotherapy* 22, 415–32.

Menninger, R. W. (1985). A retrospective view of a hospital-wide group relations training programme: costs, consequences and conclusions, *Psychiatric Annals* 38, 323–39. Reprinted in A. D. Colman and M. H. Geller (eds), *Group Relations Reader 2*. Washington, D.C., A. K. Rice Institute, 1985.

Menzies, I. E. P. (1960). A case-study in the functioning of social systems as a defence against anxiety: a report on a study of the nursing service of a general hospital. *Human Relations* 13, 95–121.

Miller, E. J. (1976). The open-system approach to organizational analysis with special reference to the work of A. K. Rice. *In* G. Hofstede and M. Sami Kassem (eds), *European Contributions to Organization Theory*, pp. 43–61. Assen/Amsterdam, Van Gorcum.

Miller, E. J. (1977). Organisational development and industrial democracy: a current case-study. *In* C. Cooper (ed.), *Organizational Development in the UK and USA: A Joint Evaluation*, pp. 31–63. New York, Macmillan. Reprinted in A. D. Colman and M. H. Geller (eds), *Group Relations Reader 2*. Washington, D.C., A. K. Rice Institute, 1985.

Miller, E. J. (1980). The politics of involvement. *Journal of Personality and Social Systems* **2**, 37–50. Reprinted in A. D. Colman and M. H. Geller (eds), *Group Relations Reader 2*. Washington, D.C., A. K. Rice Institute, 1985.

Miller, E. J. (1986a). Making room for individual autonomy. *In* S. Srivastva and Associates (eds), *Executive Power*, pp. 257–88. San Francisco, Jossey-Bass.

Miller, E. J. (1986b). Society and the inner city. OPUS Conference Report, March 8–9, 1986. Bulletin No. 22–23, Part II. London, OPUS.

Miller, E. J. and Rice, A. K. (1967). *Systems of Organization*. London, Tavistock.

Morris, B. S. (1949). Officer selection in the British army 1942–45. *Occupational Psychology* **23**(4), 219–34.

OPUS (1980–86). Bulletins 1–25. London, OPUS.

Palmer, B. (1979). Learning and the group experience. *In* W. G. Lawrence (ed.), *Exploring Individual and Organisational Boundaries*, pp. 169–92. Chichester, Wiley.

Rice, A. K. (1958). *Productivity and Social Organization: The Ahmedabad Experiment*. London, Tavistock.

Rice, A. K. (1963). *The Enterprise and its Environment*. London, Tavistock.

Rice, A. K. (1965). *Learning for Leadership*. London, Tavistock.

Rice, A. K. (1969). Individual, group and inter-group process. *Human Relations* **22**, 565–84.

Rice, A. K. (1970). *The Modern University*. London, Tavistock.

Richardson, E. (1973). *The Teacher, the School and the Task of Management*. London, Heinemann.

Rioch, M. (1979). The A. K. Rice group relations conferences as a reflection of society. *In* W. G. Lawrence (ed.), *Exploring Individual and Organisational Boundaries*, pp. 53–68. Chichester, Wiley.

Roethlisberger, F. J. and Dickson, W. J. (1939). *Management and the Worker*. Cambridge, MA, Harvard University Press.

Srivastva, S., Salipante, P. F. Cummings, T. G., Notz, W. W., Bigelow, J. D., Waters, J. A., in collaboration with Chisholm, R. F., Glen, R. H., Manring, S. and Mulloy, E. S. (1975). *Job Satisfaction and Productivity*. Cleveland, Case Western Reserve University.

Sutherland, J. D. (1985). Bion revisited: group dynamics and group psychotherapy. *In* M. Pines (ed.), *Bion and Group Psychotherapy*, pp. 47–86. London, Routledge and Kegan Paul.

Trist, E. L. (1981). *The Evolution of Socio-technical Systems*. Toronto, Ontario Quality of Working Life Centre, Occasional Paper No. 2.

Trist, E. L. (1985). Working with Bion in the 1940s: the group decade. *In* M. Pines (ed.), *Bion and Group Psychotherapy*. London, Routledge and Kegan Paul.

Trist, E. L. and Bamforth, K. W. (1951). Some social and psychological consequences of the longwall method of coal-getting. *Human Relations* **4**, 3–38.

Trist, E. L. and Sofer, C. (1959). *Exploration in Group Relations*. Leicester, Leicester University Press.

Trist, E. L., Higgin, G. W., Murray, H. and Pollock, A. B. (1963). *Organizational Choice*. London, Tavistock.

Turquet, P. M. (1974). Leadership: the individual and the group. *In* G. S. Gibbard, J. J. Hartman and R. D. Mann (eds), *Analysis of Groups*, pp. 337–71. San Francisco, Jossey-Bass.

Turquet, P. M. (1975). Threats to identity in the large group. *In* L. Kreeger (ed.), *The Large Group: Therapy and Dynamics*, pp. 87–144. London, Constable.

Wilson, A. T. M. (1951). Some aspects of social process. *Journal of Social Issues* **5** (Suppl.).

Wilson, A. T. M., Trist, E. L. and Curle, A. (1952). Transitional communities and social reconstruction: a study of the civil resettlement of prisoners of war. *In* G. E. Swanson, T. N. Newcomb and E. L. Hartley (eds), *Readings in Social Psychology*, 2nd edition, pp. 561–79. New York, Henry Holt.

CHAPTER 11

SELF-HELP GROUPS

Nona W. Ephraim

INTRODUCTION

One of the significant features of the last 20 years has been the growth in welfare services. This expansion has taken place both in the statutory and the voluntary sectors, and not least in the most informal sector of all, namely that of self-help groups. These are groups of people who share a common problem and who come together to do something about it. For the purpose of this chapter the term *self-help group* will refer to those groups which are formed around health, social or behavioural concerns. It is now possible to find a self-help group for almost any condition one might wish to name; there are groups for sufferers of backpain, premenstrual tension, cancer, groups for carers of handicapped children, the elderly, those suffering from severe mental distress or parents of hyperactive children; groups that help people either to cope with or challenge their problems in living, and groups that challenge existing orthodoxies in the manner that women's health groups have done.

The growth in the number of self-help groups has been seen by some commentators as heralding a libertarian revolution at a grass-roots level, while others have expressed concern that the growth signifies a return to the Victorian ideals of Samuel Smiley, eulogizing individual effort and the benefits of helping one's self, but with the accompanying risk of becoming a cheap substitute for professional services.

Many contradictory claims are made on behalf of self-help groups, and in a sense all the claims are correct, making the self-help group an elusive animal to define. While these groups do have characteristics in common, their diversity sometimes results in contradictory features.

DEFINITIONS

Definitions are important to ensure that all can agree on the subject being discussed, but the diversity of self-help groups has tended to produce elaborate typographies. The result is that some self-help groups are included in one definition, but excluded by another. From the recent research into self-help groups the definition offered by Richardson and Goodman (1983) is probably the most pragmatic.

Self-help groups are 'groups of people who feel they have a common problem (typically concerning a medical, social or behavioural condition) and have joined together to do something about it' (Richardson and Goodman, 1983, p. 2). Silverman (1978) has drawn up a typology around the basic activities that groups undertake: fund-raising, political action, consumer advocacy and personal help. Others have constructed definitions based on the reasoning behind the existence of groups as opposed to their activities. For example, Sagarin (1969) is interested in those groups that have been set up for people who are labelled as deviants and this is reflected in his typology. According to him people join groups either to seek support in helping them conform to the norms of society, such as the members of Alcoholics Anonymous, or to help change these norms to include the values of the deviant group such as *Gemma* which offers support to lesbians with physical disabilities. The Gay Movement is a good example of how it is possible to affect prevailing social norms. Homosexuality used to be classified as a psychiatric disorder, but the Gay Movement has been able to exert considerable influence in achieving change in the traditional medical view of homosexuality.

Killilea, in Caplan and Killilea (1976), has based her definition on those characteristics which self-help groups stress, and has produced a very comprehensive classification which identifies seven properties.

(1) The common experience of the members.   This is the bedrock of self-help groups. All the members share a common problem or concern. They may be sufferers of a certain illness, carers of others who have a particular condition, or having been labelled as deviants for one reason or another share a common life situation. People in self-help groups include those who have addictions, those who suffer from depression, those who have phobias, those who abuse their children, women with post-natal depression, divorced men who have lost access to their children and teenagers who have an alcoholic person either in the family or among their friends. The list is enormous and increasing all the time. The common experience is crucial in helping the members feel less isolated and to know that they are not alone. Before joining groups members frequently experience an almost overwhelming feeling of being quite alone and also of believing that no one else is able to understand how they feel.

Membership of a self-help group helps to dispel these assumptions; members value greatly the shared experience of 'being in the same boat' and of being with people who 'know what it's like'. What is also very important, and what makes these groups unique, is that the supporter and supported, or helper and helped, share a common experience or problem.

(2) The helper principle. This is regarded as a form of therapy whereby the person who does the helping is helped more than the person who receives the help. Many professional people find this concept difficult to comprehend. How can an individual suffering from depression for example be able to give support to another depressed person? Surely such a person's private burden disables them from offering help to another. But this is not the case. The helper-therapy principle works on the basis that through advocating a particular position one becomes more committed to it. It also enables the helper to be less dependent on another, and through seeing the problem in another allows the helper to see his/her problem at a distance. In common with all the helping professions, helping someone else gives the individual a feeling of being useful and thus helps to start strengthening self-esteem that is fragile.

At different times in the group a member will be both helped and helping. However, it is more likely that they will start by being helped before assuming the helper role. A good example of this is Alcoholics Anonymous (AA) where a veteran member is assigned a new member to sponsor, meaning that a new member always has someone who will help to introduce the AA philosophy and programme, and be available in crisis situations. Even when telling one's own drinking story a new AA member is helping by transforming past experience into something which can be used constructively by all the group.

(3) Mutual help and support. This is provided through being a participating member of a group which meets regularly for the expressed purpose of providing mutual help. As has been suggested above, self-help groups have a variety of ways of functioning by engaging in different activities. Some function as self-help therapy groups, perhaps based on a particular orientation, such as those women's self-help therapy groups who have taken *In Our Own Hands* (Ernst and Goodison, 1981) as their guide, or who have used *The Barefoot Psychoanalyst* (Southgate and Randall, 1976). Some groups like AA are very structured, others much less so.

Some of the members of *Depressives Anonymous* do not have a group in their locality but are able to participate in the mutuality of the self-help group through a regular newsletter. Contact can be through a telephone network or even the radio. Some groups put their energy into campaigning, others fund-raise for research into their condition. A common activity for groups is the exchange of information, which can be either formal or informal. For example, there are many groups like the Anorexia and Bulimia Nervosa Association (ABNA) or Lesbian Line which operate telephone lines and offer information, advice and also counselling. Others exchange practical ways of coping with specific situations during the course of a meeting. Those groups that have been set up to support people, mostly women, who have become addicted to the benzodiazapine group of minor tranquillizers, have through personal experience built up a wealth of information about how to try to reduce the impact of the withdrawal symptoms they experience. Although the term self-help is sometimes associated with somewhat selfish motives, in fact self-help groups are mostly about sharing. Information is shared, experiences are shared, ways of coping or of changing are shared.

Robinson (1978) in his article 'Self-help and Health' describes how sharing benefits the members not only because of the altruism that it signifies but also because sharing involves what he calls deconstruction and construction. Deconstruction involves concentrating on whatever the common problem is, identifying it, admitting to it and thus bringing it out into the open. Once this first stage has been worked through then the second stage can begin which involves sharing information about practical ways of coping with technical difficulties. A third stage which is perhaps the most difficult is to destigmatize the problem. This involves changing self-perception, and being part of a group of people who are 'in the same boat' contributes to this process. Robinson also recognizes that self-help groups can aid the reconstruction of people's lives, 'which may be more or less explicit and more or less detailed but at whatever level, enabling and encouraging a new way of living, a new way of seeing one's self and one's place in the world' (1978, p. 26).

(4) Differential association – or the reinforcement of normality. People who join self-help groups do so because they are considered by society to be rejects, non-conformists or deviants in some manner.

This image is internalized and a person becomes an alcoholic, an ex-psychiatric patient or physically handicapped, losing their individuality under the weight of a label. Association with others in a similar position, especially those who are able to live what is regarded as a 'normal' type of life despite the problem they have, helps new members to identify with this, to set about distancing themselves from previously held deviant identities, and to begin to develop positive images of themselves. Groups like the Campaign for Homosexual Equality have worked hard at changing the social prejudice experienced by their members. They have campaigned for change in the negative and often hostile attitudes held towards homosexual men and women, demanding equal treatment and the end to prejudice commensurate with full citizenship. While the changes are not by any means complete, attitudes have changed for the better in the past few years.

(5) *Collective will-power and belief.* Being a member of a self-help group and having contact with other people who share one's problem or concern, allows the individual to refer to the group and to have validation of one's attitudes and beliefs. Other members provide a living example that their commonly shared problems can be faced, come to terms with or perhaps even overcome entirely. This identification with the group is especially important for new members or for those who are in a period of particular difficulty. It also places a greater onus on the individual not to fail, because failing would mean not only failing oneself but also other group members.

(6) *Importance of information.* The exchange of information is highly valued in self-help groups, and is given greater prominence than intrapsychic understanding. Facts are more highly valued than feelings. Information is used in several ways; for a greater understanding of the illness, problem or situation, about how to cope, how to bring about change, and about what to expect. Such information can enable the individual to view his or her situation from a new perspective and alleviate much suffering or discomfort. For example, the Association for Hyperactive Children is able to offer dietary advice to parents. Groups such as DIAL are predominantly information-giving services, in this instance for people with physical disabilities.

(7) *Constructive action towards shared goals.* The emphasis in most self-help groups is on action. This is based on the belief that members learn by doing and are also changed by doing. Ideally each member works in a manner that will be of benefit both to him/herself and also the group. Activity can take many forms from making the tea, to being responsible for publicising the group, through to acting as social advocates in the pursuit of political objectives.

It should be apparent from the above classification and examples that self-help groups undertake a wide range of activities, and frequently one group will be undertaking several of them at the same time. Often there may be more than one type of group dealing with a similar problem but from a different perspective. Some groups advocate conformity while others are radical in their stance towards prevailing social values. This is reflected in the widely differing claims that are made for groups as well as the differing political perspectives of their supporters and critics.

WHY SELF-HELP GROUPS?

People joining together to form co-operative groups offering mutual assistance is as old as the human race itself, no doubt. What is remarkable is the growth in the number of self-help groups that have formed in the last 25 years or so around issues pertaining to physical conditions, mental and emotional conditions and social status conditions. This growth was very well established prior to the cuts in services which began around 1974–5. A survey carried out by Levy (1982) in 1979 showed a steady growth in the number of groups being formed since the end of the Second World War, with only three groups in his survey predating 1940.

Why is it that at the very time there was growth in expenditure on health and social services some people also felt a need to join together to form organizations where they could do something for themselves?

Some of the researchers investigating the growth of self-help groups have identified particular trends which are characteristic of life in the second half of the twentieth century and have suggested that they are connected (Sidel and Sidel, 1976). It is suggested that self-help groups are a response to feelings of powerlessness as experienced by those who exist outside the institutions of power and knowledge. Others talk of the 'cultural rudderlessness' endemic of the decline in community networks, the isolation produced by the nuclear family and the diminishing role of the church. Membership of a self-help group provides some form of compensation to these alienating trends by establishing new alliances based on common needs and situations. Others have regarded the growth in self-help groups as part of a wider social movement linked up with a coalition which includes the women's movement, the black movement, and the movement for peace, ecology, and so on. As previously mentioned, self-help groups as a concept are embraced by both the left and the right of the political spectrum; by the left as part of a movement away from the shackles and control exerted by the state accompanied by a search for a meaningful, emancipatory political movement, and by the right as a means of achieving economic reality by decreasing dependence on the State.

Self-help groups have also been regarded as a response to a growing cynicism in the ability of professionals, especially the medical profession, to be able to respond to the needs of their client groups. The warnings issued by Ivan Illich (1974) about the dangers inherent in medical practice resulting in iatrogenesis (disease caused by medical practice) are seen as having been taken up at a grass-roots level by the increasing numbers of people who now belong to self-help groups.

The pace of modern living, the relentless growth and expansion of technology and the high degree of specialization is thought to produce in people a feeling of losing control over their own personal destinies. Lack of trust germinates very easily in such an atmosphere, and the suspicion inherent in such a situation only adds to the wider feeling of anomie.

While it is no doubt true that these elements have had some significance in the growth of self-help groups there is a danger in over-eulogizing their importance. The majority of self-help group members operate within the dominant view of health and illness and do not regard themselves as being in any way a radical force. However, this is not to deny the existence of radical groups, but it is important to place them in the right context, namely as being part of a movement which holds a bewildering range of views.

Many have endured prejudice as a result of their particular condition. A typical example is of someone who has experienced some sort of mental breakdown, recovered, and feels ready to re-enter the employment market. However, the attitudes of prospective employers can make that extremely difficult, if not at times impossible, if the applicant is truthful about his/her medical history.

Partly, it is this devaluation or loss of personal value accompanied by various technical difficulties that attracts individuals to self-help groups. The rejection encountered in the outside world is counteracted in varying degrees by the sense of belonging within the self-help group. The value placed within contemporary society on being 'normal' forces those who are regarded as being outside this category to seek some sort of sanctuary: self-help groups are the answer for some.

However, it would be wrong to create an impression that self-help groups are full of rejected people who withdraw into an isolated sanctuary. Many groups have a high public profile and actively campaign for a change in attitudes, for changes in services which affect them, or for the creation of new services. Other groups try to effect change through fund-raising, either for research into their particular problem or for equipment which will provide relief for themselves and other sufferers. Fund-raising can be the central project for some groups, but may also provide support as people work together, get to know each other and talk about their particular problems and ways of coping.

People also choose to join self-help groups because they frequently experience a lack of empathy in their contact with professional workers. Many people have become aware of the discrepancy in power between the professional and the client and wish to find a way of establishing a more democratic relationship between the helper and the helped. The ethos of professional conduct and attitudes includes adherence to a systematic knowledge-based approach which involves having an objective relationship between the professional and the client. There is no room for identification with the client. In contrast, self-help groups regard this identification as central to their philosophy. However, most group members regard their membership as complementing the relationships they have with professionals.

Self-help groups are able to offer a democratic and trusting environment in which the members can start to deal with their particular situations. This emphasis on identifying with the other group members results in the wide range of groups that currently exist. Each group member belongs to his/her group because they share a similar world view, which extends to different ways of working and dealing with their individual situations. The range of groups might explain why many different and often mutually exclusive claims are made on behalf of self-help groups, all of which can be accurate.

WHAT DO SELF-HELP GROUPS DO?

The wide range of activities undertaken by self-help groups has been alluded to in previous sections of this chapter, but will be looked at in more detail here. What is characteristic of self-help groups is how the relationship between the need for help and the giving of help is altered and how the other members share similar psychological or social problems, some of which arise from the attitudes of non-sufferers. The attitudes of the outside world and the degree to which they are expressed can influence the cohesiveness of some groups.

Becoming a member of a self-help group means being with people who share a particular experience in a manner non-sufferers are unable to do. This commonality produces a bond and a commitment to doing something. What the group does can vary enormously; what is important is that it is being done collectively. The bond does not occur spontaneously, but needs to be forged through sharing experiences and perhaps by working on specific projects. Seeing other people cope and knowing that one's own successes can be shared with other group members is a strong incentive not only to continued group membership but also to spur people on to find new solutions to old problems. Benefit is not only for the individual but for the other group members.

To be able to share a common problem, it is first necessary to identify that problem. The sufferer has to admit that there is a problem and focus on it. This is usually a process that occurs before joining a group, for only then does the individual know that group 'X' might contribute towards helping to cope with or overcoming situation 'Y'. Someone who drinks excessively may regard themselves as heavy social drinkers; before going to Alcoholics

Anonymous they must at least entertain the idea that they could be an alcoholic. But resistance to accepting that there is a problem may persist and some groups start off their meetings by each member's declaring what the problem is, and what form it takes. 'I'm Joe and I'm an alcoholic' is probably quite a well-known phrase. Parents Anonymous, which exists for parents who abuse their children, helps its new members to face up to their particular problem by asking them to say, 'I've got problems as a parent and I want help. My problem shows itself in the form of . . .' Another format is used by Depressives Anonymous, who at the start of their meeting will read out a short statement to remind themselves why they are there. New members who have to make some sort of declaration feel a sense of relief when they are able to state what their problem is.

Having accepted the immediate social reality new members are then in a position to start to find solutions or means of coping as appropriate. Partly this is done through being socialized into the ways of the group, ideally through learning how to perform assigned roles. Especially in the early stages of membership, this means learning from older members new and more gratifying behaviour. Along with the above-mentioned benefits of being with people who are bonded because of unsympathetic or even hostile attitudes encountered in wider society, members start to have the strength to develop a more positive self-image. Taking up particular responsibilities within a group assists this process through uncovering or discovering skills and abilities. Over a period of time individuals are able to take on more responsibility and, in so doing, increase their coping abilities, thereby creating the opportunity to develop new and enhanced levels of self-perception and status, first within the group and then outside it.

In addition to the sharing of experiences, information is often the central axis around which the group revolves. Information is offered in a variety of ways: through leaflets and booklets, telephone advice lines, cassettes, newsletters and of course in the groups themselves. Information might be based on what group members themselves have learnt through their own experiences or through contact with professionals or specialists in the relevant area. For example, the National Eczema Society identifies education as being one of their main aims; their leaflet states that: 'Through talks by experts and discussion among members it is possible to learn a great deal about the control of Eczema and its general management.'

The sharing of information contributes to the process of demystification which has been identified by many commentators as an important aspect of self-help philosophy. This sharing of information and techniques also gives group members new skills and increases their independence. Quite simply it empowers them and this in turn has a positive effect on self-esteem. For some, the effect can be strong enough to help them find a new identity.

Self-help groups, if well run, are an opportunity to find new confidence and to tap hidden resources.

It is not an unusual phenomenon in the self-help world for people with no previous experience to find themselves, through membership of a group, dealing with the media, giving talks, sometimes to groups of professionals, and writing articles about their particular problem or situation. Within the group, members learn new skills, often organizational, and have to take on new responsbilities. From being receivers, members become givers, they give support, they give their own experience, they give information. Those who do the helping are helped the most in this situation. They become worthwhile members, not individuals who have to depend on someone else. The emphasis is on group members having to develop the self-reliance and self-determination to cope with the stigma, whether it be through adapting to or confronting society's norms: 'You can't do it on your own, but only you can do it.'

NATURAL HISTORY OF SELF-HELP GROUPS

While self-help groups have frequently been described as spontaneous grass-roots movements, someone or a small group of people has to have the initiative to establish them. Especially in the area of health, social and emotional problems which we are dealing with here, the initiative is a response to perceiving that particular needs are not being met. What is peculiar to self-help groups is that the initiative usually comes from a sufferer, although sometimes a professional may be involved. To start a group there has to be agreement that a group is needed. Potential group members have to be aware that the impetus exists, and that either there is no other organization available to fulfil the need, or if there is, there is some disagreement about its ideology or practice and the need for another group or organization is anticipated.

Sometimes new groups are branches of larger organizations. The same criteria as above apply except that guidance is likely to exist about how to proceed. National self-help organizations may wish to start a group in a particular area and make their resources available to an interested local person to that end. However, without at least a core of interested people the project is likely to be doomed to failure.

Having decided that a self-help group is needed, success or failure can hinge on being clear about who the members will be, what the group's goals should be and how they will be achieved. The more specific a group is about eligibility for membership, its goals, objectives and priorities, the more likely it is to be successful. Prospective members will be more certain whether this group will answer their own needs; those who do join share a stronger common bond and it is likely to be easier to agree a programme of activity.

A small nucleus, perhaps two to four people, is more likely to be effective in achieving this than is an individual alone. Forming such a nucleus may arise by chance as the result of an article or correspondence in a local newspaper. A few individuals may already be in contact with each other through involvement in another organization and decide to form a group. Someone might appeal for help to start a group, or they may be introduced to each other by a professional.

The next step, having agreed on criteria for membership, objectives and how best to achieve them, is to consider the practical organizational aspects and the resources that might be needed. Help with these tasks is available. A recent publication, *Self-help Groups; Getting Started, Keeping Going* (Wilson, 1986), is a guide which covers most of the practical issues a group is likely to have to deal with. Sometimes a professional worker may be at hand to offer guidance, and increasingly there are specialist workers and projects who offer advice and sometimes resources to self-help groups.

If groups are to have regular meetings, as most do, a suitable venue will be needed and most likely to be paid for. Publicity for the group will have to be organized and again probably paid for, although a local newspaper might consider publishing an article or letter without charge. Lack of suitable transport to the group's meeting place might sabotage its survival. It may seem to anyone wanting to start a group that there are an overwhelming number of issues and practicalities to work on. However, sharing the tasks will not only lessen the load but also ensure that responsibilities are shared from the beginning.

It is important that everyone has the chance to participate and that the group is not dominated by one or two people. Sadly, in some groups, it is the presence of one or two dominant individuals who keep the group going, and while this in itself is not a bad thing, it does not allow the full potential of a self-help group to be realized as it would if the opportunity for self-development through taking on responsibilities is present.

Assuming a self-help group is successfully started, how is it to be successfully maintained? Much will depend on how well the group's structure can be utilized in obtaining help for its members. The cohesiveness of a group is partly dependent on ensuring the structure allows members to participate. Members evaluate themselves and their peers according to the degree they are active in the group. They are expected to conform to standards of mutual helpfulness and co-operation. In small groups of up to 12 people this should be easy to achieve.

Bigger groups can present a problem for which a more formal structure is required, such as forming a committee to ensure that the group's aims and objectives are being achieved, and to plan the programme of activities. In these instances there is a tendency for active members to be concentrated almost solely in the committee. If a group is too large for everyone to participate at a meeting, having time for an informal chat over a cup of tea might at least ensure that everyone has a chance to talk to someone else. Other possibilities include having two meetings at different times, or for the group to split in two.

There is no single model for a self-help group. Each group needs to decide for itself how its goals can best be achieved. (Something that all groups should consider though, and many do, is confidentiality. It should be clear to all members if the meetings are confidential, otherwise trust will be very difficult to build, and confidences broken, albeit unthinkingly.) Some groups like AA and GROW (a mental health group comparatively new in Britain) are very structured, and have a well-worked out set of beliefs, practices and codes of behaviour which members are expected to follow.

At AA meetings a leader begins by reciting a part of their creed, a speaker is introduced who uses as a text one of the accepted writings, and this is followed by a session of general participation which includes the members identifying themselves as alcoholics and then recounting their progress since the last meeting.

Other groups develop a much freer style more in keeping with their ideology. For example, many feminist health groups use such a structure; the style and content of the meeting is determined by the desires of the participants which allows more spontaneity.

The turnover in membership depends on the nature of the condition or problem for which the group has been formed. Both high turnover and static membership present their own problems. If the condition is short-lived it is likely that the need for a group will also be short-lived. Unless recovered members are willing to stay on to provide continuity the group may disintegrate. However, this is not inherently a bad thing. Self-help groups exist for the benefit of their members; if there is no benefit then the need for a group ceases.

A problem that can arise when recovered members run groups is that they become out of touch with the needs of the newer members. This can also occur in groups that have a steady membership. Changes occur in individual circumstances. Over the years a group for parents of young children with mental handicaps may transform into one for parents of young adults with mental handicaps. This has two implications. The first is that new members with young babies may find the group inappropriate for them and, secondly, the aims of the group will have to change to suit the altering circumstances of its members.

Reviewing goals – especially when they have been achieved – is an activity all groups should consider. A change in the circumstances of members or a change in membership may mean the old goals have become inappropriate.

When people join a group they usually want either support, social activity or political involvement. If the group does not provide what they are looking for, and they are not willing to accept it as it is, they may either leave or attempt to steer it in the direction they desire.

People require and are able to give different things at the various stages of their membership. In the early stages members have a greater need for support and information, they give through participation but may not recognize that participation in itself is a form of giving. As time goes on the commitment to the group tends to increase – often the reason which precipitated membership is less acute which facilitates this increased commitment. More experienced members are usually happy to pass on their experiences to newer members. Richardson and Goodman (1983) identified a pattern which they called 'serial reciprocity', whereby established members of a group provide help to newer members by drawing on their own earlier experiences in coping with or overcoming particular problems.

Maintaining a group demands both commitment from its members and a sense of purpose. The old adage 'nothing succeeds like success' is very apt. Successful groups usually have a full programme of activities and have little difficulty attracting new enthusiastic members. But what of those which are not so successful?

Groups end for a variety of reasons. If the group is formed around a transitory condition (for example, being a new mother), the life of the group is likely to be short-lived. A fixed number of meetings may have been agreed upon, termination of which the group would be disbanded. The group may have achieved what it set out to do. Difficulties between members, such as personality clashes or incompatible beliefs, can destroy a group as can pressure from without, from unsympathetic families or professionals, for example. It may be that the reason for the group's existence turns out to be the reason for its demise (for example, agoraphobia) or that apathy drains the group of any energy that may exist to the extent that there is no point in continuing. When members of a group cease to be satisfied, they tend to stay away. A problem exists for self-help groups when experienced members drift away, because the process of 'social reciprocity' is destroyed.

Many people experience group endings negatively. They feel a sense of failure. Groups that disintegrate leave people feeling dissatisfied because of the existence of 'unfinished business'. If it is evident that a group is going to end it is better to accept it and prepare. Arranging a final meeting where members can say their goodbyes gives an opportunity to attend to unfinished business.

Undesirable group endings may possibly be avoided if groups assess themselves. Should the membership start to fall away it can be a good time to evaluate whether or not the group's goals are still appropriate, whether the means by which they are being achieved are effective and if not how best to make the group responsive to its members' needs once more. A group is started by its members, can be ended by its members, and can be changed by its members to suit their needs.

SELF-HELP GROUPS AND LEADERSHIP

The question of leadership in self-help groups can be a troubled one. Ideally groups should conform to the recognized and valued attributes of self-help, such as democracy, power sharing and providing the opportunity for development through taking on responsibilities. However, a group can very easily be taken over by one or two strong personalities who dominate meetings and may drive new members away. In some groups it is the dominant members who keep the group going, but at the expense of the above-mentioned attributes.

Leadership can refer to a quality possessed by an individual who can influence the direction a group takes, or a series of tasks and functions which can be undertaken by any member. Thus control can remain with one person or be held by the whole group. In self-help groups examples along the whole of this continuum can be found, but the majority of groups rest somewhere in the centre.

Groups should choose the kind of leadership they think will best suit their needs. The larger more traditional groups usually elect to have a committee with a chairperson, secretary and treasurer. Many have particular people responsible for certain tasks such as dealing with publicity, welcoming new members or making the tea.

Smaller groups might choose not to have a leader at all but share the responsibility between them. Self-help therapy groups often follow this model. Others may have a different leader at each meeting, thus giving everyone a chance to develop this skill. Increasingly, it is being recognized that the skills of leadership are necessary for self-help groups, and training sessions and manuals are available to help teach these skills (e.g. *Problem Solving through Self-Help Groups*).

Some of the larger organizations do provide a framework for leadership skills to develop. For example, GROW, which describes itself as a structured community mental health movement, incorporates into its structure teaching the skills of running a group. Members are encouraged to attend week-end training sessions during which they learn to become confident to use GROW's format for leading meetings. This includes listening and reflecting back in a sensitive manner what is being said, encouraging more reticent members to participate fully, and identifying practical tasks to be carried out in between meetings.

In common with other types of groups leaders have different styles:

authoritarian, *laissez-faire* or democratic. The authoritarian leader in a self-help group, if allowed to, is likely to produce quick results but with the risk of sacrificing the philosophy of self-help groups mentioned at the beginning of this section. The *laissez-faire* leader will take a back-seat role, perhaps only organizing the group to come together, or offering suggestions which the group may or may not wish to take up. Although this might seem at first to be an ideal style of leadership for self-help groups, research carried out by Lindenfield and Adams (1984) suggests that this is not the case. Such a style is not very productive and may produce tension and aggression. Especially during the early stages of a group, anxiety, lack of confidence and poor communication may prevent members from taking part and contributing to the group in the way upon which this style of leadership depends.

The democratic style of leadership is characterized by a determination to include all group members in the group's decision-making. This gives real power to group members, which in turn makes them more committed to achieving tasks or goals because they were part of the decision-making process. Although well-suited to the ethos of self-help groups this style of leadership is initially frustrating because it takes much longer to reach decisions. However, because ideally everyone is involved in the long-run, it produces a more satisfying and beneficial group.

As with most groups good leaders need to be flexible and adaptable, and sensitive to the members. This may be asking too much for leaders who are inexperienced, lacking in confidence and possibly handicapped in some way by whatever condition brought the group together in the first place. A caring group will help its leaders, perhaps give them feedback on their performances, so that they can learn the skills of leadership.

SELF-HELP GROUPS AND THE PROFESSIONALS

While the rhetoric creates the impression of self-help groups being a response to the failure of professionals to be able to treat or deal with people in a way that is responsive to their needs, the reality does not necessarily support this position. Levy's (1982) survey on mutual support groups in Britain concluded that the attitudes of groups to professionals was a positive one. Of the groups in his sample, 75% viewed themselves as having a good relationship with professionals. This would appear to confirm the contention put forward by Lieberman and Borman (1979) that self-help and mutual aid is complementary to professional services, not a reaction against or an alternative to them.

But one has to qualify such a generalized statement by saying that there are some self-help groups who specifically take an anti-professional position, especially those whose members feel they have suffered at the hands of professionals – The Campaign Against Psychiatric Oppression would be a good example of such a group. However, the majority of groups function within the dominant view of health and illness, and accept the expertise of the professional, their own role being supplementary.

Increasingly, professionals are working with self-help groups. Some even start groups, in the hope that once they have been formed the members will take over the control and running of the groups themselves. This does happen, but often a relationship of dependency is created with the group not wishing to take on the responsibility, preferring the worker to carry it. However, a sensitive relationship between a professional and a group can be of great benefit.

The relationship should essentially be a supportive one, and may involve giving support to the leaders, being a bridge between the group and other professionals, and acting as a resource for the practical matters which can prove such a burden if the group members do not have the knowledge about how best to proceed. Some groups, but ones that are not self-help groups if one is going to take a purist line, have a professional such as a social worker, health visitor or doctor attending regularly. A useful role for workers is in providing training. As indicated earlier, sometimes a great deal of effort can be expended on a group which ultimately fails because the skills for running a group are not there. Basic courses on group work, leadership skills and assertion training are increasingly being made available by a variety of community projects for the benefit of self-help groups.

A new breed of worker is emerging as a response to providing support to self-help groups. Until fairly recently those who supported self-help groups did it as part of a wider brief; social workers, health visitors, occasionally doctors, and then increasingly community workers and community health workers. In the early 1980s projects whose sole purpose was to support self-help groups started to emerge, the best known being the Nottingham Self-help Team. This particular project does not initiate new groups but responds to people who have expressed an interest in forming a new group. They will help that person to clarify their objectives, predict difficulties and give them a realistic vision of what to expect. The team will also help with practical issues such as giving information about meeting rooms, advice about publicity and help in making contact with sympathetic and sensitive professionals.

SELF-HELP GROUPS AND PROBLEMS

The problems that arise in connection with self-help groups fall broadly into two groups – problems within the group and the problems that may arise in the wider community.

Within groups, lack of experience coupled with either lack of confidence or insensitivity in the leadership can lead to stress and strain for the individuals concerned. It is not only the leaders who can be disturbed by and vulnerable to other people's problems, but the group as a whole, because of their own problems. This is most likely to occur if there are too many seriously affected people in the group. It is difficult to say what the right proportion should be because so many factors are involved. A strong structure, support for the group by someone with experience of group processes and the provision of training can help contain a greater proportion of troubled people.

When under too much stress regular commitment to a self-help group can prove too difficult. People are good at protecting themselves if they sense they are going to be hurt or overwhelmed in a group, and respond by staying away. People will stay away if they feel the group is no longer answering a need. Many groups experience difficulty in retaining 'recovered' members who could give the group stability and the benefit of their experience.

Power struggles within groups also can be very problematic and lead to internal factions and schisms. Clashes of personality may highlight differences regarding the pursuing or abandoning of previously agreed group aims. But it is at the other end of the spectrum that many groups experience difficulties, namely with apathy. Richardson and Goodman (1983), in their study of four self-help organizations, reported apathy as a particular problem for groups. People were happy to let others 'get on with it', especially in between meetings when particular tasks had to be carried out.

Do self-help groups reinforce the original condition? People can get stuck in groups, going over the same territory meeting after meeting without moving on, unless they try to give themselves goals which they can work toward. Self-help groups can be too cosy. The companionship some people find in groups, of being with others 'in the same boat', might inhibit change for fear of losing that mutuality.

Lack of accountability is another criticism aimed at self-help groups. Because they are informal, they may also regard themselves as being unaccountable and under no pressure to respect the individual rights demanded of formal organizations. This is not to suggest that self-help groups are irresponsible, but some groups do become very defensive about investigations into their standards. This is especially true of groups run by one person, particularly if they are using the group to work out their own problems, despite the best of altruistic motives for starting the group.

Members who do not conform to the norms of the group can suffer ostracism and be subjected to a harsh morality. Henry (1978) reported that some groups suppress controversial behaviour in a manner which 'results in a harsher condemnation of deviance than is found in the general population' (p. 656). However, there is little evidence of self-help groups being harmful to their members. Lieberman and Borman (1979), researchers exploring the impact of self-help groups, have thus far uncovered only a few casualties.

Self-help groups may experience problems as a result of outside pressures, and their very existence might produce complacency from service providers. External pressures include not receiving any support outside the group. Support might be withheld by the family to the individual, or from the group by professionals.

If the condition around which a group forms is highly stigmatized, e.g. paedophilia, and if there is a very obvious lack of congruency between the group's norms and those of society, hostility may be directed at the group, especially if it has a high public profile. Although the media's record in handling self-help groups is comparatively good, issues do tend to get over-simplified and this can result in a disservice to non-member sufferers by reinforcing the existing stereotype, and perhaps putting off potential joiners.

While self-help groups do, on the whole, receive good press, and public opinion is favourable towards them, their very existence may have problematic implications in the planning and provision of services. For example, it is estimated that there are approximately 500 000 alcoholics in Britain. A general population survey conducted by the Maudsley Hospital in London showed that Alcoholics Anonymous was regarded as the most helpful resource for people with a drink problem. However, Alcoholics Anonymous has only 17 000 members in Britain. Henry (1978) expresses concern for sufferers who do not get satisfaction from either professionals or self-help groups. He sees a danger arising from the success of groups leading to a failure of central government, local authorities and professionals in fulfilling their obligations.

Increasingly, self-help groups are being called on to become accountable both by members and professionals. As the next section shows, self-help groups are also being drawn into the planned system of care. Over the next few years it is likely that self-help groups will experience changes in their relationships with the formal sector. Let us hope that we can learn from the forms of association self-help groups have developed, and not institutionalize them by defining them solely in professional terms.

SELF-HELP GROUPS AND POLICY

In recent years central government has started to show an interest in self-help groups and in 1984 the Department of Health and Social Security announced a scheme of grants for local support projects for self-help groups. The project and the schemes chosen are collectively known as the 'Self-Help Alliance'. There exists some cynicism regarding the scheme being supported as it is by a government better known for cutting back on services rather than developing them. However, it does also mean that recognition is being given to the role of self-help in the complex network of care given by families, informal carers, voluntary agencies and the statutory services. The case for supporting self-help recognizes that people who start and join self-help groups are often facing serious life problems, and those unaware of the burden of running groups can become more ill or distressed themselves, and perhaps through inexperience, worsen the position of others.

Other support initiatives include the National Self-Help Support Centre which was set up in 1986. They aim to develop networks for self-help support workers, including black workers who are not well represented either in the Alliance or the National Self-Help Support Network. They also aim to provide training to self-help support workers and to promote the case for providing self-help support with policy makers and funders.

More well-run groups, so the argument goes, mean that more people will receive care, for the statutory services will always be unable to meet the growing needs that communities present them with. It also provides the community with an opportunity to get involved in providing care. Another part of this argument accepts the principle of 'helper therapy', whereby group members get better by helping others. It also recognizes the manner in which people who are usually devalued, such as women, black people, people with disabilities, can have the opportunity to grow through developing skills, and increasing in status and confidence.

The preventative aspects of self-help groups are also being recognized. Joining an organization such as CRUSE or Compassionate Friends following a bereavement can prevent a person from becoming clinically depressed. In the USA, as part of a Community Network Development Programme for people with psychiatric problems which placed emphasis on self-help and mutual support, it was shown that those who participated required one-half as much re-hospitalization as a comparable group who did not participate in the programme, after a period of 10 months (Gordon *et al.*, 1982). Child abusers who participated in Parents Anonymous reported gaining insight into their reactions to the abuse they typically experienced as children, and that they learned new ways of expressing love and affection to their own children (Comstock, 1982).

Value is attached to giving people the opportunity to take more control over their own lives and treatment, and also of entering into some sort of partnership with the professionals who are treating them. Self-help groups give people the opportunity to become informed consumers who are more likely to feed back their views to the planners and policy makers. This may lead to increasing demands for either more, better or different services from people who have become better informed as to what it is they want.

The World Health Organization's interest in self-help was promoted by an international conference at Alma Ata on primary health care. Self-help and self-care are an inescapable necessity in those countries that can afford little in the way of advanced medicine. In those countries such as Britain where technological medicine is highly developed, self-help organizations have a specific role in the fields of prevention, coping with chronic conditions and making known the views of consumers.

Throughout Europe and North America, both local and national clearance houses exist providing a range of services to self-help groups, the public and professionals. The services include the provision of material resources, technical support, information and documentation, and serving as a bridge between the lay and professional support systems.

CONCLUSION

While it is true that people coming together into co-operative groups is as old as human endeavour itself, in the last 30 years a new organizational form has become established even though its constituent parts may come and go. Although I agree it would be wrong to talk about a self-help movement, self-help groups for people suffering from medical, behavioural and social conditions are very much an aspect of contemporary life. The forms that these mutual aid endeavours take are very diverse and encompass a vast array of philosophies and political positions. However, they are regarded as being important enough for national governments to take notice of them and in some cases provide funds for their support. The growth of self-help groups and organizations are not an isolated force but have to be seen as part of a wider phenomenon whereby people are looking for more meaning and are wanting to have more control over their lives.

REFERENCES

Caplan, G. and Killilea, M. (eds) (1976). *Support Systems and Mutual Help: Multi-disciplinary Explorations.* New York, Grune and Stratton.
Ernst, S. and Goodison, L. (1981). *In Our Own Hands.* London, The Women's Press.
Henry, S. (1978). The dangers of self-help groups. *New Society* **44** (820), 654–6.
Illich, I. (1974). *Medical Nemesis: The Expropriation of Health.* London, Calder and Boyars.
Levy, L. (1982). Mutual support groups in Great Britain: a survey. *Social Science and Medicine* **16**, 1265–75.
Lieberman, M. A. and Borman, L. D. (1979). *Self-help Groups for Coping with Crisis.* San Francisco, Jossey-Bass.
Lindenfield, G. and Adams, R. (1984). *Problem Solving through Self-help Groups.* Ilkley, West Yorks, Self-Help Associates.

Richardson, A. and Goodman, M. (1983). *Self-help and Social Care: Mutual Aid Organisations in Practice*. London, Policy Studies Institute.

Robinson, D. (1978). Self-help and health. *Social Work Service* **17** (October), 23–8.

Sagarin, E. (1969). *Odd Man In: Societies of Deviants in America*. Chicago, Quadrangle Books.

Sidel, W. V. and Sidel, R. (1976). Beyond Coping. *Social Policy*.

Silverman, P. R. (1978). *Mutual Help Groups: A Guide for Mental Health Workers*. DHEW Publication No. (ADM) 78–646.

Southgate, J. and Randall, R. (1976). *The Barefoot Psychoanalyst*. London, Association of Karen Horney Psychoanalytical Counsellors.

Wilson, J. (1986). *Self-help Groups: Getting Started, Keeping Going*. London, Longman.

CHAPTER 12

SINGLE-SEX THERAPY GROUPS

Jane Price

Although single-sex therapy groups (SSTGs) originated among women, there has been an increasing movement towards this form of therapy by men since the early 1970s. In 1987 there remain many more such groups for women, however, and it is this women's form of SSTGs that I will be discussing in detail in this chapter. I have had the opportunity to discuss with male leaders some of the issues raised by men's SSTGs and will be including the details they have shared with me. Obviously I have not had the experience of a men's SSTG, except in this sharing of knowledge and, therefore, the details of women's SSTGs are bound to appear more colourful.

HISTORICAL BACKGROUND

In the early 1960s Betty Friedan (Friedan, 1963) wrote about the sense of alienation and frustration experienced by a generation of American housewives. She called their experience 'the problem with no name' because these women were unable to explain why they were suffering from such distressing emotions and had usually been too ashamed of their feelings to discuss them previously with anyone else. Her description of this problem stimulated many women to seek a variety of therapeutic frameworks within which to explore their difficulties. There was a sudden realization that the problem was not based only in individual women's psyche but was also a commonplace response by women to their position in society and the stereotyped roles into which they had been forced.

SSTGs for women were part of a more general response to Betty Friedans's stimulus. These groups began to explore women's experiences of life in a non-judgemental way and, because the environment of a women-only group was so different to the context within which these women usually lived, it allowed their problems to be seen from a different perspective. The effects of sex-stereotyping and the social pressures to conform to these roles became more easily identified when women could compare their behaviour and feelings in two different contexts. Self-understanding combined with an understanding of the effects of social context became the creative solution to a problem that had previously been seen more narrowly as the psychopathology of individuals requiring diagnosis and treatment (Rice and Rice, 1973).

Since its early Californian days this kind of therapy has spread around the world. In many cultures women discovered that 'the problem with no name' was not a uniquely American experience but was a common response by women to their positions in many different societies. SSTGs allow women to discover anew the sense of strength and fun in being together as they face personal and social conflicts.

SSTGs for men rapidly followed and have run a separate but parallel course. Although sex-stereotyping is very different for men it can cause just as much personal anguish as it does for women.

Since their inception in the 1960s these SSGTs have developed a myriad of styles. There is a wide spectrum from the consciousness raising (CR) or 'rap' groups at one end to the encounter groups with their development into group analysis for women at the other.

CR groups are often formed by women who already constitute a group in a different setting (e.g. work, political or academic organizations) and therefore start by knowing each other. Many of these groups choose to be leaderless as part of a greater 'experiment' they are conducting with themselves and each other. As these groups developed it became obvious that some tended to concentrate on personal conflicts contained within the subject matter, whereas other more radical groups emphasized political formulations and solutions to the exclusion of personal solutions (Angel, 1971).

'Free Space', an American group running between 1967 and 1972, attempted to combine the personal with the political as a healing of this potential rift by describing a four-stage process to deal with each issue as it arose. The first two stages were a personal 'opening up' followed by 'group sharing'. Only when these two experiential stages seemed complete did the group move on to the third stage of 'analysing', which led to a group understanding of what had transpired between them. Finally, this was translated into the 'abstracting' stage when the socio-political implications of the issue under discussion were explored. Descriptions of this group

(Allen, 1970) reflect the depth of feeling and sense of growth each member achieved within this structure.

Encounter groups evolved specifically to emphasize the bond between women that many felt had been lost in modern Western society (Mayer, 1974; Progrebin, 1973). Women in these groups discovered that being together provoked a sense of sheer pleasure that had previously been lacking in their lives and that, without men, they quickly discarded their superficial role behaviour (Meador *et al.*, 1972). These groups developed into explorations of the relationships between women and in particular the relationships between mothers and daughters. Individual and group development became the focus of such groups (Halas, 1973; Newton and Walton, 1971).

From the descriptions of these groups it is clear that from as early as 1971 there was a sense of excitement about the new therapeutic opportunities that SSTGs were providing. In 1979, Ellis and Nichols reviewed the literature about the efficacy of SSTGs for women and concluded that it was an effective form of treatment, free of sex role bias and, therefore, potentially more helpful to women than conventional treatments. Brodsky (1973) suggested that the female need for male approval distorted any therapeutic process for women in which men played a part either as therapist or group co-member. Since then it has been assumed that the effectiveness of SSTGs for women is closely linked with the absence of men. Although I can find no research evidence to demonstrate this conclusively, all the women and men who have been members of SSTGs and with whom I have discussed their experience rate the absence of the opposite sex as an important therapeutic factor.

HISTORICAL DEVELOPMENT IN BRITAIN

During the mid-1970s Susie Orbach and Luise Eichenbaum crossed the Atlantic to live in England. They rapidly founded the first British Women's Therapy Centre in their front rooms. They were dedicated to providing therapy for women by women therapists with a feminist perspective to an analytical style. Much of that feminist understanding had come from the earlier experiences of SSTGs. The London Women's Therapy Centre[1] provided the much needed boost to the morale of women therapists in Britain who attended workshops and training sessions and then returned to their home towns with a new purpose. Over the last 8 years centres and services based on the principles of feminist psychotherapy have blossomed in Manchester, Preston, Nottingham, Birmingham, Brighton, Southampton

[1] Now based at 6 Manor Gardens, London N7.

and Leeds. These centres and the resulting publications (e.g. Orbach and Eichenbaum, 1982) have provided rich encouragement for many groups led by, advised by or supported by experienced women therapists of many persuasions.

Running parallel to this development, women's centres offering a wide range of services to women have sprung up in every part of the country. These provided further foci for groups of women to meet and to follow the examples of their 'sisters' in California 25 years earlier, as they begin the experiential journey together towards greater understanding and respect of themselves and each other.

UNDERLYING THEORETICAL ASSUMPTIONS OF WOMEN-ONLY GROUPS

(1) The high rate of mental illness in women is a reflection of their position in society, particularly their social isolation and the lack of value given to them, their actions or their feelings (Chesler, 1972). Helping agencies are likely to reflect cultural stereotypes in their interpretation of this distress and to diagnose and treat it rather than attempt to understand it (Rice and Rice, 1973). In an all-women group it is more likely that an individual woman's experience will be listened to sympathetically, affirmed and explored without cultural stereotypes intruding into that process. In this way a woman can begin to define herself without cultural bias and gain a sense of greater freedom of options than stereotypical boundaries might have previously given her. She can also experience the difference between her behaviour and feelings in the 'real' mixed world and within the context of a women-only society. This comparison will enhance her appreciation of what part of her problems truly lie within her psyche and need analytical understanding, and which part of those problems are a reflection of the position she holds in society and, therefore, are in need of social change to improve them.

(2) There are a number of reports, the most recent being in 1984 (Women's National Commission, 1984), that suggest that women would prefer to be treated by women doctors, nurses, midwives and health visitors when experiencing psychological, gynaecological or obstetric difficulties. This choice may well reflect a desire to be understood by someone likely to have had a similar life experience. In an all-women group there is a pool of shared life experiences and it is unusual for a woman to feel isolated because she alone has had some experience shared by no other in the group. This is particularly true of events that have been sexually traumatic. Despite having been the victims of abuse these women often feel guilty, ashamed and responsible for their own suffering. They all feel that they have been

humiliated by a man or men, many of whom were well-known to them and in a position of trust in their lives. Hence, to share the experience with male co-members or a male leader, however caring such a male figure, will add to the trauma of recounting and make it less likely to occur.

Incest and rape represent two important areas of experience that women appear to find universally more easy to discuss in the absence of men. However, there are many experiences such as abortion, miscarriage, infertility, childbirth, breastfeeding, etc., that the majority of women prefer to explore in all-women groups. Intimacy between women, both emotional and physical, is often ignored or avoided by both male and female members of mixed groups, making mixed-group therapy particularly difficult and unrewarding for those women with a homosexual orientation or those women who are in confusion about their sexuality. Added to this is the more general need to be able to regress emotionally when exposing such vulnerability and the accompanying need to be enclosed by mother figures, as reported by Davis (1977). I think it is clear that all women have a need for the love, support and acceptance of other key women in their lives. SSTGs may provide the first uncritical environment within which a woman can explore that fundamental need without anxiety.

(3) In a review of the attitudes towards women that are reflected in the theorectical assumptions of many forms of therapy, Gilman (1971) concluded that these assumptions were subject to the same forms of anti-women bias as the cultures that produced them. Given that we are all products of our culture and our time this is hardly a surprising finding. Views about what constitutes a mentally healthy or psychologically normal woman may well have altered profoundly over the last century. Such an on-going change means that our theories are always behind our practice and also behind the reality of our women patients' lives. Many therapists may be unaware of the extent to which culture and history have shaped the theories with which they work and may, therefore, continue to reflect outdated models of normality with potentially puzzling and hurtful interpretations.

An example of this occurred in a group in which I was a member. The group had a male leader with a Freudian background. There was a male client in the group who told stories about the women in his life, stories which could hardly avoid offending the women in the group. It was noticeable (although never mentioned by the leader) that whenever this client began to speak the men in the group would be interested and involved while the women became quiet and unhappy. Whenever a woman client confronted this situation her actions were interpreted as castrating to and/or envious of the male client and to the group leader himself. Such interpretations were based on the leader's assumption that psychologically mature women would be happy to accept male protection from himself or other male clients if, in their judgement, the protagonist's behaviour became unacceptable. Alongside that primary assumption there was also a more covert message to all the women in the group who 'dared' to defend themselves, that this need was based on their psychopathology and not the situation within which they found themselves. Finally, it was suggested that the women clients who confronted this man were secretly envious of his behaviour and would like to humiliate other women and/or be humiliated themselves. Even 70 years ago such interpretations probably reflected a male distortion of their view of female psychology. Certainly, today, they sound outdated and unlikely to be helpful to women who are actively involved in questioning their roles as women in the 1980s.

Sadly, I do not think that such distortions are uncommon in mixed-sex therapy. If the male leader shares the stereotypical view which shaped the theory within which he operates and if that is the dominant view of the surrounding culture, including the male and some of the female clients within the group, a woman wishing to question the cultural status quo is likely to be undermined by the strength of the opposition to such questioning. For many women who are already on their way to active questioning this might represent no more than a passing irritation as they seek more therapeutic environs in which to work. For a woman who has not yet made the leap to the understanding required to begin questioning her role and position in society as possible aetiological factors in her distress, a group that functions to impose stereotypes is unlikely to be helpful and may only repeat messages of helplessness and dependence to her, throwing her back into the very quagmire from which she was seeking some form of escape.

(4) The effects of cultural stereotypes on men and women have consequences for perceived mental health and affect the workers within the field of mental health as much as they affect the patients. The Broverman *et al.* (1970) study asked psychiatrists, clinical psychologists and social workers in mental health settings in the USA to assign various personality traits to either men, women or mentally healthy adults. Men were generally seen as strong unemotional types, whereas women were seen as more emotional and less rational. The traits attributed to men were more likely to hold cultural value and acceptability than those attributed to women. The profile of a mentally healthy adult matched that of the male, i.e. the study demonstrated that key workers in mental health considered it impossible to be both a normal woman and mentally healthy.

Such attitudes reflect the view that women's feelings are merely an extension of the reproductive function and, in particular, are dependent on levels of circulating hormones. The theory of hormonal vulnerability in women (Nott *et al.*, 1976) is often advanced as a possible explanation for the greater levels of emotional distress demonstrated by women in all cultures. However, Jenkins and Clare (1985) have thrown considerable doubt over any theory that connects women's emotional experience with their hormones. The Broverman *et al.* study suggests that 'normal' women who live within cultural stereotypes and perform accepted and time-honoured roles are not expected to be mentally healthy by those workers most likely to have responsibility for diagnosing their symptoms. Such views lead to a society which tells large groups of women, e.g. mothers with young children, that it is normal for them to be sad, distressed or despairing. This, of course, releases the society from any responsibility to change in order to improve the lot of these women.

Many of the women I see complain that their distress is either diagnosed as a psychiatric disorder or dismissed as 'all part of being a woman'. Interestingly, most women experience both of these reactions to their presentations as a form of rejection of their experience. Most talk about the need to be heard and the sensation of being perpetually invisible or ignored. Professional reactions based on the bias demonstrated by the Broverman *et al.* study may well be a chief source of the difficulties which greet any woman attempting to make herself understood to a male practitioner (and women practitioners who fail to question the imposed male stereotypes of their training).

It is not unusual for women to report feeling misunderstood and of having their actions or feelings re-interpreted to them by professionals (Wahrman and Pugh, 1974; Wolman and Frank, 1975; Kiesler, 1975). Such re-interpretation serves to uphold stereotypes by actively distorting the experience the woman is trying to communicate and by then labelling the woman's part in the communication in a way that is likely to be prejudicial to her. This means that any future attempts by the same woman to seek help with and understanding of her problems can be dismissed in one of the ways detailed at the beginning of this section. Many women patients are in no doubt that present-day psychiatry distorts their experiences in ways that collude with the dominant culture and leave the male mental health workers feeling comfortable while the women patients are denied individually and denied a separate and different validity as a group (Levine *et al.*, 1974; Oakley 1980).

(5) There is evidence to suggest that women have valid complaints about the experience of seeking help from male-dominated agencies when at their most vulnerable. We know from the work of Bardwick (1971) that low self-esteem and fear of failure are important in the aetiology of depression in women. From Kagan and Moss (1971), we are aware that being passive and having unmet (and sometimes unidentified) needs are also implicated. We are also faced with the evidence from at least a decade of research that tells

us that women experience evaluation of their problems by a male professional as likely to increase their sense of helplessness and alienation
(Wahrman and Pugh, 1974; Oakley, 1980; Women's National Commission,
1984). We also know from critical studies of the major psychological theories on the 'mature female psyche' that 'true' women are meant to be passive
and to meet the dependency needs of others (Gilman, 1971; Chesler, 1972)
even though the involved professionals can acknowledge that such personality traits are not compatible with mental health (Broverman *et al.*, 1970).

Despite all this evidence I have often met with studious disbelief from male
colleagues when trying to set up women-only groups or treatment centres.
'Why do you need to exclude men?', they ask, experiencing the quest for a
more suitable treatment environment for women as a rejection of themselves.
I sense that behind this reaction lie psychological problems for men that are
too easily avoided at the expense of providing less than suitable treatment for
women patients. The sense of exclusion from the female world may well be a
major source of infantile despair for the young male child and women
practitioners and women patients who dare to suggest a need for separation in
treatment may re-activate that sense of alienation in male professionals.

Such responses also underline another widely held basic assumption in the
relationship between men and women. Society expects women to be the
carers and to look after the needs of men. This expectation continues even
when the male is the paid care-giver and the woman the patient. It is
certainly frequently upheld in mixed-sex groups where women function to
contain and care for the male patients. I have witnessed ill and distressed
women unconsciously reacting to the needs of their male 'carers' and male
patients too often to think that this is an unusual circumstance. I tend to
think that the conditioning of many women to be good carers is so extreme
that they respond in that fashion whatever the level of their own pain and
needs. Males receive such unconscious caring without acknowledgement or
even conscious awareness because they are equally conditioned to expect it.
Given this situation, male workers and male patients may experience a lack
of women in any environment as counter-therapeutic to themselves and,
therefore, protest loudly about any plans to segregate part of their care.

(6) Orbach and Eichenbaum (1982) have drawn our attention to the focal
nature of the mother/daughter relationship. They see this as the basic
building block of any woman's personality and, therefore, a necessary focus
of therapy whatever the presenting problem. Within an all-woman group
there are numerous opportunities for transference and countertransference
relationships that reflect that original relationship, and it is my observation
that such relationships tend to be more intense, develop more rapidly and
provide an easier source of therapeutic work in a totally female 'culture'. I
suspect this is because women so often use the caring of and understanding

of men as a defence against having to look inside of themselves. When there are no men present to provide a focus for avoidance of self the women have no alternative but to begin working on themselves and each other instead. They may also be more willing to demonstrate and explore the violent feelings they often have towards their mothers with other women. This is partly because they expect to receive understanding and a sense of universality from such sharing. It is also related to the desire many women express to protect men from the depths of their rage. Therefore, the absence of men allows these women a greater sense of expressive freedom while at the same time the all-female culture stirs up those feelings of rage, dependency, love and hate that were first experienced in the mother/daughter relationship. In my opinion it is this combined effect that potentiates therapeutic work on this focal relationship.

(7) Cohesiveness is of central importance in the functioning of any group (Yalom and Rand, 1966). Mayer (1974) reports that SSTGs are experienced by clients as achieving cohesiveness more quickly than mixed-sex groups. I have been impressed by the rapid build-up of warmth and support between group members in all-women groups. Not only does this serve to enhance the functioning of the group it also seems to act as a protection for the women involved that extends from feeling safe and understood within the group to feeling more confident and sure of themselves in other situations at an early stage of group development.

(8) Therapists have also benefited from SSTGs. The theories of personality development in women have changed as a direct result of the observations of women therapists who work in women-only groups. Issues such as inter-female sexuality and competition between women were largely ignored in earlier theories. The unique intensity of the mother/daughter transference and countertransference in all-women groups has stimulated much thought. I have often heard women comment that the group has changed their attitudes to other women as a direct result of a change in their relationships with their mothers. I think women therapists involved in women's groups have similarly had to change their attitudes, question all they had previously been taught about women's psychology and come up with new theories in the light of their experiences. Some of these fresh perspectives are discussed later.

UNDERLYING THEORECTICAL ASSUMPTIONS OF MEN-ONLY GROUPS

(1) Men are equally subjected to sex stereotyping as are women in any culture but with very different consequences. Men are supposed to be strong

and aggressive if they are to be accepted as healthy. They are encouraged not to demonstrate emotions or dependency needs and, because such training starts in their relationship with their mother, the taboo is often experienced as particularly strong in their relationship with women (Broverman *et al.*, 1970).

The message given to young boys is that 'men don't cry' and therefore many men fear they will receive contempt and disregard if they take the risk of exposing strong feelings. Some also fear that it will bring their virility into dispute.

(2) Men-only groups allow an exploration of a male view of sexuality that is uncontaminated by women's needs and perspectives. A greater spectrum of forms of sexuality can therefore be explored with less guilt or embarrassment than would be possible if women were present.

(3) The role of father in Western culture is only vaguely defined. Many of the men-only groups formed in the UK over the last decade have been based on groups of new fathers wanting to seek a clearer model for themselves as fathers compared to that their own fathers provided. The presence of women in such groups might well persuade them to form models of second-class mothering rather than to find different but equally valid models of fathering.

(4) Men are often encouraged not to be warm and tender with each other. The awareness of the vulnerability of other men in conjunction with a recognition of their own vulnerability often enhances a man's ability to share more intensely with male friends and relatives. Many of these men would have chosen to have only shared with women previously and, therefore, this represents an important learning point.

KEY CONCEPTS IN SSTGs

Many of the concepts that are important in other groups are also important in SSTGs. Group processes such as disclosure and feedback are commonly used tools in enhancing group and individual understanding. Individual processes such as projection may be interpreted in the groups that take an analytical model as the basis for their understanding. In SSTGs, however, there is an important third dimension which surrounds the usual dimensions of individual and group. This dimension is the socio-cultural background in which group members live out their day-to-day lives. SSTGs are often criticized on the basis that they are in some way fundamentally abnormal and therefore likely to distort individual and group processes in an unhelpful way. Such a criticism misses the point. The process of comparison between the special circumstances of a one-sex culture within the group and the 'normal' mixed-sex world outside of the group is a key feature of such groups. It is their very 'abnormality' which makes them so highly valued and useful. Within the context of being able to make this comparison, an unusual and often unique opportunity for the individual, lies a wealth of material for each group member about their differences in behaviour and feelings between the two worlds to which they now have access.

Most members are initially surprised at how rapidly the absence of members of the opposite sex alters the behaviour of the remaining sex. The years when women were asked to leave the dinner table to allow the men more freedom in their behaviour acknowledge that mankind has always known that much of our behaviour is conditioned only for the benefit of the opposite sex. This is undoubtedly true for both men and women. Such 'conditioning' starts young. Little girls and boys begin to reflect adult patterns of behaviour towards each other even in the pre-school years. Hence this behaviour is not mere social gloss applied in adolescence or adulthood but represents part of the personality structure: the rules of behaviour between the sexes is part of our cultural super-ego. Within SSTGs, this part of the super-ego can be discarded effortlessly. Because it has only been conditioned as important in our interactions with the opposite sex, most group members find surprisingly little resistance within themselves to behaving in a less inhibited way within SSTGs.

This key concept allows a number of important issues to be explored in an environment that is experienced as different and, therefore, not part of socio-cultural 'rules'. These issues can be seen as the secondary key concepts for SSTGs:

(i)   Many leaders who have functioned in both mixed groups and SSTGs report an intensification of the same sex parent/child relationship within the transference and the countertransference.

(ii)   The issue of sexual identity is regarded as an important area for exploration in SSTGs. There is a general underlying assumption that acceptance of your own sexual identity is enhanced by acceptance of and identification with the sexuality of others of the same sex. Issues that might cause embarrassment or guilt in mixed-sex groups become easily available for work. In women's groups the power of female sexuality and the guilt which often accompanies the realization of that power are frequently areas of interest. In men's groups the discomfort many 'macho' men feel with their roles and the discovery that these roles have been assumed specifically to hide their neediness from their womenfolk are often topics to be discussed.

(iii) Homosexuality is a particularly important area of sexuality that SSTGs can give attention to. Within any culture there is evidence of homophobia. These fears and prejudices are not only experienced by heterosexuals. Many homosexuals share cultural beliefs about their sexuality and have difficulty finding the inner freedom to explore all aspects of their sexual experience because their internal sense of self-criticism is cruelly in tune with the outer evidence of homophobia. I think it seems easier to share both the experience of homosexuality and the results of homophobia in a constructive group exchange when other parameters of stereotypical sexuality are absent.

(iv) There are physical events which are felt to be sexually specific and therefore more appropriately shared in SSTGs. Certainly women fail to disclose experiences of incest, rape, miscarriage and abortion in the presence of men. Men often report difficulties in listening sympathetically to women who want to discuss these issues in any depth. Their discomfort is often disguised by criticism of the woman's behaviour and apportioning blame to women generally for the violence of men. Women who have survived such ordeals need time to share the horror of their experiences in a warm environment which values them in a positive fashion before they are ready to 'fight back' verbally in mixed-sex groups. Men also need time together to share their own sense of horror at the behaviour of members of their own sex and explore the meaning of violence in their own lives before being able to allow women an empathic hearing.

The second key concept of SSTGs is their focus of change. As the sweep of their interest reaches out into the culture surrounding the group so too does the desire to bring about change. Hence alongside the need for individual and family change is an explicit understanding that social change will also be necessary if individual members are to achieve their full potential. Together with that initial and exciting recognition is an accompanying secondary, sad and frustrating recognition that social change may be painfully slow for an individual whose personal change rate is suddenly accelerating.

THE PRACTICE OF SSTGs

The goals of the group

The goals of any SSTG can be divided into three categories.

Knowledge of and acceptance of self
First and foremost there is the desire to increase knowledge of and acceptance of self. That sense of self is defined by the individual within the context of the group and may be a very different self to that which has

previously been formed by cultural stereotypes. Such self definition in an environment designed to validate the individual's experience will, of necessity, tend to undermine all the basic social assumptions that have been actively harmful for that individual, releasing them into 'free space' to discover themselves (Allen, 1970; Halas, 1973).

Harmony with members of the same sex

Secondly, there is the goal of increasing the sense of harmony with members of the same sex. Growing in love with and understanding of same-sex individuals provides a bedrock on which to base both a belief in your own internal sense of strength as a woman or man and also a sense of belonging to a large group which shares your interests and will support you. Over the last 6 years I have been a member of two women's groups and it was and is to the women of the group I often turn for both practical help and psychological support in times of crisis. Over the years acceptance of self within such groups has made me feel I have the right to ask for help, to say 'I can't cope' and to expect that the resources of the group will be available in practical ways as well as the listening, sharing ways of most groups. Such reality of caring, the practicalities of nurturing as well as the theory, which often extends to the children of group members as well as the members themselves, is a positive aim of many women's groups. Meador *et al.* (1972) noted the importance for women of this practical support combined with the psychological.

Sex stereotyping

A final goal is an increased understanding of the role of sex stereotyping in our society and the effects this has on individuals. Increased support and a sense of peer group loyalty helps individuals to find the courage to make the social changes they believe to be necessary. These changes may well mirror the individual and family changes that were the primary aim of the group. Loyalty and support often continue long after the group has disbanded (Newton and Walton, 1971).

I think it is probably true to say that the majority of people seeking SSTGs already have a sense of 'not fitting' prescribed roles and/or of being uncomfortable within their present network of relationships. As Nicki, a woman in her late 20s commented: 'We're all fairly weird!' The desire to search beyond the dictates of culture, religion and history on the roles of men and women remains a relatively unusual undertaking. The people doing it are self-selected and, therefore, powerfully motivated from the beginning.

The focal aim of each group is to acknowledge the pressures that have brought the individual to seek this form of help and exploration at this moment of their lives. These pressures are always a complex mixture of the personal, the family network and the socio-political. SSTGs aim to approach all three of these areas acknowledging the equal importance of each.

Hilary, an Australian play director and writer commented: 'I want to be with and work with women in a way that is not possible in the so-called "normal" world. That indicates to me that I have a real need that society does not meet right now.'

The role of the leaders

Many SSTGs decide to be leaderless. There are a number of reasons for such a decision. It may be that a leader with the relevant training and understanding is not available, but it is equally likely at the present time that there will be an active choice to be leaderless. There is a general feeling that to have a leader may reproduce the dominant culture within which the group is enacted and make it difficult to work successfully on issues of sharing and helping.

The word 'help' is usually taught at school as either a cry for help, e.g. 'Mary falls over and cries for help', or as a command, e.g. 'John, go and help Mary'. There are two underlying assumptions in such teaching. First, it implies that helping is an activity that one person needs and another provides. The word help is not usually taught as a mutually supportive concept. Group leaders of all sorts are aware of group members believing that the leaders have the answers to their problems and should help them in an active way. The concept of salvation is connected to a belief in this form of help. Some SSTGs believe that having a leader fosters this form of need and belief in group members. Lack of a leader means that the fact that there is nobody there to 'save' you except yourself is underlined from the start. This, they believe, means that needs of and beliefs in help as active salvation can be dealt with realistically without any distortion by the presence of a leader.

Secondly, the teaching of the word 'help' is often heavily laced with sex stereotypes. Men 'save' women. For both men and women this presents problems in life which may be reflected but unchallenged in group therapy, particularly if the group leader is male and the majority of members are female, which is often the case in both patient and staff groups. This is a complex issue that can easily trap the unwary leader in a web of transference and countertransference. Underneath the conscious and taught notions of help being given from men to women lies another layer of experience which suggests the contrary. This contradiction is a reflection of the difference in our experiences as children, when mothers provide most 'help' and, as adults, when men are given the role of 'protectors'. The unfulfilled expectations of both sexes and the resulting disillusionment and fury add fuel to this situation, sweeping away any possibility of understanding or interpretation for all but the uncommonly gifted or brave leaders (Progrebin, 1973).

If the group decides to have a leader, the role of the leader will depend upon the stated goal of the group. If individual change is pursued the group leader will function as a facilitator initially but will encourage reflection both on individual and group processes in an attempt to make sense of whatever transpires.

The presence of a leader intensifies issues of competition, the struggle for power (apparent or denied), and fears of being powerless and helpless, i.e. it awakens the specific elements of the relationship between parent and child of the same sex. There has been some suggestion (Price, 1986) that the desire to be leaderless may be an avoidance of these issues. This can be especially true in women-only groups where issues of power and competition can indeed be painful. It may be that long-term avoidance of these issues has led individual women within the group to undermine their true adult potential for many years prior to the group. Once in their 40s or 50s it is difficult for such women to recover the socio-economic ground that has been lost by this lifetime's avoidance, and fierce confrontation of what has been lost and why may only tragically add to the woman's sense of failure. Hence a leader may need to walk the narrow path between confrontation of these issues for members who have the internal and external space and resources to use the resulting insights, and protection of those members for whom such insights come too late to be anything but painful. This is particularly difficult if the leader is much younger than some of the group members. Many women who tread the hard path towards increased personal freedom have a great need to 'educate' their mothers into agreeing with their new stances. This need may fail to take into account just how much of the mother's life would need to be dismissed as 'slavery' for such an understanding to occur. It is important that the leader remembers that the group is committed to hearing and valuing all the experiences related within its confines, and failure to find that balance of accepting the 'old' while striving for the 'new' can easily lead to the group fragmenting with jealousy and envy.

The leader also needs to be able to recognize the inevitable envy aimed at her/himself and to be able to deal with the reality base for this issue as well as the psychological basis. Group leaders often seem more sociologically successful in groups of this sort. They may have already made at least part of the journey that others wish to follow. Because of this the group may use them as models of the perfect traveller in this foreign country. This is, of course, very flattering to the leader who needs to be aware of this process and recognize its limitations both in facilitating useful change in the members and also in preventing further change in the leader.

Issues of competition in SSTGs throw interesting light on many areas of sexuality. We are used to considering sexuality in terms of seduction of the parent of the opposite sex and yet, within SSTGs, it is often obvious that sexuality is employed either implicitly or explicitly in competition for leadership generally. The leader needs to be aware that the sexuality aroused towards her/himself is not simply of the loving/caring/understanding variety but also equally based in the need for mastery and power. Encouragement of group members to view their sexuality as a more rounded emotional experience may require intuitive handling from the leader. Both men and women are frightened of the connection between aggression and sexuality. This fear produces a primary splitting in their internalized view of intimacy. That split is then given much social credence by the way our culture portrays all intimacy between adults as caring and happy on the one hand or evil and perverted on the other.

For women, the acknowledgement both of sado-masochistic fantasies and of the power of their aggression towards their male partners for what they perceive as thoughtless domination can release much pent up sexual energy. For men the confusion between sexuality and aggression is often extreme. It is an issue clouded with guilt about the amount of acting out that has already occurred in their sexual lives. Group leaders are exposed to this confusion and pain in ways likely to seduce them into a variety of collusive patterns with the group. One safeguard to this problem has been to encourage 'assertiveness' within the group as an alternative to aggression. This can be helpful as long as members and leaders alike bear in mind that what passes for assertiveness within psychotherapy groups may still be seen, and responded to, as if it were aggression in the outside world. Many leaders will want to confront the presence of aggression within the group's experience of sexuality and make the connections with individual and group needs to compete for power and mastery without providing alternative methods of expression. Groups are often united in disliking any depth exploration of experiences of aggression and a leader may need to challenge that comfortable 'disliking'. As one male leader commented to me: 'disliking feelings of aggression is not the same as owning it and taking responsibility for it'. Such explorations need safe limits within the group and a sense of containment.

The role of group members

Honesty, willingness to listen and commitment are as fundamentally important in SSTGs as in any other form of group therapy. Hence, the role of members is to attend regularly and respond to each other in a straightforward fashion. Given the distressing nature of the material discussed and the emotions evoked these criteria are sometimes hard to achieve. This may be particularly difficult in leaderless groups if there is a reluctance to challenge individuals who depart from the ideals.

Maintaining trust and confidentiality are also important prerequisites for group interaction. Members of the group may well come from the same social and/or working group, and this makes being able to trust each other to maintain confidentiality even more important. Some members will share material that they have not told close friends about outside of the group, who may be mutually close friends with other group members. Others will share material that is unknown to their family and spouse. This sharing in the context of other overlapping social groupings requires that each member makes an especial commitment to behave with integrity towards anything related within the group.

Each group member needs to be able to maintain the group in a central position of her attention for its duration each week. This becomes a difficult task when group members are engaged in active relationships outside of the group in several different contexts. The problems for both individuals and the group when such a relationship is sexual are discussed on pages 275–6.

It is not unusual for partners of group members to feel excluded by the group. They envy the closeness between their partner and the group and experience anxiety about the likely effects of the group on their relationship. I have heard husbands comment that they were frightened that their wives might be 'turned into lesbians' by women's groups, but often their fears are far more generalized and less verbalized, being the fear of any imposed change. These feelings often reach their peak in the mid-phase of the group when changes in the group member may be becoming evident. These partners may seek to cause considerable practical difficulties to the member's continued attendance, e.g. by refusing to aid in child care at the last possible minute, or by becoming verbally or physically aggressive towards their partner on the day the group is held each week. Members need to be aware that such difficulties may arise and undertake, with the group's help and support, to look at and then attempt to resolve outside efforts to stop the process of change within themselves. These situations are often more easily dealt with when they arise if they have been predicted and discussed prior to the event. It is part of each member's responsibility to deal with the outside pressures that may prevent her attendance just as much as trying to look at and resolve inner issues which might keep her away.

Group development over time

As in all groups issues of trust and confidentiality are often the first topics to be covered. As suggested in the previous section these issues can present particular problems for groups of this sort for practical reasons of overlapping relationships in and out of the group. At another level of understanding many of us have been brought up to believe that we are competing with members of the same sex for partners of the opposite sex, or for work, status and income. Hence to learn to trust members of the same sex may in itself represent a considerable barrier in the group's early weeks.

Once trust has been established SSTGs often move on to issues involving sexuality and intimacy. Members may share their experiences of developing sexuality, a topic that is often mutually enlightening because of the wide range of differing prohibitions experienced by different members. An appreciation of how illogical and even humorous some of the prohibitions embedded in the teaching of sexual matters are often leads to members reconsidering issues which they had previously accepted as 'right', 'true' or 'proper' in a different light.

This form of sharing paves the way for a sharing of more painful and traumatic experiences. In groups of young women experiences of incest, rape and general humiliation are common themes while topics such as abortion, miscarriage and child-bearing feature in groups when the members are in their 30s or more. These stories are often told with a sense of guilt and shame as if the woman is to blame for her own pain because she has dared to be sexually active. The group will usually act to refocus the feelings aroused by these experiences, to enhance the woman's self-esteem and to lift the burden of guilt by seeing the act as part of the larger picture of male/female relationships rather than any individual woman's fault. The group also searches for an understanding of the role of early life experiences and socialization in causing particular individuals to be at risk of particular insults. Different styles of coping for the future are explored but there is always a great need to acknowledge the pain, fear and humiliation of the past before going on to look at ways of improving the future.

As was mentioned on page 268, there then comes a time when issues of hetero- and homosexuality emerge, often twinned with themes of power, control and competition. In the early stages group members almost always have a strong positive reaction to group membership, but as these issues emerge and the group begins to struggle with problems within itself, as well as problems from without, such positive feelings may evaporate for a while.

Jealousy and envy are also common themes in the group's mid-life. Many women are fiercely envious of the position of their brothers within their families of origin, and most particularly in their mother's esteem. It would be easy to see such a reaction as 'penis envy', an emotion that is selectively envious of the brother's maleness, until women discover that they can experience a resurgence of that emotion within all women groups if one of the 'siblings' seems especially valued by the leader: There is often a painful reality in these women's perception of their family's inability to value them because they were girls. Grappling with that reality both within the group and then within their own families often leads to family acknowledgement of the unfairness of past judgements. Given the strength and support of the group as a whole I have known many women fight their way into positions of greater respect within their own families, which in turn allows them to relate in a fresh and less bitter way with siblings and pseudo-siblings.

Within most SSTGs there is a wide range of abilities and differences in achievement. Different lifestyles may feel the need to struggle for supremacy and the cohesion of the group can be threatened by such power struggles. Resolving these competitive conflicts within the group enhances the individual's ability to accept and then use creatively their more aggressive and assertive personality traits in the outside world. I have seen a number of women suddenly become more successful in their chosen careers at this stage of group development as if the group's acceptance of and ability to survive a competitive struggle makes each individual less afraid of that form of behaviour. It is also not unusual for members to report an improvement in close relationships, both with partners and children, that seems to run parallel to these other external changes and probably reflects an increasing sense of fulfilment in areas that are not directly connected with interpersonal relationships.

After threatened fragmentation the group may enjoy a further period of closeness and during this phase comes acknowledgement from some or all members of women's groups that they have, at least in part, been searching for a source of mothering. This may be particularly true of those individuals who have had traumatic childhoods or disastrous relationships, experienced as betrayals, with their mothers. Many women report huge, overwhelming disillusionment with the discovery that their menfolk are incapable of mothering them. This is sometimes a realistic assessment of men who, by personality or upbringing, are incapable of responding in a nurturing way to another human being, even children. However, with group encouragement, some women discover that their families are more capable of being appropriately nurturing if given the right signals. Women who intuitively know when a member of their family requires their care may be amazed to discover that they need to tell the family in clear terms exactly what they require, that intuitive sense not being part of the average family's repertoire with 'mum'.

However warm and supportive the group it will not have achieved total nurturing and will have, at times, led to feelings of disillusionment in some group members and a feeling of failure to provide adequately in others. It is important to the functioning of the group in later stages that these experiences are explored in the light of the individual's early experiences of being nurtured and providing nurture. It is not unusual, particularly among the daughters of mothers who were depressed during the daughter's childhood, to discover that a woman's earliest memories are of being the carer-giver rather than being cared for. This pattern may have been repeating itself throughout the woman's life, leaving her ever more empty and desolate. The group can give a new experience of warmth and caring at the same time as maintaining the need for each individual to be separate and self-sufficient.

Groups then often proceed from strength to strength, and members feel increasingly confident about the group's 'survival' with each problem that is recognized and resolved With this increasing sense of trust in the group, individuals become aware of a parallel growth of strength within themselves. The group acts to validate and underline that growing sense of a strong self.

Finally, the group has to turn to issues of separation and growing away from each other. Most SSTGs do not set termination dates at the start, although as members move during the course of the group the majority of groups will have experienced single separations and may have developed rituals for dealing with those. For many groups, although the formal meetings end, the relationships formed within the group continue over a period of many years. This is seen as a positive and beneficial fact rather than something to be avoided.

In SSTGs the issue of separation, particularly from the parent of the same sex, often evokes memories of earlier angry and traumatic separations. Murderous rage at the absent, abandoning or inadequate parent are all expressed. In mixed-sex therapy groups I have often witnessed women appearing uncomfortable if one of their number reports raging, vengeful feelings as if they believe this is not a part of 'womanhood' that should be exposed to men. In women-only groups it is noticeable that expressions of feelings, however fierce, cause considerably less anxiety in other members, giving the member who is expressing those feelings more positive feedback about such expressions. The ending of the group may lead to a psychological separation from the parent concerned. For example, Jackie, a young mother of three with a critical and intrusive mother commented 'There is no going back. I realize that I can never have the mother I want. However much I hang on she will not be magically transformed now.' Earlier experiences of facing disillusionment with inadequate nurturing have often paved the way for statements of this sort in the group's final weeks. The acceptance of the ferocity of the feelings seems to be an important part of this work.

When the group is designed to produce social as well as personal change, separation is not a valid aim. Strength for change can only come from a sense of unity with others who desire similar change. From these groups come sad reflections that members have had to make the journey of coming close to strangers rather than find the unity they seek among their mothers and biological sisters. For example, Susan, a doctor in her early 40s said:

> I realize I am living in a world that my mother has never experienced. In some ways I am already older than her. I am sad she did not get there first and I am even sadder that I don't believe she will be following me there. It means goodbye to my dream of unity with my mother but it is only by saying that goodbye that I can be separate enough to unite with someone else.

Mechanisms of change

In leaderless groups there is a gradual growth of a sense of responsibility for self and others. The group environment, therefore, encourages a combination of self-reliance and interdependence which may be very different expectations to those the group members meet in their external environments. The discovery that there is fun and support in SSTGs is often the greatest single factor for change. This factor is said by many to be only available in groups that exclude members of the opposite sex as part of a more general experiment with themselves (Ellis and Nichols, 1979). The insights thus promoted generalize to many other forms of change including a reappraisal of the role of sexuality in the individual's manner of relating to both men and women and a change in the way that that individual regards the roles they play in life. Members of such groups often move away from the more stereotypical roles for their sex and explore different avenues of occupation in life with the new perspective that a SSTG has given them.

A SSTG can also underline the validity of the life experience of individuals from the perspective of that sex. If, for reasons of sex or sexuality, an individual lives in a society that fails to perform this function, they experience a sense of alienation and frustration which is often difficult to pinpoint and deal with. It is common for people coming into SSTGs to feel that they have been repeatedly dismissed, to wonder if they are 'abnormal', but to also feel angry at their alienation.

Women often come into SSTGs knowing that there is something wrong with themselves and/or their lives, although all the important people around them may be telling them that everything is alright (i.e. the woman's perception of herself is, according to others, wrong), or that there is an illness diagnosis which covers her sense of discontent (i.e. that the woman is unwell and not unhappy (see Levine *et al.*, 1974). Part of the excitement of the early days of SSTGs is the discovery that other people share perceptions of life that have been previously invalidated by everyone around. This discovery has been repeatedly reported as an important factor for change (Brodsky, 1973; Ellis and Nichols, 1979).

Sometimes, the need to define and find acceptance for a particular experience of life is even more extreme than usual and many groups of women living in cultures foreign to their own have attested to the value of meeting with each other to discuss the joint difficulties of being female and alien to the surrounding culture in which they are resident. Practical help and support, e.g. with language barriers, may be as important as psychological support in these groups (Alibhai, 1984). In SSTGs with a leader, there is a further powerful mechanism for change. The relationship between the group and the leader in a single-sex group seems particularly intense. This may be due to the lack of a second parent figure. For group members who have idealized their parent of the opposite sex from the age of three or four, as an avoidance of the anxiety which dealing with their disillusionment with the parent of the same sex at that age may have evoked, it is a challenging environment within which to rework that early avoidance and then work through the inevitable sadness. Many women report failing to deal with their disillusionment with mother during childhood and these women have commonly gone on to idealize fathers who were geographically or psychologically absent and, therefore, never likely to become familiar enough to make real relationships. These women have commonly consoled themselves with the notion that even if mother did not love them father did, even when all the evidence is to the contrary. Such a working through of this parent/child confusion, accepting the strength of the need to be mothered, which has often been denied since early childhood, and looking at the reality of care giving within the family of origin often changes a member's relationship with both parents simultaneously. As Janice commented: 'My father has come off the mountain top and my mother has come up from the mire!'

For women to challenge and change long-held notions about their mothers leads to a reappraisal of the mother within themselves as well as their real mothers. They can begin to allow themselves to be less than perfect mothers and feel less guilty when they sometimes fail their own children once they can begin to understand and forgive their own mothers. Looking at the impact that heterosexuality has on their own lives allows women to reconsider their mother's styles of coping within the context of similarly difficult relationships with their fathers. Again, as Janice said:

> I now realize that my mother used me as a place to vent her frustration with dad and with her limited and humiliating life. Attempting to vindicate myself in her eyes has led me to far greater choice and freedom than she ever had. For her generation I now feel some sadness and much less bitterness. My father is less of a God to me now. I can see that he did to my mother exactly what Pete [her husband] tries to do to me.

Allowing her mother and herself freedom to fail without fearing rejection and alienation often opens the way for great change in a woman's view of what is possible in life. She may become more assertive, more successful or simply less worried about how people view her. For example, Paula commented:

> I feel I have regained myself. Nobody will ever have the power to judge and hurt me like they did in the past. I am strong enough now to say 'hang on a minute, I don't agree with that'. Strangely I think my mum has gained something too. She stands up to dad much more now she knows that I will not always be supporting him.

For many women the desire to be different to their mothers is a ruling force in their lives. The discovery that mother and daughter are both equally and sometimes similarly flawed is at first traumatic but leads on to a sense of history and of being rooted. Parenthood is often a voyage towards such discoveries about your own parents, but for many people in SSTGs the opportunity to grow via the experience of parenthood has either not yet occurred or is actively unwanted.

The pros and cons of parenthood, which are sometimes connected with a need to seek or avoid reappraisal of the parenting that the individual has received, are often discussed with much feeling in SSTGs. Hopefully such discussions and explorations in this environment lead to a new understanding of the roots of self without implying that there are 'mature expectations' of what each person 'should' want in terms of their own potential parenting.

Within all-male groups the issues surrounding father/son relationships are approached with a similar intensity. Several male leaders have described to me the sense of both being battered by the group for being powerful and dominant at the same time as being equally punished for any sign of weakness.

SSTGs are seeking to promote group and social change as well as individual change. The mechanism by which this occurs is associated with the strong sense of identification between group members. The strength of this identification may initially surprise members, although given that each has made a positive decision to be in the environment it is not so surprising. Individuals must be starting along the road to a more positive identification with members of their own sex to be seeking such an experience. Issues that are raised, once explored at the personal level, are often then generalized to socio-political and economic levels. There is an acceptance that these issues underlie the psychology of the individual and, while they should not be used as an avoidance of the personal, it is equally unhelpful to deny or ignore them. Hence there is active encouragement to make changes not just within themselves but within family groups, within groups of friends and within other social and working constellations. Such changes may bring the individual into direct conflict with social norms and it is only by long-term support of the group that these changes can continue to be helpful to the member rather than serve to isolate them. Generally, the greater the change the longer the time needed to work through and integrate that change within the life of each member.

Typical problems and their resolution

SSTGs have most of the problems experienced in all groups, e.g. drop-outs and fragmentary attenders. They also have more specific problems. For instance, in women-only groups, there is a definite tendency for one woman to take on a 'helper' role. There may even be active competition for this role. Another member may then be tempted to become 'victim'. These roles are usually all too familiar to the individuals concerned but also have elements of familiarity for all group members who then proceed to project that part of themselves into the chosen member. Such roles distort the growth of the group and need to be confronted as soon as they are recognized.

Cultural stereotypes invade the group and can lead to members having unrealistic expectations of each other or themselves. Coming to an understanding that much of what you have been taught about your own and the opposite sex is untrue is a repeatedly painful process, and there is always a temptation to run back to the reassuring familiarity of stereotypes, however damaging these may be. Warmth, genuineness and a sense of humour are all necessary if the group is to survive the sense of horror that goes with the recognition that the parameters by which we have been measuring ourselves, our roles and our functions need dismantling and rebuilding.

SSTGs need to be able to refocus continually on the personal and this is often difficult if consideration of the social and economic becomes too pressing. Keeping a balance between these areas of equal importance is necessary if group integrity is to be maintained. The most successful groups are often those who lay down a structure that allows exploration at many levels. Many leaderless groups function better if members take turns to perform the basic limit-setting functions, e.g. responsibility for timing.

It is not unusual for SSTGs to contain one or more on-going close relationships. It is also not unusual for such a relationship to be formed in the early days of group development. Opinions vary on the appropriateness of allowing or even encouraging sexual relationships between members. In most other groups such relationships would almost certainly be frowned upon and interpreted as a form of resistance to the work of the group and yet, in SSTGs, they tend to be looked on more kindly. If the group is designed to foster good and openly intimate feelings between members of the same sex then such relationships might be seen as a measure of success for the group. Such a relationship within the group certainly provides a cathartic focus for group members to explore their feelings about homosexuality in a here-and-now sense, which often leads to considerably more energy and honesty in the exchange than might otherwise be possible.

I have come to view on-going sexual relationships within the group as a particular reality in SSTGs. The group needs to explore rather than ignore the presence of such relationships, however, because not only do they have a powerful impact on group dynamics, but the group will exert an equally powerful although often more covert influence on the relationship. Working through this issue often leads on to discussions about the differences between sexual and non-sexual intimacy and opens up the theme of exclusivity of relationships to others, often reawakening feelings of being excluded from the parental relationship.

Limitations of the approach

In a single-sex group, it is possible for the absent sex to become a scapegoat for all problems, personal and otherwise. It is important that groups are aware of this possibility while at the same time not inhibiting themselves from exploration of the consequences for members of their relationships with the opposite sex.

Conversely, difficulties can also arise if one or more members are strongly and positively identified with their opposite sex parent. The opposite sex can then become the idealized and psychologically untouchable object for the group, which will obviously limit the amount of work a group can do.

If an individual member's problems seem to be rooted in family or marital relationships there may be benefit in seeing the SSTG as merely a starting place for exploration, with family or marital therapy to follow.

Membership of an SSTG can become something of a way of life and I think this is particularly true of groups which start off from other social or working constellations and whose members are therefore involved with each other in multiple contexts. As in most group therapy there are undoubtedly advantages in starting off with a stranger group, even if the group becomes increasingly socially intimate as well as psychologically close as time goes on.

SSTG should never be seen as a retreat from external reality but rather as an interesting harbour in which to observe, explore and replenish prior to setting sail once more.

Typical qualities of effective leaders

The need for some form of personal therapy in training is never more necessary than when conducting SSTGs. Acknowledgement of self-conflicts, particularly in areas of sexuality, competition with the same sex, needs to nurture *vs.* be nurtured, and all aspects of the relationship with the same-sex parent is vitally important. A theorectical knowledge of present-day understandings of male and female psychology is also helpful.

I have felt the need for peer group discussion between leaders of such groups and opportunities for this remain scarce. Perhaps most importantly leaders of SSTGs need to have a genuine interest in and love of their own sex, while being able to maintain that position without either scapegoating or idealizing the opposite sex. Such a position is an ideal towards which most of us continue to struggle. It is, as ever, the presence of honestly expressed warmth and interest which make the difference between a good and bad therapist.

CONCLUSION

SSTGs allow a different milieu to that which we normally encounter in day-to-day life. It is that difference which allows for much interesting and thought-provoking work. Group members can explore their life experience within an environment that can respond empathically and appropriately to that exploration from the depths of the combined member experience.

SSTGs also offer an opportunity to look at the impact of cultural stereotypes on the behaviour of individual members. This allows participants to gain a view of themselves within a socio-economic context as well as in terms of their own personal development. There can be little doubt that such groups are a valid and helpful model for many people.

ACKNOWLEDGEMENTS

Thank you to the women of many different groups who have allowed me to use their quotes and taught me much. Thank you also to the male leaders who have discussed men-only groups with me.

REFERENCES

Alibhai, Y. (1984). Asian women's therapy: talking among themselves. *Nursing Times* 28 Nov, 44–46.

Allen, P. (1970). *Free Space*. New York, Times Change Press.

Angel, J. (ed.) (1971). *The Radical Therapist*. New York, Ballantine.

Bardwick, J. M. (1971). *Psychology of Women. A Study of Bio-Cultural Conflicts*. New York, Harper and Row.

Brodsky, A. M. (1973). The consciousness-raising group as a model for therapy with women. *Psychotherapy: Theory, Research and Practice* **10**, 24–9.

Broverman, I. K., Broverman, D. M., Clarkson, F. E., Rosencrantz, P. S. and Vogel, S. R. (1970). Sex role stereotypes and clinical judgements of mental health. *Journal of Consulting and Clinical Psychology* **34**, 1–7.

Chesler, P. (1972). *Women and Madness*. New York, Doubleday.

Davis, M. S. (1977). Women's liberation groups as a primary preventive mental health strategy. *Community Mental Health Journal* **13B**, 936.

Ellis, E. and Nichols, M. (1979). A comparative study of feminist and traditional group assertiveness training with women. *Psychotherapy: Theory, Research and Practice* **16**, 467–74.

Friedan, B. (1963). *Feminine Mystique*. New York, Dell.

Gilman, R. (1971). The feminist liberation case against Sigmund Freud. *Times Magazine* 31 Jan, 10.

Halas, C. (1973). All-women's groups. A view from inside. *Personnel & Guidance Journal* **52** (2), 91–5.

Jenkins, R. and Clare, A. W. (1985). Women and mental illness. *British Medical Journal* **291**, 1521–2.

Kagan, J. and Moss, H. A. (1971). *Birth to Maturity*. New York, Wiley.

Kiesler, S. (1975). Actuarial prejudice toward women and its implications. *Journal of Applied Social Psychology* **5**, 201–215.

Levine, S., Kamin, L. and Levine, E. (1974). Sexism and psychiatry. *American Journal of Orthopsychiatry* **44**, 327–34.

Mayer, E. (1974). Some insights into an all-women's group. *Voices* **10**, 7–11.

Meador, B., Solomon, E. and Bowen, M. (1972). Encounter groups for women only. *In* L. Solomon and B. Berson. (eds), *New Perspectives on Encounter Groups*. San Francisco, Jossey-Bass.

Newton, E. and Walton, S. (1971). The personal is political: consciousness-raising and personal change in the women's movement. *In* B. G. Schoepf (chair), *Anthropologists Look at the State of Women*. Symposium presented at the American Anthropological Association, November 1971, USA.

Nott, P. M., Franklin, M., Armitage, C. and Gelder, M. G. (1976). Hormonal changes in the peurperium. *British Journal of Psychiatry* **128**. 379–83.

Oakley, A. (1980). *Women Confined*. London, Fontana.

Orbach, S. and Eichenbaum, L. (1982). *Outside In, Inside Out*. Harmondsworth, Penguin.

Price, J. (1986). Women's therapy in Britain. A talk delivered to the First Annual 'Making Women Well' Conference. June, USA.

Progrebin, L. C. (1973). Rap Groups. *Ms* **1** (9), 80.

Rice, J. and Rice, D. (1973). Implications of the women's movement for psychotherapy. *American Journal of Psychiatry* **130**, 191–5.

Wahrman, R. and Pugh, M. (1974). Sex, non-conformity and influence. *Sociometry* **37**, 137–47.

Wolman, C. and Frank, H. (1975). The solo woman in a professional peer-group. *American Journal of Orthopsychiatry* **45**, 164–70.

Women's National Commission (1984). *Women and the Health Service*. Cabinet Office, London, HMSO.

Yalom, I. D. and Rand, K. (1966). Compatibility and cohesiveness in therapy groups. *Archives of Geneal Psychiatry* **13**, 267–76.

PART 3

RESEARCH AND TRAINING ISSUES IN GROUP THERAPY

CHAPTER 13

RESEARCH IN GROUP PSYCHOTHERAPY

Sidney Bloch

INTRODUCTION

This chapter is based upon a premise, the value of which I have appreciated increasingly with years of clinical practice, namely that psychotherapy is an intricate blend of art and science (Bloch, 1982). Without the art, the therapist is reduced to a mere technician, the patient to an object for manipulation. Without the science, the therapist is subject to the current fashion or bound inflexibly to his preferred belief system. The plethora of schools of psychotherapy testifies to the former risk; the intrusion of ideology into the clinic reflects the latter.

Ideology, in particular, is a great inhibitor of progress in psychotherapy (as it is in psychiatry generally). Unambiguous condemnation is what it warrants and, indeed, receives from the late Sir Denis Hill (1982): 'What I regard as a great sin is to hold a total ideology. In psychiatry, if you have a total ideology, you are just no good' (p. 96).

Seymour Halleck (1982) spells it out most cogently when he remarks that ideologues:

> . . . may be constantly battered by new ideas and discoveries which do not fit into their particular belief system, but if they adhere strongly enough to their theories they can ignore contradictory data or can eventually find some way of arguing that such data is not compatible with their theories. These practitioners may get better and better in learning a limited set of techniques but their overall growth as clinicians is permanently stunted (p. 23).

To avoid such stunting, I would suggest that, while the *art* of group psychotherapy is unceasingly cultivated through clinical experience and sensitive self-reflection, its scientific dimension should also be maintained in clear focus, and the findings therefrom critically appraised. My remit in this chapter is to highlight this scientific dimension, and more particularly to show that:

(i) a tradition of conducting research into group therapy exists, especially over the last 25 years (Dies, 1979; Frank, 1975);

(ii) notwithstanding its great complexity, many facets of the group are amenable to systematic investigation (Bednar and Kaul, 1978; Kaul and Bednar, 1986); and

(iii) the researcher has something solid to contribute to the group therapist, in as much as his findings can either yield clinical guidelines or stimulate the careful re-evaluation of aspects of clinical practice.

Before pursuing these goals, I must justify my opting to focus on two basic areas of research in group therapy: process and outcome. In any event, limitations of space preclude a consideration of many other competing topics such as, who should be treated in groups, how should groups be composed, what makes for effective leadership, how does group therapy compare with other modes of psychotherapy in terms of effectiveness, and do different forms of group therapy have different effects? (see Bednar and Kaul, 1978; Kaul and Bednar, 1986).

First, why a focus on process? It is a prerequisite in conducting group therapy that the therapist attempts to clarify how it works. The greater his (and indeed the patient's) understanding of the processes involved, the more likely is his treatment to be effective, cost-effective and safe (Burlingame *et al.*, 1984). As for outcome, and it can be seen immediately that process and outcome are directly interrelated, the therapist needs to know the degree and quality of improvement he can strive for with particular types of patients – and the potential hazards involved for them. Moreover, he is obliged, both clinically and ethically, to disregard any form of treatment that proves to be less effective or less safe than an available alternative (Glatzer, 1976).

I must deal with one other preliminary, that of definition. It may seem odd to attempt to define group therapy at this point in the book but it will help us to avoid the longstanding limitation that has so bedevilled research into group therapy, namely poor conceptualization. Marvin Shaw (1976) serves us well here. He sets out by offering a representative sample of different approaches to the definition of a group. Thus, a group may be seen in terms of its members' shared perception of their existence as a corporate entity, and their potential to engage with one another. Some theorists would wish for additional criteria such as *motivation* – that group membership will meet a need or bring a reward – or *purpose* – membership being based on the pursuit of one or more common goals. Other theorists postulate the salience of structure and refer to a group as an organized system of interrelationships and roles embodying norms to regulate its functions. A related view emphasizes the interaction of verbal, physical, emotional and other forms as the hallmark of a group. Shaw's (1976) own definition, derived from the above, is apt for our purposes: '. . . a group is defined as two or more persons who are interacting with one another in such a manner that each person influences and is influenced by each other person' (p. 11). Thus, interaction and mutual influence are at the heart of the matter.

This definition is clearly applicable to the therapy group. Both interaction and mutual influence are inherent features but their precise roles and emphases may vary substantially. For instance, the interactional focus may be mainly between each individual patient and the therapist, or between the group as a whole and the therapist, or between the patients themselves (Bloch, 1986c). The issue of definition is more than one of mere variation of emphasis. The uniformity myth of Kiesler (1966), that all forms of psychotherapy are alike, is highly pertinent to group therapy. Consider the wide range: insight-oriented, supportive, sensitivity training (e.g. in terms of the group's purpose), psychoanalytic, existential, gestalt, cognitive-behavioural (in terms of theoretical schools), in-patient, out-patient, encounter, self-help (in terms of membership), and so on. The pie can be cut in many different ways. In order to dispel the uniformity myth, I have advocated the concept of 'the group therapies'. Shaw's definition of a group is retained to reflect the common denominators of interaction and influence, but the sense is conveyed of a group format being applied in several different therapeutic ways. In each case the following are clearly defined: the group's purpose, the conceptual framework of the group process – especially the therapeutic factors involved, the associated techniques required, and the criteria by which the group's effectiveness will be determined.

The uniformity myth is probably the most crucial issue to bear in mind as we proceed to consider group therapy research; and I offer no apology for periodic reiteration of it in the pages that follow.

HOW DOES GROUP PSYCHOTHERAPY WORK?

A consideration of research on group process precedes that on outcome but in some respects splitting the two is contrived. In the final analysis we are interested in noting the relationship between *how* a group works and *how well* it works. Consider a simple example. It is intrinsically interesting to study the factors contributing to group interaction: how it comes about, how it is maintained, what role the therapist plays in influencing it, and so forth. But most salient too is the link between the interaction and outcome. For example, do members of highly interactive groups benefit more from their experience than their counterparts in less interactive groups?

In this chapter, however, I wish primarily to consider the nature of the research on process and on outcome and I therefore take the liberty of treating them separately. The process of group therapy is a complex matter and has been researched along a vast range of dimensions. Instead of a superficial comment on each, I propose to look more extensively at one fundamental aspect, namely the elements of the process that lead to change in group members, variously labelled curative factors, change mechanisms or therapeutic factors.

Before embarking on this task, a general point about the role of theory in the study of group process. Theories about how a group works have been either devised from within the group therapy tradition itself or transplanted from other spheres. An illustration of the former is the Group Focal Conflict Theory of Whitaker and Lieberman (1964) (see Chapter 2). They propounded the notion that a group evolved by grappling with a series of common, unconscious conflicts whereby a shared wish of the members (the disturbing motive) is reacted to with shared anxiety (the reactive motive). The resultant conflict is handled ineptly (a restrictive solution) or effectively (an enabling solution). The therapist assists his patients to appreciate the focal conflict preoccupying the group, and their involvement in it, and facilitates the achievement of an enabling solution.

The transfer to the group of theory from another tradition is well exemplified through brief mention of General Systems Theory (Durkin, 1981). Devised by von Bertalanffy during the 1920s to overcome the conceptual limitations of reductionism in biology, General Systems Theory has appealed to many other disciplines. Its application to the therapy group revolves around the notion that the group can be construed as a system in which an 'organised arrangement of elements, consisting of a network of interdependent and co-ordinated parts' function as a unit (Barnes, 1985). The system is characterized by the following: it is more than the sum of its parts; the parts are also systems, albeit on a lesser scale (e.g. the co-therapy team constitutes one system); the group system is in turn part of much larger (supra-) systems (e.g. the hospital in which the group meets); boundaries exist between the sub-systems and between the group and the supra-systems across which varying levels of communication occur; although the system tends to homeostasis (returning to its original state), it is often capable of transformation (e.g. adopting new patterns of interaction). Astrachan (1970) has written illuminatingly about the optimal incorporation of these dimensions of General Systems Theory into group therapy, and stressed the pivotal role played by the therapist as a central regulatory agent.

I have entered into some of the detail of these two theoretical contributions in order to show their relevance to group process research. These types of theories offer the therapist a means of understanding aspects of the process and thereby of enhancing the effectiveness of his interventions. They offer the researcher a source of propositions which can then be converted into testable hypotheses. The consequent systematic study may then help to confirm or refute the validity of aspects of that theory and lead to its further refinement.

THERAPEUTIC FACTORS IN GROUP THERAPY

My decision to deal with therapeutic factors is far from arbitrary: a *sine qua non* of any understanding of how group therapy exerts its effects is the identification and validation of a finite set of change mechanisms which comprise the therapeutic process. The varied assortment of theories that seek to explain that process tends to obscure the notion of core underlying factors at work. Much as Jerome Frank (1971) has sought to differentiate a set of common basic factors in psychotherapy generally, so a similar approach is applicable to group therapy. An appreciation of the concept of group therapeutic factors is best achieved by noting their evolution. Prior to the mid-1950s, research on the topic was rare but many group therapists had begun to report what they saw as fundamental mechanisms of change. A review of this literature by Corsini and Rosenberg (1955) was a landmark, in that a unifying classification of factors was produced for the first time. Their approach was as follows: first, they identified statements reflecting thera-peutic factors; secondly, they combined identical statements; thirdly, they created categories via a series of hypotheses suggested by a study of the statements; and, finally, they assigned the statements to one or other of the resultant nine categories.

It is important to note that Corsini and Rosenberg did not highlight any particular theoretical model and that their classification applies to group therapy as a whole. A corollary is that the relative importance of these factors in a particular form of group therapy is a function of, *inter alia*, the group's purpose, the members' clinical needs, the duration of treatment, and the stage in the group's development.

In examining the nine categories of Corsini and Rosenberg, and attempting to refine their conceptualization, my colleagues and I have defined a *therapeutic factor* as 'an element of group therapy that contributes to the improvement in a patient's condition and is a function of the actions of the group therapist, the other group members, and the patient himself' (Bloch and Crouch, 1985, p. 4). Distinctions between a therapeutic factor, a condition for change and a technique are useful in further clarifying this definition. A *condition for change* is an aspect of the group, such as a shared

Table 13.1.   Classification of Therapeutic Factors

1	Self-disclosure: revealing personal information to the group
2	Self-understanding (insight): learning something important about oneself
3	Acceptance (cohesiveness): sense of belonging and being valued
4	Learning from interpersonal action: the attempt to relate constructively and adaptively within the group
5	Catharsis: ventilation of feelings, which brings relief
6	Guidance: receiving information or advice
7	Universality: the sense that one is not unique in one's problems
8	Altruism: the sense that one can be of value to others
9	Vicarious learning: learning about oneself through the observation of other group members, including the therapist
10	Instillation of hope: gaining a sense of optimism about the potential for progress

sense of motivation or commitment that – while not inherently therapeutic – allows therapeutic factors to operate effectively. A *technique* similarly lacks direct therapeutic import (except as a possible spin-off), but is rather a means for the therapist to bring therapeutic factors into play. For instance, the use of role play may enable the patient to benefit from the factor of interaction.

Most published classifications of therapeutic factors consist of between 9 and 12 factors, and contain similar constructs, although the terminology used and varied emphases may obscure the similarities. Our own classification is seen in Table 13.1. Using this particular set we now turn to the type of research carried out on each of them, and on therapeutic factors as a group, especially their comparative evaluation by different clinical samples.

Insight or self-understanding

The immensely broad scope of learning about oneself and one's relationships accounts for the difficulty in defining insight precisely, and for the inconsistent pattern of research findings. After all, a patient can learn anything from the origin of a symptom to how he is seen by his peers. Moreover, various theoretical schools emphasize different aspects of learning.

The ample theorizing on the topic has not been matched by empirical research. Certainly, the manipulation of insight as an experimental variable has been carried out but occasionally. Still, some useful pointers have emerged which buttress clincial observation. Chief among these is the differential relevance of insight for various clinical groupings. An impressive study by Meichenbaum and his colleagues (1971) illustrates this issue rather well. Their purpose – to investigate the value of insight in group therapy –

was achieved by recruiting volunteer subjects complaining of speech anxiety and randomly assigning them to one of four treatment conditions: insight, systematic desensitization, these two treatments combined, and a placebo control. To fulfil the requirement for a highly specific form of insight treatment, a derivative of Rational-Emotive Therapy was selected in which the patient learns that his thoughts have a self-defeating quality, and contribute to his problems.

At the end of treatment and at follow-up, insight and desensitization emerged as most effective. Further, detailed inspection of the results reveal the complexity of insight as a therapeutic factor, even in the case of a relatively straightforward problem like speech anxiety. The research subjects could be differentiated according to the diffuseness or otherwise of their difficulty. Thus, in those in whom speech anxiety was only one aspect of a general pattern of shyness, insight or the combined treatment were most efficacious, whereas the speech anxiety-only group benefited most from desensitization.

This result, in conjunction with the findings of other relevant studies, indicates that insight is potentially valuable in group work but only in relation to certain categories of patient, and that other issues are also pertinent, namely, the form of the insight offered, to whom, how, and at what point in a group's development. Another way of making this point is the following: the therapy group provides a forum for a wide range of learning; what a particular patient accomplishes in terms of insight is associated with the sort of problems he tackles and the goals he sets for himself. Furthermore, the route he takes and the methods he adopts to acquire insight will vary.

One obvious method, especially relevant to the acquisition of interpersonal insight, is the feedback offered by fellow patients and the therapist (Yalom, 1985). The contribution of Jacobs (1974) in this context is noteworthy, and is recommended to the reader. Suffice to say, he distinguished between positive (complimentary) and negative (constructive criticism) feedback on the one hand, and emotional (a personal reaction) and behavioural (pointing out a particular pattern of behaviour) feedback on the other. In a series of analogue studies with students, positive feedback was found to be more credible than its negative form, and behavioural more than emotional; positive–emotional feedback had the most impact of all. Although the relationship between these two forms of feedback and outcome was not examined, we could assume that more credible feedback is apt to be more readily acted upon by the recipient than less credible feedback, contribute to self-understanding, and in turn to change. Video feedback is a potential tool in this regard and has been used clinically, but only rarely been subject to experimental valuation (Stoller, 1969).

Learning from interpersonal action

That interaction is a basic feature of group process became clear from our earlier comments on definition. The corresponding therapeutic factor is most suitably entitled 'learning from interpersonal action', and involves the patient's attempt to relate constructively and adaptively within the group, either by initiating new potentially positive behaviour with fellow patients (e.g. acting more assertively) or by responding to them in new, more effective ways (e.g. acting more sensitively to them). Such initiatives are followed by their appraisal by the patient in collaboration with the rest of the group. Theoretically, there is wide variation in where the optimal source of interpersonal learning is located, including the 'individual patient to therapist' in the psychoanalytic model, the 'group as a whole to therapist' in the Tavistock model, and the inter-patient in the dynamic-interactional approach (Bloch, 1986c).

As in the case of insight, considerably more theoretical than empirical work has been done on learning from interpersonal action; and it is not possible to draw any solid clinical implications from the latter.

Measuring or classifying interactional patterns in groups is presumably a useful step in the study of interactional learning. A typical effort is that of Lorr (1966), who drew up a classification of nine dimensions of relating. Applying his classification to small groups containing a total of some 200 patients, observers were able to rate members' interpersonal behaviour. A factor analysis of these ratings, which more or less confirmed the original dimensions, yielded eight factors: dominance, hostility, leadership, support, help-seeking, submission, withdrawal and disorganization. While this sort of work is potentially relevant to the study of interaction *per se*, it is not immediately clear how it can be applied to the factor of interactional learning.

Of more practical value is research on the potential of the therapist to promote interaction within his group. Assuming, for instance, that the inter-member interactional axis is an important source of interpersonal learning, then it would be useful to know if specific therapeutic strategies could promote such interaction. Heckel *et al.* (1962) have indeed demonstrated this. When the therapist of an in-patient psychiatric group referred comments directed to himself back to the group, there was a corresponding increase in interaction between patients. When, as a control, he did not so redirect, the interactional level declined. That one cannot generalize from this finding is shown by a similar study (see Bloch and Crouch, 1985, pp. 88–9), but which differentiated between acutely and chronically ill patients. With the former, the findings resembled those of the Heckel study; the chronic patients, however, did not interact upon redirection, probably because of their greater sense of reliance on the therapist's leadership.

Clearly, inter-member interaction is a function of the patients' ability to manage it, and its level and quality will vary according to the group's composition and goals.

Apart from redirection, the intensity and quality of the therapist's verbal interventions also appear to be important. Research has shown that critically toned statements led to a diminution in positive forms of interaction between group members, whereas more discreet, gentle, critical expression was associated with greater interaction overall. Moreover, greater mutual trust was experienced when negative statements were of low rather than high intensity. The assumption follows that the therapist models particular interactional patterns, as well as the degree of interaction.

Other facets of the topic which have briefly been researched involve the relationship between interaction and personality factors in the patient, the size of the group, and outcome (see Bloch and Crouch, 1985, Ch. 3 for an account of this work).

Self-disclosure

This is defined as the revelation in the group of highly personal information about, *inter alia*, the past, embarrassing or worrisome problems, fantasies and fears which would otherwise not be shared. The theoretical contribution of Sidney Jourard (1971) is most helpful in understanding the relevance of self-disclosure in group therapy. He postulated that self-disclosure is a cardinal aspect of mental health, and a feature of the integrated personality, in that it facilitates self-awareness, which in turn allows for greater authenticity.

Since self-disclosure is relatively easy to define (it is necessarily a public event and therefore directly observable), considerable empirical research has been carried out on it. What follows is a brief account of the main themes that have been explored.

Inevitably, revealing intimate details about oneself entails risk, and clinical observation suggests that large discrepancies in self-disclosing is potentially problematic (Allen, 1974). Analogue studies with volunteer students bear this out. The investigators drew up the hypothesis that liking and self-disclosure should correlate positively on the premise that: receiving a self-relevation is a social reward; greater rewards are associated with social attraction; therefore, a person providing rewards will be perceived as attractive; at the same time the discloser will offer more rewards to those whom he finds attractive. In two ingenious experiments (see Bloch and Crouch, 1985, pp. 147–8) the findings were identical: the students at first divulged information only to those to whom they felt attracted. At the end of the experiment, students preferred peers from whom they had received more personal information. Moreover, students exchanged progressively more intimate information with their peers if they acted similarly. If there is any clinical guideline emerging from this line of work it is that the therapist should prevent any major discrepancy in the tendency to be self-revealing whether this is done as part of the selection process or during the course of treatment itself.

Reference to the therapist's role brings us to the issue of how he can influence his group members to act self-disclosingly. The results of a series of studies are inconsistent, most likely attributable to differences in sample and methodology. Modelling by the therapist of self-disclosure appears to be a relatively ineffective way of trying to promote the same in patients, and it may even have the undesired 'side-effect' of the disclosing therapist being viewed as 'mentally unhealthy'. Setting explicit norms on the other hand may be more efficient. Ribner's (1974) approach involved the provision of explicit instructions designed to facilitate self-disclosure in members of eight experimental groups whose levels of self-disclosure were then compared with those in control groups. Both the frequency and depth of self-disclosure were greater in the former after a single session. In another study in which modelling (a videotape of the desired behaviour was shown) and instructions were compared, the latter condition was more effective in generating self-disclosure.

An important issue in this work is the multidimensionality of the process. As Dies (1977) suggests in a helpful review, the question of how the therapist should use himself to promote self-disclosure can only be considered when broken down into more specific sub-questions such as: in what type of group, with what sort of patient, with what purpose, and at what point in the group's development?

Finally, a word on the self-disclosure–outcome relationship. From the very limited work done on this topic, the emerging picture is unclear. But out of the inconsistency stems one clinical implication. Self-disclosure does not appear to be uniformly advantageous. In one study (Truax and Cark-huff, 1965) an identical research design was applied to two clinical samples. In the case of psychiatric in-patients, their self-disclosure and outcome did correlate positively, whereas the opposite was found with institutionalized juvenile delinquents. In another study, of a chronic psychiatric group, mostly schizophrenics, higher self-disclosers did less well than their more reticent counterparts (Strassberg *et al.*, 1975). Valid explanations for these inconsistent findings are elusive though it could be hypothesized that, at least in the case of chronic schizophrenics, poor social adjustment is a relevant factor, e.g. disclosures are made in socially inept ways and this provokes critical feedback or the discloser misconstrues the group's helpful reactions as criticisms. We are reminded thus of the obvious point that self-disclosure is always a 'public' event and occurs in a particular social context.

For other research work on the association between self-disclosure and other therapeutic factors, on the relevance of the need for social approval for self-disclosure, and on its measurement, see Bloch and Crouch (1985, Ch. 5).

Acceptance or cohesiveness

A distinction needs to be made between the therapeutic factor of acceptance, the feeling of being valued, cared for, supported and understood by other group members, and cohesiveness, a condition for change which reflects a shared sense of belonging and of loyalty to the group.

A large body of research points to the importance investigators attach to group cohesiveness (Bloch and Crouch, 1985, Ch. 4). By contrast, work done on acceptance has been scanty. Let us examine a few of the principal themes of the subject overall.

As a condition for change, cohesiveness should, theoretically at least, be associated with various therapeutic factors. And this has indeed been found to be the case. For instance, it correlates positively with self-disclosure and also, though not quite so consistently, with interaction. The correlational nature of the relevant studies does not answer the question as to how these variables relate, but in all probability a circular process operates whereby cohesiveness as a condition for change facilitates the two other therapeutic factors, and in turn is an effect of increased self-disclosure and interaction.

The experimental manipulation of variables would shed light on these relationships but is rarely done. An imaginative study by Rich (1968) exemplifies what is needed in the field. A group member propounding a deviant viewpoint, it was hypothesized, would interact in a certain way with his fellows by being more tolerated in a cohesive group. But the contrary was found; the low cohesive group tended to accommodate the deviant whereas the high cohesive group challenged him overtly. Perhaps this parallels clinical observation in that cohesive groups enjoy a degree of security which enables interaction to encompass mutual challenge and even confrontation between their members.

If cohesiveness is a desirable condition for change, its promotion should ideally occur early on in the group's development. What strategies can the therapist deploy to this end? Investigators have tackled this in various ways. Liberman (1970), for example, has shown how verbal operant conditioning can foster cohesiveness. In an experimental group, the therapist's prompting and reinforcement of any statement reflecting patients' mutual attraction led to greater cohesiveness than in a control group. Some therapists might resist such a role, preferring to leave the main responsiblity to the patients, while others would opt for a certain style of leadership to encourage cohesiveness. One investigation has shown two aspects of leadership as relevant: caring and self-expressiveness. Moreover, both co-therapists had to manifest the caring style for the effects to succeed (Hurst 1978).

Clinical experience suggests that certain organizational variables are relevant. For example, the selection of patients for a particular group is often done in such a way as to avoid deviance. One line of research revolves around the issue of compatibility: is cohesion a function of how compatible group members are with one another? In this context, the Fundamental Interpersonal Relations Orientation-Behaviour Scale (mercifully known by its acronym of FIRO-B) has been widely used. William Schutz (1966) originally theorized that we relate to one another along three dimensions: inclusion (the need to belong), control (the handling of power) and affection (the need for intimacy), and produced the FIRO-B to measure these dimensions.

Several research teams have hypothesized that compatibility in terms of these basic ways of relating is closely bound up with group cohesiveness. The experimental design has been similar throughout. Members complete the FIRO-B prior to the beginning of the group, and rate cohesiveness at a later stage. The findings would tend to support a link between the two variables but the picture is more complex in at least two respects – compatibility is not necessarily stable over time, and it is in all likelihood not a unitary factor (see Bloch and Crouch, 1985, pp. 117–21 for a fuller account of this topic and relevant bibliography).

Alternative organizational factors are more straightfoward. For instance, it may be that cohesiveness develops more rapidly in an extended marathon session compared to the conventional programming of group meetings. On the other hand, a marathon session scheduled at the beginning of a group's life appears to pose too much of a threat because it demands a level of intimacy for which the participants are not yet prepared.

Pre-group preparation – providing the prospective patient with appropriate information about the rationale of treatment, the roles of the patient, other members, and the therapist, etc. (see pp. 295–6) – is yet another possible means to speed up the achievement of the cohesive group, a procedure repeatedly demonstrated to be of distinct advantage. Indeed, this is one of *the* most consistent findings in research on group process, and an example, *par excellence*, of how a clinically relevant issue can be investigated systematically, the results replicated and a firm guideline made available for the clinician. (We shall return to this question of the bridge between research and practice in the final section of the chapter.)

Finally, what about the effect of cohesiveness on outcome? Although the clinical consensus supports a positive effect, the research findings are inconclusive. When the group member rates both the level of cohesiveness he perceives in his group and his own outcome, their correlation is significant (Kapp *et al.*, 1964). In another study (Yalom *et al.*, 1967), such a positive correlation only pertained in the case where the patient assessed his own outcome but not where his rating of cohesiveness was correlated with outcome as assessed by the therapist. This may be due to the patient perceiving all aspects of his group experience in a consistent fashion: thus, if he feels he had done well, everything about the group appears rosy; and correspondingly the converse. The occasional finding of a negative association between cohesiveness and outcome makes it all the more difficult to be confident about the precise role of cohesiveness (see, for example, Roether and Peters, 1972). Perhaps we should not be altogether perplexed if we remind ourselves that cohesiveness *per se* is not a therapeutic factor but a condition for change and as such should at least theoretically not be associated directly with outcome. The type of study we do need concerning outcome should involve acceptance rather than cohesiveness.

Other therapeutic factors

Research on the other six factors listed in Table 13.1 have been relatively under-researched. Only brief mention will therefore be made of them (a fuller account is available in the relevant chapters of Bloch and Crouch, 1985).

Catharsis
The release of strong feelings which brings relief has a long tradition in psychotherapy generally but has tended to be usurped in group therapy by the cognitive dimension of the group process. Most clinicians would contend that catharsis *per se* is of limited value, and requires complementary cognitive reflection. This is borne out empirically. In the Stanford Encounter Group Study, catharsis on its own was not associated with change (Lieberman *et al.*, 1973). On the contrary, certain forms such as the expression of aggressive feelings occurred more commonly in group members with a negative outcome than in those who did not change or improved. A similar result was found in a study examining the effects of an emotionally arousing weekend group experience on subsequent individual therapy; intense catharsis without an opportunity to make sense of the expressed emotion produced harmful effects (Yalom *et al.*, 1977).

Guidance
The imparting of useful information about mental health and ill health or giving advice has been viewed by most group therapists as relatively unimportant and even disadvantageous in that it may promote undue dependency on the therapist. This position is probably reasonable in the longer term out-patient group whose goal is personality change. In this context we may again note the relevance of the concept of the 'group

therapies'. The question of whether guidance of a specific type has a potential role in certain therapy groups has still to be answered. It is indeed conceivable that highly structured, didactic groups might suit certain clinical populations such as the chronically disabled. An appropriate illustration of this is the relatives' group, studied by Leff and his colleagues (1982) in the case of schizophrenia. Here, guidance of a specific type is regarded as an important element in the attempt to reduce certain intra-familial be-haviours, which have a deleterious influence on the schizophrenic patient.

Little attention has been paid to this issue of specificity and yet clinical experience would suggest its relevance. Similarly, the question of how to impart information or advice has barely been tackled. One exception is the work of Flowers (1979), who compared the effects of different forms of advice on sex offenders. Guidance proved advantageous overall but offering alternatives or detailed instructions were more beneficial than direct advice.

We alluded to the preparation of patients for group therapy earlier. More strictly, a condition for change, pre-therapy preparation is somewhat akin to guidance in that the patient is provided with the requisite information which will enhance the quality of his group experience, and (this is an assumption only) pave the way for benefits to accrue. An impressive body of work has been done in this area, and the reader is referred to Bloch and Crouch (1985, pp. 177–83) for an account of it.

Universality, altruism, vicarious learning and instillation of hope
These four factors have been relatively neglected by the researcher and hence the brevity of the ensuing discussion. The self-help group has brought *universality*, the realization of not being unique with one's problems, and *altruism*, the benefit derived from the sense of helping one's fellow group members, into greater prominence. A few illuminating theoretical contri-butions have been the result, among which those by Robinson (1980) on universality, and by Killilea (1976) on altruism stand out. The empirical testing of ideas proposed by these authors remains to be done.

Vicarious learning – the learning stemming from a patient's identification with a fellow member's therapeutic experience or the imitation of desirable qualities in other group members including the therapist – is an inevitable feature of the group process but, surprisingly, it has attracted only minimal interest from theorists or investigators. The study by Falloon *et al.* (1977) is a notable exception. Modelling by co-therapists of desirable social interaction coupled with actual training of patients experiencing interpersonal prob-lems, proved more effective than a guided discussion group. The experi-mental condition also enhanced interpersonal aspects of the group process, such as members' attraction to the group, and this facilitated further the modelling procedure. The conclusion that vicarious learning of this type is 'undoubtedly helpful' is well founded, but probably more relevant to the form of group therapy used in the experiment, that is short-term, structured and highly focused on a specific target area (see Emmelkamp, 1986, p. 410). By contrast, implicit therapist modelling is more appropriate with long-term psychodynamic group psychotherapy in which didactic methods are eschewed.

Finally, we comment on *instillation of hope*, the patient feeling optimistic about his actual or anticipated progress as a result of his group experience. While the role of hope in psychotherapy generally has gained substantial attention (Frank, 1968), its more specific place in the group process remains open for investigation. Obviously, a patient's fellow members have the potential to show him that the group can be helpful and provide a forum to work constructively towards personal goals. The effects on process and outcome of mobilizing hope and how this could best be promoted are unanswered as yet, and warrant careful investigation.

The comparative evaluation of therapeutic factors

The 1970s and 1980s have witnessed a growing body of research on how the above therapeutic factors are evaluated by the members of different sorts of therapy groups. The underlying assumption is this: patients are as valid a source of information about the group experience as the therapist or an independent observer. Therefore, it is profitable to seek their views on what helps and hinders them in pursuing their goals. Two main methodological procedures have been deployed: a questionnaire on therapeutic factors which require the respondent to rank the items in order of their perceived helpfulness (Yalom, 1985); and the more indirect 'most important event' questionnaire, whereby the patient identifies that aspect of his group experience regarded as most important or most helpful for him personally, this account then being assigned to one of a number of categories constituting a basic classification of therapeutic factors (Bloch *et al.*, 1979). Apart from the choice of questionnaire, it is likely that the timing and frequency of its administration, the availability of several classifications, and the many differing samples studied have all contributed to the mixed findings. The results can, however, be unravelled to some extent, with the emergence of certain trends. What follows is a brief summary of what we have learned thus far (for a fuller account, see Bloch and Crouch, 1985, Ch. 9).

If we apply a temporal perspective, we may note that in relatively *short-term* groups (groups mainly composed of more severely ill patients), universality, acceptance, and to a lesser extent altruism and self-disclosure, are viewed as most helpful, whereas guidance and vicarious learning are regarded as least helpful. In relatively *long-term* group therapy (with the less psychiatrically ill), insight, learning from interpersonal action and self-disclosure emerge as the most valued factors; again guidance and vicarious learning are rated as least helpful, together with universality. In terms of the group's setting, we can see the following pattern: altruism, and to a lesser degree acceptance and insight, are rated highly by members of *in-patient* groups and insight, learning from interpersonal action and self-disclosure are especially valued by members of out-patient groups, In both settings, guidance and vicarious learning are, as usual, bottom.

Of course, patients' perceptions are one thing, the factors *actually* related to outcome are another, and we have seen above that the data are disappointingly scanty in this regard. But the 'consumer' should be heard because he offers (at the least) (1) clues as to how models of therapy may be conceptualized for various clinical groups, and (2) information from which specific hypotheses may be derived for experimental testing. The work of Maxmen (1973, 1978) provides an excellent illustration of how this type of approach can be effectively applied.

OTHER ASPECTS OF GROUP PROCESS RESEARCH

Limitations of space preclude any discussion of research on other aspects of group process. What follows are some guidelines to reading on certain key topics.

Leadership is obviously a central feature of the group process. Issues that have attracted the researcher's attention include: the leader as model, the optimal degree of self-disclosure he should permit, styles of leadership and their effects, and co-therapy. Dies (1983) has done a splendid job of reviewing these and other topics, and of drawing out clinical implications. Although limited to short-term group treatment, much of the material can be readily extrapolated to other forms of group therapy.

Group development – the identifiable stages through which a group passes from inception to termination – is closely bound up with other aspects of group process. Theories have been advanced which attempt to explain the nature of these stages, and some empirical work has been done in order to examine the subject systemically (see Bednar and Kaul, 1978, pp. 793–801 for a useful account of the latter, and also Ch. 4 by MacKenzie and Livesley in Dies and MacKenzie, 1983, and Smith, 1980).

There are a variety of other aspects of group process which are difficult to categorize readily because of their overlap with one another, e.g. inter-actional group patterns, group norms, group climate or atmosphere, and group composition. Several chapters (see especially Chs. 5–8) in Dies and MacKenzie (1983) are a handy means of becoming acquainted with the relevant literature (see also Fuhriman *et al.*, 1984; Burlingame *et al.*, 1984; and Melnick and Woods, 1976).

Much of the research on the above topics utilize *instruments* devised to measure specific variables. Fuhriman and Packard (1986) have contributed a useful survey in which more than two dozen procedures are dealt with. Their chief focus is on the measurement of interactional patterns between group members or between members and the group leader; examples of relevant instruments are the Hill Interaction Matrix, the Group Interaction Profile and Interaction Process Analysis.

In the review article by Dies (1983) on leadership, some of these instruments (plus others – a total of 42) are also discussed, and usefully tabulated with reference to researchers who have deployed them in their studies. A study of the articles by Fuhriman and Packard (1986) and Dies (1983) will enable the interested reader to gain a good impression of the wide scope of research on group process.

IS GROUP THERAPY EFFECTIVE?

I pose the question in this way only to re-emphasize its ill-conceived basis. In the light of our early discussion concerning the uniformity myth (Kiesler, 1966), we must accept that there is no such thing as 'group therapy' *per se*, and it follows axiomatically that the question of its efficacy is a non-question.

This point can readily be demonstrated by conducting the following exercise: comparing two studies of outcome which show contradictory results, and noting in the process the ill-conception of the whole enterprise. In one comprehensive review of outcome studies (Bednar and Kaul, 1978), 14 reports were identified which satisfied specified research design criteria – a control group, random assignment of patients to treatment and control conditions, and a statistically acceptable outcome measurement. Only two of these 14 studies involved psychiatric patients (volunteers, college students and delinquents were among the other samples treated). Let us now compare these two investigations.

Haven and Wood (1970) worked with a highly specific population of hospitalized military veterans with a median age of 42 who participated in a median number of 16 group sessions, held twice weekly. The therapists adopted a directive role with the chief goal of promoting reality testing. The rate of readmission during the 12 months following discharge was used as a measure of outcome. The main finding was clear: the experimental and control patients did not differ at follow-up. Presumably we are led to conclude that in-patient group therapy had no additional effect over and above the rest of the treatment programme.

The second study involving psychiatric patients differed in virtually every respect (Vernallis *et al.*, 1970). Although only men were involved as well, they were younger, with an average age of 31, and were living in the community. The form of group treatment they received differed radically to that used with the in-patients. First, it consisted of 15 hours of treatment each week for 16 consecutive weekends, a total of about 200 hours (recall the median of 16 hours in the Haven and Wood study). Secondly, the theoretical orientation was 'psychodynamic–eclectic', and the associated goals were self-understanding and behavioural change. Assessment also differed – a depression scale and ratings of social adjustment were used. Perhaps not surprisingly, given this 'saturation group therapy', Vernallis and his colleagues found that patients in this group treatment programme showed greater improvement than their control counterparts.

What shall we conclude from this comparison – that group therapy works or does not work? Clearly the question is not worth asking in this form. Other questions are more likely to yield relevant answers. These include: does group therapy work only with certain types of patients (e.g. younger and not hospitalized); or work only under certain conditions (e.g. necessary duration and amount); or work only if its theoretical foundation is psychodynamic; or work only if the therapist adopts a particular leadership style, and so forth?

These more specific questions take us closer to the heart of the matter, but when posed separately from one another, are again ill-conceived. For instance, it does not aid our enquiry concerning the effectiveness of group therapy to examine the issue of leadership style independently of other variables. A directive and active stance may be wholly suitable with a certain type of group membership, say the chronically disabled who require supportive therapy over an extended period (Bloch, 1986a). That same style would intrude considerably in an out-patient group composed of motivated and psychologically sophisticated members who are being encouraged to achieve greater self-awareness as a result of the dynamic interaction between them (Bloch, 1986b).

In teasing out these questions we realize how complex is the task of evaluating the group therapies (to revert to the more useful terminology we adopted at the outset). Indeed, a range of methodological desiderata have to be satisfied, but the obstacles en route are many and troublesome. Let us briefly consider a few. A host of factors are entailed in the functioning of a therapy group, many if not most operating concurrently. Elsewhere I have illustrated this point by discussing the close, often interwoven relationship between the therapeutic factors of catharsis and self-disclosure (Bloch, 1986c). A patient reveals something highly personal, perhaps for the first time, and this is coupled with the release of intense feeling which brings relief. Teasing out the effects of these two factors is demanding in itself. The disentanglement becomes more complex in the light of the several other variables that are pertinent, e.g. the type of patient involved, the reaction of his co-members, the role the therapist plays, the theory he applies, the norms set for the group, etc.

Furthermore, there are substantial methodological difficulties in the specification of these variables. Little headway can be made in outcome research until such variables as the patient's level of psychological-mindedness, the nature of the composition of the group, and the therapist's leadership style can be properly identified and reliably measured. The criteria of improvement are equally problematic (Fielding, 1974). In our comparison exercise we noted the radically different measures used: hospital readmission rate *vs.* ratings of depression and social adjustment. While the former may be relatively objective, all three parameters of outcome, typical of the nomothetic approach, suffer from the limitation of not doing justice to the specific changes that a particular patient may need to accomplish. A use of standard measures of outcome at the expense of this latter ideographic approach may be too insensitive to tap the specific areas of change relevant to specific group members (Bloch *et al.*, 1977).

One final matter relates to the need for controlled conditions whereby the effects of group therapy can be compared with those of being placed on a waiting list or of receiving minimal intervention. Because many group therapies are of lengthy duration – 1, 2 or more years – the clinical and ethical hurdles to a fully-fledged control condition are virtually insurmountable.

This brief digression into the immense difficulties facing the investigator of the effectiveness of the group therapies will help to explain two prominent features of the work done hitherto: the relatively small quantity of it and the methodological compromises that typify virtually all the studies. In terms of the volume of work, the picture has hardly altered since Sethna and Harrington (1971) commented nearly two decades ago: 'The paucity of studies dealing with evaluation of group therapy is startling when compared with the vast amount published on every other aspect of group psychotherapy' (p. 641).

Parloff and Dies (1977) in their review of outcome research covering the decade 1966–75 found a similar dearth of studies, particularly with regard to neurotic and personality-disordered patients. They observe rather pointedly: 'While it is generally assumed, and probably correctly, that by far the greatest effort of group psychotherapy practitioners is directed toward the treatment of neuroses and personality disorders, remarkably little research has been reported with these patient categories' (p. 311).

As mentioned earlier, Bednar and Kaul (1978) found only 14 studies in their major literature review which satisfied their reasonable criteria of experimental design, and then only two involving conventional psychiatric samples. Given their requirement of a controlled condition it is only to be expected that whereas student volunteers presenting with test anxiety for instance can be allocated on ethical grounds to a no-treatment control group, patients attending a psychiatric clinic and in need of long-term group treatment cannot be so assigned.

Thus, methodological compromises abound, and investigators regard it as still worth the effort to examine the outcome of patients who have undergone a programme of group therapy, without comparing them to control patients. They have also tackled the question in other ways – especially by comparing the effects of group therapy with other forms of treatment, usually individual therapy, and by noting which members of a group benefit and which do not.

Bearing these points in mind, what can we learn from the reviews of outcome research that have been carried out in recent years? Unfortunately, most reviewers have confined themselves to the relatively unilluminating question of whether 'group therapy' works or not. Thus, Bednar and Kaul (1978) conclude that the 14 studies under their scrutiny provide 'further justification of group treatment and a stimulus to further research' (p. 780); also, 'evidence for the legitimacy of selected group treatment forms' (p. 773). In fact, in most of these controlled trials, the group treatment led to greater rates of change than non-treatment (and, in some cases, to another mode of treatment) on one or more measures of outcome. Mindful of their broad-brush strategy, Bednar and Kaul qualify their conclusion in pointing out that the data on which it was based had been gleaned under various conditions, from a broad range of individuals, and in many different ways.

Parloff and Dies (1977), in their review, took the additional step of examining the effectiveness of group therapy for particular clinical populations: neurotics, delinquents, addicts and schizophrenics. On the other hand, they relaxed the criteria for the inclusion of studies by not insisting on a control condition. None the less, of the more than 100 studies screened, only 38 were deemed adequate for review, and of these only 6 dealt with the treatment of neurosis. From these studies on neurotic patients, the reviewers concluded that: 'The limited sample of studies provides little basis for drawing any inferences and offers few clues for extrapolating any particular merits of group therapy over other forms of psychosocial interventions tested' (p. 311).

Parloff and Dies were hamstrung by aspects of the research reports, about which I have already commented, particularly the lack of specification. The poor definition of group therapy, and therefore the probable variation in theoretical approach and leadership style, makes it exceedingly difficult to ascertain what the treatments were like. Not surprisingly, they end with the argument that I used to introduce the section: raising the question of whether group therapy works is unhelpful, and it requires replacement by a series of more specific questions concerned with well-defined aspects of treatment.

What do we find upon focusing on these more specific questions? Space does not permit more than a few illustrative examples. Because group therapy is applied frequently in two clinical arenas – in the out-patient clinic, where it is usually long-term and geared towards the acquisition of insight and some personality change, and the in-patient ward, where it is of necessity short-term and more limited in its objectives – let me use these modes of treatment as my examples. (We should note, however, that there are specialist in-patient centres such as the Henderson Hospital in Sutton, England, where long-term intensive group therapy is an important component of the therapeutic programme.) Even when differentiating between group therapy in these two clinical settings, there is a further need for specificity in terms of the particular form of treatment applied, and the specific clinical population comprising the group.

Prominent among the outcome studies of long-term, out-patient group therapy is that by Malan and his colleagues (1976). They examined the effectiveness of a psychoanalytic model which had evolved over a period of years in the Tavistock Clinic. The model is spelled out in considerable detail in their report, leaving fellow researchers and the general reader in no doubt as to its theoretical underpinnings and the role of the therapist. In brief, the group is regarded as more central than the individual and the chief therapeutic strategy is interpretation about transference patterns, especially transferences of the group to the leader. In practice, the leader identifies unconscious feelings experienced by the group as a whole, and through interpretation makes these obvious to the patient. It is also clear from the report, particularly through the several case examples, what sort of patients were selected for this form of group therapy. Mainly young adults with all manner of neurotic disturbance, assessed as able to communicate with one another in terms of intelligence and educational attainment constituted the groups' membership. Exclusion criteria are similarly well laid out.

Thus, we know both the specific form of group therapy applied and the specific clinical population catered for. Did this treatment work? In the absence of a control group (too difficult to incorporate in a treatment exceeding 2 years), a prospective study was simulated by using a customary tactic: patients who had less than 6 months of treatment were assumed to have been inadequately treated and were designated as controls (for some critics this would be too large an assumption); they were compared to those who stayed a longer period (the original intention was to restrict this latter group to those who had spent at least 2 years in their group but the common compromise ensued in order to increase the sample size). Patients were assessed 2–14 years after termination of their group therapy, indeed an impressive follow-up period.

Evidence for some therapeutic effect was found, but as Malan *et al.*, (1976) put it: 'The results have not been impressive' (p. 1314), and '. . . we can only conclude that so far we have obtained no evidence for the effectiveness of this form of group treatment whatsoever' (p. 1308). This also applied when the short-stay patients were compared with those whose duration of treatment extended beyond 2 years. Moreover, most patients expressed their dissatisfaction with the experience, specifically pointing to the vagueness of the model and their associated ignorance about what was intended, and to their therapists' lack of support and warmth.

The patients' poor outcome and their sense of resentment combined to suggest that the Tavistock model was either inappropriate to meet their clinical needs or was applied ineptly. The latter is unlikely: although the degree of training and experience varied, all therapists were psychother-apeutically sophisticated and they included consultants who were qualified psychoanalysts. The more likely explanation lies in the nature of the conceptual model. When group processes are deemed more central than the patients who comprise the group, and their individualized clinical objectives are not a primary consideration in the group's work, it would seem to militate against those objectives being adequately dealt with. Malan and his colleagues perhaps are more blunt in their summing up when they comment that:

> . . . therapists ought to feel less constrained by what they have learned in their classical psychoanalytic training, and should feel free to offer greater warmth and encouragement, greater participation in the group interactions, and individual sessions when the need arises, without the fear that such interventions will result in disruption of the group or interference with the group transference relationship (p. 1315).

Should this lead us to assume that the psychoanalytically oriented model of group therapy is inapplicable for our patient groups? Theoretically, arguments could be offered on either side, but because we are here concerned with empirical issues of effectiveness, it is to other outcome studies that we must turn. The snag is that there is precious little to turn to.

Another study conducted at the Tavistock Clinic, of patients who participated in group therapy for 2 or more years, showed that a little over half of them were substantially improved (Phillipson, 1958). But it should be noted that the assessment of outcome was carried out while the patients were still in treatment, rather than at its termination or after a follow-up period. Sethna and Harrington's (1971) outcome study, while not directly comparable because patients were in- or day-patients (with various diag-noses, but chiefly neuroses or personality disorders), found that for those who had completed a 7-month programme and attended an average on 114 'analytic' group sessions (and who had received no physical treatment), about half showed moderate to considerable improvement, as rated by their therapists. These results must be viewed with the following in mind: the groups were led by trainee psychiatrists, assessment of outcome was carried out at the time of discharge, and by therapists rather than by independent judges, and 37 patients who dropped out during the course of treatment were *not* included in the study. The researchers were aware of these issues and this no doubt influenced their conclusion that group therapy achieved results which were 'modest but worthwhile' (p. 655).

A Canadian study is worthy of our attention in that it concerned long-term group therapy and was controlled, but the latter feature also limited the study's scope because assessments were made after a mere 3 months of therapy, that is the period of being placed on a waiting list (Piper *et al.*, 1977). The 48 patients involved in the trial were diagnosed as neurotic or personality disordered, they were in their 20s and 30s, and most were working or studying (reflecting the usual composition of the long-term out-patient group).

They were matched in terms of sex and ratings on certain selection criteria including verbal skill, psychological mindedness and motivation. When eight pairs were formed, patients were randomly assigned to group therapy or to a delayed treatment control condition. Five measures of outcome were then administered, and repeated after 3 months of treatment or of waiting for treatment. This procedure was carried out on three other pairs of matched groups. A comparison of all treated patients and control patients showed a greater degree of improvement in the former, but the only statistically significant difference was on one of the measures of interpersonal functioning. Moreover, control patients also showed improvement over their 3 months of waiting, suggesting the probable influence of the assessment itself, and/or of environmental factors.

Despite the industriousness of the researchers, the data obtained reveal only limited information about the effectiveness of long-term group therapy, but the choice of 3 months for the delayed treatment condition was obviously necessary from an ethical point of view. The pity, however, was that patients were not followed up through the course of their group treatment and beyond so that their outcome could be assessed at points more relevant to the study of the effectiveness of long-term treatment.

If the picture concerning the effectiveness of relatively long-term out-patient group therapy is blurred through a sparseness of data coupled with a set of contradictory findings, the corresponding picture of short-term, in-patient group therapy is barely visible! In his useful survey of the subject, Erickson (1982) was only able to find a mere handful of outcome studies covering more than 25 years of research. The review by Marcowitz and Smith (1986) excludes any mention of the question of effectiveness.

Again, as was the case with the long-term out-patient group, the application of psychoanalytic concepts in the in-patient setting have proved to be inappropriate. For instance, Pattison *et al.* (1967) studied patients (mostly chronic personality disorders or chronic schizophrenics, admitted for an average of 3 months), half of whom were assigned to group therapy (the frequency and average number of sessions attended were not cited). But, importantly, both experimental and control patients participated in a comprehensive psychotherapeutic programme including various group activities. Perhaps, not unexpectedly therefore, both groups showed equal rates of improvement. If anything there was an apparent trend for group therapy to exert a negative effect. Considering the type of patient treated, the short duration of admission, and the limited goals set by the ward team, a more structured, supportive approach would probably have better served this population than the psychoanalytic one.

Similar considerations pertain to the clinical sample studied by Kanas and his colleagues (1980). Their patients, acutely ill schizophrenics or with personality disorders, were randomly assigned either to a 3-hour per week group therapy programme based on a dynamic-interactional model (Yalom, 1985), or to an activity-oriented task group, or to a control condition. Assessments were made at the time of admission and 20 days later. No differences were found between these three conditions on a variety of measures – not a particularly illuminating finding considering the relative brevity of the treatment period. More interesting was the deterioration rate among the acutely psychotic patients attending the therapy group compared to patients in the task or control groups. The authors conclude, quite correctly, that insight-oriented therapy is a hazardous procedure for patients who are psychologically vulnerable because of their fragile hold on reality. Thus, what appears to be a well-intentioned initiative – to provide in-patients with something more substantial than merely the 2 M's (medication and milieu therapy) – is in fact potentially harmful for certain categories of patient.

Fortunately, pragmatic clinicians have recognized this, as well as the marked constraints that typify the short-term in-patient unit. Maxmen (1978) is one notable clinician who has devised an approach which, at least theoretically, seems more suited to this clinical context. His 'educative' model aims to enhance the patient's ability to think clinically and to respond effectively to the consequences of his illness. In this pursuit, the group's purpose and methods make sense to its members, the group complements coherently other modes of treatment on the ward, the goals are set realistically so that even the severely disturbed patient can attempt to achieve them, and therapeutic factors which appear helpful to the group are highlighted (Maxmen, 1984).

Similarly, Yalom (1983) has offered models of group therapy for in-patients which take into account their special needs. Moreover, he has differentiated between two main clinical groups in terms of group therapy provision – a relatively high functioning one capable of self-exploration, and a more disabled one in need of a structured and task-oriented group experience (akin to the activity-oriented task group in the Kanas *et al.* study). See also Marcowitz and Smith (1986) for a useful account of recent conceptualizations of in-patient group psychotherapy.

The value of these new models for in-patients in terms of outcome has yet to be examined systematically but at least we have moved beyond the application of theoretical frameworks that fail to take cognisance of the particular features of group treatments in the hospital setting.

Although this discussion began with the effectiveness of long-term out-patient groups, no mention was made of the equally important question of *cost-effectiveness*. Is the idea necessarily valid that the patient – who seeks to achieve insight and some possible personality change – needs to remain a group member for a couple of years or more? Recently, we have been presented with a theoretically attractive proposal which could potentially shorten the duration of therapy without any diminution of therapeutic effect. Budman and his colleagues (1980) have emphasized the central importance of promoting cohesiveness rapidly in this approach. This is most suitably achieved by forming homogeneous groups in respect of the stage of the life-cycle of the members. Thus, groups are composed for the young adult, or for the person in mid-life, or for the person in post-mid-life. Presenting problems may vary in each stage but certain developmental themes are shared and help bind the group. For example, the mid-life group members have in common the task of reappraising their careers and social life, whereas those in post-mid-life are faced with the task of mourning over past losses and disappointments.

Commendably, Budman (Budman *et al.*, 1984) has lost no time in subjecting his model to empirical enquiry. In a well-executed controlled study involving 36 patients, mostly diagnosed as neurotic and many also with associated personality disorders, the group therapy programme was limited to 15 weeks. Because the two treatment groups involved were restricted to young adults (with an average age of 30), the main focus was on relationship issues, especially intimacy. The therapists ensured through their active, directive stance that the main source of learning was inter-member; group transferences to the leaders were correspondingly down-played. Assessment at termination and at a 6-month follow-up revealed significantly greater improvement in treated patients compared to controls.

In noting these results, the group therapist may enthusiastically be swayed into setting time limits for all his groups. He would be advised, however, to address himself to the following caveat. Budman and his colleagues are careful to point out the nature of the clinical sample under their care: although many presented with low self-esteem and difficulties in relationships, the patients were highly motivated and only a few were in acute crisis at the time of referral. This is not to diminish the importance of the Budman initiative. On the contrary, it is argued, as I have done repeatedly throughout the chapter, that there should be a close match between the patient and the form of group therapy. Budman and his colleagues have steered us in the right direction: a cost-effective treatment devised in such a way as to 'provide patients [of a certain kind] with the opportunity to begin to change aspects of their lives about which they feel dissatisfaction or demoralisation' (p. 601). A modest, albeit realistic goal for both patient and therapist. Replication of their work by other investigators would be an important contribution to this exciting new field.

DETERIORATION EFFECTS IN GROUP PSYCHOTHERAPY

In the previous section we alluded to the potential for patients in groups to be harmed by their experience. This 'deterioration' or 'negative' effect in psychotherapy was first raised as part of the controversy about effectiveness (Strupp *et al.*, 1977). The assumption was made that psychotherapy was for better or for worse: if it has potential for producing improvement, it should also have the potential for causing harm.

The definition of the deterioration effect is not as straightforward as one would expect in that at least two aspects must be obvious: the patient's condition is definitely worse after treatment compared to pre-therapy, and this change is *directly* attributable to the treatment (Hadley and Strupp, 1976; Crown, 1983). A causal association is inherently resistant to proof but a consensus has evolved over the past two decades pointing to genuine deterioration effects as a result of treatment effects, which may take various forms. In the context of group therapy a concern about deterioration first revolved around the potency of encounter groups in the 1960s. Impressionistic accounts soon suggested that a proportion of participants might be damaged by the experience. Several investigators thereupon examined the question in relation to encounter and sensitivity-training groups and indeed confirmed the impressions (see Bednar and Kaul, 1978, for a review of these studies). Most found a low rate of between 1 and 2% though the conceptualization of deterioration varied and included self-report, rate of medical consultation, group leader's assessment, and an evaluation done by independent judges.

In the most scientifically rigorous research of 17 encounter groups, a relatively higher casualty rate of 9% was found, suggesting that either the independent assessors involved were better equipped to identify deterioration or certain factors in the Stanford encounter groups were distinctive and responsible (Lieberman *et al.*, 1973). In fact, Lieberman *et al.* (1973) located such factors, mainly aspects of leadership. Casualty status was defined as an enduring and marked negative outcome which was directly attributable to the experience in the group. Assessment, including a follow-up 8 months after the group, was conducted via several sources including self-report, ratings by peers, and evaluations by the group leaders and independent judges. Seven of the 16 casualties were associated with four group leaders. These leaders all shared certain characteristics which were markedly manifest throughout the 30 hours their groups met. They were confronting, aggressive, authoritarian and intrusive. They typically pushed their group members into immediate self-disclosure and emotional catharsis. At the same time, the leaders displayed a charisma and a caring attitude, and they also revealed much personal information about themselves. They seemed oblivious of their power to promote negative effects and were apt to label hesitant participants as stubborn and resistant.

Another group leader who customarily assumed a confrontative role produced no casualties in his group. Interestingly, he differed from the quartet of like-minded colleagues by refraining from his usual stance upon the realization that his group contained several apparently vulnerable members.

Unrelated to these leadership qualities were two other identifiable factors: first, profound disappointment in casualties in not achieving goals which they had (unrealistically) set for themselves and, secondly, an inability to cope with the sheer 'overload' of intense stimulation (three of the five casualties in this category actually decompensated into transient psychosis). An additional finding of relevance was the significantly lower level of self-esteem, measured before the group experience, among the casualties compared with those who did not deteriorate.

The implications of this work, which can be reasonably extrapolated to forms of group therapy with 'real' patients, are obvious. Care must be taken at the point of selection with prospective patients who may be especially vulnerable (admittedly a loose term but a condition identified through astute clinical judgement) to that form of group therapy involving self-disclosure, intense emotional involvement and self-exploration; and certain forms of group leadership, specifically 'aggressive stimulation', are hazardous to mental health! The latter caution is not to negate the cogency of challenge in insight-oriented group therapy, but to emphasize the sensitivity required in submitting patients to it. Ultimately, it is the therapist who bears responsibility for the patients in his group, and he is best placed to prevent their coming to harm (Grunebaum, 1975).

CONCLUSION

This chapter is perched somewhat uncomfortably at the end of a book whose chief thrust is the clinical practice of various forms of group therapy, and it would be unfortunate if it were regarded as a mere tag. If tag it must be, in as much as it is attached to the 'main piece', I would hope for an alternative understanding of the term, namely tag as 'instructive ending for a story'. Research indeed has the potential to contribute significantly to the 'story' of group therapy practice but a *sine qua non* for such a development is the erection of a sturdy bridge between them; moreover, a bridge upon which the traffic passes in both directions.

Traffic from the practice side ideally consists of clinical observations, intuitive hunches and theoretical conceptualizations which inform the researcher about what is relevant for empirical study. The greater the relevance of the investigations, the more likely is the free flow of traffic from the research to the practice side. By contrast, inconsequential research fuels the therapist's (perhaps) traditional resistance to the scientific dimension, which in turn cannot be particularly reinforcing to the investigator. There is understandable anxiety about long-cherished modes of practice being jeopardized in the wake of definitive research findings. Ideal is the embodiment of both pursuits in the same person or, at second best, the closest of collaboration between researcher and clinician in the actual identification of the topics for study, and in the selection of experimental designs and procedures which parallel the clinical experience.

In this chapter theory has had to give way to empiricism because of my remit; but it would have become obvious that without theoretical advance, empirical research is apt to be uninformed and haphazard. Theory is especially advantageous if testable hypotheses can be derived from it since this allows facets thereof to be examined systematically with the results serving as a potential source for further conceptual refinement. Coche and Dies (1981), in their useful paper on the integration of research into practice, put it this way:

> The role of theory . . . is paramount: solid theorising, marked by conceptual clarity, can make sense out of the – seemingly or truly – contradictory findings and provide guidance in attempts to apply empirical results to practical work. It also gives direction and consistency in future research and treatment. But in order to be useful, a theory has to be continually validated, modified, and refined through empirical investigation (p. 415).

Solid theory and conceptual clarity are key points if the theoretical contribution is to lead to advances in the field. An esoteric theory or one remote from clinical experience are usually as tantalizing as they are unhelpful to the investigator. Bednar and Kaul (1978) have bemoaned the primitive state of theoretical development and referred to 'a conceptual malaise regarding the primary, unique and defining characteristics of group treatments' (p. 673). They are perhaps overly pessimistic but still prod us into the uncomfortable notion that the researcher is not being sufficiently guided by the theorist. (For a sobering account of the conceptual issues, see Kaul and Bednar, 1986).

Another form of traffic could be traversing the research/practice bridge more commonly than hitherto. I refer to the clinical implications to be drawn from the findings of empirical work. Obviously, a caveat interposes itself for the therapist: he is obliged to act cautiously in the absence of consistent and replicated results. On the other hand, he can confidently incorporate into his work a wide range of well-established findings.

Consider two illustrations, both mentioned earlier in the chapter. First, preparation of the patient for group therapy has been demonstrated repeatedly to confer beneficial effects on the group process; the evidence is more than adequate to conclude that '. . . a form of orientation which enables the patient to obtain an idea of what therapy is about and what his role and that of the therapist will be in the process warrants a routine place in clinical practice' (Bloch and Crouch, 1985, p. 183). Secondly, some patients may be ill-served by group therapy and emerge scathed from the experience. This finding in itself is of sufficient import to inject a sense of caution in the therapist about the potential power embedded in his treatment but additional findings inform him that among the forces responsible is the style of leadership (see p. 309).

If the therapist were to wait for *irrefutable* evidence before he modified his practice, his wait would be unendurably long. 'Clinical implications' is a commonly used phrase for good reason: research generates guidelines at best, and more usually offers a pattern of findings which enables the therapist to reappraise some aspect of his work. It is this 'critical eye' that the responsible practitioner keeps wide open, thus permitting the product of research to impinge (Bloch, 1982, pp. 166–9).

This critical eye should indubitably focus on the two research areas which constitute the main part of this chapter – outcome and process. In my view, the group therapist has an obligation to ensure that his treatment is as effective, cost-effective and safe as it possibly can be. Thus, if one form of group treatment is shown to be more beneficial than another in a consistent fashion, then that form should be adopted as a matter of course. Moreover, if group therapy can be shortened at no cost to efficacy, and this can be buttressed by research evidence, then the more efficient option should be adopted. In the case of an approach that is demonstrably hazardous, and again the research evidence reinforces clinical impression, that approach should be avoided or modified.

All this may appear quite obvious but clinicians may lack the 'critical eye' or prefer to avert their gaze from research data which do not accord with their predilections. Consider these two examples. As we noted in the section on outcome research, the psychoanalytic model of group therapy for in-patients has been found in more than one study to yield minimal benefit.

Yet, to my knowledge the model is still widely applied. When *Encounter Groups – First Facts* (Lieberman *et al.*, 1973), a scientifically rigorous study, was published with the disturbing finding of a substantial casualty rate among those participating in encounter groups (discussed on pages 308–9), one of the leading Encounter leaders of the day (Schutz, 1977) dismissed the work with the derisory comment that: 'unfortunate is the seriously flawed yet widely publicized study . . . which under the guise of well-controlled research comes up with the outrageous findings about "casualties" of encounter groups, leaving the impression that joining a group is a quick channel to the mental hospital' (p. 42).

All this is not to insist on an empirical revolution whereby each and every research result leads unthinkingly to altered clinical practice. Group therapy would rapidly become a jerky, incoherent affair. What I have in mind is the therapist scrutinizing research reports published in reputable journals and having the critical wherewithal to discern those findings that warrant more assiduous attention and possible clinical integration.

Parloff (1967), always an astute commentator on research into psychotherapy, lamented the state of research in group therapy by concluding that the work he had reviewed was inadequate, non-cumulative, and not particularly useful to the clinician. The group therapist, he contended, had a basic responsibility to overcome his reluctance to specify his objectives in therapy, and he should therefore proceed further beyond an interest in group phenomena *per se* by trying to relate group process to specified goals.

Jerome Frank (1975), himself a pioneer investigator into group therapy, was more optimistic in the mid-1970s when commenting that, notwithstanding the then relative paucity of group therapy research, it still had the potential to contribute to clinical practice. Since that time, the situation has further improved and much has been accomplished both theoretically and empirically; the research product has grown correspondingly (Dies and MacKenzie, 1983).

In the hope that we will witness a continuation and reinforcement of this development, I can do no better than quote the concluding remarks of Hans Strupp (1968), a doyen of psychotherapy research, from his paper 'Psychotherapists and (or versus?) researchers':

> What sets psychotherapy apart from other forms of 'psychological healing' . . . is the planful and systematic application of psychological principles, concerning whose character and effects we are committed to become explicit. As psychotherapists and researchers, we want to learn more about what we are doing: we want to be able to do it better; we strive to be objective; and we are willing to work hard towards this end. To me, these are the beginnings of science, if not its essence (p. 32).

Group therapists must also necessarily act as 'scientists' (at the same time as pursuing the 'art' of group therapy) if they wish their patients to benefit optimally from their group experience.

REFERENCES

Allen, J. G. (1974). Implications of research in self-disclosure for group psychotherapy. *International Journal of Group Psychotherapy* **24**, 306–21.

Astrachan, B. (1970). Towards a social systems model of therapeutic groups. *Social Psychiatry* **5**, 110–19.

Barnes, G. G. (1985). Systems theory and family therapy. *In* M. Rutter and L. Hersov (eds), *Modern Child Psychiatry*, pp. 216–28. Oxford, Blackwell.

Bednar, R. L. and Kaul, T. J. (1978). Experiential group research: current perspectives. *In* S. L. Garfield and A. E. Bergin (eds), *Handbook of Psychotherapy and Behavior Change*, pp. 769–815, 2nd edition. New York, Wiley.

Bloch, S. (1982). *What is Psychotherapy?* Oxford, Oxford University Press.

Bloch, S. (1986a). Supportive psychotherapy. *In* S. Bloch (ed.) *An Introduction to the Psychotherapies*, pp. 252–77, 2nd edition. Oxford, Oxford University Press.

Bloch, S. (1986b). Group psychotherapy. *In* S. Bloch (ed.) *An Introduction to the Psychotherapies*, pp. 80–112, 2nd edition. Oxford, Oxford University Press.

Bloch, S. (1986c). Group psychotherapy. *In* P. Hill, R. Murray and A. Thorley (eds), *Essentials of Postgraduate Psychiatry*, pp.739–57, 2nd edition. London, Grune and Stratton.

Bloch, S. and Crouch, E. (1985). *Therapeutic Factors in Group Psychotherapy*. Oxford, Oxford University Press. (Paperback edition, 1987.)

Bloch, S., Bond, G., Qualls, B., Yalom, I. and Zimmerman, E. (1977). Outcome in psychotherapy evaluated by independent judges. *British Journal of Psychiatry* **131**, 410–14.

Bloch, S., Reibstein, J., Crouch, E., Holroyd, P. and Themen, J. (1979). A method for the study of therapeutic factors in group psychotherapy. *British Journal of Psychiatry* **134**, 257–63.

Budman, S. H., Bennett, M. J. and Wisneski, M. J. (1980). Short-term group psychotherapy: an adult developmental model. *International Journal of Group Psychotherapy* **30**, 63–76.

Budman, S. H., Demby, A., Feldstein, M. and Gold, M. (1984). The effects of time-limited group psychotherapy: a controlled study. *International Journal of Group Psychotherapy* **34**, 587–603.

Burlingame, G., Fuhriman, A. and Drescher, S. (1984). Scientific inquiry into small group process: a multidimensional approach. *Small Group Behavior* **15**, 441–70.

Coche, E. and Dies, R. R. (1981). Integrating research findings in the practice of group psychotherapy. *Psychotherapy: Theory, Research and Practice* **18**, 410–16.

Corsini, R. and Rosenberg, B. (1955). Mechanisms of group psychotherapy: processes and dynamics. *Journal of Abnormal and Social Psychology* **51**, 406–11.

Crown, S. (1983). Contraindications and dangers of psychotherapy. *British Journal of Psychiatry* **143**, 436–41.

Dies, R. R. (1977). Group therapist transparency: a critique of theory and research. *International Journal of Group Psychotherapy* **27**, 177–200.

Dies, R. R. (1979). Group psychotherapy: reflections on three decades of research. *Journal of Applied Behavioral Science* **15**, 361–73.

Dies, R. R. (1983). Clinical implications of research on leadership in short-term group psychotherapy. *In* R. R. Dies and K. R. MacKenzie (eds), *Advances in Group Psychotherapy: Integrating Research and Practice*, pp.27–78. New York, International Universities Press.

Dies, R. R. and MacKenzie, K. R. (eds) (1983). *Advances in Group Psychotherapy: Integrating Research and Practice*. New York, International Universities Press.

Durkin, H. (1981). *Living Groups: Group Psychotherapy and General Systems Theory*. New York, Brunner Mazel.

Emmelkamp, P. M. (1986). Behavior therapy with adults. *In* S. L. Garfield and A. E. Bergin (eds) *Handbook of Psychotherapy and Behavior Change*, pp. 385–442, 3rd edition. New York, Wiley.

Erickson, R. C. (1982). Inpatient small group psychotherapy: a survey. *Clinical Psychology Review* 2, 137–51.

Falloon, I., Lindley, P., McDonald, R. and Marks, I. M. (1977). Social skills training of out-patient groups: A controlled study of rehearsal and homework. *British Journal of Psychiatry* 131, 599–609.

Fielding, J. M. (1974). Problems of evaluative research into group psychotherapy outcome. *Australian and New Zealand Journal of Psychiatry* 8, 97–102.

Flowers, J. V. (1979). The differential outcome effects of simple advice, alternatives and instructions in group psychotherapy. *International Journal of Group Psychotherapy* 29, 305–16.

Frank, J. D. (1968). The role of hope in psychotherapy. *International Journal of Psychiatry* 5, 383–95.

Frank, J. D. (1971). Therapeutic factors in psychotherapy. *American Journal of Psychotherapy* 25, 350–61.

Frank, J. D. (1975). Group psychotherapy research 25 years later. *International Journal of Group Psychotherapy* 25, 159–62.

Fuhriman, A. and Packard, T. (1986). Group process instruments: therapeutic themes and issues. *International Journal of Group Psychotherapy* 36, 399–425.

Fuhriman, A., Drescher, S. and Burlingame, G. (1984). Conceptualizing small group process. *Small Group Behaviour* 15, 427–40.

Glatzer, H. (1976). Presidential address: service to patients – the ultimate priority. *International Journal of Group Psychotherapy* 26, 267–80.

Grunebaum, H. (1975). A soft-hearted review of hard-nosed research on groups. *International Journal of Group Psychotherapy* 25, 185–97.

Hadley, S. W. and Strupp, H. H. (1976). Contemporary views of negative effects in psychotherapy. *Archives of General Psychiatry* 33, 1291–302.

Halleck, S. L. (1982). The search for competent eclecticism. *Contemporary Psychiatry* 1, 22–4.

Haven, G. A. and Wood, B. S. (1970). The effectiveness of eclectic group psychotherapy in reducing recidivism in hospitalized patients. *Psychotherapy: Theory, Research and Practice* 7, 153–4.

Heckel, R. V., Froelich, I. and Salzberg, H. C. (1962). Interaction and redirection in group therapy. *Psychological Reports* 10, 14.

Hill, D. (1982). In conversation with Sir Denis Hill: Part II. *Bulletin of the Royal College of Psychiatrists* 6, 94–7.

Hurst, A. G. (1978). Leadership style determinants of cohesiveness in adolescent groups. *International Journal of Group Psychotherapy* 28, 263–77.

Jacobs, A. (1974). The use of feedback in groups. *In* A. Jacobs and W. Spradlin (eds), *Group as an Agent for Change*. New York, Behavioral Publications.

Jourard, S. (1971). *The Transparent Self*. New York, Van Nostrand.

Kanas, N., Rogers, M., Kreth, E., Patterson, L. and Campbell, R. (1980). The effectiveness of group psychotherapy during the first three weeks of hospitalization. *Journal of Nervous and Mental Disease* **168**, 487–92.

Kapp, F. T., Gleser, G., Brissenden, A., Emerson, R., Winget, J. and Kashdan, B. (1964). Group participation and self-perceived personality change. *Journal of Nervous and Mental Disease* **139**. 255–65.

Kaul, T. J. and Bednar, R. L. (1986). Experiential group research: results, questions, and suggestions. *In* S. L. Garfield and A. E. Bergin (eds), *Handbook of Psychotherapy and Behavior Change*, pp. 671–714, 3rd edition. New York, Wiley.

Kiesler, D. J. (1966). Some myths of psychotherapy research and the search for a paradigm. *Psychological Bulletin* **65**, 110–36.

Killilea, M. (1976). Mutual help organizations: interpretations in the literature. *In* G. Caplan and M. Killilea (eds), *Support Systems and Mutual Help: Multidisciplinary Explorations*, pp. 37–93. New York, Grune and Stratton.

Leff, J., Kuipers, L., Berkowitz, R., Eberlein-Vries, R. and Sturgeon, D. (1982). A controlled trial of social intervention in the families of schizophrenic patients. *British Journal of Psychiatry* **141**, 121–34.

Liberman, R. (1970). A behavioral approach to group dynamics: I. Reinforcement and prompting of cohesiveness in group therapy. *Behavior Therapy* **1**, 141–75.

Lieberman, M. A., Yalom, I. D. and Miles, M. B. (1973). *Encounter Groups: First Facts*. New York, Basic Books.

Lorr, M. (1966). Dimensions of interaction in group psychotherapy. *Multivariate Behavioral Research* **1**, 67–73.

Malan, D. H., Balfour, F. H., Hood, V. G. and Shooter, A. M. (1976). Group psychotherapy. A long-term follow-up study. *Archives of General Psychiatry* **33**, 1303–1315.

Marcowitz, R. J. and Smith, J. E. (1986). Short-term group therapy: a review of the literature. *International Journal of Short-Term Psychotherapy* **1**, 49–57.

Maxmen, J. (1973). Group therapy as viewed by hospitalized patients. *Archives of General Psychiatry* **28**, 404–408.

Maxmen, J. (1978). An educative model for in-patient group therapy. *International Journal of Group Psychotherapy* **29**, 321–38.

Maxmen, J. S. (1984). Helping patients survive theories: the practice of an educative model. *International Journal of Group Psychotherapy* **34**, 355–68.

Meichenbaum, D. H., Gilmore, J. B. and Fedoravicius, A. L. (1971). Group insight versus group desensitization in treating speech anxiety. *Journal of Consulting and Clinical Psychology* **36**, 410–21.

Melnick, J. and Woods, M. (1976). Analysis of group composition research and theory for psychotherapeutic and growth-oriented groups. *Journal of Applied Behavioral Science* **12**, 493–522.

Parloff, M. B. (1967). A view from the incompleted bridge: group process and outcome. *International Journal of Group Psychotherapy* **17**, 236–42.

Parloff, M. B. and Dies, R. R. (1977). Group psychotherapy outcome research 1966–1975. *International Journal of Group Psychotherapy* **27**, 281–319.

Pattison, E. M., Brissenden, A. and Wohl, T. (1967). Assessing specific effects of inpatient group psychotherapy. *International Journal of Group Psychotherapy* **17**, 283–97.

Phillipson, H. (1958). The assessment of progress after at least two years of group psychotherapy. *British Journal of Medical Psychology* **32**, 210–21.

Piper, W. E., Debbane, E. G. and Garant, J. (1977). An outcome study of group therapy. *Archives of General Psychiatry* **34**, 1027–32.

Ribner, N. J. (1974). Effects of an explicit group contract on self-disclosure and group cohesiveness. *Journal of Counseling Psychology* **21**, 116–20.

Rich, A. L. (1968). An experimental study of the nature of communication to a deviate in high and low cohesive groups. *Dissertation Abstracts International* **29**, 1976–A.

Robinson, D. (1980). Self-help health groups. *In* P. B. Smith (ed.), *Small Groups and Personal Change*, pp. 176–193. London, Methuen.

Roether, H. A. and Peters, J. J. (1972). Cohesiveness and hostility in group psychotherapy. *American Journal of Psychiatry* **128**, 1084–87.

Schutz, W. (1966). *The Interpersonal Underworld*. Palo Alto Science and Behaviour Books.

Schutz, W. (1977). Encounter. *In* R. Corsini (ed.), *Current Psychotherapies*, pp. 401–43. Itasca, Ill, Peacock.

Sethna, E. R. and Harrington, J. A. (1971). Evaluation of group psychotherapy. *British Journal of Psychiatry* **118**, 641–58.

Shaw, M. (1976). *Group Dynamics: The Psychology of Small Group Behavior*. New York, McGraw-Hill.

Smith, P. B. (1980). *Group Process and Personal Change*. London, Harper and Row.

Stoller, F. H. (1969). Videotape feedback in a group setting. *Journal of Nervous and Mental Disease* **148**, 452–66.

Strassberg, D. S., Roback, H. B., Anchor, K. N. and Abramowitz, S. I. (1975). Self-disclosure in group therapy with schizophrenics. *Archives of General Psychiatry* **32**, 1259–61.

Strupp, H. H. (1968). Psychotherapists and (or versus?) researchers. *Voices* **4**, 28–32.

Strupp, H. H., Hadley, S. W. and Gomes-Schwartz, B. (1977). *Psychotherapy for Better or Worse*. New York, Jason Aronson.

Truax, C. and Carkhuff, R. (1965). Correlations between therapist and patient self-disclosure: a predictor of outcome. *Journal of Counseling Psychology* **12**, 3–9.

Vernallis, F. F., Shipper, J. C., Butler, D. C. and Tomlinson, T. M. (1970). Saturation group psychotherapy in a weekend clinic: an outcome study. *Psychotherapy: Research, Theory and Practice* **7**, 144–52.

Whitaker, D. S. and Lieberman, M. A. (1964). *Psychotherapy Through the Group Process*. London, Routledge and Kegan Paul.

Yalom, I. D. (1983). *In-patient Group Psychotherapy*. New York, Basic Books.

Yalom, I. D. (1985). *The Theory and Practice of Group Psychotherapy*. 3rd edition. New York, Basic Books.

Yalom, I. D. (1986). Interpersonal learning. *In* A. Frances and R. Hales (eds), *Psychiatry Update: Annual Review*, Vol. 5. Washington D.C., American Psychiatric Press.

Yalom, I. D., Houts, P. S., Zimerberg, S. M. and Rand, K. H. (1967). Prediction of improvement in group therapy. *Archives of General Psychiatry* **17**, 159–68.

Yalom, I. D., Bond, G., Bloch, S., Zimmerman, E. and Friedman, L. (1977). The impact of a weekend group experience on individual therapy. *Archives of General Psychiatry* **34**, 399–415.

CHAPTER 14

ISSUES IN THE TRAINING OF GROUP THERAPISTS

Mark Aveline

INTRODUCTION

This volume documents the considerable variation that exists between different modalities of group approach; some are more cognitive, some more behavioural, some stress intrapsychic processes and some emphasize interpersonal transactions and the search for meaning. In some, the prime role of the leader is that of analyst or interpreter of the social matrix, in others facilitator of interpersonal transactions, director or educator. Just as the emphasis will differentially appeal to members and will inform their choice of group should they be so fortunate as to have a variety to choose from, so will the different formats provide settings where the substantial variation between therapists can find fruitful expression. If the aim of therapy, as the author believes, is to assist with the process of individuation and the development of the capacity to love and to work, then the therapist needs to know himself and recognize in what direction his talents lie.

Training should help the therapist make explicit his model of help-giving, examine how it may be integrated with the group situation and identify natural preferences that may obstruct his therapeutic role (Lakin *et al.*, 1969).

At this point, I must declare my bias towards interpersonal and analytic small groups. These modalities provide a rich conceptual framework for understanding the interpersonal and group processes that are present in all groups and which may be harnessed in the therapeutic service of the group. I contend that whatever direction the natural talent of the trainee group therapist finally takes, his later performance will benefit from a close familiarity with these modalities early in training. They will provide a frame of reference against which special approaches may be deployed; the frame may or may not be explicitly referred to in practice but is there to be drawn on in case of need. It follows that a suitable foundation experience would be as leader of a closed small group meeting for 18 months; the same point is made by Yalom (1985). Moving from a specialized format to a general perspective is much more difficult once perceptual sets and practice habits have been established.

For the above reasons, the major focus of this chapter is on small group psychotherapy. Most of the points made come from that field whose training literature in contrast to others is conspicuously systematic in its coverage. While different approaches will need to teach the specifics of their way, the issues raised by the orthodox group therapy trainings have implications for the entire field.

This chapter, first, considers the qualities of the good leader which are to be looked for in the trainee and brought out by the training; these are on two planes, one in personal characteristics and the other in the ability to conceptualize on several levels. Secondly, the typical problems of inexperienced leaders are described, because this is the point from whence training begins. Thirdly, the elements that make up a balanced training are critically examined, together with some comments on the perspective of the leader. These sections are addressed to trainers as much as to trainees. They also serve as template against which a training may be chosen, the subject of the fourth section which also lists some of the opportunities in Britain.

THE GOOD LEADER

Personal characteristics

In general terms, the good leader will be characterized by an abiding interest in people, a fundamental conviction that people have it within them to change and to grow and, significantly, that group members can assist each other in this endeavour. In his interactions he should embody these attitudes; the good model he presents to the group is essential to the therapeutic process. He should enjoy being in the group, that is once the severe anxiety that afflicts all group leaders early in their career has abated. He must have a highly ethical attitude.

As Grotjahn (1983) says, the ideal therapist must be reliable as only then will he invite trust and confidence; he must trust and have confidence in himself and in others; he must be an expert in communication and a master of dynamic reasoning. In his interactions within the group, the leader needs to be spontaneous and responsive; being responsive also means being responsible. Though the leader will reflect upon the session afterwards, in the moment to moment exchange within the group he will need to respond honestly, openly and intuitively. Such spontaneity is bedded in trust and depends upon courage and the ability to withstand bad experiences without despair. A firm identity, the capacity to identify with others, the ability to laugh at oneself and acknowledge mistakes, and a willingness to be a bystander in the interactive focus completes this portrait. The picture is far distant from the harmful profile identified by Lieberman *et al.* (1973) in their meticulous study of psychological casualties among members of encounter groups led by experienced leaders. Leaders who were intrusive and aggressive and who demanded rapid self-disclosure, emotional expression, and attitude change when combined with members who were particularly vulnerable or who had unrealistic expectations accounted for all but one of the casualties who totalled 9% of the sample of 219 subjects. The leader who is aloof and distant also contributes to negative effects (Dies and Teleska, 1985).

The complexity of a therapy group far exceeds that of individual therapy. Whereas in the latter the therapist has to strive to comprehend the conscious and unconscious selves of one person, in the group the database is multiplied eight or more fold. Furthermore, the group as a whole has a reality whose form illuminates individual and shared personal difficulties and which, in most approaches, needs to be addressed if the full potential of the group for therapeutic change is to be realized. In contrast to individual therapy, the leader achieves the therapeutic effect in work with and through group members rather than directly out of the single relationship between the therapist and patient or help-seeker. For some, these elements constitute the attraction of group work; for others, the complexity and the seemingly inevitable chaos is aversive.

While training may improve the competence of the leader by increasing knowledge, inculcating skills and reducing defensive personal strategies which may inhibit the good development of the group, there is no evidence that training, itself, can remedy a basic lack of aptitude for group work. For those with aptitude, much hard work needs to be done before the craft of group leadership is learnt and the reward of fully using this powerful instrument for improving interpersonal relationships is gained.

An individual and a collective perspective

In judging whether or not and how to intervene, the leader of a small therapy group needs to examine what is happening in the group from several perspectives. The perspectives are assessed against the context of (1) the developmental stage and (2) the history of the group. Thus, the priorities of the leader will vary with the stage of the group; in the beginning, building a secure, cohesive base and establishing facilitative ground-rules will be the dominant task; later, once a working group is formed, fine tuning and a gentle insistence that termination issues be faced may be the chief activity. Similarly, the history and composition of the group will weight the leader's decisions – a group that scapegoats and punishes will require different corrective action from one that cannot tolerate sadness. Also, possible interventions are subject to two overriding principles: (1) what is the most emotionally charged issue, and (2) what intervention in the best judgement of the leader would be most likely to facilitate the fruitful development of the group? Generally, it may be said the good functioning of the group as a whole takes precedence over individual concerns.

To illustrate the complexity of the dual perspective ideally required of the leader, a schema of the decision-making process is presented.

- The leader takes an individual and a collective perspective.
- The leader attends to process as well as content
    in the individual,
    and in the group.
- *Content* delineates surface concerns which have a certain importance. They may contain the individual's and the group's understanding of what the difficulties are, what they signify and how they have come about.
- *Process* reveals the nature of the underlying fears that, unconsciously, moves the group as a whole, or mobilizes defensive strategies in the individual or prompts him or her to tell a story which indirectly conveys an experienced but unacceptable feeling.
- Thus, the leader needs to remember
    (a) the history of the group, its drama, personalities and stage;
    (b) the histories of the members, their particular sensitivities and concerns;
    (c) the sequence of interactions, feelings and focus
        within members,
        and within the group
            from one session to the next,
            and from moment to moment within the session.
- The leader attends to the content and the process of the session,
    facilitating its expression,
    its exploration,
    and looking for shared central themes.
- Furthermore, the leader derives an understanding of what are the important, perhaps unrecognized, issues in the group
    by being aware of his inner feelings,
    by recognizing the role-relationships that
        the group,

and members encourage him into,
and by noticing the emotionally charged issues that
the group,
and the individual avoids.

● The leader considers the relationship of the group as a social system to the larger social and institutional systems of which it is a part and between which there is a two-way exchange (Kernberg, 1975). The leader considers the group in its context.

● From the above the leader decides to intervene
individually,
or collectively
or to wait for the situation to clarify itself
or, frequently, to wait for the group to act,
bearing in mind the developmental
stage of the group, its strengths
and the personalities of its members.

It is recognized that this schema will be modified by the imperatives of different forms of group therapy.

INEXPERIENCED LEADERS AND THEIR PROBLEMS

The inexperienced leader often has difficulty in making sense of what is happening in the group. In part, this is a function of the immense size of the phenomenal field in group therapy. But, also, he is subject to strong emotional pressures. The group may be hostile or resistant; it may doubt his competence. The relationship with the co-leader or leaders may be tenuous or frankly rivalrous. Colleagues may doubt the validity of what is being done and professional standing may be in jeopardy. Supervision, itself, may be a further source of performance anxiety. Hopefully the leader will be sustained by positive, expert supervision, having seen more experienced therapists at work and achieving good results, or the internalized memory of a good personal group experience, but sometimes this will not be the case.

The views of 100 experienced supervisors on the difficulties experienced by inexperienced group therapists were elicited by Dies (1980a). The two most frequent problems were insensitivity to group process and inappropriately attempting to do individual therapy in a group setting; this may be a function of greater familiarity with individual therapy among leaders before commencing group training. Role problems, in particular of being overactive – in other words, overstructuring as a way of containing the therapist's anxiety – or being excessively concerned with projecting a competent or powerful image, and countertransference fears of scapegoating or being unable to confront intense group issues followed in rank order. Technical errors, such as in the form or timing of interpretations and inaccurate preparation for the role, were less frequently mentioned. Similar findings have been previously reported. As well as emphasizing the burdensome sense of responsibility that the leader has for the group, Brody (1966) pointed to conflicts over the degree of therapist transparency. The six fearful fantasies identified by Williams (1966) were (1) encountering unmanageable resistance, (2) losing control of the group, (3) excessive hostility breaking out, (4) acting out by members, (5) overwhelming dependency demands on the leader and (6) the group disintegrating. Hunter and Stern (1968) focused on problems within the supervision group; these included fear of exposure and criticism by peers and the supervisor, threats to self-esteem and sibling rivalry.

As well as the acquisition of complex cognitive and technical skills, group training must take full account of the powerful emotional reactions of leaders to their role. The term 'leaders' is deliberately used without the qualifier of 'inexperienced' as experience does not, and probably should not, armour the leader against the tension of the moment. Too much tension narrows the therapeutic vision of the leader, too little robs him of the spur to creativity.

ELEMENTS IN A BALANCED TRAINING

Supervised experience of leading groups, knowledge of theory and some form of personal experience in groups are the three elements that form the bedrock of training in group therapy (Lakin *et al.*, 1969; Dies, 1980a, b). Observing experienced leaders at work is, generally, considered valuable. However, the utility of solo *vs.* co-leadership, of being the junior leader, of being for training purposes a member of a patient group rather than a professionals group, and the necessity of prior training in individual therapy are hotly debated issues. This section critically examines the elements that enter into a balanced training.

Supervised practice

The small group has a character of its own, similar to, but in important ways different from, a large group or a community meeting; the differences are much accentuated by the purpose and theoretical orientation of the leader. It is self-evident that the trainee must gain experience in the modality of the group in which he is seeking to become proficient. However, as has been stated, there is much to be said for the foundation experience as leader of a small closed group with a duration of 12–18 months; group processes are easier to perceive and their recurrent nature allows interventions to be practised and evaluated, the trainee can live through the natural history of a group from its hesitant beginnings at the selection stage to the dispersal of the members at the end, and with good supervision and member selection the chance of an encouraging initiation to group work is enhanced. The author regrets that in his experience all too many potential leaders begin and quickly end their careers by attempting to lead unstructured, unsupervised large groups, often on in-patient or day-patient psychiatric units which have made a token investment in group therapy.

It is preferable to gain experience of solo and co-leadership as each form has advantages and disadvantages. Trainees of the Institute of Group Analysis in London are required to be solo leaders of their training group. Responsibility for what happens within the meeting is clearly theirs and must serve as a powerful concentrator of the mind; evaluation of that trainee's performance is made more easy. On the other hand, the processes of the group are so complex and at times the pressures so great – when, for example, the group unites against the leader – that a co-leader is a welcome additional observer and ally. Furthermore, the presence of a co-leader facilitates the good practice of reflecting on the recent history of the group before the session and reviewing the events of the meeting immediately afterwards. At times one co-leader will, by intention or experience, be junior to the other; this fact contributes its own oedipal dynamic to the group and may need to be focused on by the supervisior. Occasionally, a trainee may be placed in the room as a silent observer; this role is tenable for a brief period prior to assuming the responsibilities of leadership but otherwise soon becomes boring.

Proper record keeping is essential. This may take the form of a chronogram (Cox, 1973); the time sequence of the meeting is represented by quadrants of a circle, key interactions are noted in the appropriate segment and arrows used to link themes and active members. The author favours a written naturalistic narrative of the session which documents the form and sequence of the interactions, the feelings that were present and the interventions of the leader; countertransference feelings and hypotheses about the group process may be included (Bloch *et al.*, 1975). Alternatively, a structured report identifying key themes, group and individual inter-actions and leadership issues may be compiled (Aveline, 1986a). Circulating the written reports to group members may form part of the therapy (Yalom *et al.*, 1975; see also Chapter 3).

For the purpose of supervision, written reports may be supplemented by audio- or video-recording of the group meetings. The technical quality of the recordings in both modalities needs to be very high if they are to be usable. For audio-recordings, an overhead microphone or preferably several, centrally placed, directional microphones whose inputs can be individually adjusted for the quiet or noisy group member are necessary. A technician-controlled two-camera system is ideal for video-recordings; whole group shots should be used sparingly because rarely do they provide sufficient detail to hold the viewer's attention; medium shots and zoomed close-ups are much better. Recordings provide information on the non-verbal communications of members and leaders alike whose comprehension is so important in the practice of group therapy.

The supervisor should be involved from the outset. Improved outcome is the reward of careful preparation. The supervisior should clarify the purpose and form of the proposed group and anticipate with the leaders the problems they are likely to encounter; role plays may be a useful way of working through the latter (see below). Selection and preparation of members is equally important – the former to maintain the principle of heterogeneity of personal style and homogeneity of severity of problem, and the latter to reduce the incidence of drop-out in the early phase of the group (see Chapter 1). The supervisor will help the leaders acquire the individual and collective perspective previously outlined in this chapter. Two or even three pairs of co-leaders sharing a supervisory 1½ hours provide peer support, a further opportunity for multiple perspectives on the same event and the chance to see how similar therapeutic dilemmas are handled differently.

To help the supervisor register the cast of characters and understand the unique flavour of that group, a wise move is to observe the first one or two sessions and, if so desired, to repeat this periodically. Yalom's (1985) counsel of perfection is to observe the last 30 minutes of each session and then hold the supervisory meeting immediately afterwards.

Theory and the question of prior training in individual therapy

The theory component of a training should be comprehensive in scope, coherent in logic and critical of the tenets which underlie or are assumed to underlie the particulars of that approach. The last may be too much to ask of committed trainers in a training scheme but it is still the ideal. Often trainings are too narrow in their conceptual base and ignore the overlapping and complementary perspectives of knowledge held by other schools (see Chapters 7 and 13). Trainers tend to over-value the validity of their approach. It is worth bearing in mind that the best estimate of the contribution made by technique to outcome across the psychotherapies is only 15% (Lambert, 1985). Until such time as it can be demonstrated that certain techniques contribute a much higher percentage to the variance, the sage therapist will resist the siren call of a narrow but comfortingly secure theoretical base and instead listen to many songs before, in a critical spirit, composing a melody that tells the truth as it is then known.

It has already been suggested on pages 318–21 that only some therapists will be suited to group work. Dies, in several surveys of the literature (Dies, 1980a; Dies and Teleska, 1985), makes the point that many inexperienced group therapists do not appreciate the nature of the therapeutic factors that uniquely operate in groups (e.g. altruism, self-disclosure to peers and feedback) and, hence, co not make use of them. In part, this may be a function of prior orientation to and training in individual therapy. In the past, group training programmes have frequently emerged from institutes primarily concerned with individual therapy (Lakin *et al.*, 1969). Psycho-analysis has been the starting point for many group therapists; it has drawn attention to unconscious processes that contribute to the formation of the social matrix of the group and highlighted the transferential relationship between the leader or conductor, in the terminology of the British Group-Analytic Society, and the members. For Pines (1979), analysis is a primary discipline in training. Similarly, Grotjahn (1983) speaks of the group psychotherapist coming from an analytic background but points especially to how in the maturation of that therapist a personal group analysis will attend to the unanalysed family romance. In its training guidelines, the American Group Psychotherapy Association recommends ten times as many hours supervised practice in individual therapy than in group therapy, 1200 to 120 hours, while the Institute of Group Analysis in Britain, though being interested in a candidate's previous analysis or experience as a therapist, only requires group experience. Evaluative research should be carried out to elucidate the value in group therapy training of prior or concurrent training in individual therapy.

Personal experience as a group member

In learning to be a group leader, the personal experience of being a group member completes the training triad of supervised practice and theoretical learning. All three are essential and inseparable. The lived experience of being a member of a group not only makes sense of the theory but has the greatest chance of being integrated into the developing professional identity of the leader if it parallels in time the presentation of a comprehensive conceptual framework (Dies, 1980b). The intention of the experience is to deepen awareness of group process, enhance self-knowledge and foster sensitivity to the needs and feelings of others (Aveline, 1986b); it provides an opportunity to experience a climate of openness and inquiry, and a chance to increase the ability of the participants to be innovative (Berger, 1970). Thus, it is not surprising that all major training programmes in group therapy require a personal group experience.

The Institute of Group Analysis requires candidates for the Qualifying Course, its most advanced training which leads to full membership of the Group-Analytic Society, to undergo a personal group analysis in a twice-weekly group throughout the 3 years or more of training; the group is a patient-group with trainee members being most definitely in the minority. The duration of the group analysis is about right for a specialist professional qualification but the requirement for membership of a patient-group requires comment. In its favour is the fact that the patient-role is experienced in its entirety; on practical grounds, it is, perhaps, easier to organize entry to a therapy group meeting for 3 years than to have available a sufficient number of trainee-groups; and the anonymity of such a group may facilitate the exploration of personal issues without loss of face – certainly, sibling rivalry and concern about being judged by fellow professionals is reduced (Bathegay, 1983). However, the presence of a trainee, albeit as a full member, introduces a powerful dynamic whose resolution may be long drawn-out; spy, *agent provocateur* and leader's assistant are some of the roles that may be ascribed or assumed. Furthermore, the health care professional has some special preoccupations which need attending to during training.

In an analysis of personal themes raised by health care professionals in 21 12-week closed training groups that formed part of an introductory course for group leaders, the author found that a number of themes recurred (Aveline, 1986b). Many members took the opportunity to reveal personal tragedies that they felt could not be expressed at work for fear of being thought weak. They feared damaging their careers by self-disclosure. In their work-role as helper, they often felt unappreciated and helpless; in the group, they were able to express their experience that giving care and not receiving it was ultimately burdensome (McCarley, 1975). Just as in any therapy group, but given special poignancy by the fact that the majority of members worked in mental health and hence might be expected to be more insightful, the exploration of these personal and professional issues was obstructed by the initial tendency of members to see each other in stereotype and not as people. Despite the brief life of the group, many members entered into intimate dialogue with colleagues, sometimes for the first time; others were supported through personal crises or helped to make career decisions.

Provided that the group is well-composed in terms of heterogeneity of coping style and homogeneity of severity of interpersonal difficulty, membership of a patient-group affords the most realistic setting for personal learning and is to be preferred for advanced levels of professional training. However, there should also be an opportunity to explore the issues of the professional role in a group of mental health care colleagues.

In the training of group therapists, there is room for exposure to a variety of approaches and durations. An introductory 3-month or 1-year personal group experience is sufficient to acquaint that trainee with the nature of the modality and, more importantly, to determine if this is the direction in which the therapist's talents lie. Intensive 1-day or residential workshops are useful (for an example, see Lerner *et al.*, 1978), but it is only through repeated experience over a longer period that the natural rhythm of hard won personal change can be learnt.

The leader of the training group is in a position of influence and responsibility. The style of the leader is likely to be internalized – at least for a while – and the sensitivity and professionalism with which personal issues and intra-group conflicts are handled will enhance or detract from the trainee's liking for the approach. The leader needs to be chosen with care. Yalom (1985) suggests that the determining factors are talent, experience and, for the first training group, a non-specialized format. In the interests of confidentiality and to underline the fact that the organizers of the training programme will not have access to any evaluation made by the leader, the leader should be clearly seen to be independent of the training organization (Berman, 1975; Shapiro, 1978; Dies, 1980a; Yalom, 1985).

Role-play and observing experienced therapists at work

In a promising development, British group analysts have formulated a series of problematic group scenarios as part of an investigation into how different leaders may conceptualize and intervene in the group (Garland *et al.*, 1984). The discussion of these scenarios with trainees is a useful teaching aid. Issues may be explored without putting group members at risk. The exercise can be extended by role-playing the issue and then soliciting feedback from participants and observers; the techniques of psychodrama, namely role rehearsal and reversal, auxiliary ego and deroling, can be used advantageously to elucidate the minutiae of the interaction (see Chapter 5). Role play is a flexible technique which can be adjusted to the needs of inexperienced and advanced trainees (Lakin *et al.*, 1969). Further details of structured exercises may be found in MacLennan (1971), Cohen and Smith (1976) and Roman and Porter (1978).

The essence of learning is doing and reflecting on what was done but seeing can accelerate the process. Observing experienced group leaders at work has relatively low priority in group training, perhaps because of the passive status of the observer (Dies, 1980b). However, as Shapiro (1978) comments, observing a professional leader presents a golden opportunity to get a realistic picture of the true nature of group leadership; successes and failures can be seen, the results of specific interventions in specific situations examined and the whole put in the context of the trainee's developing skills as a leader. Yalom (1985) strongly advocates observation of a group for a minimum of 4 months, preferably from behind a one-way screen; the sessions being followed by 30–45 minutes of discussion between the leader(s) and the observers. This exacting task benefits both parties. If resources allow, a trainer can sit with the observers during the session and draw attention to the multiple elements entering into each interaction. As with individual supervision, the discussion period can degenerate into the *post hoc* cleverness of 'why didn't you do this or that?' instead of examining the issues and leadership dilemmas. For this reason, some trainers prefer to have the trainees each write an account of the session which brings out the interpersonal processes that they observed and have this as the basis of the discussion later in the week. Dies (1980b) lists 10 scales that can be completed by observers, 5 of which focus on leadership and 5 on group process; these scales help structure the trainees' attention. The discussion period offers an opportunity to learn how to give clear feedback in a sensitive, supportive manner, a skill whose necessity will be sharply underlined if leaders and students reverse their roles in another training exercise later in the programme.

Observing a group is always a privilege. Few if any group members welcome being observed and some feel persecuted by it. The reactions of members form another focus for exploration, but it must not be forgotten that they are being asked to accept an intrusion and that the final decision has to be theirs. Permission must be sought to have observers and, when someone is behind the one-way screen, their presence must be declared; some groups prefer to meet briefly with any new observer so that their presence is less anonymous. The situation needs to be handled with sensitivity and tact; observers arriving late and the sound of laughter are simple examples of what should not happen. Borrowing a practice from therapeutic communities, the fish bowl, the group can be offered the opportunity to change rooms and observe the post-group discussion. If this is done, it is important that all the members attend; in the author's experience, the interest of members in this extra dimension is short-lived. Once the persecutory fantasies have been dispelled and voyeuristic interest satisfied, members prefer to use their time in other ways. The fish bowl procedure demystifies group therapy and would easily integrate with most of the approaches described in this book; it might, however, be dissonant with group analysis with its greater emphasis on transference.

Evaluation

Training without evaluation is a lost opportunity for learning and an abnegation of responsibility by the trainers. At an introductory level, a certificate of attendance may be all that is looked for. At an advanced level, completion of the training should be a statement of quality and should be marked by a normative evaluation; it must be possible for trainees to fail or be deferred. At all levels, there is room for repeated formative evaluations which help the trainee make fuller use of the subsequent training. In the group course organized by the author, a written, tentative evaluation of their strengths and weaknesses as potential group leaders is sent by the leader to each member of the training group at its mid-point; the comments may be worked on in subsequent sessions (Aveline, 1986a).

The entry and evaluation procedures at the Institute of Group Analysis for the Qualifying Course is an excellent example of a carefully applied, professional system and so is described in detail. The involvement of many members of the Institute in the procedures introduces a system of checks and balances into the system. Candidates first meet with a consultant for a personal assessment and then with the Board of Assessors whose report is considered by the Admissions Sub-Committee before a final decision on entry is made by the Training Committee. Any deficiencies in experience are identified and candidates may be advised, for example, to seek a period of individual therapy before entering training or to gain experience with major psychiatric illness if coming from a lay background. Admission to seminars comes after about 1 year's membership of a therapy group and a satisfactory report from the group analyst. This report, together with seminar leaders' reports, form the key elements in the decision of the Training Committee to allow the student to conduct a weekly group under supervision. Any element in the training may be extended; supervisors', seminar leaders' and group analyst's reports contribute to the assessment that training is complete. The metaphor of the training is that the student is on a personal and professional journey and that by sharing the evaluations with the student at each stage, the journey can be facilitated.

In common with other psychotherapy trainings, objective criteria of competence and in particular of therapeutic effectiveness are lacking. At the end of the day, a global gut-feeling that the trainee is an ethical, competent therapist to whom one might safely entrust one's nearest and dearest is, I suspect, the deciding factor in the evaluator's mind. There is much to be said for retaining this as the fundamental construct in designing courses and evaluating outcomes.

Research

It is a counsel of perfection to expect trainees to be personally involved in conducting research. However, as has been stated on pages 324–5, it is important that the trainee maintain a critical – but not cynical – attitude to what is being taught. Organizers of training programmes should ensure that their students are acquainted with the findings from research and help them consider what implications they may have for practice (see Chapter 13). Certainly the trainee should be familiar with research methodology and may find it helpful in their learning about therapeutic factors, group development and group processes, to apply the research instruments of the major studies to their own group or observed group.

The perspective of the supervisor and his training

The supervisor, though only participating in the group at second hand, has the great advantage of hindsight and a certain psychological distance from the action. These two elements together with the wisdom of clinical experience and depth of theoretical knowledge are brought to bear on the responsible task of facilitating learning. As has been advocated, the supervisor should be closely involved from the outset. Just as the leader of a group fosters helpful group norms and draws attention to important but neglected aspects of the group exchange, so does the supervisor attend to aspects that are not fully in view by the trainee. Bascue (1978) suggests eight therapeutic dimensions that need to be considered: past and present, external and internal, cognitive and affective, verbal and behavioural, individual and group, leader and member activity, manifest and latent meaning, problem solving and personality change. The present author stresses the importance of the individual, collective and contextual perspectives (see pp. 319–21).

Training for supervision is a neglected issue. To be made a supervisor on an established course is an honour, but rarely is preparation given for this role or support continued as the supervisor hones his skills. Several precautionary steps can be taken. Two supervisors leading a supervisory seminar may learn from each other as well as offering different perspectives; a junior supervisor may serve an apprenticeship period with a more experienced one. Written yearly evaluations by the supervisee of the supervisor and vice versa ensures that an appraisal is made of the work that has been done. Problems in supervision should be discussed at regular meetings of supervisors. Finally, the exacting challenge of leading a training group of experienced therapists is an excellent postgraduate training (Grotjahn, 1983).

GUIDELINES IN SELECTING A TRAINING

At an advanced level, the leader will know what kind of group work he is most suited to and will seek training in that, but the beginner has a greater need for variety. The foregoing sections offer a guide to what a trainee might look for in a training. The principal points are now reiterated. Trainings which offer the opportunity to experience and evaluate critically their approach are to be preferred. The training should provide extensive practice as a leader with more than one supervisor. Theory should be comprehensively taught and high ethical and normative standards adhered to. A personal group experience should be offered, as should the opportunity to observe and discuss the work of experienced leaders. Commitment to a training should only follow the affirmative answering of the private question 'Will this training help me to know more clearly what my talents are as a therapist and develop them?'

Some British trainings and professional associations

The following list includes selected trainings in the public and the private sector. Formal specialist trainings in particular forms of group therapy tend to be found in the latter, but both sectors provide introductory and advanced training. High-level practical training can be found in the NHS as a staff member in specialist psychotherapy units. A number of professional associations are listed which do not offer full trainings but do bring together people with similar interest and advises them of educational events.

National Health Service
Most teaching districts in the NHS now have specialist departments of psychotherapy, many of which offer training to staff with a generalist or specialist interest in group therapy. An example of the former is the training group component of the 1 day a week, 2-years general psychotherapy training offered by the Uffculme Clinic in Birmingham, and of the latter the group track in the 3-year South Trent Training centred on Nottingham, Leicester, Derby and Lincoln. Staff employed at the Henderson Hospital in South London, the Littlemore in Oxford and Dingleton in the Scottish Borders will gain experience in therapeutic communities, and at the Cassel in London in an analytically informed therapeutic milieu. These institutions sometimes offer training attachments for non-employed staff.

Academic courses
The M.Sc. in Psychotherapy offered at St. George's Hospital in the University of London and in the Department of Psychology at Warwick include a training group comprised of the students. Similar provision is made in the Diploma in Psychotherapy at Sheffield, Leeds and Aberdeen Universities. A M.Sc. in Psychological Counselling with either an

individual or a group track is offered by the Roehampton Institute of Higher Education in London.

Institute of Group Analysis
A very active institute founded in 1971 which organizes scientific meetings, workshops and training. It has its own journal – *Group Analysis*.

(a) Introductory general course.   Annual course on 30 afternoons during the academic year. Theory seminars, weekly small group, and also one term in a large group. Courses held in London, Cambridge, Glasgow, Manchester, Northampton and Oxford.

(b) Qualifying course.   Successful completion leads to membership of the Institute. Duration: at least 3½ years. Candidates must have completed an introductory course and, generally, have a university degree. After selection, students are required to attend twice-weekly personal group analysis throughout the training. After an adequate year of this, students join theory seminars for a minimum of 2-years and 3 months. A supervised once-weekly group has to be conducted for at least 2 years and two papers presented, one theoretical within the group analytic frame of 3000–5000 words and the other of 5000–10 000 words on a clinical aspect of their supervised group.
   Address: 1 Daleham Gardens, London NW3 5BY.

London Centre for Psychotherapy
Founded in the 1950s and registered as a charity in 1974. Offers training in analytic psychotherapy, either individual or group. Trainees on the 3-year part-time qualifying course in group therapy have to have successfully completed the 1-year Introductory Course in Analytic Psychotherapy and been a member of a weekly psychotherapy group for 1 year. The qualifying course, which commences every third year, continues the personal group experience, provides seminars on theory, and provides supervision of a group conducted by the trainee for five terms. On satisfactory completion of the course, the trainee may apply to the Council for Associate Membership.
   Address: 19 Fitzjohns Avenue, London NW3 5JY.

Dramatherapy and psychodrama
(a) *Holwell Centre for Psychodrama and Sociodrama.*   Established in 1974. Offers introductory and advanced residential and 1-day workshops. Accumulation of credits from attending advanced workshops leads to qualification as a director. Awards two Diplomas of Competence, one in Advanced Psychodrama and the other in Group Action Methods; both

require 780 practicum hours, a thesis and a demonstration of clinical competence.
Address: East Down, Barnstaple, North Devon EX31 4NZ.

(b) British Association for Dramatherapists. Promotes training events and will provide a list of approved courses.
Address: c/o Hertfordshire College of Art and Design, Hatfield Road, St Albans, Herts.

(c) Shape. Promotes training events.
Address: 7 Fitzroy Square, London W1P 6AE.

Gestalt
The English Gestalt Institute offers part-time training in gestalt therapy over 3–4 years, plus further training and supervision.
Address: c/o Barrie Hinksman Associates, 67 Cubbington Road, Leamington Spa, Warwickshire CV32 7AQ.

Educational and behavioural
The British Association of Behavioural Psychotherapy is a multidisciplinary organization founded in 1972. It has its own journal – *Behavioural Psychotherapy*. Acts as a forum for discussion and is committed to the advancement of theory and practice of behavioural psychotherapy. Organizes conferences and workshops, and promotes training.
Address: Howard Lomas, Membership Secretary,
Craig House, Bank Street, Bury, Lancs BL9 0AB.

Women's Therapy Centre
The London Centre was founded in 1976. Local centres in several parts of the country, including Leeds, Southampton, Oxford and Nottingham. No organized training but runs many workshops on various aspects of feminist psychotherapy.
Address: 6 Manor Gardens, London N7.

Person-centred
(a) Facilitator Development Institute (British Centre). The Institute was founded in 1974 and currently offers: (i) residential summer workshops on the person-centred approach to small and large groups, and (ii) a 2½-year part-time course in counselling and psychotherapy, which includes a high percentage of small and large group work and also offers a specialist option in group counselling or group facilitation.

Address for information: F.D.I. Administrator, The Norwich Centre,
7 Earlham Road, Norwich NR2 3RA.

(b) Person-centred Approach Institute International (Great Britain). The
Institute, which runs courses throughout Europe, offers a 2-year programme in psychotherapy and group work for British participants. A
co-director is Dr Charles Devonshire, founder of the Center for Cross-
Cultural Communication, whose summer programmes also provide training
experience in both small and large group work.

Association of Therapeutic Communities
Founded in 1972, it provides workshops, training meetings and conferences,
publishes the quarterly *International Journal of Therapeutic Communities*,
and generally acts as a network for support, information and debate for
people who work in therapeutic communities or are interested in them. The
ACT became a registered charity in 1982. Membership is open to anyone
working in a therapeutic community or with a special interest in this field.
Individual and group membership are available. Membership includes free
subscription to the above Journal.
Address: Henderson Hospital, 2 Homeland Drive, Sutton, Surrey
SM2 5LT.

Certificate in Therapeutic Community Practice
Launched jointly by the Association of Therapeutic Communities and the
Royal College of Nursing in 1986, this is a part-time course extending over
one academic year leading to a certificate awarded by the RCN in
conjunction with ATC. It is a multidisciplinary course open to all disciplines
working in the therapeutic community field and may also be of interest to
nurse tutors.

Candidates should normally possess a professional qualification. The aim
of the course is 'to enable participants to acquire the knowledge and skills
necessary to work in a community setting in such a way that the group
experience itself becomes therapeutic for the clients involved'. The course
comprises a weekly workshop, lecture and experiential group, plus two
residential weekends. Assessment procedures include two essays, two
written tests, and a practice report describing work in members' own
settings.

Holders of the Certificate may be eligible to submit a dissertation for
reclassification of their award to a Diploma.
Further details from: The Registrar, Institute of Advanced Nursing
Education, 20 Cavendish Square, London W1M 0AB.

Other Therapeutic Community Associations and courses

● *Standing Conference on Drug Abuse* (information on therapeutic communities for rehabilitation of drug abusers/addicts).
   Address: 1–4 Hatton Place, London ED1N 8ND.
● *Planned Environment Therapy Trust* (mainly concerned with children and adolescents).
   Address: New Barns School, Church Lane, Toddington, Gloucestershire.
● *Association of Workers in Maladjusted Schools*
   Address: Glebe House, Shudy Camps, Cambridgeshire.
● *Henderson Hospital* runs a one-term Group Work Course which includes ideas relevant to therapeutic community work.
   Address: Henderson Hospital, 2 Homeland Drive, Sutton, Surrey SM2 5LT.
● *Richmond Fellowship* provides a 2-year in-service training for staff plus regular short courses for therapeutic community workers.
   Address: 8 Addison Road, London W14.
● *Arbours Association* provides therapeutic community placements for those training on its dynamic psychotherapy course and others.
   Address: 41A West Park, London N8.

REFERENCES

Aveline, M. O. (1986a). The use of written reports in a brief group psychotherapy training. *International Journal of Group Psychotherapy* **36** (3), 477–82.

Aveline, M. O. (1986b). Personal themes from training groups for mental health care professionals. *British Journal of Medical Psychology* **59**, 325–35.

Bascue, L. O. (1978). A conceptual model for training group therapists. *International Journal of Group Psychotherapy* **28**, 445–52.

Bathegay, R. (1983). The value of analytic self-experiencing in the training of psychotherapists. *International Journal of Group Psychotherapy* **33**, 199–213.

Berger, M. M. (1970). Experiential and didactic aspects of training in therapeutic group approaches. *American Journal of Psychiatry* **126**, 840–45.

Berman, A. L. (1975). Group psychotherapy training. *Small Group Behavior* **6**, 325–44.

Bloch, S., Brown, S., Davis, K. and Dishotsky, N. (1975). The use of a written summary in group psychotherapy supervision. *American Journal of Psychiatry* **132**, 1055–57.

Brody, L. S. (1966). Harrassed! A dialogue. *International Journal of Group Psychotherapy* **16**, 463–500.

Cohen, A. M. and Smith, R. D. (1976). *The Critical Incident in Growth Groups: A Manual for Group Leaders*. LaJolla, California, University Associates.

Cox, M. (1973). The group therapy interaction chronogram. *British Journal of Social Work* **3**, 243–56.

Dies, R. R. (1980a). Group psychotherapy: training and supervision. *In* A. K. Hess (ed.) *Psychotherapy Supervision: Theory, Research and Practice*, pp. 337–66. New York, Wiley.

Dies, R. R. (1980b). Current practice in the training of group psychotherapists. *International Journal of Group Psychotherapy* **30**, 169–85.

Dies, R. R. and Teleska, P. A. (1985). Negative outcome in group psychotherapy. *In* D. T. Mays and C. M. Franks (eds), *Negative Outcome in Psychotherapy and What to Do About It*, pp. 118–41. New York, Springer.

Garland, C., Kennard, O., Roberts, J. P., Winter, D. A., Caine, T. M., Dick, B. and Stevenson, F. B. (1984). What is a group analyst? A preliminary investigation of conductors' interviews. *Group Analysis* **17**, 137–45.

Grotjahn, M. (1983). The qualities of the group therapist. *In* H. I. Kaplan and B. J. Sadock (eds), *Comprehensive Group Psychotherapy*, 2nd edition, pp.294–301. Baltimore, Williams and Wilkins.

Hunter, G. F. and Stern, H. (1968). The training of mental health workers. *International Journal of Group Psychotherapy* **28**, 104–9.

Kernberg, O. F. (1975). A systems approach to priority setting of interventions in groups. *International Journal of Group Psychotherapy* **25**, 251–75.

Lakin, M., Lieberman, M. and Whitaker, D. (1969). Issues in the training of group psychotherapists. *International Journal of Group Psychotherapy* **19**, 307–25.

Lambert, M. J. (1985). Implications of psychotherapy outcome research for eclectic psychotherapy. *In* T. C. Norcross (ed.), *Handbook of Eclectic Psychotherapy*, pp. 436–62. New York, Brunner/Mazel.

Lerner, H. E. Horwitz, L. and Burstein, E. D. (1978). Teaching psychoanalytic group psychotherapy: a combined experiential didactic workshop. *International Journal of Group Psychotherapy* **28**, 453–66.

Lieberman, M. A., Yalom, I. D. and Miles, M. B. (1973). *Encounter Groups: First Facts*. New York, Basic Books.

MacLennan, B. W. (1971). Simulated situations in group psychotherapy training. *International Journal of Group Psychotherapy* **21**, 330–32.

McCarley, T. (1975). The psychotherapist's search for self-renewal. *American Journal of Psychiatry* **132**, 221–4.

Pines, M. (1979). Group psychotherapy: frame of reference for training. *Group Analysis* **12**, 210–18.

Roman, M. and Porter, K. (1978). Combining experiential and didactic aspects in a new group therapy training approach. *International Journal of Group Psychotherapy* **28**, 371–87.

Shapiro, J. E. (1978). *Methods of Group Psychotherapy and Encounter*. Itasca, Ill, Peacock.

Williams, M. (1966). Limitations, fantasies and security operations of beginning group psychotherapists. *International Journal of Group Psychotherapy* **16**, 150–62.

Yalom, I. D. (1985). *The Theory and Practice of Group Psychotherapy*, 3rd edition. New York, Basic Books.

Yalom, I. D., Brown, S. and Bloch, S. (1975). The written summary as a group psychotherapy technique. *Archives of General Psychiatry* **32**, 605–13.

INDEX

In the following index, 'group therapy' is abbreviated to 'g.t.'

Index compiled by Peva Keane